LIFE
INSIDE

A Memoir

Mindy Lewis

ATRIA BOOKS

New York London Toronto Sydney Singapore

ATRIA BOOKS

1230 Avenue of the Americas,
New York, NY 10020

Library of Congress Control Number: 2002104389

ISBN: 0-7434-1149-8

First Atria Books hardcover printing October 2002

10   9   8   7   6   5   4   3   2   1

ATRIA BOOKS is a trademark of Simon & Schuster, Inc.

For information regarding special discounts for bulk purchases,
please contact Simon & Schuster Special Sales at 1-800-456-6798 or
business@simonandschuster.com

Printed in the U.S.A.

For those who got lost . . .

CONTENTS

I. LIFE INSIDE

Intake   3
Testing   11
Days Like Any Other   15
Life Before   28
Adolescents   46
Inappropriate Behavior   65
Outside Communication   86
Inside Out   101
Deep Dirt   108
Desperate Measures   124
Backlash   139
Celebrities   147
Procrustes in Coconut Grove/The Buddha/Hic Phat!   156
Progress   161
Parting Shots   173

II. LIFE AFTER

Released   187
Roots   208
Crazy   226

A Member of My Tribe   235
The Clitoris of the Heart   240
Work   251
The Train to Bellevue   257
Personal Mythology   264
Follow-up   271
Reunion   274
Forgiveness   279
My Father's Keeper   288
Floating   303
Toward or Away?   308
Rockland Revisited   312
Old Friends   316
Seduction   324
For the Records   330
Facing the Enemy   339
Appointment with the Past   343

A Note to the Reader   351
Acknowledgments   353
Selected Bibliography   355

What's madness but nobility of soul
At odds with circumstance.
　　　　　　　　　　—Theodore Roethke, as quoted in
We've Had a Hundred Years of Psychotherapy and the World's Getting Worse,
　　　　　　　　　James Hillman and Michael Ventura

Having stripped myself of all illusions, I have gone mad.
　　　　　　　　　—Friedrich Nietzsche, *My Sister and I*

Man is sometimes extraordinarily, passionately in love with suffering.
　　　　　　　　　—Dostoevsky, *Notes from Underground*

Forty thousand headmen couldn't make me change my mind.
　　　　　　　　　　　　　—Steve Winwood

I

LIFE INSIDE

INTAKE

THE TAXI ROLLS NORTH ALONG the West Side Highway. I sit in the back-seat next to my mother, six inches of highly charged space between us. Turning my face away as far as possible, I look out at the Hudson River, the George Washington Bridge growing larger by degrees. I'm filled with conflicting emotions: fear, anger, defiance. My life as I know it is about to end. They're going to lock me up. And it's all *her* fault.

My mother's face wears a familiar shutdown blankness. For just a second I wish I could reach out and touch her, ending the war between us. I would revert to the nice, accommodating child I'd been, adoring my stately, beautiful mom. But it's too late. On her lap is a folder containing papers and forms, among them the court order placing me in state custody. A suitcase in the trunk of the taxi holds my belongings. Aside from summer camp, this is the first time I will live away from my mother.

It's been a busy day. We spent the morning at the Department of Child Welfare Services. Our destination: Family Court. With each click of my mother's high heels against the tile floor I ambled more slowly, dragging my feet, trying to dispel the middle-class aura that surrounded us. My fashionable mother and my bedraggled hippie self stood out among the welfare mothers and others who had fallen through the socioeconomic cracks. When our turn came to appear before the judge, my mother pressed charges against me for truancy, smoking marijuana, and unmanageable behavior. The judge raised her eyebrows at me before placing me on Court Remand, making me an official ward of the state.

3

As the cab swerves onto Riverside Drive I see the yellow-brick building, its windows staring like blank, unreflecting eyes. I imagine this is how
convicts feel on their way to the electric chair, at once suspended in time
and rushing inevitably forward. But in some way, I know this is what I
want—to cut the cord, get away—even if I have to go all the way to hell
to do it.

The taxi turns onto West 168th Street and rolls to a stop. My mother
pays the driver and turns to me.

"Let's go," she says, as if there's a choice, but I've already slammed the
door against her voice.

"Mindy was always a well-behaved child, but lately she's stopped performing." My mother addresses this remark to a small group seated on
plastic hospital chairs: three psychiatrists, a psychologist, a social worker,
a nurse. As my mother pronounces this last word—*performing*—I stiffen in
my chair. Does she think I'm some sort of puppet?

It is December 6, 1967, three months before my sixteenth birthday.
We are gathered for my intake conference at the New York State
Psychiatric Institute at Columbia-Presbyterian Medical Center. Because
P.I. is a teaching hospital, it's supposed to be better than the other state
hospitals. Dr. L., my former shrink, said I should consider myself fortunate to be accepted here. He said I'd be part of a community of others
like me: adolescents and young adults, mostly from middle-class backgrounds, unable to cope well enough to continue living with their families.

"Your education won't be interrupted. There's even a school on-site,"
he'd added, then wished me luck and shook my hand as if I were going off
to college.

The hospital agreed to accept me on the condition that I'm placed on
Court Remand, so my mother, in a moment of weakness, will not have
the power to sign me out. Here I will remain until they decide to discharge me, or until I turn eighteen, whichever comes first.

"She could be here as little as six months," one of the psychiatrists
reassures my mother.

My heart pounds defiantly, each beat the slamming of a door. I had
seen the impending date of my admission as a token of a battle won, a
badge of victory in my rebellion against my mother and the mundane

conventionality I despise. Until this moment, it has never occurred to me that I would have to live, as usual, through each day.

———————

The Institute is built into the side of a cliff along Riverside Drive. The main entrance is on the tenth floor; to get to the fifth floor, you must descend. We live underground, nestled into rock. On one side locked windows overlook the Hudson; on the other is a wall of stone.

Up to thirty men and thirty women live on one floor divided into two mirror-image halves. On each side long hallways, their walls uninterrupted by artwork or decoration, connect two dorms, five private rooms, a bathroom, a shower room, a utility room, a locker room, an isolation room, a nurses' station. The North and South sides converge in a central area (Center) where patients sit around in couches and chairs. From Center it's a few steps to the kitchen and dining room, the elevators and locked staircase, and two living rooms that house TVs, a Ping-Pong table, a piano, and heavy, padded chairs and couches upholstered in orange, gold, and green vinyl.

The intake conference was almost more than I could bear, everyone talking about me as if I weren't there. My stepfather showed up and spouted his bullshit. And my mother—so charming, so innocent, with her high heels and makeup. What a hypocrite! She tried kissing me good-bye, but I walked away. Then I was fingerprinted, like some kind of criminal, by a little bald man in a white jacket wheeling a squeaky portable fingerprint cart. Kafka would have loved it.

As I walk down the corridor I trail my fingers along the wall, afraid that if I'm not touching something solid, I might just float away. Walking next to me, slightly ahead, is my new psychiatrist, Dr. A., a clipboard tucked under his arm. At the end of the hall, he unlocks a door, flips a switch to turn on the overhead lights, and steps aside to let me enter.

The room is just like all the other rooms in this place. Just . . . bland. Beige walls. The same heavy padded chairs I saw in the living room. Hot air hisses from the radiator. It's stifling. I ask if he can open a window.

"I don't see why not." He searches for the key that will unlock the wire gate over the window, then pushes the window diagonally out, just a crack. The window reflects the lit room, so all I can see of the sky is a little strip of blue.

Dr. A. seats himself and gestures to me to sit across from him.

"For the next seven months, I will be your psychiatrist."

Seven months. The minutes are so long. How will I survive seven months?

I look him over. It's hard to tell how old he is. Maybe in his late twenties, with blue-gray eyes and curly blond hair. I'd prefer it if he weren't so good-looking. How am I going to talk to him? Even if I wanted to talk to him, I don't know what I'd say.

I chew the threads hanging from the cuff of my favorite sweatshirt, comforted by its soft, tattered familiarity. Nestling my face in the crook of my arm, I breathe the faint smells of laundry soap and cigarette smoke, smells of home. I breathe deeper and catch the tiniest whiff of fresh air, rain, and trees. Then it disappears. All that is behind me. Now I'm a blank. Now I'm truly nothing.

Dr. A. sits there, watching me. Does he think he can tell from the outside what goes on inside of me? Like how scared and lonely I am right now, here in this place where I don't know anyone, where all the doors are locked and the sky is a little stripe.

Who is he, anyway? I steal another look. Dr. A. wears a white jacket over his blue pin-striped shirt and red tie, and a gold wedding band. Red, white, and blue—real straight, like some kind of narc. He's cleanly shaved, combed, proud of his appearance.

I look down at myself, at the holes in my sweatshirt, and feel ashamed. I don't want him to look at me. I tuck my feet up under me and hug my knees.

Dr. A. opens a file folder and looks through it. A thin folder, containing all there is to know about me. He takes out a pen and writes something on his clipboard—probably something about how "sick" I am. Does he think he's going to "cure" me? I want to tell him this is a masquerade that's gone too far. But it's too late.

He gets down to work, asking me questions about my childhood, my parents' divorce, what kinds of drugs I've taken. He writes down my answers carefully, barely looking at me. When he's finished, he asks if I have any questions. Just one: When can I go outside?

"We'll see," he says, and falls silent. The sound of his breathing makes me queasy.

He gets to go home at night, but I have to stay here. I hate him, just like I hate the stupid plastic chairs we're sitting on and the ugly blandness of everything around me.

I prefer the heat of anger to the cold paralysis of fear. Riding my anger,

I've succeeded in getting away from my mother. I thought this was a kind of victory. Now I'm not so sure.

Dr. A. leans forward. "Did you want to say something?"

I give him my worst malevolent smile. "Fuck you," are the only words I can find.

MENTAL STATUS EXAMINATION

The patient is a tall, slender, ascetically pretty 15½-year-old white female with long dirty blond hair which hangs down to her shoulders. This together with her dark stockings and turtleneck sweater contributes to her image as "hippie." While conversing with me it was quite obvious that she is more genuinely wrapped up within herself. She toys with her hair, unconsciously and aimlessly, winding strands about her fingers. She is very self-conscious and is usually unable to face the interviewer. Rather she hides behind her hair, peers off into space or buries her face on her chest. Her walk is a sort of bedraggled shuffle which makes me think of someone being led off to their execution. She smokes a great deal.

She is sullen and for the most part nonverbal. Her responses are quite unpredictable. She can be cooperative, helpful and verbal at one moment, and then suddenly she'll refuse to answer a question entirely or tell me that the query was "God-damned stupid." Her profanity comes in bursts, often corresponding to rises in her anxiety. It is as if she uses it part of the time to shock, and dares the therapist to curtail her.

The patient is fearful, extremely anxious and depressed. At times her anxiety rises to such heights that she begins to tremble. Occasionally she smiles or giggles inappropriately. Her rage is generalized, poorly controlled and inappropriately expressed. The patient is well-oriented in all spheres. It is presumed her intelligence is above average.

Doctor's Orders: E.O. in pajamas. Restrict to ward. No privileges. No phone calls. No visitors.

—Arthur A., M.D., NYS Psychiatric Institute

I'm delivered back to the head nurse, who tells me to get undressed for a medical exam and unlocks a closet-sized room next to the nurses' station. I change into a hospital gown and sit shivering on the exam table. My hands are blotchy purple, and sweat trickles down my sides. The door opens, and in walks Dr. A. I can't believe *he's* going to examine me! I don't want him to see me without my clothes.

Dr. A. presses a stethoscope to my chest and leans in close. I look up, away, anywhere but at his face, holding my breath to slow my heart, which is beating too fast. I hope he doesn't think it's because he's close to me. He looks in my mouth with a little flashlight and tells me to stick my tongue out, but it's hard to do without it shaking. Even my tongue is out of control! He shines a light in my eyes, then sticks an instrument with a tiny light into my ear. I imagine the light shining in one side and out the other. I try to resist an urge to laugh, but it comes curling out the edges of my mouth. Why do I think such stupid things? Maybe he really will find something wrong with me. Maybe I'm brain-damaged from all the drugs I've taken.

Dr. A. scrapes a needle along the bottom of my foot, leaving a long scratch. I stare at the thin line seeping blood, then at him. "Sorry," he says. "Just testing your reflexes." There must be something wrong with my reflexes. If they'd been working right, I would have pulled my foot away, or kicked him. I hope he's a better shrink than he is a doctor.

The nurse comes in and hands me a pair of cotton hospital pajamas. She gathers up my clothes and explains that for the time being I am on observation so they can make sure I don't run away. I tell her I won't wear them. They're pink—I never wear pink—and too small, besides. I follow her to a closet filled with stacks of folded pajamas. I choose a pair of pastel green, size large. The sleeves hang over my hands, which is fine with me—the more that's hidden, the better.

I ask for my cigarettes. The nurse pulls from her pocket an enormous bunch of keys, unlocks a cabinet and finds the carton of Marlboros marked with my name. She removes a pack, hands it to me, and offers me a light. She puts the matches in her pocket and locks the cabinet. Everything here is under lock and key, including me.

"Can't I have my own matches?" I've been here two hours, and I can't open a window or wear my own clothes. Now this. It's worse than being a child.

"Not yet." She puts her hand on my shoulder, but I pull away.

"Fuck you!" I can't seem to come up with anything else today.

"That's not a nice thing to say," the nurse says.

Good, I think, because I am not nice. Once I was a nice little girl, but those days are over. Before I can stop it, that nice little girl's tears fill my eyes. I blink them away, hoping nobody saw.

The nurse shows me the dorm where I will sleep. Ten beds line the walls, beside each one a dresser, like a stripped-down version of some children's story—*Snow White* or *Madeline*. Only a few personal possessions are allowed on top. Here and there stuffed animals sit on hospital bedspreads, huddled together: silly little-girl things, symbols of nonexistent comfort. I arrange my books on top of my dresser to remind myself who I am. Since I'm not allowed my clothes, all I have to put away are socks and underwear, shampoo and soap. As I put them in the empty dresser drawers, I have a sense of how little space my life takes up.

I wait outside the nurses' station. With its large windows, it's like a glassy eye, always watching. The head nurse scribbles in a book. I hate her, her stupid curly hair, her fat ass. Every once in a while she looks up at me. I'll have to give her something interesting to write about, something she can really sink her teeth into. I open my eyes wide and give her a hateful stare.

A girl with long brown hair comes over and says hello, a stupid smile on her face. She says if I have any questions or need any help to ask her. Maybe she's in cahoots with the staff. I stare just past her, then turn my face away. I won't conspire with the enemy. If I have to be here, I'll just be a body, a piece of matter. I won't talk to anybody.

I can't take another minute sitting out here in the hallway. Privacy is as important to me as air, and I'm suffocating. I jump up, knock on the nurses' station door, and ask permission to sit in the little room at the end of the hall. The nurse answers yes, as long as I keep the door open. What does she think I'm going to do in there, commit suicide by hitting myself with my book?

Fortunately nobody else is in the end room, just a table, two chairs, a lamp, me, and my book—Pär Lagerkvist's *The Dwarf*, about a twenty-six-inch-tall servant/adviser to a princess, who secretly despises and mocks those people who seek his counsel. He considers himself one of a superior race, beyond reproach even after committing a treasonous crime.

I sit here in my chains and the days go by and nothing ever happens. It is an empty joyless life, but I accept it without complaint. I await other times and they will surely come, for I am not destined to sit here for all eternity. . . . I muse on this in my dungeon and am of good cheer.

I close the book. As much as I'd like to emulate the dwarf's acceptance of his fate, I'm afraid. I cannot see my future.

TESTING

"THE TEST YOU ARE ABOUT TO TAKE is in three parts and will take about three hours."

The psychologist, Miss M., is too perky for her own good. Her voice is too friendly, too singsong, like she's reading from a script. She tells me she'll be giving me an IQ test and some psychological tests.

"Some of it will be fun," she says. When I don't smile back, her face goes tight.

If there's one thing I hate, it's phoniness. It's obvious her niceness is fake. She's just one of a long line of social workers, psychologists, psychiatrists, and neurologists who pretend to be friendly but are really just trying to figure me out. They think they can measure my intelligence, measure *me*. I don't want to take their damn tests! I'm here. Isn't that enough?

She places some paper and a pencil in front of me and asks me to draw a person. It's hard enough to draw people when I'm looking at them, but when I have to draw them from imagination or memory they come out looking like stick-figure cartoons. It makes me want to tear myself to shreds! How can I call myself an artist if I can't draw people? Besides, I don't draw on command. Drawing is personal, a kind of poetry that comes from deep inside me. I never let anybody watch me draw or paint. I tell her some bullshit about why I can't draw. Then I look away.

Since I don't respond to her chitchat, Miss M. grows quiet. She lays a small black suitcase on the wooden desk between us, flicks open the latches with an official-sounding *click!* and unpacks some spiral-bound books, stacks of cards, wooden blocks, a clock. She fusses a little with her things, arranging them.

"We'll start with Picture Completion." She takes a pile of cards and taps them on the desk to make a neat stack. The tapping sound reminds me of other cards from long ago, puzzles, game cards. Does she think I want to play games with her? I haven't played games in years and I don't intend to start now!

"Look at each picture carefully and see if you can tell me what's missing." She flips the first card. It's an illustration of a man's face. He looks like the father in Dick and Jane, only he's wearing glasses. The area over the bridge of his nose has been airbrushed out.

They've got to be kidding. Do they think I'm an idiot? Only a complete moron would miss this. "His glasses are missing their nosepiece," I say icily.

She makes a notation and flips the next card. This time it's a chair with three legs. Another piece of cake. I do several others; with each the missing thing becomes less obvious. Trees in the snow, with no snow on the branches. A woman who leaves no footprints. A man who casts no shadow. A chimney without smoke. Does a chimney always have smoke? And how should I know? I live in an apartment. I've never seen a real chimney.

The stack gets smaller and smaller, until . . . it's a picture of a locomotive, but I can't tell what's missing. It seems to have all its windows, its headlights, the little thing that sticks out in front, whatever it's called. This isn't fair. I've only seen subways, never locomotives. How should I know what's missing? I check and recheck, but I can't figure it out.

These cards are creepy. They presuppose a perfect world, where everything is so symmetrical it's surreal. If something isn't symmetrical, is it wrong? That's their world, not mine. Not all faces have perfect features. The right side does not always match up with the left like it's supposed to in their Dick and Jane world. People who can't go outside don't leave footprints. People who never see the sun don't cast shadows.

Sometimes what's missing is invisible. Like me. What's missing in me? I don't know, and neither do they. And they're not going to find out with their stupid tests.

She asks me to memorize long strings of numbers, and recite them forward and backward. I define words, try to guess the meaning of clichés, some of which I've heard a million times but don't know what they mean.

Maybe I'm not as smart as I think I am. My brain feels sluggish and slow. I look at trippy-looking geometrical patterns, I play with blocks, I rearrange pictures that tell a story, but in the wrong order. Is there only one order? Where is their imagination? When she asks me to look at some pukey inkblots and tell her what they look like, I've had enough. I refuse to answer any more questions.

The patient is currently functioning at the bright normal level of intelligence. Although there was little discrepancy between her verbal and performance IQ scores, there was a marked discrepancy within certain tests in which the patient answered more difficult questions correctly while missing more simple ones (she did not know how many weeks there are in a year but did know that Goethe wrote *Faust*). The patient showed little ability to concentrate and had limited tolerance for frustration; that is, when things become difficult for her she gives up immediately.

Many of the patient's responses are vague and arbitrary which suggests she has difficulty in defining boundaries. Some examples from the Rorschach test follow:

"It looks like a witches face on top of another face and it looks like the witch is drinking somebody's brains." (Card VIII)

"It looks like somebody's face on fire." "Two men's faces with mutilated noses." (Card IX)

"It looks like a colony of snakes and crabs and frogs and things, or two people throwing up." (Card X)

The patient has pronounced ungratified dependency needs, which lead to anger, resentment and frustration. Many problems with interpersonal relationships arise because, as is illustrated in the following Rorschach response, she does not know whether she should be friendly and loving, or reject others before she is rejected by them.

"It looks like two people dancing, or two people playing tug-of-war—two women." (Card III)

Currently the patient is overwhelmed by impulses. Some examples of her impulsiveness follow: Asked, "What would you do if while in the movies you were the first person to see smoke and fire?" she replied, "I'd either yell 'Fire' or go and get some water . . . I suppose I'd yell 'Fire.'" Asked, "Why should we keep away from bad company?" she said, "'Cause they drag us down, which is a lot of bullshit." She had no idea why the state requires people to get a license in order to be married.

Program for social recovery appears favorable. Motivation for personality change is minimal, and the patient is more likely to try to change the environment than herself. Since she does not show generalized deterioration, a supportive well-structured environment may help her to pull herself together.

Diagnostic Impression: Acute schizophrenic reaction with marked pre-morbid hysterical features. General deterioration is not apparent, and prognosis within a supportive and structured environment seems favorable.

DAYS LIKE ANY OTHER

"TIME TO WAKE UP." The attendant standing in the dorm doorway snaps on the overheads. One by one the patients in the surrounding beds get up, reach for bathrobes and slippers and gather toothbrushes, soap, and towels. The last thing I want to do is get up, but the attendant comes over and shakes me. Thoughts and dreams swirl in my head. I sit up, swing my legs over the side of the bed. If I stand too quickly, I feel dizzy and have to sit back down. The attendant waits until everyone's ready, then herds us to the bathroom. I avoid looking at my reflection in the long metal mirror above the row of sinks. I don't want to see the puffy, pale moon of a face with its dull eyes and stringy hair.

I sit in a stall and try to pretend I'm alone. It's hard to relax when strangers are listening to you pee. If you're on suicide watch an aide or nurse holds the door open. Then it's impossible to squeeze anything out, even when you really have to. Every day I ask if I can go to the bathroom by myself, but they won't let me.

There are three types of observation: S.O., suicide observation, is constant; you're never alone for a second, and you must wear pajamas. C.O., constant observation, is a little less stringent; you can sometimes go to the bathroom by yourself or wear your own clothes, depending on the staff's decision. E.O., elopement observation, means you have to wear pajamas, so you can't escape. I'm on E.O., which makes sense—you can bet I'll run away the first chance I get.

Showers are scheduled in advance. I ask if I can take a bath, but they say a bath takes too long. Since I'm on observation, an attendant has to stay with me the whole time. I get my soap and shampoo from my dresser drawer but have to ask the nurse for my razor. What does it matter? Nobody can see my hairy legs under my pajamas anyway.

At home I stayed in the bathtub a long, long time. I liked to lie on my back and submerge, letting my hair fan out around me, listening to the amplified sounds: bubbles, drips, my own heartbeat. Soothing sounds. I'd hook a washcloth on the index finger of each hand and swirl them around like graceful sea creatures in an underwater ballet. I'd pretend I was a mermaid, holding court with seals and dolphins, rescuing innocents from the evil giant squid. My father, wise old Neptune, would praise me for my deeds. I had a suitor, a handsome merman. When I caught him admiring me, I'd avert my gaze and swim away, and he'd fall in love with my modesty and grace.

The shower room is creepy. The white tiles glare when the lights are on, and when they're off it's even spookier, dark and echoey. The bathtub is ugly and uninviting, with long metal faucet handles and some kind of strange attachment. I wonder if it's something they use to chill people out when they get really crazy, like the ice packs in *I Never Promised You a Rose Garden.*

In my soap dish is the bar of Dial soap my mother packed. I pop open the lid and inhale. The smell reminds me of home. When I lather up, I feel like I'm washing away some of the dreariness of this place, getting rid of the tiredness, the stale smell. I stand under the shower with my eyes closed and let the hissing water block everything out. Water streams down, making my hair flow over my breasts like seaweed.

"Time to get out," the attendant calls. "I can't stand here all day."

Afterward, the smell of soap and shampoo on my skin and hair reminds me how it feels to be a normal girl. I still have my skin, my smooth breasts, and body. I still have my long, clean hair.

It's a hard time between sleep and meds, a kind of limbo within limbo. We line up for breakfast, do the patient-shuffle, stand in clumps outside the dining-room door, avoid each other's eyes. Male and female patients wear the same hospital pajamas and robes in pastel shades: white, yellow, blue, green, pink. Some wear street clothes, and shoes instead of slippers. I see some kids my age wearing jeans. The boys have long hair. They seem like regular kids, not at all crazy. I don't know what to say to them. I slump, hug my arms, look at the floor.

An attendant unlocks the door and we file past the food cart. I take a tray and some utensils—a bent knife and a fork with prongs that go every which way—and hold out my plate to receive a scoop of overcooked scrambled eggs, undercooked home fries, and white toast. The toast revolves slowly on the creaky merry-go-round mass-production toaster; I watch it inch along for what seems like an eternity before my two slices fall onto the disordered toast pileup. I carry my tray into the dining room and blink at the sunlight filtering through the curtained windows. Patients sit at rows of tables, most with empty chairs between them. A group of kids are sitting together, but I eat by myself, or try to eat, my stomach in knots. Too many people for me. I don't like people. I don't know what to say to them.

After breakfast the men go to the North side, the women to the South, and assemble outside the nurses' stations. I join the line of women restlessly shifting, sighing, rocking from foot to foot. Everyone is so docile, lined up like sheep. Not me, I tell myself, I won't ever be like that. I bite split ends off my hair, chew my nails, jiggle my leg. An increasingly familiar, nagging buzz fills my ears.

The nurse, busy behind the glass, emerges pushing a metal cart. "Meds!" she calls out, ringing a bell. She hands out the morning dose— tiny white pills, round yellow ones, red capsules, blue ovals—that rattle in little paper cups before being tipped into mouths and washed down with water poured from a frosted metal pitcher.

When I try to peek at what other patients are getting, they shield their cups with their hands. It's nobody else's business what you take. Just as long as you swallow. Mouths are checked for pill retention, names checked off the list. Patients who have trouble swallowing or a history of resistance get liquid meds, clear or gem-colored cocktails that burn as they go down. I watch one woman make a face, swish water in her mouth, swallow, hold out her cup for more water, please.

The nurse hands me a cup containing a round red pill that looks like an M&M. When I ask what it is, she says it's the medication my doctor prescribed. I tell her I don't want it. "That's your choice," she says, "but if you don't take it, we'll have to give you an injection." Assholes! Do they think they can fix what's wrong with me by giving me pills? I tip the pill into my mouth, hold out my cup for water, and try to wash away the bitter taste of my impotence. After, she asks me to open my mouth, pushes my tongue aside with a tongue depressor, and peers into my mouth.

Medication is the rule, the burning absolution. There is a drug for every physical and emotional state. Their names have a certain poetry. Elavil, for example, elevates you from depression—I'm envious of the patients who get that. Thorazine, the king of drugs, hurls thunderbolts into your brain. Chloral hydrate, for sleep, comes in a clear green bubble like a bath-oil capsule, but I envision a floral-scented handkerchief laced with ether—a sniff, and you float into oblivion.

Patients ask for aspirin for headaches, Gelusil for heartburn, Valium for anxiety. It's a form of entertainment, a break in the routine. Sometimes people demand more medication betweentimes, begging for it tearfully. I try to resist, hiding the pills in my cheek, under my tongue. I hate them for trying to deaden me, extinguish my spark of life. *Let them have a taste of their own medicine,* I pray, wishing on the doctors a forced experience of the flatness, distortion, and lack of luster. My body turns leaden, my mind hums numbly. Objects sprout halos. I am on Thorazine, the standard-issue drug for psychosis.

After breakfast and meds there is a brief bustle of energy. We check the list for morning chore assignments, a feeble attempt to make us feel useful. Then the ward divides into patients going to activities and those who will stick around. The mood shifts to quiet concentration as those left behind settle into chairs in the common area. Soon you can hear the humming of the electric clock, the tap tap of cigarettes on ashtrays, the rustling of pages.

I look around at my new community. They could be a random group of commuters awaiting their train—wearing pajamas. A bulky man sits motionless, staring, mouth open, dribbling a little. Every few minutes a twitchy woman, wrinkling then releasing her face, calls out "Nurse!" but everyone just ignores her, except for two adolescent boys who taunt, "Noisse! Noisse!" in high-pitched nasal squeals. Mrs. G., the attendant on duty, frowns, raises a hand in a mock slap, then waggles her finger. "Bad boys! Stop that!"

Some patients wear silk or flannel bathrobes brought from home. One guy actually wears an ascot. If you don't try to look good, you've already started to sink. Like those with stubbled, unwashed faces. Slack mouths, unbrushed teeth, stinking body odor. Spines that refuse to support the body. Bad children! Unable, or unwilling, to take care of themselves. But they are the minority. For most of us, the damage is invisible.

Why are we here? That's the big question. Sometimes I catch people looking at me, x-raying me with their eyes, the same way I look at them.

I already know a few patients from my dorm. Liz, her straight brown hair tucked behind her ears, pulls her bathrobe tight around her ample form as she settles into a chair with a thick book. Liz makes it clear that though she's large, she's not jolly, and though she likes The Mamas and the Papas, she's not Mama Cass. When she's annoyed, she has a caustic tongue. Usually, though, she's depressed. She's been here for more than a year, in pajamas most of the time.

I head for an empty chair near Liz, but a tall guy with glasses gets there before me. I sink into the chair next to him, pull my knees into my chest, wrap my arms around my legs. He tilts his head to peer at me over the top of his black-rimmed Buddy Holly-style glasses.

"Hi. I'm Ted." He smiles and extends a large, damp hand for me to shake, then peels the cellophane off a new pack of Benson & Hedges Golds. It makes sense for a tall guy to smoke tall cigarettes. He holds out the pack, knocks it on his knee so several slide partway out.

"Smoke?"

"Yes, thanks." My voice is barely audible, even to me. Ted flicks his lighter, a Zippo, like the one I used to have. The flame shoots out and almost singes the tip of my nose. I pull back, surprised, but find myself smiling—even his torch flame is tall. "Sorry." He adjusts the flame, lights his, then mine. I inhale deeply, welcoming the dizziness, like taking an elevator down inside myself. Ted takes a deep drag on his cigarette, sucks some of it up his nose, and exhales, adding to the communal cloud. Smoke signals, all around the room.

I make regular trips to the water fountain to take a break from sitting and because the medication makes me thirsty. On one of my runs, Ted asks me to bring some back for him. I drink and drink the warmish water, then take a cup from the dispenser, but the tiny fluted cups, the same ones they use for meds, hold only a sip. A dozen wouldn't be enough, especially for a tall thirsty guy. So I cup my hands and fill them, trailing water on my way back. When I get to Ted there's little left, but he slurps it up like a thirsty deer. "You're a deer," I say, and we laugh out loud. The nurse frowns and makes a note on her clipboard. I laugh louder and go get another drink.

"Fea!" the Spanish-speaking maintenance crew say to me as I pass them in the hallway. I smile at their greeting, until Ted tells me they're calling me ugly. They must hate us for being privileged and spoiled, for being fed without laboring, for abusing everything they work for. Every day they clean up our mess, buffing away the spills and scuffs on the speckled linoleum to a dull sheen.

Half the patients are on high doses of Thorazine. It's easy to tell who. Their faces are bloated, their skin an unnatural pink. That's because Thorazine makes you hypersensitive to light. It dries you out, sucking out all of your life force, replacing it with a chemical stupor. I don't get it. We're here because we don't have enough life force to begin with. They should be helping us have more, not less.

There are other side effects. Trembling hands. Itchy skin. Tongues that won't work, just get in the way—dry, swollen slabs of muscle flopping uselessly in parched mouths that all the water in the world can't quench. If you get dehydrated, your bowels refuse to work and your skin erupts. You're in trouble when you can't bring yourself to get up and go to the water fountain.

The Thorazine zombies sit motionless for hours. That's what they are—the living dead. Even worse are the pacers, trudging back and forth, back and forth until you want to kill them, just to get them out of your line of vision.

Patients who are able to talk compare dosages. Some patients take 2,000 milligrams or more a day. I can only imagine how they feel. I'm on much less, and I feel like I've been nailed to the chair I sit in. I get dizzy when I stand and stagger when I walk. My skin feels three inches thick. My speech is slurred. When I complain, they take my blood pressure. It turns out I have hypotension—low blood pressure, caused by the medication. They take me off it and I feel much better . . . until they decide to start me on Mellaril, which in spite of its name doesn't make me feel mellow.

They add other pills to counteract the side effects, but I still feel dull and distorted, so I do a pretty good act of swallowing, and spit them out later. When they catch me, they make me drink a nasty liquid. After a day of that, I promise to swallow my pills from now on. It's strange that they're so dedicated to pumping me full of drugs, when taking drugs is partly what got me into trouble to begin with.

The drug company that makes Thorazine also makes most of the other drugs we take here. Ted tells me that this same drug company, SmithKline & French, is a major funder of P.I.'s research studies.

"SmithKline and French I adore you. Right from the moment I saw you. . . ." Ted and Liz sing a duet, waxing operatic in their bathrobes.

The ward has one record player, kept on a table in Center. Liz has brought a stack of her own records from the dorm. She slides one out of the sleeve, and after a few static-crackling seconds, Laura Nyro's voice rolls out into the room—a transfusion of melody, filling me with energy, clearing my head. In the next song her voice changes to a bluesy wail, and my pessimism returns.

The adult patients prefer classical music, and the adolescent boys want rock or heavy metal, but almost everyone likes folk songs, especially haunting, melancholy songs. Today's lineup includes Otis Redding, James Taylor (that sweet baby James, rumored to have been in a nuthouse himself, whom we cherish for his suicide ballad "Fire and Rain") and Peter, Paul and Mary. *"I'm leaving on a jet plane,"* Liz sings, swaying to the music. Ted and some others join in on the next song. I know all the words but would never sing aloud in pubic. *"So I'd best be on my way in the early mornin' rain."* Funny to be singing songs about leaving, when nobody's going anywhere.

We sit and wait. The hands of the clock sweep the seconds slowly. The silence buzzes, the air is heavy; medication makes it heavier. We wait, we pace, we jiggle our legs. We wait for meals, for meds, for appointments with doctors and social workers. We wait to be escorted to the bathroom, to school, to O.T. and P.T., and back to the dorm for rest-hour. We wait for sleep. Mostly we wait to get out of here. Dark-browed Aram, inert in his chair, slides to the floor every few minutes, thinking he is committing suicide.

There is little to look forward to: only the craving for coffee, cigarettes, sugar, anything that gives a little jolt. Chain-smokers exhale billows and clouds, fingers brown, breath rank. Cotton-mouthed from medication, we amble to the water fountain but prefer something caffeinated, preferably Coke. The coffee is weak swill, but it's guzzled in abundance. Vending machines on the third floor dispense instant coffee, sodas, candy, and chips, which we purchase with coins from our allowances, if we can find a staff member to accompany us.

———

There is a hierarchy of staff, our keepers. At the top, Dr. Lothar Gidro-Frank, complete with requisite Eastern European accent, his rangy presence looming Lincoln-like above the other psychiatrists. His name is mentioned in hushed tones, like that of a king. Then come his various assistants and underlings, down to the residents: young male psychiatrists-in-training, our doctors. The female social workers, unlikely angels, play an intermediary role. Next, the Virgin Mother: our solid, officious head nurse, who I call "Woodridge" or "Woodfuck," depending on our level of battle. Then the other nurses, in their white uniforms and little white hats, their huge key rings jingling as they bustle down hallways in squishy-soled white shoes; sometimes disgruntled, but mostly helpful and concerned, like white-clad nuns. Finally, those closest to us, the attendants: Mrs. G., with her Irish brogue, big bosom, and conciliatory mothering, tries to be stern but is usually unable to repress a smile. R.J.—a large, powerful black man, capable of wrestling the most difficult patient to the floor in no time flat; sometimes inscrutable, sometimes pleasant; in any case, you *listen.* Curtis Thompson, known as C.T., tall, skinny, and street-smart, a former backup singer with the Cadillacs (*"Well, they often call me Speedo but my real name is Mr. Earl, bop-bop-a-diddleit . . ."*). Sylvester Gabriel ("Sly," for short), handsome, jive, bebop strut in his step; his method of persuasion: charm. "Be cool," he warns if someone's getting out of line; "Slap me five!" his greeting; we slap his open palm once in front, once behind before he struts away. Oliver, blond and refined, a conscientious objector whose exemption from fighting in Vietnam is being paid for by his sentence of public service work: taking care of us. These are our key-bearing keepers, on whom we depend.

———————

Big John stands six feet three, at least 220 pounds. He strides back and forth in a state of agitation, scowling. He's perpetually in motion, as if on wheels, performing ritualistic touching of objects: the walls, his own ear, intensive nose-picking, more furious with each repetition. "I've got liquor in my locker," he repeats as he paces. I wonder if he really does have liquor in my locker, but I don't think the nurses listen to what he's saying.

Izzy, a melancholy wraith, practices scales and arias in an attempt to keep his operatic studies alive. "Ahhh . . . ahhhh . . ." His moaning vocalizing wanders and bends, unable to stick to one key. He waves his hands in the air, conducting a symphony—a tragicomic Jewish Pagliacci.

Izzy is practicing his opera. Big John paces by, fingers in his ears. "Shut up! Shut up!" he mutters, swerving around him. On his return trip, John growls, "Outta my way, damn you!" just a second before he runs into Izzy, knocking him to the floor. Izzy sits there, stunned, a wounded look on his face. John steps around him and continues his furious pacing. R.J. strolls over, hitches up the waist of his white pants, and calmly places himself in John's path, crossing his arms like Mr. Clean. "Once more, my man, and you're in seclusion. Got it?" John stares into space. "Apologize to Izzy," R.J. continues. John mutters something to the floor. Izzy smiles sweetly. "That's okay, forget it, no harm done." He stands and brushes himself off. The show is over, the room exhales, and the rattling of pages and tapping of feet begins again.

Beneath the constant restlessness on the ward there is a suspension of anticipation; we are caught in the sludge of the slow-moving present. Something is missing—that force that keeps a moving bicycle balanced when your feet aren't touching the ground. The innate belief in forward motion has been damaged, replaced with belief in other realities: pain, dark forces, the power of gravity—pulling people from their chairs to the floor, from tops of buildings to sidewalks.

Some of the patients frighten me. Like Howie, who, with his low brow and perpetual dark shadow of beard, resembles a hedgehog. He appears of indeterminate age—though I'm told he's in his mid-twenties, which to me is pretty old. His movements are stiff and zombie-like. Like a just-awakened sleeper, when you talk to him he can barely mumble a few slow, inaudible syllables in reply. Congealed spit collects in the corners of his mouth, and crust lines his eyelids, like forgotten shelves gathering dust. I try not to stare, but he's right across the room.

I sit watching him, my gaze connecting us. After a while it's hard to tell who's who, both of us sitting, staring. I start to get scared. Stiff as stone, I can't move, as if I'm somehow metamorphosing into Howie. Tears trickle down my face, but I still can't move. Mrs. G. comes over and asks me how I am, but I can't speak. She calls a nurse, who talks loudly at me for a while. Her face looks like a mask, and her words sound like they're coming from far away and don't make any sense. I wonder why she's getting all worked up. Then R.J. comes and hauls me to my feet and bundles me off to the Quiet Room—the small square room next to the dorm. The only window is in the door and has dark wire fencing over both sides. There are padded mats on the floor, along with a bare mattress. I sit on the mattress and stare at the walls, searching for signs of others—scratches, stains, graffiti—but they are clean, and silent. Too silent.

The Quiet Room is not really quiet. It's where people go when they're upset, usually dragged there by staff and locked in. Or if you don't feel good, you can ask to go there and stay as long as you like if staff is available to watch you. Sometimes sitting in Center you can hear screaming and banging coming from the Quiet Room. When this happens, I put my hands over my ears, feeling like I need to scream too.

Now it's my turn, but I don't feel like screaming. I cry a little, hug my knees, and rock back and forth. In a little while I drift off to sleep.

In the half hour before the lunch bell is rung, we glance at clocks and watches. Then the bell! We line up and check the day's menu posted on the chalkboard, hoping for some special entree or dessert to add flavor to the day. The bedraggled, green-uniformed food lady, hairnet askew, calls out in her Irish brogue, much to Ted's delight: "Me-at, good hot me-at!" as she slaps the mystery meat du jour onto our plates. It's always the same meat in slightly different forms, called by different names: brisket, roast beef, tenderloin, Salisbury steak. For a change there's tuna casserole, sloppy joes, or spaghetti and meatballs. If we're lucky we get fried chicken; if we're unlucky, "smothered chicken"—which I envision in some agony of asphyxiation. Glutinous gravy drips over piles of potatoes. When I got here I was so skinny that my spine was black and blue from bumping against chair backs, but I already feel fat and constipated from a diet of macaroni and cheese, powdered mashed potatoes, canned vegetables, pasta, cake, and pudding. But when that Pavlovian bell rings, like everyone else, I start to salivate.

After lunch we have one hour to rest back in the dorm. Lulled to a constant drowsiness, I live for these nap-times—my one chance to escape. Sometimes I go into a half dream state, like a hallucination, with kaleidoscopic symbols, sounds, and numbers. I don't know if this is because of the meds. Whatever it is, it's better than being awake. Then the light is snapped back on, and I gradually remember where I am.

Twice a week after rest-hour the doctors make their rounds. A small group of psychiatric residents, led by the director of our ward, walk from bed to bed interviewing the patients, accompanied by a nurse carrying our charts. I sit cross-legged on my bed, hoping they'll pass me by. No such luck. The tall, gray-suited figure of Dr. Lothar Gidro-Frank stops by my bed and looms over me. Some patients call him "Loathsome Lothar," but I think of him as Gidro-Frankenstein. With his pale skin, long, dangly limbs, and disjointed way of walking, he could be made of spare body parts. The laces on the sides of his orthopedic shoes look exactly like stitched-up scars. He smells slightly of martinis.

"Hello, Mindy. How are you feeling today?" he asks in his Hungarian accent.

I don't look up. He's not getting a thing out of me.

He turns to the other doctors. "She's been consistently incommunicative since she was admitted." He turns back to me. "Do you think you will be starting school soon? Hmm?"

I look at the opposite wall. I've already told my shrink I won't go to school. If I wanted to go to school, I wouldn't be here. I feel my silence weighing on them, making them uncomfortable. They don't wait long for an answer, and soon amble over to Liz's bed. She chats with them for a few minutes, like it's some kind of teatime. They exchange smiles, then the clucking band of doctors waddle over to the next sitting duck.

The adolescents go off to school and the ward becomes quiet. The afternoon looms long.

It's important to move occasionally. The longer you sit in one place, the more like a piece of furniture you become. So if you can, you move to another room. There are three choices: Center, where patients can be easily observed, and two living rooms that afford a little more privacy. North living room has a Ping-Pong table. The pinging and ponging, if you're not playing or watching, bounces annoyingly off your brain. In South living room the ancient piano is usually idle, except for "Chopsticks," or the occasional patient who knows how to play. Both living rooms have televisions.

In Center, there are two card tables where patients and staff play poker, bridge, whist, and hearts. On another table there's a jigsaw puzzle—an enormous, complex nature scene, broken into a thousand pieces. Patients wander over to try their hand. Sometimes I try too. The puzzles go fast at first, because it's easiest to find the edges and corner pieces. Blue sky is easy, but white snow and brownish foreground mix together, and tree branches are a jumble. It's frustrating—each piece looks like it could be the one, until you find that the roundish projectiles don't exactly fit the oblong bites in the pieces—always something that doesn't fit, mocking you, reminding you of the texture of your own life. As the puzzle pieces grow fewer, the pace picks up. But in the end, there are always a few pieces missing, a few holes in the landscape. Lost, or never in the box to begin with?

Smoking is our most serious ritual, more natural than breathing: the sharp sulfurous hiss giving way to a subaudible crackle, inhalations like gasps of surprise followed by grateful exhalation. I watch people smoke. Some take deep drags, "steaming" their cigarettes, so the tip glows red. Others, frozen, forget to smoke, and their cigarette turns to one long, gray ash. The worst are those who noisily suck or chew their filters so the tip becomes slimy. Some have more exotic styles. One woman rolls her cigarette around with her tongue, making loud kissing sounds. Ted specializes in slow, lazy plumes that swirl like charmed snakes up and back into his nostrils. French inhale, he calls it. At the end of the day his nostrils are tinged a golden brown.

The ashtrays, large, dented aluminum cans with removable tops, overflow with butts. Patients smoke different kinds to suit their moods: menthol in the morning to perk them up, regular for serious afternoon contemplation, nonfilters for an espresso-like kick. Packs are stowed in pockets; hospital bathrobes provide two, pajama tops one. Matches are always in demand; lighters, prized. People trim their wicks carefully, lovingly. Lighter fluid is kept locked up, too volatile for the likes of us.

Someone is screaming, horrible piercing screams that come at regular intervals, like an alarm. The screams cut into my brain like knives. I put my hands over my ears and roll into a little ball. The nurse comes over and asks me what's the matter. Can't she hear? I ask why she doesn't do something. The nurse is calm. "We know Helen is upset, but she'll calm down soon," she says. Then she asks why it bothers me. What kind of place is this? Someone should go put their arms around Helen and tell her she's going to be all right. But they don't give a shit. They just walk down the hall like nothing's wrong, like everything's under control. The screaming fades and finally stops, but the alarm is still going on inside of me.

Is this what I have to look forward to day after day?

I have a headache, a horrible pounding throb behind my eyes. I get them every day, along with burning stomachaches. I don't know if it's because of the medication or the thoughts accumulated in my head, the fear and anger stuck in my stomach. I tell the nurse, and she gives me some aspirin and permission to go back to the dorm and lie down. Mrs. G. wakes me for dinner: more of the same starch, the same mystery meat. I fill myself up and then feel bloated. If there's any left I get seconds of dessert and wrap it in a napkin in case I get hungry later. No matter how much your stomach grumbles, there's no more food until morning.

After dinner and evening meds we watch television. On the news we witness the escalation of the war and the latest student protests. Then we negotiate which programs to watch. In one living room, they're watching game shows. In the other, we watch *Mission Impossible,* and then it's a toss-up between *The Fugitive* and *The Avengers.* We spend a blissfully absorbed hour watching beautiful, classy Emma Peel somersault her way out of hopeless situations, unrumpled and impeccable. If only I could somersault my way out of here.

Sometimes there's a movie, which we watch with lights out, taking us through two hours—almost the whole evening. There's a strict 10 P.M. curfew, 11 on weekends. If the movie runs long, we're out of luck. The attendant snaps off the TV, and we shuffle off to our dorms, stopping for last-minute sleeping meds at the nurses' station. A trip to the bathroom, then it's lights-out, and if you're lucky, the deep sleep of the drugged descends to blot out the day.

———————

At the end of my second week, I come down with a spiking fever. I am moved into a private room, my inner world taken over by visions of living geometry and alien music. Burning hot, I wake to freezing wetness. Someone is bathing me in ice cubes, wrapping me in wet sheets. An electric fan, mounted high on the wall, whirs day and night. Time lengthens into a dark corridor. Someone shakes me and asks, "Do you know your name? What day it is? What year?" Though I'm not sure I want to, I say my name and begin my return. But I am changed. It's as if my entry into the atmosphere of this new planet I am on has burned away my earthly crust, my attachment to life outside.

LIFE BEFORE

W HY ARE YOU HERE?" When asked the inevitable question, I mumble
something about taking drugs, dropping out of school, and not
getting along with my mother. More than that I can't say. Lately I've
become nearly mute, words clogging and clotting in my brain.

In my world, confusion reigns. Ask me any question and I'll have a
hard time answering. There seems to be no real me, no real self, just a
mass of unanswerable questions. A whole flock of selves fighting for
space. Or maybe there are two selves: the good me and the bad me, the
old me and the new me.

At home, my mother has albums filled with snapshots: three-year-old
me in front of our Stuyvesant Town apartment building, making a silly
face. At the beach, my ponytail pulled tight, doing the cha-cha for the
grown-ups. A profile shot, all dressed up in my patent-leather shoes and
charm bracelet, posing with my beautiful mother.

That was a long time ago. The girl in the photos, so unlike me, might
as well be someone else. Like Kafka's cockroach, I seem to have under-
gone a reverse metamorphosis, changing from butterfly to chrysalis, an
ugly pod hanging by a thread. In pajamas, no less.

A snapshot: my mother and I together in Central Park. I hold up a
flower for her to see. She wears a dress printed with large, splashy flowers,
the neckline swooping low, revealing the tops of her breasts. Her coppery
hair curls away from her face. She poses for the camera like a movie star,
her eyes obscured by dark glasses. I wear a pink dress, pink ankle socks,

and white shoes; I'm chubby-cheeked, with legs like chunky little columns.

Which picture is real? Me at thirteen, unconscious in a stairwell from too much Demerol, some neighborhood boy's hands in my pants? Or that little girl, happy just to be, dancing ballet around the living room or curling up in my father's arms.

"I've got you in my power, me fair beauty! Ha ha ha haaah!" he'd cry in a scratchy pirate's voice, and tickle me until I shrieked with laughter and mock fear, thrilled. That was heaven—my father's face close to mine, my finger tracing the square line of his jaw, ending in the cleft in his stubbly chin; the clean smell of his T-shirt with a hint of cigarette smoke; his wavy brown hair and brown eyes shining with play.

There are clues that life isn't quite as sunny as it seems: the sound of shouting, my older brother crying himself to sleep, the crash of my mother's prized ornamental china plates, cream and maroon, shattering on the floor. I don't remember who flung them, but a sense of irreparable loss was imprinted in my body.

A family portrait taken by my father: Six years old, I beam at the camera while my eleven-year-old brother looks glum, and my mother looks away, stone-faced. Not long after, my parents break the news: Daddy is moving to California, just for a while, to start his own business. I live in that hope, and a year and a half later we join my father in Burbank.

Burbank is a foreign country: hairpin turns through the foothills in my dad's baby-blue Hillman, the setting sun as huge and orange as the round Esso gas station signs. Streets that circle and wander, unlike the familiar New York City grid. I trudge home from school in rainwater up to my knees because earthquake-prone San Fernando Valley has no sewers. People speak differently, with long flat vowels, and in my class we're studying what I learned last year. All the other kids' parents are voting for Nixon, not Kennedy, like mine. I don't think it's an accident when the kids sitting behind me at the movies pour a Coke down my back. On Halloween my mom dresses up as a hobo and comes trick or treating with me, and I don't care anymore about the other kids.

Though I love being near my dad and watch, shyly thrilled, as my parents slow-dance across the living room, I don't like California. I miss my friends in New York, my school, and my familiar surroundings. After six months, my mother, brother, and I return to New York.

"You're the reason Mommy and Daddy are getting divorced," my brother accuses me the day before we leave California. It's just another variation on the usual big brother/little sister torture, yet somehow I do feel responsible. For the first time, I become aware of myself as a player in the family drama. When I say good-bye to my dad at the airport, I ham it up like a love scene in a movie. "Stop those crocodile tears," my mother says as we board the plane.

Back in our New York apartment, I move into my mother's room to give my now thirteen-year-old brother, with whom I'd shared a bedroom, some privacy. My mother and I become roommates.

I love my mother with fierce adoration. When my best friend taunts me, saying my mother is *divorced,* I bring my fist down hard on her back and shout that her mother is ugly.

My mother is beautiful. When I was little I thought of her hair as slices of apricots, the bright waves pointing toward her face. She is her own work of art. I watch with fascination as she does her makeup standing in front of the sink in bra and panties, examining her face in the medicine-cabinet mirror, opening her eyes wide as she applies mascara; tilting her head back; stroking, plucking, smoothing, powdering; smiling as the lipstick glides on, then blotting. I watch as she throws the square of toilet paper she blotted with in the toilet bowl, the paper turning transparent, the red imprint of her lips floating on the water's surface. She rubs any stray lipstick marks off her teeth with her finger. Finally, spritzes of perfume, which make me sneeze, on neck, wrists, breasts. Sometimes I get a sprintz too.

I watch as she gets dressed. Stockings shimmy up to garters over long, shapely legs. Slips and blouses and skirts or dresses rustle carefully over her head. She ties a protective scarf over her head and face to keep from mussing her hair and makeup. Then comes jewelry, a scarf, perhaps a belt. High-arched feet slide into spike heels.

My mother is up on the latest fashions and strolls the department stores with presence and purpose, dragging me in tow. She knows all the best creams, lotions, and perfumes. She belongs in a scented, laundered, powdered place. She taps red fingernails on glass tabletops. She finds wisdom in the articles of the monthly women's magazines: *Glamour, Mademoiselle.* She belongs to that secret society of which I am not yet a part—she is a woman.

"Who's the best mommy in the world?" my mother asks.

"You are!" comes my fervent reply. What other mother looks so beautiful, keeps the apartment so clean, and goes to work every day? My mother works hard at her secretarial job. Everybody admires her proud presence. "Big Red," the men at her office call her. When they take her out for dinner, I wait up for her good-night kiss, and inhale the smell of drinks and dinner mingling with her perfume.

My mother spends her nonworking hours making order at home and browsing the fashion pages and *House Beautiful.* She redecorates regularly. The credenza and drum table, with their dark wood, leather, and brass tracks, are replaced by Danish modern around the same time the walls and upholstery are redone in colors named for vegetables and plants: avocado, bittersweet. I help my mother choose paint chips and fabric swatches.

My mother wages constant war against disorder. Each hiss of the steam iron impresses her will into the wrinkled sheets. The kitchen is always left spotless, the dishes dried and stacked. Sometimes I open the door of the linen closet, inhaling the scent of the folded sheets and towels, and run my fingers over the spools in my mother's sewing basket, marveling at the perfect uniformity of the colorful, tightly wound thread.

On weekends, delicious smells float from the kitchen. My favorite meal is shepherd's pie and a dessert called ambrosia, made with mandarin oranges, marshmallows, and coconut. While she works, my mother sings along with Ella Fitzgerald or Harry Belafonte records, and all is well in the world. But there's another version of my mother: the one who comes home and vents her frustration while cleaning the apartment. "Ungrateful kids!" she shouts above the whine of the vacuum cleaner. "I only wish one day you'll have children like yourselves!" My brother and I look at each other. What did we do now? I tiptoe around until the storm passes.

Marie, our black "cleaning lady," comes three days a week. She cooks, cleans, walks me to school and to the playground. On the days Marie doesn't come, my brother, five years older than me and newly assigned man of the house, watches me after school. Resentment blooms and explodes. We fight so loudly my mother can hear my screams floating toward her from our window as she walks home from work. Then we both catch hell, but it's usually worse for my brother.

Before falling asleep, I hug my favorite stuffed animal and vow to do something special to make Mommy feel better—make her a present, or be extra neat and clean.

When my father was still around things were comfortably neat and lived in, but after he left, the apartment became spotless. The comfortable overstuffed gray sofa was replaced by a "contemporary" couch with slab-like cushions, sheathed in clear plastic, that made unwelcoming sounds when sat on. Tiles in the entry hall and new carpeting required the removal of shoes. No smudges allowed on mirrors or windows. Spills and crumbs met with charged disapproval.

My mother applied this same meticulousness to my physical appearance. When I was little I wore dresses with Peter Pan collars and little pearl buttons down the front to match the pearl buttons on my white shoes, which were supposed to *stay* white, my hair brushed back into a ponytail so tight that my eyes slanted up. "You're so pretty," my mother would say, tying a pink ribbon around my ponytail. "She's just a doll," said her friends. "A real doll," my relatives gushed, pinching my cheek. This did not seem such a bad thing to me. I loved my dolls, whom I tenderly thought of as my babies. I was happy playing with my dolls and stuffed animals. I wrote them poems and sang them songs. And I loved to draw, and read.

Afternoons after school, and on the weekends, I immerse myself in books. A trip to the library is my greatest treat. I love being able to take home any book I want—and there are so many—for free, as long as I take good care of them. Every night before saying my prayers with my mother, I read. Even after lights out, I read under the covers with a flashlight: *Nancy Drew*, my brother's *Hardy Boys* books, Pearl S. Buck, and my mother's own copy of *A Tree Grows in Brooklyn*.

When I read *Little Women*, I cry buckets of tears at the death of saintly, sickly, beautiful Beth. Dying young and innocent seems to me the most romantic of fates. When I'm sick I get special attention. My mother brings me mashed potatoes and carrots and warm ginger ale, and best of all, I get to stay home in bed, reading and drifting off into sleep, imagining I am as good and beautiful as poor, doomed Beth.

Once a year my dad comes to New York. I await his arrival with joy, staying up late in my favorite pajamas, beaming at the camera when he takes my picture. How lucky I am—five whole days with my dad! Snapshots: My brother, Dad, and I on the observation deck of the Empire State Building, the city sparkling below us. After a challenging climb up the arm of the Statue of Liberty, a breathless ride on the Staten Island Ferry, the wind whipping my hair. I slurp up a frothy ice cream soda at Rumpelmayer's, then my dad takes me shopping. I wear my new dress when we visit his relatives on Long Island. While he stands chatting, I loop my arm around my father's leg and hug him tight, my cheek against his trousers. I can't get enough of him.

The next day he takes off for his bachelor's life in sunny California.

"We'll go shopping for a new daddy at Macy's," my mother promises. Instead she goes out on dinner dates. Only one, a tall gray-haired man who talks in a phony British accent, starts to come around regularly. My mother says he's good-looking, but that's not what I see, just watery, pale-blue eyes and a carefully trimmed steel-gray mustache that makes his unsmiling lips even thinner, especially when he's criticizing me and my brother. They date for almost a year—much too long, from my point of view, though I'd never tell her that. Finally, my mother breaks up with him after he slaps her face for slamming the door of his well-cared-for car. This happens on her birthday—the same day the radio broadcasts the news of Marilyn Monroe's death. When I ask why she's crying, she says it's because Marilyn is dead. The apartment fills with a mournful mood. I try to cheer her up, but I feel sad too. Nothing is worse than seeing my mother upset.

My mother has lots of friends and enjoys throwing dinner parties. After helping clean bowls of shrimp and dressing up for the party, I make my appearance. Later, in bed, I listen to the hum of grown-ups talking and laughing. It's as if there are two sets of us: the shiny, show-off ones, and the unhappy, simmering, explosive private ones.

"You'll never be eight again," I say to my nine-year-old face in the mirror. I smile at myself, and the eyes in the mirror smile back. Nine means free-dom: I can ride my bike wherever I want, as long as I stay in Stuyvesant Town. I ride up and down the landscaped hills, into quadrants with build-ings identical to mine, except they smell different. I run my fingers through the tassles on my bike's handlebars, bring my face close and mur-mur, "Good horse, steady, boy," then I ride and ride and ride.

Stuyvesant Town is an oasis of suburban safety, right in the city. Guard stations stand at every entrance. Twice a day sprinklers douse the well-groomed lawns; the sweet smell of freshly mowed grass tickles my throat. There's plenty of green grass I'm not allowed to walk on and trees I'm not allowed to climb. Acorns, leaves, and winged "noses" twirl to earth in autumn. Earthworms surface after spring rain and caterpillars spin cocoons and burst out as butterflies. Sparrows chirp and squirrels scam-

per. This is nature as I know it: tantalizing, but untouchable. Signs are
everywhere: DO NOT ENTER, DO NOT WALK ON GRASS. There's a sense of
someone always watching; a higher power, a melding of God, Mom, and
Metropolitan Life.

Aside from dirt and germs, my mother's major anxiety is physical
injury. She is terrified that I'll hurt myself, and I absorb her fear. I'm hes-
itant and awkward, and can never quite lose myself in roller-skating, running, or playing.

Sometimes my mother comes home on her lunch hour to make me
lunch. On one of these special days, I fall in the schoolyard playing
ring-a-levio and slide along the pavement on my face and arm. Terrified of
my mother's reaction, I let myself into the apartment and, shielding my
face with my hand, head straight for the bathroom. When she sees my
face, her alarmed cry, "What did you do to yourself?" is worse than the
sting of my scrapes.

On afternoons when I don't go to a friend's house after school, I walk
the few blocks home, stopping for ice cream or a piece of fruit from the
produce stand on First Avenue. I let myself into the apartment with the
key I wear on a ribbon around my neck. Then I'm alone in the quiet,
gleaming apartment. I get a snack from the refrigerator and settle on my
bed to do my homework. Soon after the light fades, I hear a key in the
door—Mom is home. She kicks off her shoes, changes out of her work
clothes, turns on some music, and the apartment comes alive. I set the
table while she heats up the dinner Marie has prepared.

I do what my mother tells me, and usually I don't mind. But starting in
sixth grade, I'm tempted to take some chances. One afternoon, a group of
kids invite me to go with them to Murphy Park, a place I'm expressly forbidden to go. It's not really a park, more like a paved playground with ten-
nis courts. It's located on Avenue D near the East River, south of
Stuyvesant Town, in the big, wide, unprotected, unknown, forbidden
world. These kids are not my usual group of friends—they're tougher,
more daring and worldly. I tell them I can't come, because my mother
won't let me. Come anyway, they say—she'll never know.

How could she not know? I can't help feeling that my mother knows
and sees everything. But I don't want to be a drip, so I say okay. It's not the
first time I've lied to my mother.

Murphy Park turns out to be a disappointment. The concrete playground is gritty with soot that floats in from the highway with the *whump,*

whump of passing cars. I work at pretending to have fun, but mostly watch the others running around playing tag. Then they take turns climbing through the broken window of an adjoining garage. "Come on," they call, "it's fun."

I climb unsteadily onto the concrete ledge, unsure of my body and afraid of heights. In spite of my friends' urgings, I don't want to do it. It's not just because it's dark and scary inside. My clothes could get torn on the jagged glass; if they just get dirty I'll have a hard time explaining it to my mother. All I want to do is get home, but I'm afraid to go by myself, afraid I'll get lost or some nameless bad thing will happen.

Luckily I get home before she does. I immediately change my clothes, which smell faintly of garage. When my mother gets home and asks what I did after school, I tell her I was at my friend Susie's house. She doesn't suspect a thing.

Soon after that I start lying, mostly about small things. "Where were you?" my mother asks, and I tell her I was at the library—even though I wasn't. Or if I had been to the library I tell her I was at a friend's house. I feel a new space between her and me, a kind of insulation like the inside of corrugated cardboard, each lie another little air pocket. I start to stand apart. And as I do, things change. My blond hair darkens to a tawny light brown that we set with rollers into a flip. My body expands to fill the dresses that used to look pretty, but now look ugly, and the little bulges on my chest embarrass me.

I always feel like hiding when my mother's dates come to pick her up, neither of us knowing what to say when we're introduced. But I rarely see them more than once or twice, until she meets the one who'll become my stepfather. He arrives at the door one night with a huge smile and a bunch of flowers, smelling like Canoe.

"He drags his leg a little, so please don't stare," my mother forewarned me, but when he greets me I'm so shy I hardly look up from watching *Bonanza*.

My mother remarries when I'm eleven. We move into a larger apartment just a few blocks away, and I sadly say good-bye to the one that's been home all my life.

My new stepfather is nice, almost too nice. He has a hard time keeping jobs but is always cheerfully optimistic. "Don't worry, gorgeous," he tells my mother. "I'll get a better job."

He has his good qualities. Every week he gets new books from the library. Sometimes I pick up what he's been reading. I read a little bit of *Lolita* and am intrigued; I can tell right away there's something dirty about Humbert's feelings. I shut the book when my stepfather finds me reading it, but he doesn't seem to mind. "It's a classic!" he exclaims, ignoring my mother's frowns. To him everything is "a classic." Songs, books, jokes, stories. "Classic!" he says about everything.

When my stepfather finds me engrossed in his copy of James Agee's *A Death in the Family*, he's especially impressed, and announces to my mother and anyone else who'll listen how "precocious" and "bright" I am. "Dollgirl," he says, pulling me close for a cuddle, "I always wanted a daughter, and when I married your mother, I got you."

It's confusing having a new father. I partly want him to love me, and I partly want him to go away. I'm reluctant to invite my girlfriends over after school. He embarrasses me, answering the door in his boxer shorts, singing "Fly Me to the Moon"—one of his favorite "classics." He joins us in the kitchen, conspiratorially bringing the conversation around to sex . . . nothing very explicit, just enough to make us explode into giggles.

My stepfather is proud of having been in Freudian analysis twice a week for more than twenty years. He loves to show off his psychoanalytic jargon in everyday exchange. He's not, he cheerfully insists, "anal retentive"—he makes sure of this with his daily use of suppositories.

He also extends his Freudianisms to others.

"You have penis envy," he informs me, as if it's an established fact. I check myself for traces of this condition, but if it's there, it's invisible to me. Why should I envy that wormlike thing that causes such embarrassment when it accidentally flops out of boys' underpants?

"Why did you have to marry him?" I ask my mother.

"It was time to get a father for you and your brother," she says. Since my brother started high school, he and my mother often engage in screaming battles that end in blows and bitterness. Sometimes at night I hear him sobbing himself to sleep. These days I'm the "good" child, my brother the "bad" one. I capitalize on this arrangement, commiserating with my mother after the fireworks have died down.

Snapshots show my brother as a cute, happy little boy, mugging for the camera in his cowboy hat and holsters. In one photo taken when I was an infant, he hugs my chubby body in his arms, smiling lovingly at his new little sister. In later photos his face became sullen and unhappy. Instead of playing, he bullied me and made me cry. Now my brother has a flat-topped crew cut and hardly talks to me.

The same year my mother marries my stepfather, my sixteen-year-old brother graduates high school and goes off to California, where he lives with my father and gets free tuition at UCLA, majoring in philosophy. I look up to him. He reads literature—not magazines or bestsellers like my mother, or the Reader's Digest Condensed Books (just add water, like Campbell's soup) my father reads. My brother gives me a clothbound anthology of modern poetry—my most treasured possession. I read the poems aloud, reveling in their sound.

Just as I'm discovering that my brother is my ally, he is leaving. The focus will now be on me.

I stand in front of our foyer mirror, watching the ache that fills me overflow down my cheeks, and recognize this new sadness as something uniquely my own, something nobody can take from me . . . but also something nobody else can understand or share.

Suddenly, everywhere I look I see suffering. I see—really see—my first homeless person, smell the stale alcohol and sour flesh. On the bus, I sit across from a woman with a severely disfigured arm; she cradles the gnarled, twisted limb in her lap. Horrified, I blink back tears. When she rises to get off the bus and I see the "arm" is just a piece of driftwood she is carrying, I weep with relief.

I start to wander farther afield. I'm not allowed to go near the East River, so that's where I go. Crossing the highway is scary, but sitting on the deserted pier is divine; there I can be alone in the salty air, just me and the seagulls on the weathered pilings, casting their rippled reflections. I'm happiest by myself, with a book or a sketchbook and some watercolors, painting the moody sky and river, savoring the silence, away from yelling mothers and ridiculous stepfathers.

At home, I feel a kind of oppression. The stillness in the apartment makes me sluggish and dull. The smell of furniture polish gives me a headache. And there is the ever-present tension, my mother's constant dissatisfaction.

"Look at this place! Pick up your shoes! Is this what I work so hard to come home to?"

I start to hate the sound of my mother's voice, the way she phrases things, with all her little nuances: Nagging. Annoyance. Distaste.

Criticism. I know it all by heart, as if her voice has worn a groove in my inner ear. The way she says my name: "Min-*day*," ending in a little growl of disapproval. The way she taps her red-lacquered fingernails on tabletops and glasses, the *click-clicking* marking her territory, assuring her of her importance, claiming her rightful place at the center of the universe. It makes my stomach clench.

Underneath, a different voice nags me, asking questions I can't answer. How can I suddenly hate what I used to love? It can't be her fault. She's the same mother I've always loved. The answer is a simple equation: She is good. I am bad. Or is it the other way around? I'm not sure of anything anymore.

A new me emerges. At thirteen I start drinking, smoking cigarettes and marijuana. By fourteen I wear all black and carry with me a pack of Marlboro cigarettes and a Zippo lighter. My grades drop. I can't pay attention in school and I can't sleep at night. My weight falls to ninety-eight pounds, my flesh shrinking on my big-boned five feet seven and a half-inch frame.

"What will the neighbors think?" my mother yells after I'm arrested for smoking marijuana, shaking my shoulders so my head bangs against the wall. Some criminal. When an officer at the police station, suspecting needle tracks, asked about some marks on my arm, I answered truthfully: "My cat scratched me," trying not to cry.

It's not just me. Other kids smoke dope. My new friends—tough kids, "greasers," not the "nice" kids I used to hang out with—teach me what they know about all sorts of ways to get high.

In the afternoons, I come home from school to our spotless apartment, the smell of furniture polish, and the hum of empty hours. After Marie finishes her ironing and goes home, I stay in the dark living room and carefully put a record on my mother's stereo. I sip a little out of the bottles in her liquor cabinet: crème de menthe, sherry, Kahlua—easier to swallow than vodka or scotch. Then I find a bottle of cleaning fluid. Soaking a rag, I breathe the sweet, suffocating fumes until I no longer know who or where I am.

"Wear your love like heaven," Donovan sings in his white robes, flowers entwined in his hair. I seem to be going in the opposite direction. I have nothing but scorn for the alarming superficiality of what most people, particularly my mother and stepfather, have to say. I resolve to be different. While the rest of the world sleeps, I am wide awake, reading poetry

by Eliot and Yeats and existentialist writings by Kafka, Sartre, and Camus. I accompany Harry Haller, the *Steppenwolf,* on his inner journey and draw pen-and-ink illustrations of *The Hollow Men* and the cave of Barabbas. Or I'm busy memorizing the sayings of Buddha or listening with illicit rapture to the subversive ramblings of Steve Post or Bob Fass on WBAI, the volume on my transistor radio turned down low. When I light a cigarette, I lean out the window and cough to disguise the sound of striking the match. I smoke anything from jasmine tea to banana peels to tobacco mixed with aspirin, in a corncob pipe I hide behind a book in my bookcase.

Daytime is harsh, with its pressures and confusion. I come alive at dusk. From my bedroom window I paint the streetlights glowing through the purple drizzle on First Avenue. I love everything about painting—my brushes and tubes of watercolors, the thick, textured paper. When I'm painting I lose track of everything but the paint swirling in my palette tray, and the colors entering my eyes and flowing from my brush onto the wet paper. When I emerge from my trance, I look at my work and see the glow of streetlamps reflected in wet pavement, rows of buildings, empty streets. The painting has something else in it, something extra that I hadn't been aware of putting in it—loneliness.

Emotion is my own private poetry. I love rain and the city at dusk, the moody urban sky, the seagulls circling my secret East River pier. I love sadness, and sad songs, and being alone. I sip jasmine tea, burn incense, put a red lightbulb in the lamp next to my bed, and read late into the night. All I want to do is think, dream, and read. I hate any interruption into my inner world. Lying in the backseat of my parents' car, sunbeams flashing red through my eyelids, imagining a thrilling future, I tune out their voices until I can't stand it any longer. "Shh! Please be quiet! I'm thinking!"

I write a poem for my ninth-grade English class:

DAYDREAMS

In a fog,
Invisible fingers repress me,
Envelop, massage, conduct me away.
It is not night, nor is it day.

Coming nearer,
Almost within my frantic reach
Voices once heard, faces once known—
I'm caught in a vortex, whirling, alone.

On the shore—
The water flows, glows for tomorrow.
Waves slap, tease at my feet.
I waver with weakness, attempt no retreat.

I must find reality.
I blink my eyes, cough, feel a breeze.
Yet I am gone, swallowed by a soothing sea,
In my nest of solace, waiting for me.

In the morning when my mother and stepfather are in the kitchen drinking coffee and listening to AM radio, I sleep, undaunted by my stepfather's escalating attempts to wake me—first verbally, then stripping off my covers, and finally sprinkling me with cold water. In the kitchen I switch the dial from my mother's news and Muzak station and hear the black national anthem, "Lift Every Voice and Sing." I stand in a state of thrall as the music passes through me.

There is a passion, an intensity in the air that is almost religious. Blues and gospel, rock, and folk pour from the radio—not the same old love songs, but bearing a new message.

"*Come mothers and fathers throughout the land, and don't criticize what you can't understand. Your sons and your daughters are beyond your command. . . .*" Bob Dylan, prophet of the new age, intones the new order. The times have changed, in the blink of an eye.

Suddenly the whole world is different. The war in Vietnam rages. Conscientious objectors burn flags and draft cards. Peaceful demonstrators are beaten by cops. I grow flagrantly scornful toward my mother's plastic-wrapped world. What matters to me is inside. I want to acquire inner beauty, the kind that has nothing to do with makeup and fashion. Truth and love are what's important.

I wander into Washington Square, wearing the paisley dashiki I sewed by hand over my jeans, carrying my sandals. I try to look hip, but when one of the local characters, a black man reeking of alcohol, puts the moves on me, I get scared and hurry home, feeling like a moral failure. Why was I so frightened? Am I a racist? Should I have let him kiss me? I don't understand why I'm always so fearful.

My mother meets me at the door, checks the soles of my feet and sniffs me. I try not to laugh, but she's dead serious. She's taken to policing my person for foreign matter: dirt, smoke, subversion. She seems afraid of me—even to hate me. I'm starting to realize who the enemy is.

When I take the admission test for the High School of Music and Art, I know I'll get in. I'm well prepared by the art school I've been attending on Saturday mornings since eighth grade, mornings spent engrossed in quiet concentration, inhaling the smell of fixative and turpentine, hooked on the magic of charcoal, pastel, watercolor, oil.

Excitement and fear accompany me on my first day at Music and Art. As I climb the 126 stone steps up the hill in Harlem to the castle-like building, its two towers marking the sky, I feel myself stepping toward my destiny. Streams of kids climb with me—aspiring artists and musicians, all chosen to attend this special school. Older kids greet each other, looking cool and confident. A friend from junior high points out a girl standing on the front steps, surrounded by a small crowd—Janis Ian, already a successful musician. In our first freshman assembly my skin tingles with a sense of honor and opportunity. I have stepped away from the materialistic world into the world of art and ideas.

It isn't long before the dream gives way. The kids surrounding me appear hipper, more creative, more savvy than me. Shyness strikes me dumb in the lunchroom. I tremble when kids speak to me, or don't speak to me, and try to concentrate on swallowing my food. It's a relief when the bell rings and the mob scene called lunch is over. During the shuffle between periods, the metal staircases echo with talking and singing—the music students are unfettered and exuberant. I envy them. If only I could feel free, instead of tied up in knots.

At Music and Art a revolution is taking place. Marijuana smoke seeps out from beneath the girls' bathroom door. Miniskirts give way to bell-bottoms, in spite of the fact that girls wearing pants to school are threatened with expulsion. I get into the habit of stubbing my cigarette out on the sole of my boot, then stowing the butt in the pocket of my khaki army shirt to smoke later. I iron my hair so it's stick-straight, my bangs hanging low into my eyes. I wear Erase on my lips and line my eyelids with black.

At first I do well in my classes, especially studio art. When the teacher holds up one of my watercolors as an example to show the class, I'm caught between pride and self-loathing. It's as if I'm still a child pleasing my mother. I scowl when the teacher praises my work to show I don't care for her approval.

It's a long commute from Stuyvesant Town to Music and Art, a circuitous route involving three subway trains. On my way to school a pressure builds inside me. The train lurches, screeches; bodies press against me. When the train finally pulls into Columbus Circle, I surface like an air bubble, emerging right next to Central Park. I'd been to Central Park a handful of times when I was little, and a handful more in junior high, with friends. But I've never come just by myself. My only witnesses are the pigeons atop the bronze statue of Columbus at the park's entrance. As I follow the path into the park, trees obscure the buildings, and the sounds of traffic fade behind me.

Alone in the park, I'm suddenly part of nature. Here, I can breathe, and everything breathes along with me: trees, sky, rocks—everything breathing peace. I gaze across the Sheep Meadow at a vista so wide it's dizzying. Each color shines: vivid blues, soft greens, muted browns. I take my watercolors from my backpack and get to work. If only my brush could capture this beauty! Sycamores, oaks, and maples make a tracery of branches against the sky, each tree a world in itself: gnarled and crooked or smooth and straight, with almost human limbs and intricately tangled roots. Rocks, smooth or striated, the same ones we learned about in Earth Science, are like primordial sleeping creatures. How absurd to sit in classrooms when the world is alive and waiting.

Soon I'm in the park more often than school. There's always more to explore. I get lost in the Ramble, with its twisting paths that tunnel through rocks and over bridges, but always manage to find myself again. I pass other wanderers, as deep in their thoughts as I am. There are endless quiet places to sit and read. If I get lonely I go to Bethesda Fountain where a crowd of kids hang out, always on the lookout for the police. A smorgasbord of drugs is available—grass, hash, ups, downs, and sideways (amphetamine, Demerol, Seconal, Benzedrine poppers, mescaline, and LSD), sometimes for free if you're female. Sometimes I wake up, clothing disheveled, foggily aware that something or other has transpired between me and some long-haired boy. I've rejected the boys my mother likes; I like the ones who call themselves "freaks." For every six who want to make it with me, there's one who protects me. A long-haired freak named Lee guides me on my first acid trip.

There are moments of great joy walking barefoot and unprotected in heavy spring downpours, drenched to the skin. I resonate to the raw anger in Dylan's voice, the redemptive poetry of Phil Ochs's protest songs, the Beatles' harmonies, Judy Collins's loneliness, the electric wail of Jimi Hendrix's guitar. Seas of diamonds, emeralds, rubies tumble down Fifth Avenue at dusk as I emerge from Central Park high on LSD.

"She's disturbed," says my stepfather, urging my mother to send me to a psychiatrist.

It takes a while to get myself to talk to Dr. L. At first I sit smoking Marlboros, clicking the lid of my lighter. Dr. L. smiles. "I know what you're really saying. With each click, you're saying, 'Fuck you.'" In addition to his private practice, Dr. L. is a staff shrink on the prison psych ward at Bellevue. For all his compassion and humor, he's a bit hard-boiled. I like him. I wish he could enter my mind, hear my thoughts, experience my loneliness and pain. But I can only speak to him in code, bouncing my leg furiously up and down, my hair covering my face. Minutes tick by, each breath amplified. I try to impress him with my weirdness.

"People are strange when you're a stranger. . . ." Jim Morrison's lyrics could have been written just for me. Being strange has its advantages. Boys fall in love with me and offer to save me. "You're an artist without a medium," says one, as he tries to kiss me.

"You're so vague," a girlfriend criticizes my spacey dreaminess. I learn in French class that the word "vague" means wave, and decide I'm wavy— like the sea, I have my ups and downs. It's just that the undertow is becoming stronger, its pull more powerful. I try to figure it out. Am I superficial or deep, a real person or a fake? The self-judgments pile up. I'm a horrible person, a nonperson.

I test myself: Holding the tip of a lit cigarette inches from my arm, I bring it close enough to feel the heat. Will I be able to do it? I watch, and as if on its own, the cigarette touches my skin. The sting is overridden by a thrill: I'm claiming power in a radical new way. I show the burns to my mother and watch the confusion and fear flicker across her face.

I ask Dr. L. if he thinks I'm crazy. He says he doesn't think so.

"Well, what am I?"

"Confused. Frightened. Phobic. And I also think you're angry."

I don't like any of these words. I try to model myself on the

Buddhist and Hindu concept of nonattachment. I despair that I'm not more spiritually enlightened. "It's human nature," Dr. L. reassures me. "Animals find good use for aggression. Do you think we're so different?"

Little by little I open up. When I tell him how much I hate *them*, and how different from *them* I am, Dr. L. seems to understand. I like that he doesn't judge me. But I don't dare confess that he reminds me of my absent father, who's become more and more a stranger.

My mother and I no longer talk—she screams at me and I scream back. The old me is completely gone. I hate that good little girl, and I hate the person I've become. Above all, I hate my mother. She takes up all the space, breathing all the air, telling everyone what to do, her anxiety suffocating me.

We now refer to each other as third-person pronouns:

My mother: "I can't understand what's gotten into her. She's not the same child."

Me: "She thinks she knows everything, but she's full of it! I don't care what she says."

My stepfather chimes in. "Do not call your mother 'she'! It's disrespectful! Do you hear?" He raises his hand to slap me. I throw my lit cigarette at him and mouth the words "Fuck you." My mother grabs my arm, digging her nails into my skin. Our shrieks ring, hanging above us in the startled air.

I'm suddenly the cause of all the trouble in the family. There's a tension in the air that rarely breaks. My stepfather and my mother argue constantly about what to do with me. When they're tired of fighting with each other, they gang up on me. My stepfather is just trying to look good in my mother's eyes, as if his taking charge would make her forget that he can't hold a job. He's grotesque, with his suppositories and his skinny legs sticking out of his boxer shorts. He tells my mother over and over how sick I am, calls me a "problem child," and says that if I don't straighten out I may need to be hospitalized. He pretends to be concerned, but I know he wants me out of the way.

I try running away but wind up staying overnight at my best friend's house. Her parents make me call my mother to let her know where I am. She's so uptight that if I come home even a couple of hours late she calls the police.

I have to get away—but where? After I'm suspended from high school, there aren't many options. The private school I visit with my mother won't take me. I'm too much of a risk.

Dr. L. tells my mother about an "institute" where they specialize in adolescents and urges her to apply. When he asks how I feel about this, all I can think of is *I Never Promised You a Rose Garden*, about the girl with multiple personalities (I wish I were as interesting as she is), and *David and Lisa*, a movie about a schizophrenic boy and girl living in a mental institution. Lisa can only talk in rhyme, and David can't bear to be touched. They're supposed to be crazy, but I think they're exquisitely sensitive. I'd rather be like them than live in the mundane, stupid, artless world.

ADOLESCENTS

12/7/67 Little change in patient's behavior or attitude. Unable to talk about general topics other than her situation. Negative comments include: "I hate being closed in." "I refuse to go to school." "Nobody here likes me." She seems as frightened as she is angry.

I'M SITTING OUTSIDE THE NURSES' STATION, staring at the lights reflecting off the glass panels when a girl sits down next to me. She has straight, shoulder-length brown hair and a pretty, heart-shaped face.

"Hi. I'm Marjee. My real name is Margaret"—she wrinkles her nose—"but I call myself Marjee." She spells it out for me. I like that she doesn't spell it the usual way.

I ask how old she is. Thirteen, she answers. Two years younger than me. She seems older, more developed, with a curvy body and round breasts swelling beneath her pajamas. Her voice has an unfamiliar twang. She's from Oklahoma, but before the hospital she lived with her mother in Greenwich Village. I feel a pang of envy—she actually lived in the Village! I can't imagine why she's here.

"It was only twenty aspirin, but they pumped my stomach anyway," she says, smiling a beautiful smile. "I never want to go through that again. I'd rather die."

Looking into Marjee's huge, long-lashed brown eyes, I recognize a friend.

I've never met anybody from Oklahoma before. I try to imagine what it's like there, but all I see is flat expanses of corn and dust. Marjee tells me how boring life was in Oklahoma City, how everybody knew everybody else's business. "They smile at you in church, then talk about you behind your back." She asks if I believe in Christ.

I tell her I'm Jewish—or at least my parents are. I consider myself more a Buddhist.

She glances at my forehead. "When I was growing up, they taught us that Jews had horns. You know, like Moses." Can she be that naive? She seems more intelligent than that, pretty sophisticated for a thirteen-year-old "Okie," from my New York point of view.

My new friend, leaning toward me, says there are lots of pigs in Oklahoma, and that in fact, aside from being extremely smart, the pigs are very pretty. "Much prettier than her," she says, pushing her nose up with her finger and giving a little snort, gesturing toward our solid head nurse. "She's *porcine,* don't you think?"

I ask why she moved to New York.

"After my parents got divorced, my mother had lots of boyfriends. You can't blame her, though. She's young and pretty. And my father is such a bastard. He used to beat me when he was drunk—with his belt. It hurt like hell, but I taught myself not to cry." Marjee twirls a strand of hair around her finger. "When my mother left, she sent me and my younger brother to live with my grandmother. She was very strict, but she loved us."

Marjee says her mother came to New York to start a new life with her boyfriend, who happens to be black—things like that don't go over too well in Oklahoma. When she was settled, she sent for Marjee. Although Marjee misses her brother, she was glad to get away from the stultifying, small-town atmosphere. But once she was in New York, in a new school, with new kids, the loneliness she thought she'd left in Oklahoma caught up with her. That's when she took the aspirin.

Marjee doesn't mind being in the hospital; she says it makes her feel safe. "It's not so bad once you get used to it." She holds up her wrist, showing off a beaded bracelet. "I'm making jewelry in O.T. Why don't you come?"

Occupational Therapy? We're obviously on a different wavelength. Doing nothing represents my serious commitment to the vacuum, the void, the nothingness I know to be the true nature of things. I tell her I've been refusing to go to any activities, including school.

She says she likes school, and that I ought to give it a try. "English class is really good. We're reading *Hamlet.* It's a lot better than just sitting around."

I tell her I'll think about it.

The O.T. room is really the dining room on the floor above us. Maggie, the occupational therapist, asks me what I'd like to do. I don't want to copy Marjee, but aside from bead-stringing, I can't think of anything. I don't want to sew or stitch a wallet from a kit. I categorically refuse to weave a basket. When I put a pencil to paper, I draw a line that curls around in tight concentric spirals, until it ends, trapped within itself. Maggie offers me some tiny plastic beads, jet and amber, blue and green. One by one I pierce them with a needle and watch them drop, glittering, onto the thread, making something sleek and shiny of my minutes. When I leave I wear a strand of beads over my pajamas, like Marjee's.

> 12/9/67 Very withdrawn. Sits with knees drawn up and peers out over them in a frightened way. Frequently looks at her hands as if examining them very closely, turning them slowly. Appears preoccupied, lighting cigarettes and letting them burn until someone reminds her to put them out. Marge W. showing much concern for her.

I have a headache. The slightest bit of light is excruciating. I sit all scrunched up with my face buried in my arms. Occasionally I'm aware of someone coming over, asking how I am, but don't have the energy to answer. There's a tremendous struggle going on inside me, two forces pulling in opposite directions. One tells me I'm okay, that all I have to do is move and everything will be fine. The other tells me I'm all fucked up, and that I always will be. I feel like I'm encased in some incredibly heavy stone, and I don't know if I'll ever be able to move again.

Marjee crouches down next to me, her face level with mine. I look at her with frightened eyes. Does she understand what I'm feeling? Marjee puts her hand on my arm, and the spell is broken. Tears fall from my eyes.

"Sometimes it really stinks, I know, but there are also good people here. Don't worry. It'll get better. You're not alone. Really." She taps my arm. "See, there's Woodridge! She counts for two people." I lift my eyes just a hair, and there's Woodfuck walking down the hall, her big bosom and hips truly enough for two. She fixes her eyes on me and Marjee. "I thought of the perfect word for her. *Officious.* That's *her,* isn't it? I can think of a few others. Obsequious. Obnoxious. Odorous." I can't help it, I have to smile. Marjee's been reading the dictionary, and she's obviously into the O's. She leans in a little closer and whispers, "There's going to be a party tonight in Laurie's room, and you're invited."

Laurie's room is two doors down the hall from A-dorm, across the hall from the Quiet Room. On our way to brush our teeth, Marjee asks the night attendant if we can visit Laurie for half an hour before we go to sleep. The attendant says okay, for half an hour, as long as we keep the door open. On our way back from the bathroom, we knock on Laurie's door. When the door opens, it lets out a cloud of cigarette smoke. Laurie gestures us inside.

Only a few patients have private rooms. I wonder what Laurie did to get it. Inside there's the same furniture as the dorms, but Laurie has hung pictures on the wall: a big poster of Mick Jagger, a few glossy photos of Laurie and some sexy-looking guy. Another photo shows him shirtless, flexing. A makeup case shaped like a small trunk lies open on her dresser, overflowing with bottles, jars, and tubes. There's a wardrobe filled with clothes, some of which are strewn around the room. Clothes—a luxury. Except for the wire mesh over the window and the fan mounted high on the wall, it's almost like a regular room. Most important, there are four walls and a door, which we've left open a crack.

"Smoke?" Laurie tosses us her pack of Marlboros, a pack of matches slipped under the cellophane. She puts on a record—the Stones. Laurie's really into Jagger. She sticks her lips out like Mick's and bops her head up and down.

Though Laurie's only a year older than me, she seems more grown-up, especially with her makeup. Every morning she puts on foundation, powder, lipstick, false eyelashes, black mascara and liquid eyeliner, and three shades of eye shadow—even more makeup than my mother. She shaves off her eyebrows and pencils them back on. Laurie's face is mostly makeup. Without it, she looks pale and kind of scary, like her features have been erased, especially her missing eyebrows. Made-up, her face looks too perfect and kind of hard.

Laurie's tough. When she tells me she used to shoot heroin, I'm impressed. I ask her if it's hard to do.

"Nah, you get used to it. You tie off your arm to make it easier." She tells me to make a fist, rolls up my sleeve, and taps my inner elbow. My vein pops up, big and blue. Laurie says it's too bad I never did it; I have great veins. "Virgin veins," she says with a laugh.

The attendant pokes her head in the door and says we have fifteen minutes. Laurie smiles at her, a big shit-eating grin. As soon as the footsteps fade, Laurie shakes a cigarette from the pack, squeezes out half the tobacco, fills it with some pot she's stashed inside a box of matches, and twists the end into a joint. We smoke it fast and try to be quiet but can't help laughing when one of the seeds pops really loud. We're almost done when the girl who came to talk to me my first day—the one I thought was a spy—sticks her head in the door. "What are you doing in there? It stinks!" Then she goes off down the hall. Paranoia bursts over me like a freezing shower. You can't trust anyone here. I have to remember that, have to remember, have to . . .

As if things weren't bad enough, now I'm restricted to South side for smoking pot, which means that I'm all alone on the bench in front of the nurses' station while Marjee goes off to school. And now I'm on constant observation. *Observation.* How I hate that word! Like some kind of specimen they're always scrutinizing. What are they trying to see? Proof that I'm fucked up? I thought they already knew that.

They're always observing me, but they can't even see me. They can be sitting right next to me, writing in their chart that I'm scratching my head, and they have no idea I'm doing it just for them. They think I'm really scratching my head, but in fact I'm just pretending to. Pigs! They're like the Thought Police, watching my every move, but they'll never win. They can take away my clothes and restrict me to South side, but they can't stop me from thinking. So I tell them, "I'm not on observation!" and laugh in their faces. And of course they think I'm crazy for saying that. Let them! I say it to let them know that their rules don't apply to me. I don't have to believe in their reality.

I feel like an animal in a cage, but even zoo animals get to go outside once a day. I can't just sit here forever! When the nurse isn't looking I get up and start walking down the hall toward Center. When she sees me and orders me to come back, I start to run. Then R.J., the big powerful attendant, grabs me, drags me back down the hall and plunks me down on the bench.

"Do that again, and I'll carry you to the Quiet Room. Got it?"

"Okay, okay. I got it."

Every once in a while Ted wanders down to South side to smoke a cigarette with me. Otherwise, there's nothing to do but sit on this bench or pace the hall in front of the nurses' station, and nobody to talk to but the student nurses. They're so nice, it's sickening. It's fake nice; I can see in their eyes they're scared. I get off on acting crazy, to scare them even more.

I sit smoking, flicking my ashes on the linoleum. They blend right in with the linoleum's pattern: beige squares with little gray flecks alternating with squares of gray flecked with beige. At first beige is the main color but as I stare, suddenly the gray comes to the foreground. It's a weird feeling when it switches—the same as when I try to figure out whether I'm good or bad, crazy or sane. One minute it's one way, and the next minute the reverse. In a way it doesn't matter which I believe, because it will always change to the other. I don't have any control over it. I just have to wait to feel good while I can before I wind up back in hell.

———————

I'm standing on line for lunch when a couple of boys line up behind me.

"Hi," one of them says. "I'm Harold." His round face is framed by straight brown hair cut in a Dutch-boy style. His bangs fall slightly over his eyes, which flash a guarded blue. We peer at each other from behind our hair.

"You been here long?" Harold's voice is soft, with a certain flatness that matches the distracted look on his face. Every few seconds he twitches his head to flick the hair from his eyes.

I shake my head. "You?" He tells me this is his first day. Oh God, I want to say, how horrible. But I don't. Instead I just look at him. His face is pale, and it looks like there are tears in his eyes. I can see he's scared, the way I was on my first day. Watching him, my own eyes fill.

The other kid, Bobby, is small and slight, with dark, darting eyes. He sucks in the smoke with a vengeance. "I've been here three months. It really sucks," he says, shooting his words out at top speed. He takes several fast, deep drags of his cigarette, drops the butt on the floor and stomps on it. I've never seen anyone smoke a cigarette so fast. I think he's trying to impress me.

I ask Harold why he's here. He flicks his head left and right as if the answer might be just over his shoulder, then tells me in his soft, flat voice that he's here because he fought with his parents, took drugs, and dropped out of school.

Maybe I'm not so unique after all.

The next morning, I join the group assembled by the elevator to go to P.T.—short for Physical Therapy, long for gym. They're always herding us around in groups. I don't like groups. An individual *person* is one thing, but *people*, the mindless crowd, are something I want no part of.

C.T., the day-shift attendant, his white uniform dazzling against his ebony skin, jokes with some of the boys. "Yo, Bobby, what you been smokin' this mornin', man? Look sharp!"

C.T.'s real name is Curtis Thompson. Curtis L. Thompson, really, though we never learn what the L. is for. C.T. doesn't like his first name. Sometimes when a nurse addresses him as Curtis, he looks like he swallowed a lemon. Mostly they call him Mr. Thompson. The other male attendants call him Thompson, or C.T.—which the boys translate into Cutie, as in "Oh, Cutie! Cutie Pie!" His full initials, C.L.T., sometimes translate into Clit, like now, when Bobby calls out, "Yo, Clit-head!"

C.T. is well over six feet tall, and his long arms come in handy. He grabs Bobby by the collar and pulls so Bobby is on his tiptoes. "Hey, let me tell you something, my man. Number One: Don't go callin' me none of them nasty names or I'll knock you upside the head. Number Two: You ever think what those initials spell backward? Think on it a minute, man. T.L.C. Tender Lovin' Care. That's what the ladies call me, 'cause that's what I give 'em. I keep 'em young, I keep 'em happy. You got a lot to learn, my man. And don't you forget it!"

Bobby's face cracks a grin. C.T.'s cool. You can tell he has a good heart.

The elevator operator pulls back the door with authority. He's friendly but kind of formal, like he's proud of his job. It must be like being a gatekeeper of hell, ferrying people down to the underworld. "Abandon all hope, ye who enter here." That's what they should put over the entrance to this place.

The elevator is crowded. Staff people with name tags pinned to their jackets and patients in pajamas, all crammed in together. I try to make myself as compact as possible. How can they expect me to do this? They know I freak out in crowds. I hold my breath and pray we get there soon. The elevator is stopping on every floor. "Next stop, Forty-second Street!" Bobby calls out, and laughter ripples through the car. I stiffen. Do they think being in a nuthouse is funny? At last the doors open and we pile out.

In the gym, cold air filters in through the large, fenced-in windows. I shiver and huddle against the wall. The P.T. leader, Luis, bounces a basketball and blows a whistle, trying to get us to move. Harold and Bobby do some dribbling and start shooting baskets, then Luis assigns teams and a game starts, but I stay on the sidelines, sitting with my back against the wall. I hate team sports. I consider myself too much of an individual to join the herd. Besides, I always fumble and screw up, so people don't want me on their team. This is one team I *definitely* don't want to join. It's absurd: a bunch of slow-mo Thorazine zombies trying to block the adolescent boys' passes, always too late. Luis tosses me the ball. I catch it, then let it drop from my hands. Luis doesn't push me, just says, "Don't want to play? Okay, maybe you'll change your mind," which of course I won't. I feel the pull toward immobility, the air pressing down. *Why do? Why go? Why be?*

Maybe I *will* go to school, just once, and see if I like it. If I don't—if it's stupid or beneath me—I won't go back.

As we straggle into the classroom, the teacher, perched on the edge of her large wooden desk, stands to greet us. She wears jangling Moroccan bangles, huge hoop earrings, a Chinese pendant, a navy skirt ending above her knees, a brightly woven textile vest over a snug-fitting maroon sweater, and a wide, soft leather belt that emphasizes the curve of her hips. Her curly brown hair, streaked with gray, fluffs out around her head in a Jewish Afro. She smells of some spicy-sweet perfume. Her glasses sit low on her nose.

"Good morning." She smiles at the attendant accompanying us. "And who is this?" she asks, turning to me. I look down at my feet, thinking maybe it isn't too late to go back to the ward. The attendant hands her a slip of paper—my letter of introduction.

"Hello, Mindy," she says. "Welcome. I'm Mrs. Gould. Have a seat, dear." She points to a desk, one of those desk-and-chair combos where it's really hard to get comfortable. It looks like a real classroom, chalk, blackboard, wastebasket, and everything. For an instant I almost forgot I'm in a hospital.

"Do you know everyone here?" She gestures to each student. "Nick, Rocky, Marjee, Nora, Laurie, Bobby, and Eric, who'd better sit down right now if he knows what's good for him!"

Eric, who'd been creeping up behind Mrs. Gould with two fingers held up like devil's horns, ostensibly to throw away a crumpled piece of paper, does an overhand toss, lands the paper in the wastebasket and returns to his seat. Mrs. Gould smiles broadly at him, then turns to me.

"Occasionally we're allowed to have fun here—when we're discussing literature! Have you read *Hamlet?*" I nod. "Good! Feel free to join the discussion." She turns back to the group. "Bobby, would you please read line 222 on page 46? Polonius . . ."

Bobby thumbs through his book and reads: "Though this be madness, yet there is method in't."

"And what does that mean? Anybody?"

Nick raises his hand. "Hamlet appears mad, but maybe he isn't. Maybe he's doing it on purpose." I feel uncomfortable, blurry. Maybe it's the Thorazine.

"Good!" Mrs. Gould continues. "And why would he be doing it on purpose?" Silence. "Anyone?" More silence. Mrs. Gould is undaunted. "Let's look more closely. What are the signs of his madness?"

Bobby picks it up. "He's disheveled, talking with ghosts, he's insulting people, saying crazy things, he's scaring Ophelia, walking around with a bare bodkin . . ."

Titters from the group. Mrs. Gould smiles. "And? Anything else?"

Marjee raises her hand. "He's thinking about killing himself."

"Yes, and he talks about it—can anyone find where?" I start to fade out, the discussion around me an annoying buzz. I just want to go back to the ward and lie down. Mrs. Gould walks over and stands in front of me. I feel her energy, and sit up.

"So, my brilliant children, what do you think Hamlet's problem is? Is he really mad?"

I can't believe she's asking us about madness. I look at the floor, clasp and unclasp my sweaty palms.

Eric raises his hand. "Maybe he hates his mother. That's what Freud would say."

Nick, slouched into a long, low S with his legs protruding from under his desk, sighs loudly and rolls his eyes.

Mrs. Gould perches on the edge of her desk. "Nick, do you disagree?"

Nick runs both hands over his long, light brown hair, smoothing it back from his high forehead. He slides farther down, his legs straight out in front of him.

"He hates his *stepfather* for murdering his father. He despises his mother for marrying so soon. Who knows, maybe he's jealous. Maybe he wants to fuck her himself." Nick runs his tongue over his wide, curvy lips. The boys all snicker. I try to look above it all, intelligent beyond words.

Harold raises his hand. "Why would he want to do that when there's Ophelia, who, you know, she's so very ripe, you can tell she really needs to get some! Do you think it might be because they're all sort of *repressed*, or maybe he has some kind of mother-*complex?*"

Mrs. Gould raps on her desk. "All right, enough! Does anybody have any other ideas? Laurie?"

"You kids are all such idiots," Laurie laughs, then takes her compact from the pocket of her sweater, opens it to check her makeup, licks her finger, and runs it over her eyebrow.

"Anybody else? Nora? Rocky?"

Nora sits quietly drawing designs in her notebook. Rocky stares listlessly. Mrs. Gould walks over to her, takes her chin in her hand and looks into her eyes. "What's the matter, darling? Not feeling well?" She presses a motherly palm to Rocky's forehead.

Rocky does not look good. Her pale skin has bright red patches, and she looks listless. Usually she is quick and clever, her hip-length dark hair swinging around her like a whip around a reed. Nick looks at her with concern. He and Rocky are inseparable friends.

"Do you want to go back to the ward?" Mrs. Gould asks. Rocky shakes her head, then puts her head down on her desk.

"Okay, dear, just let me know if you do." Mrs. Gould returns to the front of the room, picks up a piece of chalk and energetically scrawls on the blackboard in large letters: TO BE OR NOT TO BE. Her bangle bracelets jangle as she writes. I like the sharp sounds the chalk makes as it hits the slate. Clear and decisive, unlike the whirling muddle of my mind.

Mrs. Gould asks Eric to read the soliloquy. His voice goes up and down the scale from croaky bass to cracked soprano like Spanky in *The Little Rascals.* I listen extra hard when he gets to the part that goes: "Thus conscience doth make cowards of us all, and thus the native hue of resolution is sickled o'er with the pale cast of thought. . . ."

Everybody's paying attention. Marjee chews thoughtfully on her pencil. Nick has a serious look on his face. Even Rocky has lifted her head. When Eric gets to: "With this regard their currents turn awry, and lose the name of action," Bobby mutters, "Amen."

Mrs. Gould points to the sentence on the blackboard. "Why do you think Hamlet is asking himself this question?"

Marjee raises her hand. "I think Hamlet both loves *and* hates his mother. He feels betrayed. He knows the truth but speaks in riddles so everyone thinks he's crazy. He's cut himself off from everybody. He doesn't know whether life is worth living, because he's lost his innocence."

I can't believe it. That's my story exactly. In spite of myself I say something aloud.

"Yes," I say, "that's it."

It's a fair bargain: I continue with school, and my restriction to South side is lifted. A week and a half of sitting on the bench in front of the nurses' station almost drove me crazy (if I'm not already), and Marjee was right—going to school is a lot better than just sitting around.

In every class, Mrs. Gould makes literature come alive. She reads sections of the *Canterbury Tales* in Old English, Dante's *Inferno* in Italian, and Calderón's *Life Is a Dream* in Spanish before we discuss the English translation. She reads with feeling, digging down deep for what the words stand for. The juicier the subject matter, the more Mrs. Gould gets into it. Alienation, guilt, despair: Kafka, Camus, Sartre. Social mores and taboos: Hawthorne, Orwell. Conformity, duty, and rebellion: Dostoevsky, Tolstoy, Pasternak. Even suicide. One day Mrs. Gould has us read aloud and discuss Dorothy Parker's poem "Résumé," a cool consideration of methods of suicide, culminating in the world-weary resolution: "You might as well live." Surprised as much by Mrs. Gould's casual approach to this loaded subject as by the poem's directness, I shiver with the recognition that writers are able to express thoughts and emotions I know well, but don't know how to say.

Classes aren't always as raucous as the first one was; most of the time they're serious discussions. We write essays about what we're reading. After Mrs. Gould gives them back to us with her comments, she'll often ask someone to read their essay aloud, and the discussion goes to deeper levels. Everybody works hard in Mrs. Gould's class.

Mr. Bardell's American history class is less boring than history was in junior high, mostly because he doesn't mind if we challenge him. "That's an excellent question. I'm glad you asked," he says, and opens it up for discussion—a relief from the tedium of memorizing facts and dates. I can tell by Mr. Bardell's long sideburns that he thinks he's hip. He mumbles things like, "It's cool," and "I can dig it," and talks about his dream of taking a break from teaching to travel cross-country on his motorcycle. I think he may be trying a little too hard.

The math teacher and I don't get along. He throws me out of class when I insist on understanding what the X and Y symbols in the equations stand for. "Just take my word for it," he says, but I can't solve the problem until I know the meaning of the symbols. I don't understand why he won't tell me—unless he doesn't know. "Okay, that's enough," he says, red-faced, and phones for an attendant to take me back to the ward.

Back from school, we usurp the stereo, blasting Eric's new album, *Fresh Cream*. The boys play pretend guitars along with the wailing guitar riffs, the falsetto vocals sending them into some kind of trance. *"I feel free, I feel free-ee."* The music, like a siren's call, beckons dangerously toward what we can't have.

Tall, skinny Eric is all angles and joints, big hands and feet, a pole of a neck and long, stringy hair. His Adam's apple pokes out sharply and bounces when he speaks, as if he's swallowed a Ping-Pong ball. As it turns out, he's something of a Ping-Pong shark. He plays for blood, choking the paddle, two long, skinny fingers flat along the length of the handle. He's so into Clapton that the other guys call him Clap—unless there's some other reason.

Harold likes Clapton, but Jagger is his idol. He can dance just like him, sliding, shimmying, whirling in place, one belligerent finger held high. Harold is athletic and muscular, with a boxer's build. He had a football scholarship to Horace Mann, and before he dropped out of school, he was president of his class. But he has doubts about his intelligence.

"I had encephalitis when I was five and I was *brain-damaged*. Yeah, it's true! Maybe I'm fucked up because I'm *stupid*." Even when Harold's brain scan comes back normal, he's still worried about it. But there's always an antidote to worry: "What difference does it make? I'm *fucked*, anyway." Harold's not alone. He speaks for all of us. When the Stones play "Paint It Black," we all sing along. It's our anthem.

Music keeps us going. It's not just the words. It's the sound—*our* sound. Drums, like blood. Guitar strings, like nerves: picked, plucked, screeching. Notes, like thoughts: questioning, caressing, building, racing, clashing. Janis Joplin screams and moans the new, electric blues: our own. But when the boys blast Led Zeppelin I can't take it and have to put my hands over my ears. I'd rather listen to John Fahey, Jefferson Airplane, or the Beatles.

"Dear Mr. Fantasy, play us a tune, something to make us feel happy. Do anything to take us out of this gloom. . . ." Steve Winwood is another of our favorites. I blush when Eric tells me I look like the bare-breasted girl on the *Blind Faith*

album cover. She has long, wavy blond hair, spaced-out blue eyes, perfect boobs—and doesn't seem at all embarrassed. Unlike me.

I listen to Jagger singing "You Can't Always Get What You Want," backed up by the London Bach Choir. Who else could get away with such audacity? Taunting, mocking, shaking his ass at the world. No matter how outrageous he acts, nobody tries to stick *him* in a nuthouse.

12/26/68 Patient generally more appropriate and friendly. Her profanity has remained in check and she continues to go to classes, looking quite neat and womanly.

Marjee and I graduate from observation at the same time, and move from small A-dorm to larger B-dorm, which is subdivided into cubicles with low partitions. We find an empty cubicle, with adjacent beds. When she gets into bed, Marjee piles blankets on top of her, although there are already two on her tightly made bed. I ask if she's cold. To me it feels warm, with all the windows locked and the steam on. "I can't sleep without lots of blankets," she explains. "I need their weight to hold me down." We read until lights out, then we whisper—gossip, thoughts, secrets— until the other patients shush us. "Sweet dreams," we wish each other before sleep.

With Marjee as my friend it's not nearly as bad being here. Marjee can do just about anything. She likes to draw and paint and read; she cooks, sews, sings, and tells stories with imaginative, humorous plots. She doesn't think of herself as a writer, but I am in awe. We discover we've both been reading the same books. We read aloud, write notes and giggle, weep, and comfort each other. I give her one of my Rapidograph pens; Marjee sews me a pair of elephant bell-bottoms. We collaborate on drawings: trippy doodles and ridiculous caricatures. We debate God's existence, exchange ideas about reincarnation and life after death, and declare ourselves agnostic. We sit next to each other at meals and in school, schedule showers at the same time, go together to brush our teeth and wash our faces.

I can't believe how beautiful Marjee is. She looks like she's eighteen, curvy and voluptuous, with big, round boobs. Mine are like peanuts in comparison. Marjee says I'm lucky because they won't droop when I get old—which doesn't matter because I don't expect to live that long—and says they're shaped nice even though they're small. The rest of me is like a stick. I try to keep myself that way, nothing extra to slow me down.

Marjee and I have our own way of drying our hair. First we wrap our towels around our heads like turbans and get dressed. Then, in the hallway, we unwrap the towels and shake our heads side to side real fast like saying *no!* so our wet hair twirls out around us, flipping back and forth, sending drops of water flying. It feels good, a little like getting high, waking me up and making me feel light-headed at the same time.

I love Marjee's straight, shiny hair. She likes my long, curly frizz. When I go to bed, I lie down with my hair stretched flat under my back to straighten it. At home I used to iron it, but I can't do that here, or put peroxide in it. I used to do just a few streaks at a time so my mother wouldn't know. She would have killed me. Hypocrite! She dyes her own hair. She just doesn't want to let me do anything on my own.

In eighth grade my best friend, Wendy, had been shaving her legs for months. When I asked my mother if I could start shaving, she looked at the blond fuzz on my legs and said I didn't need to do it yet. She'd tell me when I could start, and she'd show me how to do it properly, so I wouldn't cut myself.

One afternoon Wendy came home with me after school. We'd decided the time had come to shave my legs. But once we were in the bathroom together, I wasn't so sure. I had orders to meet my mother at the A&P at 5:30.

"We have plenty of time. It's so easy. You'll see," Wendy reassured me. We locked the door and ran the tap until the water was warm. Under Wendy's supervision, I squirted out a dab of my stepfather's shaving cream and smoothed it over my leg like icing on a cake, then held my breath and mowed a path up my shin. Before I knew it, I'd sheared away all the shaving cream, leaving only one small nick, which we blotted with toilet paper after trying to figure out how to use my stepfather's styptic (cryptic would be a better word) pencil. Then I noticed the time: 5:25. I pulled on my jeans, which felt funny against the naked skin of my left leg, and ran for it.

When I got there, my mother was fuming. I told her that Wendy was over and we'd lost track of the time. She calmed down enough to start picking out groceries (shopping always calms her down), but I could tell she was still annoyed by the way she muttered disapprovingly at the cans of soup. I helped picked out some items, feeling increasingly guilty. Should I tell her? She was bound to find out; all she had to do was notice my mismatched legs. My mother paid the cashier, and as we loaded bags of groceries into the shopping cart, unable to contain it any longer, I blurted: "Wendy and I, we, I mean I . . ."

"You what?"

"Wendy showed me how to shave my legs. I mean we shaved one."

My mother was livid. "How could you defy me? I wanted to show you myself!"

I had anticipated my mother's anger, but not her hurt feelings. "But Mom, I only shaved one leg. We could still do the other together." Why was she making such a big deal about this? I fussed around her, trying to help, but my mother stayed angry. Even slamming the groceries onto the kitchen counter and slapping the hamburger meat into patties didn't dissipate her wrath.

Wasn't there anything I could do on my own? Did she want me to stay a little girl forever?

My mother has always kept mementos of my childhood wrapped in tissue paper in her dresser drawer. Every once in a while she'd take them out to show me: my first baby shoes, a tiny yellow dress with white embroidery and mother-of-pearl buttons, a baby tooth, a lock of silky blond hair.

When I was little my hair was a light ash blond. As a teenager, I started noticing other colors mixed in, ranging from reddish to dark brown. The blond hairs were straight and fine, but the dark hairs were coarse and curly. The darker the hairs, the thicker and kinkier the texture. Something about these hairs made me feel ashamed. Whenever I saw one, I'd pluck it out, hoping to purge my head of everything except the golden purity of blond. Each time I plucked a hair, I was ridding myself of visible evidence of my faults. I wanted my hair, and my soul, to be like Mary Travers's— silky, straight, and platinum blond.

I tried everything. I slathered my hair with Dippity-Do and taped my bangs flat across my forehead. I laid a towel across my bed, spread my hair out on it, and scorched it with my mother's steam iron. I applied Curl Free with cellophane-gloved fingers, and set the timer, hoping the caustic chemicals reeking beneath the sugary perfume wouldn't burn my scalp or solve the curl problem by making me bald.

Beauty's only skin deep. . . . I thought I believed this, but deep down I don't. My mother's friends and relatives have always gushed over the way I looked. ("She's adorable . . . and so *good!*") In praising my little-girl cuteness, they intimated that I was not just pretty but better than other children. But I knew I wasn't as good as I looked. In junior high, when my face erupted in pimples, it was as if the bad stuff inside me was finally coming to the surface. I squeezed them, but they kept popping up, as persistent as the dark hairs I couldn't get rid of.

I don't remember how old I was when my mother began dying her hair. Originally a rich dark auburn, the goopy Lady Clairol my mother applied transformed it into a bright orange orb, like Lucille Ball's. It epitomized the persona my mother created for herself—blazing, bright, and glamorous. My stylish mother was never satisfied with the way she looked. She thought her nose was too long and not straight enough, and that her ears stuck out. She pointed out dewlaps and accused her eyelids of droopiness.

"What do you think?" she'd ask. "Should I get my nose done?" The idea horrified me. I loved the asymmetry of her nose, one side a fraction of an inch longer than the other; even the much-reviled bump on its bridge had a regal character. Examining her face in the mirror, my mother would appraise her profile, then hold her ears flat against her head. "Or should I have my ears tucked?" I'd emphatically tell her no, that I loved the way her ears looked and wouldn't want a single inch of her changed.

I pretend not to care about the way I look, but it's a lie. I can't resist checking my reflection, my hair, face, body. I care too much about how I look, and what other people think of me. I say I'm different from my mother—another lie. I'm just as big a hypocrite as she is.

B-dorm is much less supervised. Since the patients there aren't on observation, they're more independent. Next to the dorm are two private rooms—another world entirely. I doubt I'll ever get one. I'm happy just to be able to wear my own raggedy sweatshirt and bell-bottoms, so long the hems are shredded from walking on them. Marjee wears peasant blouses and long skirts and looks sexy and pretty. She has the same star quality my mother has. No matter what she wears—even a ripped T-shirt—she's still sexy. Next to her I look like a ragamuffin.

Marjee says she's part Cherokee. She's fair-skinned with faint freckles, but with her straight brown hair and brown eyes, it could be true—especially when she wears her soft-soled suede boots with fringe and her fringed suede skirt and vest. Watching her pad down the hall, fringe flipping with the sway of her hips, I envision her as an Indian maiden, living free and strong, doing ceremonial dances around the fire, cooking for the handsome Indian brave who loves her. I see it in her gift for storytelling, in her inscrutable, mysterious side, and in her clear eyes and sharp vision. Marjee's not nearsighted, like me.

I wish I could be like Marjee. I've never known anyone so original. When my mother writes and asks if there's anything I need, I write back and ask for suede boots and a fringed vest like Marjee's. We wear them together and look like sisters.

Nick is starting to pay a lot of attention to Marjee. She pulls me aside, all excited, to tell me that he kissed her and felt her up under her blouse. "I really like him," she says, her eyes shining.

"What about Rocky?"

"I don't care about Rocky," she pouts. "I'm usually not that friendly with girls."

"Me neither," I tell her, even though it's not true.

Nick is always surrounded by girls. He's kind and gentle with Nora, the girl from the fourth floor who rarely talks. He spends time talking with Gloria, the well-behaved Orthodox Jewish beauty, which surprises me because I think she's too straight for him. But Nick is democratic. Sometimes he pays more attention to one of us than another, but Rocky is Nick's best friend. They stroll the corridors slowly, arms linked, heads close together, in their own private bubble. I see the way Nick looks at her, taking a handful of her long hair and letting it sift through his fingers. What wouldn't I give for him to look at me the same way!

Suddenly there's a new reason to get up in the morning, brush my hair, dab on patchouli oil. Nick. I can't keep my eyes off him. He looks like a classical sculpture, his leonine head sitting nobly atop the strong, slim column of his neck. A straight, golden-brown mane sweeps back from his high forehead, one lock falling over deep-set eyes framed by quizzically arched eyebrows; an aquiline nose culminates in flared nostrils above a wide, mobile mouth. Bow-shaped lips curl into a smile or a sneer.

Even in hospital pajamas Nick is sexy. His pajama top is unbuttoned halfway; a V of pale, smooth chest falls from his collarbones, ribs visible beneath the skin. Long-boned arms extend from rolled sleeves; elegant hands end in bitten fingernails. Broad shoulders taper down to slim hips, the long triangle of his torso slightly concave. Pajama legs ripple over bony, slightly bowed shins. Scuffed brown loafers worn without socks flip-flop lazily against the linoleum.

Whenever I see Nick, I'm instantly flustered. What could he possibly want with me? I'm not beautiful like Marjee or Gloria, or smart like Rocky. When Jagger sings *"Look at that stupid girl,"* I blush and look at the floor.

Nick is prep-school smart. He has tremendous contempt for ignorance and a kind of x-ray vision into people's motivations. When he's angry his eyes flash darts of scorn, and from his lips come carefully chosen insults designed to wound.

But Nick surprises me. One day, when I'm sitting curled up in a chair refusing to talk, he squats down next to me and asks if I'm okay. I look up to find his intelligent hazel eyes looking into mine, unprepared for the concern in his voice and the gentle touch of his hand on my shoulder.

I become one of Nick's group of admirers—or, as he calls us, his *slaves*. Laurie and Marjee take turns ironing his clothes and shining his shoes. Marjee irons his pajamas with perfect creases, well prepared by years of doing housework after her mother left. Later I see them kissing behind the dining-room door.

Only once I see Rocky sew up a rip in Nick's bathrobe; otherwise she's exempt from the chores the rest of his slaves worshipfully perform. Even Gloria takes a turn at ironing—but never anything as demeaning as shining his shoes, the one job I do well because I used to help my father shine his. But I'm really bad at ironing. The first time I try, Nick pulls my hair back hard and asks me to do it over, *or else*. If Nick doesn't like the way something's done he finds a way to punish you, like a hard pinch on the arm or an Indian burn. But the worst punishment is when he ignores you, like you don't exist.

Something about him makes me weak in the knees. If he looks at me too long in the eyes, I have to look down. I'd like for him to kiss me, the way he kisses Marjee.

———————

As soon as you start getting used to things, someone new arrives on the ward.

Noel has long, dark blond hair that he wears parted on the side like Veronica Lake, sweeping down to cover half his face. His teeth are tinted yellow from cigarettes and look out of place in his innocent baby face. Though he's only thirteen, Noel tries to act ultracool. When I ask why he's here, he raises an eyebrow in disdain and utters one word: "Drugs." It's the usual story: Divorce, Depression, Defiance, Drugs. Like most of us, Noel is rated 4-D.

Little by little—in installments, to keep us in suspense—Noel tells the true story of why he's here. It wasn't drugs exactly . . . unless you consider aspirin drugs.

For his mother, sending Noel to a shrink was as natural as giving him aspirin. His father had abandoned the family when Noel was an infant, and his mother saw psychiatry—and boarding school—as ways of providing male guidance for her son. When twelve-year-old Noel complained to his mother that he was unhappy at boarding school, she sent him to a psychiatrist famous for his work with adolescents. Noel hated him; he could tell the big-shot shrink didn't like kids. Mid-semester, when Noel announced to his mother that he was not returning to boarding school, she phoned his shrink, who talked her into hiring a strong-arm man, a former bouncer, to "escort" Noel back to school. Noel woke up on his last day of vacation to find a strange man looming over his bed. The bouncer drove Noel back to school.

Soon afterward, Noel swallowed the only drugs he could find, a half-bottle of aspirin. The next day he was admitted to the state hospital in Waltham, Massachusetts. After that, he did some time at McLean, where Anne Sexton gave poetry workshops and stories abounded about former residents Ray Charles and James Taylor. Noel met some interesting characters and had a chance to learn blues guitar before his mother had him transferred to P.I.

Noel is the only adolescent I know here who isn't on meds. Maybe it's because he's so well-behaved. I don't get it. If he's so well-behaved, why is he here? Then again, why are any of us here?

After a while the stories start to blur together. It's all a variation on the same theme. Only the details—the D-tales—change.

INAPPROPRIATE BEHAVIOR

IT'S EASY TO GET DRUGS ON THE WARD. Attendants bring them in for us—grass, hash, or coke, if we have enough money. Four or five of us, including Sly, the attendant who bought us the stuff, cram into Laurie's room and smoke some opium-laced hash, trying not to splutter loudly when we exhale, laughing as we get higher and higher. Then we become desperately paranoid, at every sound certain that we are busted. The next day we avoid Sly, who is suddenly cool and formal with us too.

We give our allowance money to patients who have neighborhood privileges, and they bring things back for us. Booze can be difficult to smuggle in, but over-the-counter cough syrup with codeine is easy and has the advantage of fitting inconspicuously into a pocket. Marjee and I get high on Romilar several times without being caught. It's a dizzy feeling of freedom to be able to get high right under their noses. I slip a bottle of cleaning fluid in my bathrobe pocket and inhale it in the living room when staff isn't around, watching my mind buzz out.

There are other ways to get drugs. We ask the nurse for Darvon for headache, Librium for stomachache, Valium for anxiety, Benadryl for colds or allergies or medication side effects, chloral hydrate for insomnia, even Dexedrine diet pills, like Laurie gets. We save them up until we have enough to get high. Then when we float around the ward in a drug-induced daze, they write in our charts: "Patient seemed listless today."

Occasionally there's bigger stuff: Demerol, Seconal, angel dust, speed. Jack is the biggest pusher on the ward. He doles it out for money or as gifts, establishing himself in a position of power. Jack is hard-edged and tough, a street kid from the Lower East Side with acne-pitted skin, a beak of a nose and a jutting, ridged brow that casts a shadow over his eyes. He scares me. He and Nick become tight. Together they rule, making sure we show them the proper respect.

Ted—out of pajamas with neighborhood privileges—has a peacoat with pockets large enough to stash a fifth of gin. "Would you like anything from outside, girls?" he asks me and Marjee with a wink. Getting the bottle from Ted is like espionage. When he's back from his walk, Ted calls to Marjee, "I have your sandwich, please come get it." While they're exchanging money, Marjee slips the bottle under her pajama top. Then she asks the attendant if she can go back to the dorm to get a sweater. I ask if I can go too. "Sure, girls, just come right back," Mrs. G. answers. We start out slowly, but by the time we're near the dorm we're almost running, breathless, laughing.

There's no place to safely hide the bottle, so we drink the whole thing, chugging it down fast. At the first few swallows we gasp and grimace, but then we're gagging. The world twirls. Laughing turns to retching, and we're soon found out. We throw up all afternoon and night, waking the next morning bone-dry, dizzy, and in a ton of trouble. We're put back on observation. Back into those same ugly pajamas.

"Inappropriate behavior," the doctors tell us. *Appropriate* and *inappropriate* are the standards by which we live, by which privileges are meted out or taken away. "Inappropriate acting out! No phone privileges, no clothing privileges, no outside passes." It's inappropriate to ask too many questions, to swear, to get angry, to be secretive, laugh too loudly, or have physical contact. "Inappropriate acting out," they say when we touch each other.

What is appropriate behavior? Where are we to funnel our energy, rebelliousness, intelligence, mischief, rage? Is it *inappropriate* to want to go outside, walk in the daylight, breathe fresh air, be among the living, see the sky, wander the streets? How can we explore new interests, be alone on occasion, have some privacy? And what of our need to connect?

I look up to see James staring at me from across the room. James is a classical pianist, almost twenty years old. He is quiet, gentle, and moody, with brown hair and eyes and pale skin. I have a crush on him, even though he's not my type—too clean-cut. He wears dark slacks, not jeans, and white oxford-cloth shirts. He tells me he thinks I'm beautiful and doesn't understand why I'm here. "You're so young," he sighs. When I tell him the sordid details of my life, his pale face grows even sadder. When at last he bends down to kiss me, his lips are wet, his palms moist as he smooths my hair from my face. As we slowly move our faces away, Woodridge walks by.

"What do you think you're doing? You know there's no P.C."

"No physical contact" is the rule on the ward. Patients are not allowed to touch one another, certainly not sexually. But there are ways around this.

One day after school, Nick motions me into the living room. I follow him into the corner, where I stand facing him. He squeezes my breasts, then slides both hands into my pants and pulls up hard on my underwear. Then he tells me to pull down my pants. I'm nervous about it, but nobody's around and Harold is standing guard in the doorway. So I do it, feeling funny and exposed. They're not down a second when—just my luck—Woodfuck's spy walks into the room, wheels around and is gone.

When we're caught, we're punished. We're separated, restricted from speaking to each other, and placed on constant observation. Our psychiatrists are informed. They write it in their notes, restrict us, observe us, punish us, but they can't stop us. What can they do to us? Take away privileges, make us wear pajamas? What a joke.

Sex is our most challenging entertainment, and yet the most accessible. The equipment is always available at a moment's notice. Pajamas, with their elastic and snap crotches, provide easy access. We unwrap each other like gifts.

We reach toward each other incessantly. In hallways, under tables. We are all bulging protruberances and wet gaps, holes to fill and things to fill them with. Tongues in ears, fingers in mouths. Hands slide over warm bellies into springy pubic hair. Lips meet lips, more investigation than love. We hold palms together to compare hand sizes. Take off our socks and feel each other's feet. Tickle the soft skin inside elbows and knees. Breathe each other's hair. Lick each other's necks. Squeeze each other's nipples. Left alone for a second, we flash bare chests, bellies, and asses. The boys dare us; we dare them back.

Penises come to life under my hand. They grow and harden until they stick out like flagpoles at ludicrous angles. I rub them through their pajamas until I feel sorry for them and release them from captivity. They spring rubbery and tremulous into the air, exposed in the living room, of all places; the only thing keeping them from view are the chairs we sit in. Excitement is heightened by danger. From three feet behind, where the attendant sits, all that can be seen of us are our heads, facing front or looking at each other, as if we're watching TV or talking, but in fact, our hands are in each other's laps, trying this, trying that, becoming more and more expert at making each other squirm. Below the waist we are in another world, open, melting, beating, burning.

We are relentlessly creative about P.C. "She had an itch," Harold tells staff when he's caught on his knees in front of me, my pajamas down around my ankles.

"I guess I blew it," I say to my shrink after I'm caught in the act of fellatio. He is exasperated by my dirty deeds. "You had just gotten clothing privileges," he sighs, shaking his head. "Now we have to put you back on observation." The look on his face asks, *why?*

I used to think sex was something you had to be still and submit to, like an exquisite death. The only way I'd let a guy do anything was by getting stoned first. Half-unconscious from too much Demerol and alcohol and grass, I'd grow tired of some guy breathing in my ear: "Let me do this to you. Oh, baby." To lie still like a baby. Was this love? If it was, I wasn't ready for it, even though I'd been imagining it all my life. Love was the ultimate self-sacrifice. What did it have to do with plastic smells, rubbery flesh, and spurting liquids?

When I was twelve, my mother had handed me a slim book about the facts of life. "If you have any questions, ask me," she said, leaving me to gawk at the schematic diagrams of vulva, labia, vagina, uterus, and branching fallopian tubes. Was this what I looked like inside? The whole apparatus looked like some kind of science-fiction lobster. There was a drawing of a man and woman having intercourse, both completely placid, like Mr. and Mrs. Dick and Jane—only cross-sectioned, so you could see their innards. The text read: "When a man and woman fall in love and get married, they can have sexual intercourse, and begin thinking of starting a family," adding that under these conditions, intercourse is the most "natural" thing in the world. From those diagrams it looked none too natural, just weirdly hygienic. The man was on top, the woman splayed open beneath him. I imagined her lying perfectly still to receive him, sort of like getting an enema or an injection—an injection of love, or sex. *Sex:* a cryptic word, like *vex,* or *hex.* I tried to think of a question to ask my mother, but I was too embarrassed to think of anything, and I could see she was relieved. I soon found other, juicier sources of information. While babysitting, I discovered the *Kama Sutra* and *The Story of O,* which I skimmed voraciously, squeezing my legs together as I read the good parts. Strange new energy surged through me, thick and sweet.

One Sunday morning I awoke with a headache, my muscles aching. The pink stain on the toilet paper explained the cramps in my belly. "Congratulations, you're a woman," my mother said, then sent my stepfather to the drugstore to buy me some sanitary napkins and a belt. Was I now a woman because of the ache in my belly and the pink stain? I looked at my mother, curvy, made-up, confident. *She* was a woman; I was still a little girl.

In eighth grade, the same bratty boys who had terrorized me and my girlfriends suddenly smelled like English Leather and clean shirts and politely asked us to dance. Their braces grazed my lips, which were slathered with Yardley lip gloss. When we slow-danced their hands wandered over my shirt and my heart raced. But when they tried to get their hands under my shirt and into my bra I had to stop them, primarily because I was terrified they'd discover the tissues I'd put there. My best friend and I both padded our bras, carefully layering the tissues, taking turns checking each others' profiles. It looked convincing . . . until the tissues crinkled and got lumped up. It would've been awful if the boys found out. They had a word for girls who stuffed their bras: *taxidermy.* Dead things. Stuffed animals.

> 1/31/68 In general, patient's adjustment to school and activities has been friendly and appropriate. On the ward, less sullen and provocative with staff. Several staff members have noted her seductive behavior with adolescent boys. She is usually surrounded by young men. Mostly she looks at ease. At times, however, she has to be warned about physical contact with the boys. On other occasions she has looked terrified and helpless when socializing. She grudgingly confirms this. Doctor's Orders: Mellaril 100 mg. po qid.

A new girl was admitted. Alyssa is taller than me, with shoulder-length blond hair. Nick notices her right away. I watch him play with her hair, piling it up on top of her head, then lets his hands drop onto her chest. She slaps his hands away, but she's laughing, and I can tell she likes him. I'm not happy about this, and neither is Marjee. I'm not sure whether to be friendly or keep to myself. But somehow we all move over and make room for her on the bench.

The guys are incredibly interested in our breasts. They cup them in their hands, feeling for weight, shape, symmetry. They rate and compare them. Mine are little, but nicely shaped. Marjee's are big and round, and so are Alyssa's, but curved differently. They're into breasts much more than asses, though that's their second preoccupation. They're also into physical aberration of any kind. B.O. is a topic of great interest, as is farting. They've narrowed both down to which precise, particular smells they evoke. "Mike's smells like roast beef, but George, oh man, his smells like rotten eggs. Lethal!" I hate hearing these boys, who possess the power to make me twitch, sound so stupid and juvenile.

Nick is different. He carries himself with a kind of aloof superiority. His parents have the same aristocratic air. On visiting day they greet each other politely and retreat into the dining room for their tête-à-tête. It's hard to imagine Nick being under the jurisdiction of parents.

People respect Nick because he's smart. He's quiet about it, but you can tell he's read a lot. Mrs. Gould adores him. He knows Latin, and enough Spanish to get in tight with the Hispanic attendants and maintenance crew. He plies them for obscene words; they laugh and share dirty jokes. Like most people, they do Nick's bidding. He has authority, charisma. He also has a private room where his friends gather to listen to music and look at his pornography collection, including both straight and boy-boy porn.

Nick is a compendium of obscure sexual trivia. He takes it upon himself to educate us by teaching us new words. First he has us guess, and if we don't know, he corrects our ignorance, then quizzes us. Some, like *jism* and *smegma*, are common penis-related terms. But others are more esoteric, like one of his favorites—*scuttles*. Nobody knows this one. Nick enlightens us: Scuttles are guys' underpants with a hole in back for easy access, a very popular item in prisons. This causes quite a sensation. Harold, Eric, and Bobby explode into laughter and high-five each other. The word is used constantly for days.

"If you want to know the difference between *frig* and *fug*, the answer is in this book." Nick is a devotee of the Marquis de Sade. He lends us his copy of *Justine*, on the condition that we report back to him on our favorite parts. He covers it in plain paper so we can read it in full view of the staff, right under their noses, which adds an extra thrill. We also get *The Story of O*—the same book I sneaked peeks at while baby-sitting now has new meaning. It's a menu of things to practice with Nick in a free moment in the living room. The idea of subjugating my body to his wishes keeps me constantly aroused.

Not all of Nick's obsessions are sexual. He owns a collection of Fats Waller records that he plays in his room, handling the rare LPs and 45s with great care. He treats all his possessions with the same perfectionism he employs when he shines his brown leather, ankle-high, zip-up boots and irons his clothes, including his jockey shorts and T-shirts, pajamas, and bathrobe. Nick is as intolerant of poorly ironed clothes as he is of stupidity. He's a perfectionist in every sense, including his investigations into pleasure and pain.

Nick is fascinated by sexual perversion of all kinds. He experiments with self-asphyxiation and fantasizes about the perfect death: strangulation at the moment of orgasm. Nick likes dark songs: the Stones more than the Beatles, Jim Morrison more than Dylan. But Nick's favorite musical obsession is the Velvet Underground. The album cover has Warhol's image of a single bright yellow, curved, phallic banana.

"Shiny, shiny, shiny boots of leather. Whiplash girlchild in the dark. . . ." The lyrics, droning along with the electric guitar, lull me, entice me, excite me.

In the North living room, a group of us line up for fainting sessions. Nick puts his hands around the neck of each willing victim and squeezes until he or she faints. I do it several times, amazed to feel my senses go thin and dissolve into a rush of darkness, my body jerking, then melting away. I barely feel Nick lowering me to the living-room floor. I awake to pairs of eyes peering down at me, and rise up slowly. It's almost as good as drugs.

We take turns strangling each other. Sometimes when I'm bored I do it to myself, my hands loosening their grip just as things start to go shimmery. Nick's influence is widespread. Eric squeezes Alyssa's knees until she yelps. Bobby plays a game with a new patient. He kisses her, then slaps her face, Kiss, slap, kiss, slap. You can see the hard-on bulging in his pants.

Marjee and I talk about Nick a lot, trying to figure him out. You never know what he's going to do next. Sometimes in the middle of a conversation he'll open his eyes wide, shake his head and go, "Woooo, wooooo!"

He has a weird sense of humor, very trippy. He can be funny one minute and serious the next—remote and cruel or kind and caring. I'm completely awed, but Marjee makes fun of him, even to his face. When she does, his face goes pale, and his nostrils flare with anger.

Nick gives me and Marjee a present wrapped in tissue paper, and tells us to open it in private. At first the curved white form, a U-shape with two long prongs, made of melted candle wax, looks like a modern sculpture. We run our fingers along its smooth surface. It looks like two penises, joined at the bottom, but we're incredulous. We ask Nick. He tells us it's a double-ended dildo, and to have fun with it. We know he's insulting us, but it's still a gift from Nick, something he made himself, his fingerprints imprinted in the wax. We decide to keep it. Marjee and I each grab an end, break it in half like a wishbone, and stash the halves in our lockers. The nurses discover them during an inspection, and although Marjee and I plead ignorance ("They're wickless candles," we protest), we're both restricted to South side for a week.

"I think I have a yeast infection. Unless it's VD." Marjee shocks me by putting her hand in her panties while we're sitting in the hallway. Her finger comes out wet, with a few dots of whitish stuff. She sniffs. I can't believe she's so open. If I thought anybody guessed I touched myself there I'd die of shame. Seeing the expression on my face, Marjee says, "What? Because I put my finger up myself?" She laughs, tosses her hair. "Don't you know everybody touches themselves? Even old Woodridge over there. Especially Woodridge! Don't you?"

"Well, sometimes . . . ," I mumble, mad at myself for feeling ashamed. I never feel cool enough, or pretty enough, or smart enough. There are so many things I've done that I'm ashamed of. In seventh grade I joined a hate club against a girl who later became one of my best friends. I let a friend talk me into screaming in the movies when we watched *A Hard Day's Night* even though I didn't really want to. I bragged about French kissing before I'd actually done it. I even told my friends I'd *done it*—gone all the way—when I really hadn't.

I hate myself for everything. For being too "nice," for being afraid, for being dull and spineless and lacking imagination, for being timid and shy. I hate myself for being uncool and inexperienced. I want to be *experienced*, to have a lover who'll take me all the way. I want the real thing. A passion that's all consuming, like fire, like death.

Rocky is back in pajamas. Her doctor has put her on observation, after months in clothes. Nick walks arm in arm with her, Rocky crying and Nick comforting her. The nurses and attendants let them be.

Nick blames Marjee for Rocky being put on observation. He says Marjee told staff that Rocky was planning to kill herself, or something like that. Marjee says she was only trying to help.

Over dinner, Nick leans forward and mumbles to Marjee, so softly it's almost inaudible: "You're the reason that Rocky was put on observation."

"What?" Marjee says, "I can't hear you."

Nick clears his throat. "I said, pass the salt without further gesticulation!" Nick is playing with Marjee's head. She ignores him, but I can see she's freaked.

Then we get the word: Rocky is being shipped. "Shipping" is hospital jargon for sending a patient to one of the regular state hospitals: Creedmoor, Rockland, Manhattan State—those awful institutions that warehouse chronic cases. "If you act out again, we might have to ship you," is the ultimate threat. *Shipped*, like packages, cargo, the word spoken in a fearful whisper.

Mrs. Gould goes to Grand Rounds to plead Rocky's case. But the next day Rocky is gone.

Nick is one of Gidro-Frank's favorites. When Gidro-Frank passes through Center on his way to rounds, he often stops to talk with him. Now I watch them face off in intense conversation, until Nick turns on his heel and walks quickly away, fists clenched at his sides.

After Rocky is shipped, Nick gives Marjee the cold shoulder, and me too, because she's my friend. When her feelings are hurt, Marjee gets cold and bitchy. No matter what I say, she answers everything with a question: "Am I?" "Are you?" "Do I?"

"You're being mean," I tell her. "Am I?" she asks, and turns away. I do my best to pretend I don't care, but whenever I see Marjee talking with someone else, all smiles, my heart breaks. I hate her for hurting me. And I can't even avoid seeing her, because there's nowhere to hide, except inside myself.

Marjee's been busted for smoking pot. Some other patients and a staff member were involved, but she won't tell who. I went to bed early and missed the whole thing. Marjee emerges from her therapy session wide-eyed and pale, sits down next to me on the bench and sobs in my arms. They're shipping her to Rockland. There's nothing anyone can do to stop them. Dr. Gidro-Frankenstein has spoken.

I sit with Marjee while she packs. She tries to pretend she's not scared, but I can see it in her eyes. "It won't be so bad," she says. "They have great grounds there. Maybe I'll get to go outside." But she can't fool me, or herself. We've heard what it's like in these places.

The next day Marjee is gone. I sit in the hallway watching the walls dissolve into molecules. Bobby comes over and asks what's wrong, but I can't move or speak. Nick and Harold come and sit with me, comforting me, asking if I'm okay. They try to get me to talk, but I have no words. I don't know what I'll do now. I don't know how I'll survive without her.

Mrs. Gould is furious when Marjee is shipped. "What were they thinking? She's only thirteen. For God's sake, even my own children smoke marijuana occasionally."

"It's not fair," I say to Gidro-Frank when I see him on the ward. "Life is not fair," he answers, and goes about his business.

I hate them more than ever. They've sent Marjee to some hellhole, and when I ask them about it, they tell me it was for her own good. There are rules to follow, they say, and we have to learn to follow them.

My shrink is driving me crazy. He raises my meds, lowers them, raises them again. If there's something wrong with me, then help me fix it! But he can't, and that's why he gives me drugs. To control me, keep me quiet. If they can't help me, why don't they just get off my back? They've locked me up, taken away my clothes, sent away my best friend. What else do they want?

Each time somebody leaves, someone new arrives. It's weird, having new people around, but you get used to it. And every once in a while I make a new friend.

Sheila's a free spirit, a stoned hippie who's smoked so much dope her eyes are permanently at half-mast—unless it's the Thorazine. I get stoned just talking with her. We groove and laugh for hours on end, which the nurses do not appreciate. They don't think our laughing is healthy. They try to separate us by restricting us to different areas; when I ask why, they say we act out each other's craziness. This is complete bullshit—how am I to survive without a close friend? It's the only thing that makes my life bearable.

Adults are such hypocrites. Who are they to talk about what's *inappropriate?* Sheila's mother and grandmother used to lock her in the closet or chain her to the bed and force her to pray. When her parents divorced, she had to testify against her mother in court, and then felt guilty. She hoped living with her father would be better, but it didn't work out because her stepmother hated her. When she was sixteen she got a live-in job as an *au pair*, but the children's father kept pulling her onto his lap and kissing her. She got so depressed she tried to kill herself.

Now that she's here, it's even worse. The day Sheila was admitted, a doctor took her into the exam room, put a rubber glove on his hand, and without warning checked her ass for drugs. She screamed and cursed him out. Later, when she walked into therapy session, there was the same doctor—her new shrink. No way was she going to cooperate, she decided, and she stayed true to her word. The more they drug and restrict her, the more resistant she gets.

Sheila reminds me of myself. When she's pissed off, she curses and gets sarcastic. Most of the time she refuses to do what they tell her. I sit with her all day on the bench on South side to keep her from breaking restriction. Otherwise they'd restrict her more.

Sometimes Sheila sits under the card table in Center for hours, refusing to come out. She cries and cries, hugging herself, rocking back and forth. When I crawl under and ask what's wrong, she says she wishes she had a mother to hug her.

For a while Sheila is so spaced-out the staff is convinced she's doing drugs. She talks funny, not making sense; wandering into the laundry room, she starts sorting through other people's clothes like she's in a trance. At first I think she's just acting, but soon I'm worried too. They try to get information out of me, but I don't have any to give—and I wouldn't, even if I did. It turns out to be a reaction to meds. It's incredible how stupid the staff can be. Another time they accuse Sheila of being uncooperative, until they discover she has the mumps.

One day in the living room I demonstrate taking my bra off with my shirt on—something I learned from my mother. When she came home from work at night she'd pop open her bra and pull it through her sleeve, like a magic trick. It's a big hit with the boys, though it's perfectly innocent. Then Sheila tries it. A nurse sees, writes it up and restricts us . . . because it's *inappropriate*. Go tell my mother that!

A lot of problems could be avoided if only they had a sense of humor.

Bobby's been waiting for months and months to get building privileges, so he can go unaccompanied to the third-floor vending machines. When he finally gets them, he's thrilled. He asks R.J. to unlock the staircase door to let him out, and fooling around, in high spirits, he puts his arm around Harold, who's standing nearby in pajamas, and says, "Come on, come with me," and starts to walk through the open door. R.J. immediately pulls Bobby back inside, locks the door, and writes him up. His doctor restricts him to the ward and revokes his privileges. Crestfallen, he stands looking out the window in the living room, watching the cars whizzing freely down the highway. Suddenly there's a crash and a loud cry: Bobby has crashed his arm through the "unbreakable" double-paned glass, cutting himself so badly he's severed a nerve. When he saw all the blood he got frightened and called for a nurse. It's Catch-22 again. They make us so angry and frustrated, of course we freak out.

After a few months Sheila's doctor decides to ship her to Manhattan State because she hasn't been making progress. What kind of sense does it make to send someone who isn't making progress to a place like that? Luckily Sheila's father gets her into Chestnut Lodge (the place in *I Never Promised You a Rose Garden*), a private hospital where they don't give anyone drugs.

———

Jane, my best friend from outside, has been admitted. I can't believe it. It's strange, almost surreal. I've severed my ties with outside, and now here's Jane, floating down the hallway in pajamas, looking dazed. It's amazing to see her, but it also throws me off balance. Now I'll have to share my world, and my new friends, with Jane.

I've known Jane since junior high, when we started hanging out on the fringes of the same tough crowd. I smoked my first cigarette with her, stolen from a pack of her parents' Kents stashed high on a closet shelf in her Stuyvesant Town apartment. That first smoke, swirling and smooth, rasped hot inside my throat and lungs, landing me in my first drugged state—disjointed, thick, and dizzy. We were thirteen. Jane had already been smoking for a while. By the time I was fourteen, I smoked a pack a day of Marlboro cigarettes, and Jane and I smoked grass together regularly. I was amazed to be included in her large circle of friends. Jane got along with everyone: the popular kids, the greasers, the intellectuals. In high school, when I went to Music and Art, Jane went to a Quaker school in Chelsea, where she made new friends: smart, hip kids who lived in the Village.

I've always admired Jane. She's really knowledgeable about literature and poetry. Next to her, I feel stupid. I always thought she was stronger and more together than me. But here she is. I guess we're more alike than I thought.

Still, it's amazing that she wound up here. Is this some kind of weird epidemic? A plague of pessimism? A scourge of schizophrenia? It's almost as if she's followed me inside. If so, she'll probably wind up hating me—especially when she realizes it's not so easy to get back out. Jane's on Court Remand, like me. We're even diagnosed the same: adolescent schizophrenic, although Jane says the shrink who put her here diagnosed her as "impulsive behavior disorder." I envy that; it's much better than Dr. L. labeling me "phobic." When I'm impulsive, at least I'm not stuck in my head. "Schizophrenic" is more serious, weighty, literary. It looks good on Jane.

I worry about Jane, but at least she has me, and I know she'll like Mrs. Gould. And she's always been into Kafka, so this place is right up her alley. In no time she's sitting and chain-smoking with the rest of us, twitchy, dazed, and dizzy from meds.

Jane and I sit in the hallway and scratch each others' arms till we bleed, helping each other wake up from the drug-induced nothingness of this place. At least we feel some *real* pain we can identify by the red streaks on our skin. The staff gets really pissed when they see us doing this and restrict us to different areas of the ward. Too late. Anything we do on our own feels like therapy.

They soon have Jane on such high doses of different kinds of medication that she can't move. She's bloated and twitchy. Her hands clutch and convulse like snapping claws. The doctors study her. They give her more meds to get rid of the side effects. Then they give her Dexedrine to try to get her to move—which is really weird, because Dex is one of *our* drugs. Jane has nosebleeds that won't stop. Then she starts having fainting spells. Finally they send her to the medical center for tests. Her white blood count is dangerously low. They give her a transfusion and keep her in the hospital until her blood count stabilizes. Another friend, gone.

Ted and I commiserate on the fearfully inept, experimental quality of the "science" of psychiatry and wonder about the sanity of our doctors. They've completely thrown Jane's chemical balance out of whack with their drugs. We console ourselves with a bottle of vodka and drink to Jane's health.

Aside from suicide attempts, physical illness commands the highest level of status, earning the undivided attention of the doctors and nurses. When Jane goes to the hospital, mixed in with my concern is a rivalry that I do my best to squelch. I can't deny my enjoyment of having the boys' attention more to myself, but I'm relieved when she returns. I already have enough guilt and self-hate to last a lifetime.

> 3/4/68 Patient discussed in Rounds. It was decided to discontinue the phenothiazine for the present. Patient had complained of increasing depression, depersonalization and illusions while on the medication. She has been generally more appropriate off the medication. Patient continues on C.O. in pajamas.

March 4—my sixteenth birthday. My friends throw a surprise party for me in the dining room after dinner, but I refuse to let it cheer me up. What do I have to celebrate? Being in a nuthouse, in pajamas? At least my shrink finally agreed to take me off medication. That's the best present. Though you'd think that when he wrote the order in my chart he might have noticed that today was my birthday.

———

I long to be alone with Nick. I idolize him, like a god—not just because he's so smart, handsome, and perfectly formed—but because he's remote, inaccessible. Like a Kabuki-master, behind his many masks there is a wise, all-seeing presence. Nick has ultrasharp vision. Foolish people disgust him. He sees their underlying motives, their fear, stupidity, and self-deception. And in that vision there's power; something splendidly, perfectly, inscrutably *male*. It's something I want, something that makes me want him so much I can hardly look at him. And he knows it, and he knows I know he knows. Even the sound of his name wounds me. Nick, a little cut in my heart.

Nick takes his time with seduction. Once he decides you're worthy, he cultivates you slowly, letting anticipation build to an unbearable pitch. When we pass in the hallway, Nick surreptitiously brushes his hand against my hip, letting it rest just a second on my ass. Or he gradually lowers his voice until it becomes inaudible, then leaning closer as if to whisper, he'll stick his tongue in my ear—his pointed, intelligent tongue—causing me to shudder with pleasure.

In the dining room, during lunch, Nick slips a foot from his loafer and slides his toes up my leg and into my crotch, which is damp. I know he can feel it through my pajamas by the curl of his lips and the look he gives me. He's looking up at me from under his eyebrows, his face down low near his bowl, slurping his soup suggestively, some of it dribbling down his chin, while he's toeing me very insistently under the table. He's very good with his toes. I have to try hard not to wriggle too noticeably. When I feel myself start to twitch, I pull away and his foot drops to the floor. Nick gives a surprised jolt, and his spoon falls from his hand and splashes soup on his pajamas. He looks at me like he's mad, but he just picks up his napkin and blots up the soup, then turns and talks to Jane. He ignores me for the rest of the meal, and that makes me so angry I want to cry. But it's hard to tell with him. Sometimes pretending to be angry is just part of his act, the performance he's always perfecting.

Nick says he can bribe the night attendant, Higgins, to leave us alone together after hours, if I want to. Yes, I say, and wait for Nick to tell me when. Later, he whispers in my ear, "Tonight." *Tonight.* . . . Desire, intense and relentless, pulls me through the day. One thought, like Maria in *West Side Story. Tonight* . . .

I lie awake in agonized excitement waiting for Higgins to come get me, but fall asleep just as the sky is getting light. All the next day I'm in a black cloud, desperately disappointed. I avoid Nick. I'm afraid he's playing with me and doesn't intend to keep his part of the bargain. I wish I could shrivel up and blow away. But later in the afternoon, as Nick walks by, he brushes against me, tweaks my thigh, and whispers, "Sorry about last night. Higgins said it was no good. Maybe tonight."

Maybe? I don't know if I can stand not knowing. In bed, I struggle to stay awake; once again my excitement turns to agony as the night narrows. The third night, losing hope, I fall asleep instantly. The fourth night someone shakes me awake at 2 A.M. It takes me a moment to realize that Higgins, the male attendant, an unlikely messenger of the gods, is standing over me, whispering that Nick is waiting for me in the living room. Am I dreaming? I gather myself from sleep and creep down the hall behind Higgins.

It's eerie in the living room with the overheads off. At first I can't see Nick, but when my eyes adjust, I see him, slouched in one of the armchairs, watching me. The EXIT sign glows above him, a square red moon. Higgins says, "All right now, I'll be back in half an hour," and disappears down North side. Nick and I are finally, amazingly, alone together. I walk over and stand in front of him. I don't know what to do, until he pulls me onto his lap.

I straddle Nick in the vinyl armchair, face-to-face. I'm afraid to look in his eyes, afraid to find myself, or Nick's appraisal of me, in their gaze. He unbuttons my pajama top, runs his hands over my breasts and belly, rubs me until I'm soaked, then takes my hand and puts it on him. "Take it out," he whispers. I pull his cock through the fly on his pajama bottoms and lean down to feel its warmth against my cheek. Then I sit up and ease myself down on top of him. He pushes himself into my tight space, past the pain, making me gasp. As he enters me I enter an inner space, the inside of my eyelids a red so dark it's black. This is what I've waited and prayed for: Nick, deep inside me. He rocks me on top of him. Together, we're a boat in the middle of the ocean, rolling on the same wave. I open my eyes a second and he stares right back, his gaze so penetrating I have to close them again. His fingers find that other place, throbbing, red hot, the sensation so powerful it's almost unbearable. My whole body is vibrating so hard I'm afraid my teeth will chatter. He's making me see flashing colored lights. Then my body's jerking, out of my control. I bury my face in his neck.

I open my eyes to the red glow of the EXIT sign. "What was that?" I ask Nick. He laughs. "What do you think?" His hips start moving again, first slowly, then faster. Inside I'm still twitching and melting, and each thrust makes me see another flashing light, another color. I open my eyes a tiny crack and watch Nick's face. His eyes are closed, his lips pressed together to stifle a moan. Then he relaxes and we rest, our bodies glued together. Nick's thighbone presses into mine, my thigh joints are stretched too wide, one leg is asleep, but I don't care. I'd like to stay this way forever. *I love you,* I think over and over.

"Mr. N.?" Higgins pokes his head into the living room. "I think y'all better be movin' along now . . . supervisor be doin' her rounds soon. It be my ass as well as yours if she find you here."

In the morning the attendant has to shake me awake. "I'm tired," I mumble, "let me sleep." I must have had a dream. . . . Slowly it comes back to me. Me and Nick, together in the living room.

I search my face in the bathroom mirror. Do I look older, more *experienced?* I look like hell, dark circles under tired eyes. I splash water on my face. As I head toward breakfast fear seizes me. How will he be with me? I approach the dining room with dread. I'm late; no eggs left, so I just put on a piece of toast and get some coffee, push open the dining-room door, eyes on the floor. I glance up just long enough for a quick scan. My heart stops. Across the half-empty room, Nick sits talking with Harold, Bobby, Jack, Jane, and Alyssa. He turns his head, sees me, and goes right on talking. Now he's laughing. My heart shrivels. What if he's already told them all about it? I set my tray down. Nick shoots an opaque glance straight at me, then returns to eating his cereal. I sink into an empty chair and blindly chew the cardboard toast.

I don't know how lovers are supposed to act. I can only adore, adulate, worship him like a god, put him on a pedestal, and lay myself at his feet. I'm not a lover, I'm a mute, passive victim.

Just as they're getting up to leave, I do too. I must find out what's going on. Nick takes a detour toward me. "Good morning, Mindy, how are you today?" he says, a little too loudly, then brushes up against me, and whispers in my ear, "That was good last night." He gives my ear a little nuzzle before sauntering away. When his lips brush my ear, an electric current runs through my body.

I'm starting to feel like sex is something I can really lose myself in—or find myself in. It's an irresistible force, like a siren's call. When I'm caught, my shrink always asks the same question: *Why did you do it?* and I always give the same answer: *I don't know; I couldn't help it.*

The boys appreciate my wriggling and squirming, and I also have the power to make them squirm. I get to examine them up close. Their penises are like little trolls, each with its own personality. Some are long and thin. Some are pointy, some blunt, some stubby, some crooked. Eric's is uncircumcised. Harold's is thick and sturdy. Nick's is beautiful, straight, just right, with golden-blond pubic hair and a very intelligent-looking tip. It's perfect, I tell him, but he says, "Not quite," and frowns, pointing to a freckle. Poor Nick. He can't escape imperfection.

———————————

Nick has been spending more and more time with Alyssa. He plays with her hair—her straight blond hair. Her boobs are bigger than mine, and her black eyeliner makes her eyes stand out so you don't notice her buck teeth. She even jiggles her goddam leg, though not as fast as me, and her big feet flap when she walks. I hate the sight of her, and I hate Nick too.

I can hate them all I want, but they're the lucky ones. At least they can laugh.

I can't blame Nick for not wanting to be with me. I hate everything about myself—even my name. It's a little girl's name, a nickname, not a real name. It sounds like what's wrong with me: *Mind-y*, like being stuck in my head. If I had a different name, maybe I'd be a different person. Someone distinctive, with real character. I wonder what to change it to: Melinda, Miranda, Amanda? I ask around. Jack says, "Oh, that's simple; you're an Alice." I'm offended. Alice, like *Alice in Wonderland*. Another little girl's name.

Is there anything about me that's interesting or unique? I used to be able to draw, but not anymore. I can recite *The Cat in the Hat* from memory, and most of *The Love Song of J. Alfred Prufrock*. I can read the newspaper upside down and sing the words of songs backward—like "tahW a yaD rof a maerdyaD" or "woR, woR, woR ruoY taoB." Otherwise, the only thing that's special about me is that I'm fucked up. And here, that's not even special.

Before I started "having problems," all people had to say about me was that I was "nice." I hate nice; that's not what I want to be. Aside from *nice*, I'm just a big black hole with nothing to say. The thoughts are in there, but when I'm around people my throat closes up and my mind shuts down. People confuse *quiet* with *nice* but it's not the same thing. It's easier for other people. They don't have the same hole in themselves, the same trouble talking to each other.

Jane is becoming one of *them*. She's gotten all buddy-buddy with staff, hanging out and playing cards with the nurses and attendants. She's on a first-name basis with her shrink. Lately she's gotten really tight with Ted. They're together constantly. And she's doing so well in school that she's becoming one of Mrs. Gould's favorites. I fade into the background, a nonperson.

Jane's doctor put her in clothes and gave her neighborhood privileges!

Now she'll get to go on walks with Nick and Ted. While they're getting ready to go, I pretend I don't care. I wait until they're on the elevator before I let myself cry. When they're around I try to ignore them, but inside the tension is tearing my head apart like I'm about to explode. Instead of exploding, I implode, shutting down and down and down. If I shut down enough, maybe I'll disappear.

Harold is my only comfort. He puts his arms around me, and I cry into his shoulder. He knows how bad I feel now that Nick is hanging out with Alyssa. I can't avoid seeing them together. Everywhere I turn they're there.

I hate Nick, and I let him know it. Whenever I see him, I walk away. One day he comes over to talk to me, and I'm so afraid I'll cry, I won't look at him. He squats down next to me and says he's worried about me. He says I'm "too fragile." I thought he liked that about me! I wish I'd never let him come near me to begin with.

Everybody I've ever loved has left me, one way or another. Family, friends—they all betray you. I want someone who'll love me back, no matter what.

One day when Harold and I are messing around in the living room, it hits me—I could have a baby. Then I'd never be alone. Harold says he'd be happy to be the father. We cuddle and kiss and fool around. Harold gives me one of his sweatshirts wrapped in a towel, to practice with. I walk around the ward with Harold's little bundle, and the nurses and doctors get all freaked out about it. "What's that?" they ask. "It's a baby," I tell them, and they scurry off to write it in my chart. Would they rather hear me answer, "It's a sweatshirt wrapped in a towel?"

Harold and I do it whenever and wherever we can, usually in the living room after school. We joke about the tadpoles swimming around inside me, racing toward an egg. For all I know a baby might already be growing inside me. My secret—a funny mixture of calm, excitement, and queasiness—makes me feel powerful. I'll finally have a reason to exist, and I'll never be lonely again.

When my period is late, fear radiates from my brain into my belly and settles on my skin. I can imagine the brouhaha when they find out. Meetings, conferences, everyone telling me what to do. They'll never let me keep it. I'll have to run away and find some way to take care of it. I realize it's impossible, but I keep trying anyway, until Harold and I are caught. When I get my period, I'm relieved. I promise not to have sex again, but my shrink doesn't believe me. He talks about putting me on birth-control pills, but first he'll have to get my mother's permission. I can imagine how furious she'll be. Maybe she'll finally have to admit that I'm not a child anymore.

Marjee is coming back from Rockland. I'm so happy. I'm also a little nervous. I don't know how she'll feel about me and Nick, but it doesn't matter. I can't wait to see her.

When Marjee arrives on the ward, she seems different. Her skin is pale and translucent, in contrast to her dark hair and eyes, which look huger than ever. She's still the same beautiful girl, but there's something remote and fragile about her.

I sit with her all day in Center, trying to get her to talk to me. I don't know what to say to her. "What was it like at Rockland?" I finally ask.

"Hell," she says, but won't discuss it.

Things soon get more or less back to normal. Marjee and I hang out, talking, reading, listening to music. We're like the song on Simon and Garfunkel's new album: *"Old friends . . . sat on their park bench like bookends . . ."* On the same album a song about a bus ride across America fills me with longing for a future I still can't see.

Marjee is on S.O., so now I'm not the only adolescent restricted to the ward. Who cares what Jane and the others do? I'll just hang out on the ward with Marjee.

I still haven't told Marjee I've been with Nick, and I'm worried sick over it. I'm afraid she'll hate me. I almost cry when I tell her. But Marjee's cool about it. "Oh? How was it?" She leans toward me conspiratorially. "Come on, tell me!" Marjee forgives me almost too easily. "I'm over Nick," she says. "Don't you think Harold's cute, with his beautiful blue eyes?" I don't dare tell her about Harold and me.

Harold and Marjee are soon spending all their time together. They sit together holding hands, eat meals together, are never apart for a minute. I struggle with my feelings. I'm jealous . . . but I'm not sure of who— Marjee and Harold for being in love, or Harold for stealing Marjee's attention, or vice versa. Nick hardly pays attention to me, and now that Marjee's spending all her time with Harold, I feel all alone, left out in the cold.

Marjee sits on her bed, her chin on her knees, making a tent of her nightgown by pulling it down to her feet. Her eyes glow.

"Harold is such a good kisser, better than Nick. He's warm and cuddly, like a teddy bear." She reaches out and takes my hands. "I'm in love. Are you happy for me?" How could I not be? She's my best friend. I love her, and I love Harold too. They're so happy that they include me in it, both of them beaming and hugging me. "We both love you," they coo, cuddling around me. We're like a family—Harold, Marjee, and me.

When Marjee and Harold get restricted after they're caught kissing, I'm their go-between, carrying messages back and forth: "He said he loves you and sends you a kiss . . ." and "Tell him I miss him so much I do nothing but think of him and send him a dozen kisses back."

"What's wrong with wanting to touch someone you're in love with, especially when we're around each other twenty-four hours a day?" Harold complains to staff. The answer, of course, is: "It's inappropriate!" His shrink says they'll have to be content with holding hands. That just strengthens their desire.

When they quarrel, Marjee is inconsolable, but sooner or later they always kiss and make up. A nuthouse is a convenient place to be during a breakup. When you get depressed, they just raise your meds and put you on observation or suicide watch.

Other people pair up. Ted proposes marriage to Jane, ceremoniously getting down on one knee right in the middle of Center. Surprised, Jane bursts out laughing. "I mean it," Ted says, but it's part real, part fun. Some people really do get engaged. Two adult patients, Anne and Aaron, were made for each other. They sit together for hours, silently looking into each other's eyes. Aaron tenderly strokes Anne's hand, as if to say, "It's all right, sweetheart, don't worry. Everything will be okay."

Even some of the sickest patients have boyfriends. But not me. Boys may feel sorry for me or want to fool around, but I'll never have a real boyfriend, never be loved.

OUTSIDE COMMUNICATION

THERE IS ONE PHONE BOOTH ON THE WARD, nestled into a corner next to the kitchen, right near the elevator. It's a regular phone booth with metal and glass walls and a door that, when accordioned shut, creates a bubble of privacy. People line up and take their turns. Tall and short, fat and thin, they fold themselves into the booth in an effort to make contact with the outside world. I don't have phone privileges, but that's not going to stop me.

I plan the moment carefully. Sly and R.J. are involved in a serious game of bridge with Liz and Mike. Mrs. G. alone is watching the living room. I ask her permission to get something from the dorm. She says okay, as long as I come right back. I stroll to the dorm, then back, humming a little tune, trying to look casually thoughtful. Then I wander back to the corridor that houses the phone booth. It's empty, nobody waiting. Bending to tie my shoe, I look around. Nobody seems to notice me. I take from my shoe the coins I've stashed in the instep.

I slip into the booth, my pajamas sliding onto the metal seat. Closing the door is out, because it squeaks. When I pick up the receiver, the dial tone sounds surprisingly loud, its monotonous hum a one-note tribute to communication. I cough to camouflage the sound of the dime dropping into the slot and dial slowly, taking care not to make any noise. Every sound is dangerously loud, as is my thumping heart. Keeping an anxious eye on the corridor, I relish the forbidden luxury of the moment.

Through the receiver I hear the phone ringing in my friend Janice's apartment—the same apartment where we hung out after school. Her mother answers and I hang up. I'd have to whisper, and her mom will know something's up. Besides, she knows I'm in the hospital. She doesn't want Janice to associate with me.

I try Josh.

Josh is one of my few close friends. He took me to the first Human Be-In in Central Park—10,000 multicolored, long-haired freaks in the Sheep Meadow, smoking grass, dropping acid. Arms entwined, we swayed together, singing, *"What the world needs now . . . is love, sweet love!"* And for a few hours it really seemed possible, this sense of my own generation banded together, a vision of peace and love.

If one of Josh's parents answers I'll stay on and ask to speak to him. His parents seem to really like me, though usually I'm so shy I can hardly talk to them. Josh's father is a theater director, and his mother used to dance with Martha Graham. They read books and talk about art. I wish I had parents like that.

To my relief, Josh answers.

"It's me, Mindy," I say as softly as possible, clutching the receiver like a lifeline.

Josh says he's happy to hear from me. We've been friends since my last year of junior high. I met him at a dance at the Y where he played guitar in a rock band. Amazing what went on at those dances, in the staircases, in the bathrooms. Smoking grass. Popping pills. Making out. I never made out with Josh, though. He's always been really nice to me and would never do anything to make me feel uncomfortable. He may even be in love with me, though it's hard for me to tell.

When I tell Josh how much I hate it here, that I can't go outside or wear my own clothes, and about the drugs they give me, I can tell he feels bad for me. He asks if he can come see me; I tell him I'm not allowed any visitors. After a moment he says he's sorry to hear that, but to cheer up—he'll be sending me something in the mail. Just as I'm asking what it is, a hand enters the phone booth and clicks down the cradle, cutting us off. It's R.J. and he's pissed.

"Okay, that's enough. You know you don't have phone privileges."

"Oh, I thought I did," I start to say, but he knows I'm bluffing so I just let it go. I wonder what my punishment will be; I'm already on observation, in pajamas, restricted to the ward. Maybe no TV for a while? R.J. places his hand on the back of my neck, which is sticky with perspiration from sitting in the booth, and steers me back to Center. He tells me he'll let it go this time, but warns me that next time he won't be so nice.

The protocol for people with phone privileges is: fifteen-minute limit. Line up quietly a respectful distance from the booth so the person talking will have some privacy. The atmosphere inside the booth with the door closed rapidly becomes a steam bath, so clean up after yourself, wiping the perspiration from the seat and receiver with a tissue or paper towel. For your own good, do not attempt to use the phone following a patient with B.O., and don't hog the phone.

Arguments break out among patients who are tired of waiting or annoyed at being interrupted by people asking when they'll be finished. Sometimes the arguments turn into fights. One day unusually loud sounds of yelling and crashing permeate Center. It turns out that Ted, angry at being told he has to get off the phone, has flipped out and *beat up* the phone booth, pounding and smashing every supposedly nonshatter-glass surface. We rush down the hall to check it out. I've never seen Ted so angry—red-faced, spluttering and shouting, shaking with rage, so full of adrenaline that it takes R.J. an amazingly long time to subdue him. It's sad to behold: Ted, a gentle giant, erupting like a volcano. When he finally gives up, Ted shrugs R.J.'s hands off him and walks to the Quiet Room, his eyeglasses crooked on his nose, one lens shattered, wearing a look of terrible defeat.

Such is the strength of our need for outside communication.

When my doctor finally gives me phone privileges, it does feel like a privilege—a rich treat, a reward. I plan who I'll call, wait my turn, then slip into the booth, clutching my nickels and dimes. I only call those I still consider good friends—those who won't judge me, who love and support me—because only the most essential connections will penetrate the isolation of this place. Knowing that Josh or Wendy or Andrew will phone me at 6 P.M. on Friday, I literally whistle a happy tune and smile at the attendants. Then there are surprise calls, which stir in me a tremulous excitement . . . unless I'm too depressed to talk or it's someone I don't want to talk to, in which case I ask an attendant to call out that I have to get off the phone.

One of the first people I phone is Dr. L., my shrink from before the hospital. I tell him I'm doing okay, that I've just gotten phone and cloth-ing privileges, and am finally off observation. I shyly tell him that I miss him, and think of him often—I push the words out in a humid rush. He thanks me and says he's fond of me too, and wishes me well. I feel wobbly when I leave the booth, teary, and a little silly. Dr. L.'s parting words had a "good-bye and good luck" quality. Does he have any concept of what his "fatherly" advice of putting me into the hospital has landed me into? What did I expect? He's not my father, not my friend. I can't help feeling that the one adult I thought was on my side has sold me down the river.

We experience the outside world in vicarious ways. We follow the weather on television instead of feeling it on our skins. We watch the news devotedly, hungry for the latest atrocities and scandals. We escape into newspapers and magazines, disappearing behind the front pages of *Times, Tribune,* and various tabloids, unless we're too restless to concentrate. Medication makes the type hard to read; the letters jump and glow. Juicy headlines engender commentary and discussion—sometimes bitter, sometimes humorous. Newpapers are delivered daily and make the rounds. On Sundays there's an intense lineup for sections. Patients become irritated awaiting their turn; testy remarks erupt into confrontations. A few patients receive their own newspaper subscriptions, and they fully devour each issue before offering it to the scavengers to read later or the next day, when it's old news.

I write to and receive letters from my friends. Reading their letters is bittersweet; I hate it when they tell me all the things they're doing, and skim down to the part where they tell me they miss me. But at the same time it's delicious to receive these remnants of my old life. I sneak off to a private corner, where I read them again and again.

Letters are usually uncensored unless they suspect you're getting drugs in from outside or are planning to escape, or if you're suicidal. Packages are routinely inspected, so staff often know what's in them before you do, and hand them over with suppressed smiles and knowing eyes. Or else they stand and watch you open them, diluting your excitement as they check the contents for contraband.

When the mail arrives, I'm surprised to be given a large mailing tube. It's from Josh. I pull out a three- by five-foot sheet of thick drawing paper, so tightly rolled that I have to kneel on the edges in order to read it. It's a beautifully handwritten and illustrated letter, in honor of my sixteenth

birthday. I marvel at how much work Josh put into it: his careful calligra-
phy and little drawings of guitars, birds, flowers. A second sheet of blank
paper is included for me to draw on. Josh always loved my spirally
Rapidograph drawings modeled on the style of Aubrey Beardsley, like my
illustrations of T. S. Eliot's *The Hollow Men*—a castle composed of fools'
faces visible through tall grass stalks—or the cave of Barabbas, or spooky
trees with spiderwebs and faces hidden in them. But I no longer have anything to express, nor any self to express it from. I roll up the paper and
slide it back into the tube.

My mother sends me letters, telling me she loves me, asking me if
there's anything I want. When I get these, I curse and crumple them up,
but later I take them out of my bathrobe pocket and smooth them out,
crying a little at the familiarity of my mother's handwriting, reminding
me of the grocery lists she'd stick on the refrigerator door.

Visiting hours are Saturday and Sunday, one to five. I sit in Center with
my book and watch the other patients' family members arrive, all rosy-
cheeked and smiling, the cool air rolling off their coats, their heels clicking briskly. They carry shopping bags of gifts and goodies, but more than
that, they lend some vitality to our sleepy, inert ward.

After a few weeks, I'm allowed visits from my mother and stepfather.
It's confusing to have them come. They bring me candies and cookies as if
I'm at summer camp. I'm not sure whether to hug my mother or sit fuming, so I do a little of each. I hate them for pretending that everything's
hunky-dory. Don't they realize where I am, and why? My stepfather is the
worst. I can feel him gloating; finally the big expert has me where he wants
me. I never want to see him again. It's better to make a clean break, I tell
myself. We've parted ways, so why try to pretend we haven't? I tell my doctor I don't want to see them, and the visits are discontinued.

I get news of my mother through Dr. A. and the psychologist who
meets with my mother twice a month. Sometimes the psychologist stops
down to the ward to ask if there's anything I need, or if I have any message I'd like her to pass along to my mother, since we no longer have direct
contact. When I see the psychologist walking toward me, I bristle and
answer her questions with silence. But when I imagine her telling my
mother, I feel guilty.

Why should I care? She stopped being my mother the day she signed

the papers in Family Court and dumped me here. She's not even my legal
guardian anymore. She should accept the fact that I'm on my own now.
But as hard as I try to sever our connection, I can't help worrying about
her. Until recently, I was the only person who could make her feel better.
How will she survive without me, especially now that my stepfather's on
the road, working as a traveling salesman, and my brother's away at college?

I push the thoughts away. I've cut the cord. My life is here now.

———————

Once in a while my brother comes to see me. That's different; he's more
like me, a rebel. Under his gaze, I feel foolish for ending up in the hospital. He never would have allowed himself to be in such a helpless position.
I was raised to be passive and dependent, but my brother was expected to
fend for himself. He's angry at my mother for locking me up, and I think
a little pissed at me too, for allowing it to happen. I know he thinks less
of me for it. He tries not to show it, but I know I've let him down.

Fortunately, my brother jokes away the tension between us. He tells
me stories about his work as an ambulance driver: cruising through the
night, red light flashing, sometimes using the siren just for the hell of it,
showing up at scenes of accidents, poverty, violence, exchanging jokes
with his black and Hispanic coworkers . . . who, from the details of my
brother's storytelling, remind me of the hospital attendants. Our worlds
are not so far apart—except, of course, that he's living a real life, and I'm
in here.

All the time we were growing up, my brother and I fought. Our interactions were peppered with betrayals and meanness, shrieks, tears, expressions of barely concealed rage. It was a trickle-down effect. My mother
harangued my brother for failing to live up to this or that responsibility.
My brother, enraged at having to come home after school to baby-sit, bullied me. Then I'd be sure to get him in trouble when my mother came
home.

In a way, my being in the hospital places my brother and me on equal
ground for the first time. He left home at sixteen to go to college, and I
left at fifteen to come here. Both of us had to get away from the screaming and yelling and anger and misery that was the air we breathed. That's
what we have in common. We communicate it with a look, a word, a
laugh, and instantaneously understand one another's scorn, hurt, and

anger. After years of venting our unhappiness on each other, we're now, strangely, on the same side.

For a long time I'm not allowed to have friends visit; I guess they're afraid they'll bring me drugs . . . or maybe that they'll catch whatever's wrong with me. My shrink is always accusing me of smuggling drugs onto the ward. A nice idea, but yeah, sure, how am I supposed to do that? I don't have any visitors. They inspect my mail. I don't have magic powers. If I was able to smuggle drugs in, I'd smuggle myself out!

When I finally am allowed to have friends come, the visits are awkward. I'm not sure what we have in common anymore. They're concerned with grades, dating, and applying to colleges, while I'm living in a world of meds, restrictions, and acting out. My friends ask well-intentioned questions and jump silences with a rush of sentences, while the gap between us broadens.

Patients scrutinize everyone coming in from outside. If a guy visits me, everyone notices and comments afterward. "He was cute. Is he your boyfriend?" or "That was the weirdest-looking guy I've ever seen! Is *he* your *boyfriend?*"—the latter referring to a friend who arrives dressed in a ratty, oversized trenchcoat, scuffed suede bucks, and a slouch hat like his idol, Humphrey Bogart. They tease me for days. For all our blurriness, we have sharp eyes, and equally sharp tongues.

For my sixteenth birthday, I request a visit with my mother. Just her alone, not my stepfather. I'm not sure how it's going to be seeing her, not sure if she'll be disappointed or angry at me for being back in pajamas. I don't want her to lecture me. I prepare myself, and decide to be polite and not to let her see it if I start to seethe—something I always fail miserably at.

When she steps off the elevator, I spot her immediately, even with her red hair hidden under a scarf. She's as stylish as ever in her slim skirt and beaver coat, her high heels tapping toward me. She carries an ever-present shopping bag, this one with a Lord & Taylor logo.

I walk toward her, and in a minute I'm enveloped in the soft fur of her jacket and her perfumed aura. We go into the dining room, the designated visitors' area. Our visit is limited to twenty minutes—doctor's orders. At first I'm wary, but as long as she doesn't ask about my future or lay a guilt trip on me, we're fine. We talk about neutral things: what the food's like, how I'm doing in school, whether I've made friends. I introduce her to Marjee and some other kids. As usual, she turns on the charm, and they all seem to like her. Noel rolls his eyes as he walks away, as if to say, "That's some sexy broad!" She looks so beautiful, I can't help feeling proud she's my mother.

She asks me what I want for my birthday. I want to get out of here, is what I want to say. "How about a nightgown? I'd like to get you something pretty, so you can feel better about yourself." Does she think a *nightgown* will make me feel better about myself? I tell her I don't want anything, but when her jaw tightens and her face gets that closed-down look I decide to ease up on her. It doesn't make sense for her to give me clothes, since I'm in pajamas, so I tell her some jewelry would be nice, maybe earrings or a necklace.

On her next visit my mother surprises me with a long strand of unusual-looking beads.

"They're bugle beads," she says as I unwrap them. The bronze beads give off a warm shimmer. Each tiny bead has eight flat facets, forming a perfect octahedron.

"I saw them in an antiques store and thought they were lovely. I had them strung for you."

I feel uneasy that she's given me something so nice. It makes it hard for me to hate her. When I look into her eyes I see she loves me, and that makes me feel worse than anything. It all comes rushing up: regret, sadness, hurt that can't be undone. A wave of hate rises like a snake inside me. I hate her for being nice to me, for reminding me I once had a mother I loved.

She loops the beads around my neck. "You can tie them in a knot like this," she says, her long fingers deftly arranging the beads. "Or you can double them up." Her perfume tickles my nose. I don't like her fussing over me. I undo the knot and place the strand over my head a second time so a long loop hangs from a tight choker, the way Marjee wears hers.

"Thanks, Mom," I say. "They're beautiful."

I was prepared to dislike her gift and have to pretend to like it. But it's clear she looked for something she knew I'd really like. Something for me, not her idea of me. I'm proud to have a mother with such good taste. I wear the beads and feel dressed up, almost pretty. They're a token, a promise that maybe one day I'll grow up, wear beautiful things, and feel good about myself.

One day as I'm hurrying down the hall to go to school, my arm catches the strand of beads, the string pops, and beads go flying everywhere. They skitter along the linoleum, bouncing fast and rolling out of sight. I feel terrible, not just because I love the beads but because I know my mother would be hurt and disappointed to know I'd broken her gift. It's the same way everything—our closeness, my parents' marriage, my innocence—has broken, the way everything beautiful and perfect breaks. I scoop up whatever beads I can find, put them in a tissue, and stash them in my dresser drawer. I try restringing them myself, but the new necklace is too short, and the string soon breaks again. I do my best to forget the beads, but my hand automatically flies up to my chest to check them several times a day. It's a while before my phantom necklace fades away completely.

My doctor tells me that my father would like to see me. He'll be coming to New York on one of his business trips from California. The visit will be limited to half an hour. If the visit goes well, my shrink says, we can schedule another one.

I'm not sure I want to see him. I'm afraid of his disappointment, his anger. He's bound to scold me, to judge me. And I'm embarrassed. I don't want him to see me in pajamas. I plead with my shrink to take me off E.O., but he refuses. As the visit approaches I'm more and more apprehensive. But I know he'll be hurt if I refuse.

When my father steps off the elevator, my heart lurches. He's so handsome, so alive. In an instant my trepidation vanishes; I jump up and go to him. He puts his arms around me and hugs me, and I breathe in his wonderful, familiar smell. I'm just so happy to see him. He holds me at arm's length, then takes my chin in his hand and tries to kiss me on the mouth, but I pull away, embarrassed.

I don't want him to think I don't love him. Pleasing my father has always been second nature for me. To please him, I'd stand on my head, but that doesn't jive with my rebel/mental-patient persona. Now, the way I make an impression is to shock, to repel.

"So what's new?" my father asks, as we sit in the dining room. What can I possibly talk to him about—the medication they have me on, or how long I've been on observation? I'm not about to tell him I'm back in

pajamas for "acting out." I feel grotesque sitting across from him in my
pajamas, trying to make small talk with this suntanned man in his
powder-blue, polyester bell-bottom leisure suit. He tells me he'd like to
see me take more pride in myself and my appearance, and reaches over to
tuck some strands of hair behind my ear.

"Anyhoo . . ." My father's voice trails off. He is obviously as uncomfortable as I am. He asks the usual mundane questions about the food and
whether I've made friends, and then tells me about what's new in his life.
He's brought things to show me: his new business card with gold lettering
("Sy Lewis & Associates, Manufacturer's Representative"), a photo of
him with his new girlfriend, who's wearing a tiny bikini, at the beach with
their arms around each other. ("I've told her all about you and she wants
to meet you.") I wonder what he told her, and how he would explain my
being in the hospital. Finally, snapshots of his recent travels, including
one of him standing next to London Bridge. "Guess where they moved it
to? Arizona!" he says with a grin. "That's what's great about traveling. You
never know what you'll find or where you'll find it. The important thing
is to take a chance." I know he's just trying to show me what's possible, but
I feel bad anyway. The photos are proof that he's out there enjoying his
life . . . unlike me.

I can tell he's at a loss to understand my situation. He can't understand
why I'm in the hospital, and I can't explain it to him. I see the questions in
his eyes: What's wrong with me? Am I sick, or faking it, or just plain lazy?
My father doesn't believe in psychiatry. He believes in simple things, like
getting to work on time and keeping his shoes shined. My father—who
taught me when I was five years old to ride the subway without holding
on, who ran alongside my bike the first time I rode without training
wheels so I wouldn't panic and fall over, and who, unlike my mother,
didn't get hysterical when I wobbled into the path of a pedestrian, knocking us both to the ground—knows how to take things in stride. One of
eight kids growing up poor during the Depression, he learned early how
to keep his balance in difficult circumstances, to look on the bright side
and make the best of things. He's the kind of man whose day is made by
finding a penny in the gutter and spending it on a two-pack of Chiclets
from a subway vending machine. Yet in spite of his warm greeting, there's
something tentative about him; I read in his face disappointment that his
lessons have been lost on me.

I watch as he gears up to act out his fatherly role—something I don't know how to deal with at all. It's too sporadic to take seriously, and too unfamiliar to actively rebel against. His face grows stern. "I hope you'll make an effort to get along better with your mother." As if it were as simple as just saying okay, as if she's played no part in getting me locked up. He thinks I can just pull myself up by my bootstraps, decide to get better, and go back and live with my mother as if nothing had happened. If we all just ignore it, whatever it is, it will go away of its own accord.

When my father glances at his watch and says it's time to get going, I'm relieved. After we kiss good-bye, I picture him riding up in the elevator, pulling his overcoat closed, and striding briskly through the hospital entrance to the welcome familiarity of the street, glad to be back in the light of day.

When it really gets to me, when I can no longer stand another minute of the boredom and confinement, I decide to elope. "Elope" is hospitalese for escape. It's a sport we all engage in from time to time. Some stay away long enough to break the spell and never return; others reappear after a few days or even as long as a couple of weeks later, sheepish to be back, trading in street clothes for pajamas. Since elopement in the romantic sense generally involves another person, who or what are we eloping with? Perhaps our freedom, our selves, our own free will.

"Have you heard? So-and-so eloped!"—the news rips through the ward like a fire; when it reaches me I am alight with admiration and envy. "Good for them!" I gloat, and the desire to accomplish this on my own builds, burns.

Eloping takes some planning: eluding the staff, thinking up a good story to tell the elevator operator, finding a place to stash and change into street clothes, ditching your pajamas, and, finally, walking out that door. Sometimes it involves an accomplice, either inside, to create a diversion, or waiting for you outside.

I've planned it carefully. One day when I'm trusted enough to go to the third-floor vending machines unattended, Marjee meets me there a few minutes later and helps me get into the clothing she's smuggled along with her. I stash my p.j.'s behind the cigarette machine, hug Marjee good-bye, wait for the next elevator going up, calmly say, "Ten, please"—even though I'm shaking with adrenaline—stroll past the guard in the lobby, and walk out the door. I come alive in the chilly autumn air. Before I know it I am blocks away. I have *eloped*.

Air has never smelled so good. Leaves and litter skitter along the sidewalk. I'm only wearing a sweatshirt and jeans; not used to the outside temperatures, I shiver, but it is a thrilling, exhilarated chill. I have to get out of this neighborhood fast. The only problem is, where to go? None of my friends have their own apartments; they all live with their parents. Most of my city friends are out of the question, because their mothers know where I am. But I have a couple of friends in Queens whose families don't know my story.

Clutched in my fist are six dollars I've saved up from my allowance, along with five from Marjee, and some change she stuffed into my pocket. Keeping my face down, I hurry to a phone booth on the corner and dial Larry.

Larry and I went to camp together the summer I was fourteen, the first summer I felt so inexplicably sad and sexual, the summer I fell in love with Larry and his best friend, Will. The three of us hung out at the theater, where I painted sets, Larry worked the lights, and Will rehearsed his lead role in *Fiddler on the Roof*. During breaks from work they sang Richie Havens, Simon and Garfunkel, and Dave van Ronk songs, told jokes and flirted with me. We smoked joints and lay in the grass on our backs looking at the stars, entranced by the bullfrogs' singing. It was love, *à trois*, achingly innocent. *This*, we agreed, was how it would always be—the Three Musketeers, in love, forever.

Larry's mother answers, but to my great relief, says hold on and hollers, "Laarrr! Phone!" and a moment later he picks up. I tell him I've escaped. He tells me to grab a cab and come to his house, never mind how much it costs. He gives me the address.

Soon I'm rolling safely toward the Triborough Bridge. I lean my forehead against the window and watch the cars speed by—everybody is on their way home for dinner. I imagine TVs being turned on for the evening news, delicious dinner smells wafting from kitchens. I'm on my way to someone else's house, because my own is off limits. It's illegal for me to go home. The police would contact my mother and she'd have to return me to P.I.

Larry tells his mom some story, and she says I can stay for one night but not more, as long as I sleep on the couch. Luckily, it's Saturday, so Larry doesn't have to go to school the next day. We hang out and eat the tunafish sandwiches his mother prepares. They taste different from my mother's. It's strange to drop in on a family that isn't my own.

Larry's room is in the basement. It's like his own world down there, with electric guitars and drum sets and clothes all over the place, ashtrays overflowing with cigarette butts and stubbed-out joints. From upstairs, I heard the muffled sound of Larry's sisters fighting and his father shouting at his mother to make them behave. Is this what a normal family is supposed to be like?

In the morning it's time for me to go. But where? Knowing I don't have the guts or independence to stay out on my own, I resign myself to returning to the hospital. I wish I were older, tougher, more self-confident . . . but then I wouldn't be in this situation to begin with.

Larry takes the subway back to the hospital with me and leaves me at the front steps. I walk in on my own, and there is a big bustle of "She's back!" The nurse hands me a pair of pajamas in exchange for my clothes. They press me to tell them where I was, but I won't say a word. Then I tell them I was at my friend Lois's place—someone I haven't been friends with in years. The least I can do is maintain some privacy.

I've accomplished something important in my first solo flight. A day and a night outside is better therapy than all their drugs and therapy sessions. It's back to pajamas and observation, until I slowly win back the trust of the staff. In spite of everything, I've earned some independence. My self grows an eighth-inch larger.

Running away is habit-forming. After Marjee is shipped and my shrink is on vacation, I decide to go on vacation too. This time I have company. Laurie's run away dozens of times; for her it's just something fun to do. We slip onto the elevator early one morning, take the subway to Columbus Circle, and go to Central Park. I show her all my old haunts: the Ramble, the Sheep Meadow, the Boathouse. It's almost like old times, but the familiar places are deserted. The smell of winter in the air makes me melancholy, all the leaves already fallen from the trees. It's freezing, and neither of us is dressed warm enough. We're just wearing sweaters over shirts and jeans. Hot chocolate in the Boathouse doesn't warm us up.

Laurie's not impressed with Central Park. To her, it's just cold and dreary. Teeth chattering, she tells me she's going back to the hospital. "Fine," I say, unable to keep the hurt out of my voice. "Just don't tell them where I am, okay?"

Before I leave the Boathouse, I call my mother from a pay phone. She's relieved to hear from me. "Go back to the hospital," she says, trying to sound calm. "Or come home." When the recording comes on asking for another nickel, I tell her not to worry, and promise to call back later. Then I notice a couple of cops and get out of there fast. I wander around the Ramble until my hands, face, and feet are numb. My brain function is down to two words: *cold* and *walk*. I follow the plume of my breath. By the time I emerge it's mid-afternoon. Cars whiz back and forth on Central Park West as I enter the subway station. I'm so frozen I don't know if I can wait for a train.

Where am I going? Anywhere, except the hospital—I'm not ready for that yet. I suddenly want to see Greenwich Village one more time, go to St. Marks Place, do the things I used to do when I was free. I cross over to the downtown track and wait, stamping my feet and breathing on my numb hands. When two tiny white pin-dots of light appear in the dark tunnel I almost weep with relief.

It's good to see the Village again, the hippies and booksellers, the little shops and cafés. It feels alive, and so do I. I have a slice of pizza in my favorite place on St. Marks, then sit in a café warming my hands on my coffee cup, still shaking with cold. I try to think what to do next. I don't even have enough change to get on a bus.

I use my last coins to call my mother at work. She asks if I'd like to come over for a meal. Food, the basic currency between me and my mother, has always been a way of neutralizing whatever else is going on. A nice warm dinner in my mother's kitchen sounds really good. She tells me to stay where I am and she'll come meet me, but makes me promise not to tell the hospital because she's required by law to send me right back.

I wait for her on a street corner. All around me strangers rush past. When I spot my mother walking toward me, in a second changing from just anybody to a familiar face, I feel a tremendous sense of relief, as if someone had drawn a line connecting two dots, making sense of a random world. I don't resist her hug.

It's bone-cold, snowing a little now, and I'm just wearing a sweater. My mother asks if I'd like to do a little shopping. I usually hate shopping with a passion, especially with my mother. But not today. Today we shop in my kind of store—a funky thrift shop on St. Marks Place. Now it's her turn to be out of place. But she quickly gets into her accustomed role, flipping expertly through the racks. I try on a fur coat made of deep brown pelts. The salesperson tells us it's skunk.

My mother tries to talk me out of it. "Are you sure you want skunk? It'll stink if you get caught in the rain." But I love the coat, the dark fur all shiny and sleek. I deliver a sales pitch: "It's in good condition, only a few ripped seams, and not expensive . . ." My mother inspects the lining with pursed lips, then gives in gracefully and buys it for me, along with a beautiful burgundy-and-gold velour scarf and matching mittens. When I see myself in the dusty thrift-shop mirror, I like the way I look. With a pang I realize I won't be able to wear these things again after I return to P.I. I try not to think about it. My mother and I have a silent agreement not to talk about the hospital. It's as if we're on an island removed from time, on reprieve from reality. As we leave the store my mother ties my scarf and straightens the padded shoulders of my new coat.

We take a taxi the twenty blocks home. The sight of my old building makes me ache with sadness. It looks slightly unfamiliar, like a place I left long ago—not just the few months I've been gone. After a hot bath, I begin to warm up for the first time since morning. Sitting in the kitchen watching my mother prepare dinner, I feel a strange sensation, as if some loud, continuous noise has suddenly stopped. For the first time in years there's no tension between us.

After dinner I take a look at my old room. All my things are still there, my books and furniture and clothes. The cat is asleep on my bed, where I'm no longer allowed to sleep. I can hardly remember why I used to hate being here. The past seems as muffled as the snow falling softly outside the window. I take a last look around, then my mother appears at the door and says it's time to go.

It's an oddly out-of-context experience walking to the subway in the snowy purple twilight with my mother, like a dream. I wish I could wake up in my own bed and everything would be normal again—I'd go to school, see my friends, sleep late on Sunday, and eat brunch in my mother's kitchen. But I know this will never be; it's just a phantom of my former life.

INSIDE OUT

Granted: I am an inmate of a mental hospital; my keeper is
watching me, he never lets me out of his sight; there's a peephole in the door, and my keeper's eye is the shade of brown
that can never see through a blue-eyed type like me.

—Günter Grass

IT'S NAP-TIME. I'm lying on my bed reading *The Tin Drum*, the story of a
dwarf named Oskar who decides (if we are to believe him) to stop
growing at the age of five, and who claims that his drumming has the
power to start wars and that his high-pitched silent screaming can drive
people mad. Does Oskar really have this power, or is he just a mischie-
vous liar? Whatever answer you choose, Oskar lives his own reality—like
all the loonies in this bin.

So you see, my white enamel hospital bed has become a norm
and a standard. To me it is still more: my bed is a goal
obtained at last, it is my consolation and might become my
faith if the management allowed me to make a few changes: I
should like, for instance, to have the bars built up higher, to
prevent anyone from coming too close to me.

Outside, the worst thing was having to be around people all the time.
When I needed to get away, I cut school and went to the park, or sat on
my East River pier. Here there are always people around, and there is
nowhere to escape to but *in*.

My favorite part of the day is the hour after lunch when we get to go
back to the dorm. It's my time to escape. I lie on my stomach with my
hands tucked under my shoulders and wait for the waves of sleep to pull
me under. Then I'm no longer in the hospital, but in that other world,

where I can understand languages I've never heard before, or fall and fall through the air from a great height but always land softly, unharmed.

When I was little I loved bedtime: the smell of clean sheets, my stuffed animals all around. Every night my mother sat on my bed while I said the bedtime prayer. After she kissed me good-night and turned out the lights, I imagined that my bed was a raft washed up on a deserted island. I built a tent of blankets and leaves and hunkered down in the forest while wind and rain whistled all around. My bed was an island of safety and love, the dark ocean of night lapping at its clean sheets.

When I was seven or eight I got into the habit of falling asleep holding my right arm straight up until it found a point of perfect balance. Then I would feel myself start to spin, slowly at first, then faster and faster. Just before falling asleep I'd have a sense of being a tiny speck in a vastness that went on and on. It filled me with a kind of contentment. Sometimes I dreamed I was spinning through star-studded space on a disk like one of Saturn's rings, only it was two-dimensional; when it turned sideways it disappeared. For a while I dreamed this dream often, always waking with wonder at having spent the night steeped in infinity.

Around this time I dreamed that everybody I knew, including myself, were marionettes jerking happily along in a puppet parody of life—until, at random, the puppeteer suddenly dropped the strings and somebody or other fell down lifeless. I woke crying. My mother came to my door and said I'd had a bad dream and that everything was fine. How could I explain my grief? When the puppeteer drops the strings, it's final.

One night, lying in bed with my head resting on my upper arm, I heard a rhythmic *thump, thump*. For a moment I wondered what it was; then I realized it was the sound of my heart pushing the blood through my veins. My own heart, keeping me alive, all by itself. But what if it should stop? What would life be like without me in it?

When I was thirteen my brother took me to the big discount book annex at Union Square to buy a book. I'd never bought a book all on my own before. I wanted it to be something really special. There were so many books, rows and rows of shelves. I walked the aisles scanning their titles, picking them up, running my hands over covers before putting them back, searching for the one that was meant for me.

When I picked up the thin volume it felt different in my hand. The cover illustration was a pen-and-ink drawing of two faces, each cut in half down the middle. *The Sibyl,* by Pär Lagerkvist (a Pulitzer Prize–winning author I'd never heard of), told the story of a young oracle of the temple at Delphi. The language was simple and solemn. I opened it at random and read these words: *"I lived only in the reality I bore within me; that was all there was."* Chills went down my spine. This was the book for me.

Something guided me to that book. It wasn't God exactly, but a nameless something I've always known was there—a spirit I felt in the smell of rain, in the feeling of sun on my skin, in spring air. It was there on bright mornings, in the long afternoons and sudden dusk. It was in our apartment, in the furniture, in the walls. Everything was alive with it.

When I get really confused, and there's no way out, I just wait for that force to come get me. I pray for it; my own form of praying. *Help me,* I whisper deep in my mind, *help me.*

Sometimes I have to wait a long time for help to come. It never used to come when I was around other people. I was more likely to find it walking at dusk or sitting out on the East River pier. When it comes, it's like an overwhelming, beautiful sadness that descends, filling me until it overflows.

Now that I'm in here, where is help going to come from? I can't go outside and breathe the air or walk in the rain. I can't be alone on my East River pier or wander in Central Park. All I can do is sleep or read. When I read, I go somewhere else. Books are another way of reaching the other world, the inner world.

Almost everybody here reads, not just magazines and newspapers, but books. They read some of the same authors I like, plus others I've never heard of. Certain books take on cult status, like Kenneth Patchen's poetic pacifist novel, *The Journal of Albion Moonlight,* and Tom Wolfe's tale of Kesey's Merry Pranksters, *The Electric Kool-Aid Acid Test.* I join the long line of people waiting to borrow one of Ionesco's surreal picture books for children. The more surreal the better, in this place. It reassures us to know there's a literary tradition for what ails us.

We read with a vengeance, absorbed in worlds and lives more compelling or cool, amusing or tragic than our own. Richard Fariña's novel, *Been Down So Long It Looks Like Up to Me,* has obvious appeal. Ted sometimes reads aloud a particularly hilarious or bizarre paragraph, so that Fitzgore and Heffalump become familiar characters even before I read Fariña's book. We appreciate the abstract, the bizarre, the arcane. We're

on familiar terms with Timothy Leary and Buckminster ("Bucky")
Fuller. We speculate whether orgone boxes enhance orgasm and if razor
blades really stay sharp if kept in geodesic domes. We mourn Wilhelm
Reich's tragic death in prison and shiver at the karmic justice of Ezra
Pound's descent into madness and death. Freud (affectionately called
"Sigmund" or "Siggy," like a brilliantly offbeat but well-intentioned
uncle) is often the butt of our jokes and anecdotes. We read his books
and discuss his ideas. But whenever we get too interested in death or
bodily functions, we're accused of "morbid curiosity."

Liz keeps a library of books and records in the bottom drawer of her
dresser. She gets up early, makes her bed, and reads before breakfast. She
reads in Center all morning, and in the dorm after lunch. I like it when
everyone else is asleep and only Liz and I are awake, reading, surrounded
by breathing.

I ask Liz what she's reading. She looks up and delivers a short synopsis
of Kazantzakis's *The Last Temptation of Christ.* "I'd lend it to you when I'm
finished, but I've already promised it to Ted. If you like you can have it
after him." Then she goes back to her book.

Too much talking makes you tired. And here I'm always tired.

In seventh grade I was beset with a fatigue that wouldn't go away.
Everything seemed to be conspiring to put me to sleep. I was in a new
school with new kids, new routines, and bewildering new classes. I managed to keep up in English and math, but American history put me to
sleep. Mostly I was fascinated by the thick layer of dandruff on the
shoulders of the teacher's dark jacket. It seemed to sprout from his ears,
along with tufts of hair. But I couldn't concentrate on anything he said,
especially the long lists of dates we had to memorize. Only my French
teacher terrified me enough to keep me awake, her sharp "Ma'mselle
Lewis!" bringing me back from my daydreams to a chorus of giggles.

Danger lurked between classes. White lines bisected the hallways, and
hallway guards were on the lookout for students imprudently going in the
wrong direction. Shrimpy little boys liked to slam the girls' books against
our chests, bruising our tender new breasts.

Gym was my worst nightmare. The locker room smelled like old socks
and rancid cheese. I undressed crouching down so no one would see my
flat chest. The navy blue gym uniforms, our names embroidered on the
breast pocket, were the ugliest things I'd ever seen. The more developed

girls looked cute in them, but for those of us in the ugly duckling stage, forget it. We lined up shivering in the cold gym, trying to hide our knees. The exercises were excruciating; I could do none of them. The gym teacher, a sadistic middle-aged man, singled out kids who were late or who'd lost their gym uniforms, and humiliated them.

One day it finally happened—I forgot the combination for my locker. I tried dozens of variations with no success. I sat on the bench in the empty locker room and sobbed. Then I went into the gym and told the assistant teacher I was sick. By this time, I truly was sick. In the infirmary the nurse took my temperature, found I had a slight fever, and sent me home.

I went to bed and stayed there. I slept and slept, but the fever didn't go away. After a few days my mother called the doctor who woke me long enough to feel my glands, listen to my heart, and take some blood. It turned out I had mononucleosis, the "kissing disease." How I got it I don't know. I certainly hadn't kissed anybody. But it saved me from having to return to school and being humiliated by the gym teacher.

At first all I could do was sleep. It felt peculiar to fall asleep in daylight and wake up in the dark. All the while I knew that normal life was going on as usual for my friends and classmates at school. In one way it was special to have the luxury of slipping into another reality. But when I felt forgotten, it made me want to cry, then drift off to sleep, to forget.

When I wasn't sleeping, I read. I read Willa Cather's *My Antonia* and then I read James Michener's *Hawaii*. Right from the start the book came alive. I smelled the rotten bananas on the long ocean voyage, felt the sway of the boat. My dreams were filled with the things I read, until I couldn't tell where my life left off and the book began. I lived and dreamed that book for four weeks, and when I'd finished its 400-odd pages, I began it all over again. When I was finally well enough to get out of bed and return to school, it was as if I'd taken a long journey. I was still a timid twelve-year-old girl, but inside I was someone else—a passionate, grown-up woman.

In high school I started having trouble sleeping. One night I stayed up to watch a movie, *The Incredible Shrinking Man.* The film's hero gets exposed to radioactive particles and shrinks a little each day, until he's so tiny that even the household cat is his deadly enemy. And he keeps on shrinking. There's nothing anyone can do. He gets so small that his wife and kids can't hear him screaming for help even though they're in the same room. And still he keeps shrinking, getting smaller and smaller . . .

As I watched, the night grew huge and echoey around me, each sound, each thought, every beat of my heart magnified. My mother and stepfather were deep asleep in the next room. The whole world was asleep. I was the only person awake, except for the drunks staggering out of the Irish bar across the street. The night was like a living creature, threatening to devour me.

I put the pillow over my head and tossed and turned, praying for sleep to blot out the image of the man getting smaller and smaller, until he's an infinitesimal dot, smaller than an atom. It was no consolation that he said in the movie's final scene: "I feel myself becoming one with God's great universe. . . ." What would it be like to shrink so small that nobody can hear or see you?

Now I know. It's the way I feel being in the hospital, and it doesn't feel like God's great universe. It just feels like rooms within rooms, walls within walls, thoughts within thoughts, fears within fears. Like the Sibyl, I'm alone with my fear and fascination, deep in a pit of my own making, trying to make out the voices in my head.

Being in the hospital is like being sick, or asleep. I'm sick with my own poison, my despair, hate, anger. My thoughts are like Oskar's high-pitched screaming. No one else can hear them, just like I can't hear anyone else's. But the screaming is there. It's like that Siqueiros painting at the Museum of Modern Art, *Echo of a Scream*. A baby with a huge head sits in the middle of a desolate landscape, a field of rubble painted in grays, black, and red. The baby's mouth is open, and from it floats another, smaller, head; and from it, another. You can't actually hear anything, but the painting is filled with invisible sound. That's what the ward is like. We walk around like zombies, but inside our heads we're screaming.

You have to be careful about going too far inside. You may not be able to get back out. Like the Thorazine zombies. They're stuck inside. They've lost the way back.

I wanted to get away from the petty, materialistic world, and I have. In our looking-glass world, we've turned *off*, tuned *out*, dropped as far *in* as you can go. We're tuned into our own inner channels. Only the radio dial doesn't always stay where it's tuned. It wanders, picking up obscure stations and static.

Outside, life is empty, all appearances. Here, we're inside out. Things are reversed. Though I'm locked up, in a way I'm free. The worst has already happened. There's nowhere to go, no farther to fall. Five floors below street level, I've reached rock bottom. Here, we're all creatures of the depths, free-floating prisoners in a cage of ironclad rules, locks, and keys.

Nine years old, my first summer at camp. A diving lesson. We line up on the dock in our bathing suits, about to go for the first time into the ominous-looking deep water. I stay at the end of the line and watch as one by one my bunkmates bow their heads, place their hands together, curl their toes over the edge, and go *kerplunk* into the dark lake water. When my turn comes, I don't want to go. I'm afraid—the water looks uninviting and cold, and though I love to swim, I'm accustomed to getting in gradually, one toe at a time. The counselor maneuvers my head and arms into the right position, but I'm not ready. "Just a second," I tell him, "wait . . ."

"One, two, three . . ." A hand on my back pushes me. I don't have time to remember to push off the dock, and graze my arm and side against it as I fall. Then a slap of cold and I'm tumbling upside down amid bubbles, water forced painfully up my nose. I churn my arms, not sure which way is up. The water is very cold, in deep shadow, pierced here and there by light green shafts. I hear voices and splashing but they're muffled and echoey. My head bumps against something. Where am I? I reach my hand up and touch a ceiling just above my head, tiny bright slivers of light shining through, and realize I've come up under the dock. It's like I'm in another world—all alone in the cool and quiet. I shiver. This is what the world would be like if I weren't here. It wouldn't really matter at all; life would just go on. I duck my head under the dock and resurface in the world of sunshine and noise, the counselor's whistle blaring in my ears.

This is what it's like being in the hospital. We're lost swimmers who wound up in the shadow world under the dock. We've chosen to stay, at least for now, in this alternate reality, where the world is an echo. We focus on the amplified meter of our own breathing, the racing of our hearts. We disappear into books and dreams, fiction and fantasy. We hold our breath and go deeper down, where things look fascinatingly distorted. And nobody seems to notice we're gone.

DEEP DIRT

Patient is considerably more disturbed than I originally felt her to be. She is anxious, autistic and intensely manipulative, when she is not too anxious to be distracted. She is an adept and slippery bargainer. In treatment, patient is alternately childlike and hostile, challenging and testing me: "Isn't this all stupid?" "How can psychiatry help? Anyway, it's none of your business." She does not trust me and cannot acknowledge friendliness towards me.

—Dr. A.

I SIT IN SESSION WITH DR. A. Silence hangs between us—like one of those heavy lead blankets dentists put over you when you're getting x-rays. Only it feels like the x-rays are coming from me, waves of negative energy. I try to suck it in, but it's useless. I hold my breath for a few seconds, but after things go sparkly I give up and breathe.

Dr. A. looks scrubbed and ruddy, like he's just come in from outdoors. I can smell it on him: trees and wind, shaving cream and coffee, air that moves, not like the stale air in here. He meets my eyes and smiles. I blush and look at my hands.

"How are you feeling?"

"Like I don't exist."

"Can you say more about that?"

What can I tell him? That I'm a complete and total void? If he doesn't know what I mean, what's the point? There's nothing to say. I'd rather talk to him about something else, anything but myself. I come up with fitting Freudian tidbits to feed him, repeat favorite lines from literature. "Full of sound and fury, signifying nothing," I quote, not quite sure of the source. I try to think of something else, a book or poem to refer to, but all points of reference seem to have slipped from my mind like furniture along a slanted floor.

I see my shrink three times a week for thirty minutes, but I'm never sure what to say to him. Usually I talk about my mother—how much I loved her when I was little, and how I came to hate her. How much I hate her, or worry about her, or miss her, or don't. I'm tired of talking about my mother and tired of talking about what's wrong with me. How I hate myself, feel sorry for myself. What self? I have no self.

"What are you feeling right now? Can you express it in words?"

Dr. A. wants me to use words to express my feelings. But what are words? Just sounds. If you repeat a word long enough, it becomes meaningless. It's amazing anybody can communicate anything at all. *Patient, doctor, illness, therapy.* Meaningless words. *Sadness, anger, fear, despair.* When all the meaning dissolves from words, they are bleached, brittle, empty shells. Deep inside, where there are no words, there is something else. Beneath the feelings, coiled snakes writhing in my guts, there's something vast and deep and endless. How can I express this in words, and why would I want to? It's mine. He thinks I'm sick and wants to cure me, but he doesn't know the beauty inside me, the beauty of my thoughts.

They're always asking how I feel, trying to get me to talk. You get extra attention for telling staff when you're "upset." If you're feeling afraid, or depressed, or hallucinating, you're supposed to tell a staff member. When I do, I feel a sort of relief, but mostly I feel stupid. Why tell *them?* They're my enemy. If I trust *them,* or confide in *them,* what does that make me? Smaller and stupider than the smallest, stupidest speck. But there's another side. If I'm bad, or sick, why let the badness out by smearing it all over them? It just makes me hate myself more.

"What's going on?" Dr. A. looks up from his notepad and waits. I tell him about the things I've been seeing. The walls and things fragmenting and dissolving, flaking apart like snow. People's faces distort, then disappear. Everything is slithery and changeable. He asks me what I think is causing it. What can I tell him? It's the way things *are.* Everything *does* dissolve. People *are* distorted. I hate his obtuseness. The way he sits there waiting for me to say something.

"Acid flashback," I tell him, just to get him off my back.

Dr. A. looks annoyed. I guess I'm a failure as a patient. What a stupid word. Patient. Like I'm supposed to be patiently waiting for something in me to change. I should be called an Impatient. Because I am. And so is Dr. A. He taps his pen on his clipboard.

Today he's stern and judicious; other times he's chummy, just-a-regular-guy. I feel like a dog: bow-wow, up on my hind legs, wag my little tail, roll over, beg for a doggy-treat smile, maybe I can even make him laugh. I can try to get his sympathy and concern . . . or just play dead.

The minutes tick by. I feel myself sinking, going cottony.

Dr. A. sighs, puts down his pen. "We can sit here silently for the rest of our session or we can end early. What do you say?"

I nod and make the corners of my mouth twitch slightly, as much of a smile as I can muster. Dr. A. rises and opens the door. The cloud of bad air I've filled the small office with rushes out into the fluorescent hallway. He locks the door behind us and escorts me back to the ward.

I'm not sure who I'm supposed to be: crazy or sane? It varies from day to day. Sometimes I live up to my label as crazy (after all, that's why I'm here). Their reactions are unpredictable, varying from concern to annoyance. If I give them something really big, like hallucinations, they treat me special. When I sit wrapped in depression, unable to move, I know who I am, and where I belong: *Here, sick, crazy.* I hear them discussing me in low voices, "She's had a setback. She's been hallucinating again." Other times it clearly pleases them for me to be sane. But when I have energy and feel good enough to rebel, they get mad and punish me.

I try to tell them that being in the hospital is making me worse. They tell me I'm paranoid, or depressed. Of course I'm depressed—*I'm here.*

Depressed, confused, anxious, frightened, phobic, self-destructive, dissociated, hostile, inappropriate. Everything I do or say, every feeling I describe, is labeled as a symptom. Can't I just simply *be?* It would be really amazing to hear someone tell me I'm fine. That's one option I'm not allowed—it was disqualified the second I was admitted.

You'd think they'd just leave you alone and let you rest, but that's not an option—instead they accuse you of being *withdrawn.* You're supposed to *interact* and *participate,* but only on their terms. Getting too close or being too active is considered *acting out*—another one of their dumb expressions. Our daily life is a ridiculous pretense at "normalcy." We go to activities as if we were going off to do important work, instead of stringing beads. *This is not summer camp,* I want to tell them, *this is serious!* Don't they realize what's at stake?

We're expected to transfer our feelings for our parents onto our shrinks, strangers we know nothing about—another miserable charade. Yet it's our job to help them save us—like the scene in *Peter Pan* when all the children say they believe in fairies and save Tinkerbell's life. If we believe they can help us, maybe it will come true.

It's such a lot of work being a mental patient. There's so much subtlety involved, so many invisible waves to navigate. In some sense I'm always busy. Because there are so many of us in here, and so little to do, there's a lot to deal with in the invisible world. Thoughts and feelings, our internal weather conditions, rule.

We invent our own therapy. Marjee and I sing a country-western yodel that we made up especially with our shrinks in mind: *"Oh, my heart is filled with odium for you-ooo, for you-ooo . . ."* Of course, it's an O-word song. Somehow Marjee's gotten hung up in that part of the dictionary. Maybe it's the roundness, the openness, the orbicular oratorio and often obscene obscurity of the O-words: Ovulation. Orthocephalic. Orvis root. O is balanced, classic, eternal. A perfect circle waiting to be filled . . . as are we all. We sublimate our anxiety by filling ourselves with food.

Marjee decides to lose some weight. She stops eating, and her flesh evaporates, leaving model's hollows beneath her cheekbones, which she accentuates by sucking in her cheeks. I'm envious. Aside from cigarettes, food is my biggest comfort . . . and it shows. I hate seeing my face in the mirror with round chipmunk cheeks, like I had in sixth grade. I ask how she did it.

"Oh, it's easy. I just think of food as something disgusting: Spaghetti is blood and guts, gravy is mucus, meat is a rotting corpse." She smiles, ravishing. "You should try it; it really works."

We therapize each other, exchanging diagnoses, poking around to unearth each others' traumas, whispering revelations when we think we've hit pay dirt. We compete to be the weirdest, the most far out, the most fucked up. It's a kind of sibling rivalry: We have our favorite doctors, nurses and attendants, and even though they're not supposed to, they too have their favorites. When my shrink smiles too warmly at another patient, my smoldering dislike can burn up hours or even days of empty time, and each intimate conversation Jane has with R.J. adds a little fuel to my rivalrous feelings. But we also confide and listen, feel each other's pain, protest unfair treatment, cover up for one another, help each other escape. The staff doesn't think this is healthy, but it's our best medicine. Our parents dumped us here, and it's easy to bullshit the shrinks. Who do we have but each other? Nobody else understands us, except philosophers and poets. Like disciples, we copy poems into our notebooks, then memorize them. Marjee recites Sylvia Plath's "Daddy" with venomous precision, her eyes shining with tears. Jane helps Marjee write a poem, in homage to Poe:

"Margaret Alice lives in a palace high above the sea . . ." that contains a stanza each about her three best friends: Harold, Jane, and me.

Television can be a form of wish-fulfillment. In *The Prisoner*, Patrick McGoohan, a retired secret agent, wakes one morning to find himself imprisoned on an island along with other people who "know too much." Confined to the Village (hospital), the prisoners wear striped uniforms (pajamas). Their every action is monitored (nurses' notes) and their dreams recorded (therapy). If they try to escape, they are chased by large white bubbles (nurses) and brought back to be brainwashed (medicated) into believing their lives in the Village are normal and real. Names are replaced with numbers. The Village is run by a series of expendable Number Two's (Gidro-Frank and his assistants), but the identity of the elusive Number One remains a mystery that the hero, Number Six (a kind of Nietzschean *überpatient*, unafraid to defy the status quo), is determined to discover.

In Episode 5: "The Schizoid Man," Number Six, unconscious, is hooked up to a machine that records his dreams so they can be observed. In his dream, he enters a room that contains the secrets of his past. Just when Number Two is gleefully certain he's about to conquer his victim's subconscious, Number Six turns toward the camera in his dream and shouts, "Who is Number One?" It's a battle of wills very much appreciated by a roomful of zoned-out Thorazine zombies. But at the series' conclusion, when Number One is revealed to be none other than Number Six, the implication that "they" are merely a reflection of our own subconscious (and vice versa) inspires a low-grade group depression that doesn't lift for days.

Once a month everybody has to go to group therapy. Adults and adolescents have separate groups. There's usually a shrink or psychologist, the head nurse and maybe a student nurse, and sometimes an attendant for good measure. We go into the South living room and shut the door. First there's some comic scrambling for seats, then changing places, like musical chairs, usually by the boys, who curse at each other. Then, after the nurse finishes yelling at them, we sit around, the usual leg-swinging accompanied by nail-biting, gum-chewing, snide jokes, and bursts of laughter. Then the doctor starts the session.

"How are you feeling, Nick?" Someone has to go first.

Nick sprawls, one leg over the arm of his chair. "Oh, just terrific," he drawls, carefully biting off the edge of a fingernail.

Giggles. Silence.

"Does anyone have anything they'd like to talk about?"

We go in turn around the room: head-shaking, shoulder-shrugging, several "nope's" and "nnmm . . . hmmm's," and "uh, uh, not a thing."

"I don't, but Bobby has," volunteers Eric. "Why don't you ask him about the size of his . . ."

Bobby jumps to his feet. "Eat shit! Fuck your mother!" he yells, simultaneously giving Eric the finger and sticking his tongue out. Bobby is the runt of the group. All the guys pick on him as a form of play, but he seems to love it. Half the time he picks the fights himself. When Bobby isn't being bullied he makes fun of patients who are too zoned-out to defend themselves.

"Oh yeah? As if you could get it up to fuck anything!" Eric croaks back. His voice has a way of sticking in his throat, as if it can't find its way out of that long, skinny neck. He reaches out a long arm and thwacks the top of Bobby's head, and all the boys crack up.

"Cut it out! No physical contact!" Woodridge stands up and shouts, spraying saliva. The boys howl with laughter.

I don't like their yelling and fighting and start jiggling my leg. Gloria sits, eyes closed, hands folded in her lap. Laurie shakes her head, mouths the word "babies," takes out her compact, licks her finger, smoothes it over her eyebrow, and applies new lipstick.

The shrink in charge focuses on me. "Mindy, you look lost in thought. Is there anything you'd like to bring up?"

"Yes, her lunch!" Bobby volunteers. The doctor ignores him.

I tell him I don't understand how they decide who's sick and who's improving. That's what I've been thinking about, but he just says that's too general a topic and asks me if I have something more specific to discuss.

After that we find some stupid thing or other to talk about, but it never amounts to much. It's just the motions you have to go through.

After group, we blow off some steam. Harold struts like a rooster, singing into his fist, *"I can't get no . . . sat-is-fac-shun,"* sticking out his lips in a Mick Jagger pout. Izzy walks by; Harold feigns a punch; he and Izzy spar for a few seconds before Harold starts singing again. Izzy loves it.

Someone puts on The Doors. When it comes to the part where Jim Morrison, bard of darkness, kills his father and rapes his mother in his oedipal epic song "The End," the boys go playfully nuts, shouting along with the crescendo, much to the nurses' chagrin.

Izzy paces by in a state of agitation, calling out, "I fucked my mother, I fucked my mother."

"Hear that, Lenny?" Bobby calls out. We all know that Lenny is in here because his unconscious got the better of him—literally. The rumor is that he awakened from a drug-induced blackout to find himself lying on top of his mother . . . whom he evidently had tried to rape.

Lenny smiles sheepishly. Unshaven and unkempt, he looks as harmless as a little boy awakened from a nap. Medicated up the wazoo, probably.

There is a burst of bitter laughter from Melvin, the former doctor who lost his license for self-prescribing narcotics. Off in the corner, Luke, resident hippie cum pirate, with his black eyepatch, strums his guitar, singing one of his original songs—a beautiful melody with ringing minor chords. "We are very young, we are very old, and our minds glow red and gold."

Sometimes I feel sorry for Woodridge. I don't think it's fair to hate her just because she's fat. We just focus on her ample rear because it's an easy target, so to speak. The real problem is that she gets angry too easily. And the more we tease her, the meaner she gets.

Eric, Bobby, and Harold have gotten into the habit of mooing when they see Woodridge—long, drawn-out lowing that sounds just like real cows. Whenever they see her, they start. This leads to a new nickname, "Moo," which they call her in respectful tones whenever she addresses them. She pretty well ignores this, but they're determined to rattle her.

Eric, Bobby, and Harold are sitting on the North side bench waiting for Woodridge to start serving meds. As soon as they see her . . . "mmmMMMooo-ooo-OOO!" Woodridge goes through various stages of red, then loses it. "Stop that!" she snaps, but as soon as her back is turned, the barnyard sounds begin again. She whirls around. "If you do that one more time, you'll be restricted to different areas."

"Okay, we'll stop," Eric assures her. Then he turns to Harold and says, "Damn it! You're sitting too close to me! Would you please mmmMMMOOOOOVE over!" Busted! They put up with whatever punishment they're given, just wait it out, in order to get it over with fast so they can be reunited with their buddies and come up with new, more clever, more annoying diversions.

The unholy three form an alliance they call the Arg Brothers. "Arg, brothers!" they greet each other, clasping each other's forearms in the official Arg salute. The name comes from the *Jason and the Argonauts* TV show. It's a manly man type of thing. Very macho. Very idiotic.

The Args have code names and code words for everything. They develop an incomprehensible kind of pig latin that they rattle off at a great speed. I tune them out. They're behaving like eight-year-olds, and it makes me uneasy. I didn't come here to be around a bunch of immature jerks.

The adolescent boys go from one form of mischief to another, mimicking and cruelly mocking the more unfortunate patients. Harold chases John, who's deathly afraid of being touched, across the ward by simply walking toward him with his index finger extended, so that John is trapped, cowering, against the wall—until one of the male attendants finally comes and releases the poor guy from Harold's spell.

The Args embark upon some mysterious mission called O.A.—short for Operation Arg—a top secret until they're busted for stealing the cash allowances of certain highly medicated victims while they sleep the unperturbable sleep of the drugged. Very unacceptable, inappropriate behavior. But there are even dirtier doings going on. Rumor has it that Dwight, at twelve the youngest kid on the ward and an honorary Arg, urinates on these same patients while they sleep.

The staff does their best to subdue them. Bobby is on 2,400 milligrams of Thorazine a day, enough to sedate a small horse. It slows him down, and sometimes he nods off in his chair, but it's not enough to make him concentrate any better in school. His mind's always wandering, and he hates having to sit still. He has to find other ways to keep his mind alive. Sometimes I see him on the ward, scribbling in a dog-eared spiral notebook. I don't give it much thought, until the day I find out what's in it.

Bobby has been trying to convince me that Nick is bad for me. He tells me he really cares about me, and that I deserve someone who'll treat me better than Nick does.

"Like who?" I ask. He looks into my eyes, blushes, and answers, "Like me."

I don't trust Bobby, and I don't know what he's up to. How could he compare himself to Nick? Next to Nick, Bobby is a troll. He's even said so himself. Of course, I feel like I'm a troll too, especially these days, plump and inert in pajamas.

"I'm not as good-looking as Nick," Bobby continues, "but I'm more sensitive. Do you know that I write poetry? I'll show you sometime, if you want to see."

I wonder if he's goofing on me. Maybe he's bet one of his friends he can get me to make it with him. He reaches for my hand and gently strokes it before I take mine away. His skin is so dry it feels like lizard skin, probably from the Thorazine.

"Sure, okay," I say. Then, to my relief, the dinner bell rings.

The next day I see Bobby pacing around Center clutching his notebook to his chest. His eyes look up toward the ceiling, and he's mouthing words. Is he trying to look cool, or is he flipping out, I wonder.

Later he approaches me. "I just wrote something new. I'm really excited about it. Do you want to hear it?"

"Okay." I have nothing better to do.

"Not here." He leads me into the North living room. It's empty. I peer around the door, looking for an ambush. I still don't trust him.

"It's based on *The Odyssey*." We've been doing Homer in Mrs. Gould's class. "It's called 'Ancient Worlds.' " Bobby clears his throat and begins to read.

> From the Tigris and Euphrates
> To the solemn hall of Hades
> Where Achilles' soul lies eternally
> From Athens to the Roman
> And the skillful Grecian bowmen
> Who fought and died so patriotically
>
> The writings of the ancient
> Tell the story of the patient
> Whose wounds were healed with herbs and magic
>   creams
> And the beauty of dear Helen
> Who was kidnapped by some villain
> Who loved her and saw her in his dreams
>
> How I worship every ruler
> Every lover every dueler
> Who lived on land or sailed the mighty sea
> But here I am just writing
> About the loving and the fighting
> And any ancient man I'd love to be.

I'm stunned. I never expected his poem to be so beautiful. I'd expected some moon-in-June sort of thing—not something as eloquent and accomplished as this. Who could possibly know that underneath Bobby's obnoxious behavior and Arg Brothers silliness, a serious, sensitive poet was hiding. Mrs. Gould recognizes it—she reads Bobby's poem to the class, beaming with pride; afterward, catching him off guard, she gives him a big hug. But *they* don't know—otherwise, why would they take Bobby out of high school and send him to work in a frame shop, to learn a "practical" trade.

What do we really know about each other? Only what we let each other see on the surface. There are telltale signals: Eric rocks himself to sleep at night. Harold sucks his thumb, and not just at night. He walks around the ward, thumb in mouth, forefinger curled around his nose, like a baby with a blankee. Harold, with his blue eyes and muscles, is cute enough to pull it off. When he pulls his thumb from his mouth, it's pink and wrinkled—"like a baby's weenie," Bobby teases.

But these are just clues. For the most part we remain ciphers to ourselves, each other, our parents, and our shrinks, who keep digging in the deep dirt of our psyches, hoping to find something concrete, some rich vein of neurosis. Instead, we keep them supplied with fool's gold.

The scene in front of me grows gauzy and dissolves; objects shimmer, threatening to vanish. I have a headache that won't go away. When I complain of these things, Dr. A. schedules a brain scan and an eye exam. I get scared that maybe something is wrong with my brain waves, but they come back normal, and the eye doctor tells me I'm nearsighted, which I already knew.

Can't they see? While they're digging around in our psyches and excavating our family histories, the important stuff is right in front of their noses. What I really need is proof that there's some sense in the world, some hope that life is worth living. Reassurance that I'm going to be okay. But they want bigger stuff. I'm supposed to have some deep, dark secrets . . . and I feel guilty that I don't. I'm so much less interesting than I pretend to be.

———————————

On a ward with sixty patients, the war against dirt is a continuing battle. We live like moles in a hole, befouling our burrow. Each day the floors are swabbed with disinfectant, but nothing can stop the accumulation of ashes, a fine, filmy layer everywhere, like fallout. There are the invisibles: shed skin and hair, dandruff, nose pickings (you have to be careful—nose picking is a popular sport, and patients without Kleenex are likely to wipe their hands on the furniture, leaving trails of green slime); and the visibles: used Kleenex, discarded cigarette packs and candy wrappers, and the ubiquitous chewing gum.

Gum—the very substance of stuckness—is stuck everywhere: on undersides of tables and chairs, on floors and walls, transferring itself to you when you least expect it. It's doubly unpleasant knowing the dead Doublemint you sat in was macerated in some Thorazine-parched mouth. Yes, we're one big family, but I draw the line at used gum. It brings home the fact that we can never get away from each other and each other's emanations . . . and secretions. Then there's the constant chewing, chewing, chewing, like crazed cows. Francine pops her gum loudly and aggressively, each angry *crack!* like gunfire. It really gets under your skin, and she won't stop even if you ask her nicely. Gum has a territorial aspect. Marjee sticks hers on her bedpost overnight (she sings me the song when I ask her about it) and pops it back in her mouth first thing in the morning.

Our bedframes have hollow posts. If you pry off the tight-fitting plastic caps, they make perfect ashtrays. Because the posts go all the way down to the floor, it would take the ashes of a thousand cigarettes, and several years, to fill one. When the stench of a filter smoldering deep within a bedpost gives us up, we catch hell. Smoking in the dorms is strictly prohibited. When night staff makes their rounds, you have to jettison your cigarette in a hurry. The linoleum around our beds is scarred with brown, caterpillar-shaped imprints of burning butts.

We're always looking for new places to hide things (razor blades, money, drugs), slipping them between mattress and bedsprings, taping them to the bottoms of our dresser drawers, sliding them into the hollows of chairs. Our fingers are always working, checking out the rips in the vinyl upholstery and the spaces between things. Coins that slipped from a pocket nestle between couch cushions or deep in the recesses of chairs amid lint and bits of tobacco. Matches are a good find, and sometimes, if you're very lucky, a bit of a joint someone stashed there when their partaking of cannabis was rudely interrupted.

Dog-eared *New Yorker* magazines are scattered around the ward. They lie around for months until they blend in with the furniture, their covers a kind of horizontal decoration. Their pages are soft and worn, wrinkled and stained. You wonder which unwholesome hands they've passed through and wish they could be fumigated. Sometimes they sit in laps for hours, unread. The *New Yorker*s have a funny way of renewing themselves; they've been around so long that after a while people forget having looked at them and reread them, experiencing a sense of déjà vu. "Déjà vu" is big on the ward. Since our routine varies so little from day to day, every day is a form of "Déjà vu, all over again," as Ted is fond of saying.

One day Gidro-Frank, passing through Center, stops, looks around, shakes his head, and frowns. A few minutes later he returns with Woodridge.

"Dr. Gidro-Frank has an announcement to make," she says.

"Thank you, Miss Woodridge." A smile cracks his serious demeanor, then vanishes. "This place is filthy," he says. "The ashtrays are full, and nobody bothers to empty them. Many of you don't even use them. There are ashes and cigarette butts on the floor, and burns on the furniture."

Patients shift in their seats, hands instinctively moving to cover the scarred vinyl.

Gidro-Frank pauses, like he's savoring a good cigar. Then he continues, crisply.

"This is entirely unacceptable. Until you learn to have some respect for your surroundings, no smoking will be allowed in Center."

Jaws drop, ashes fall. Impossible, and unfair. If we can't smoke in Center, how will we pass the time? How will we stay calm? What will happen?

Gidro-Frank is unyielding. "You can smoke in the living rooms."

He knows as well as we do that patients on observation can't go into a living room by themselves. That either means no smoking (unthinkable) or we'll have to go smoke in groups. And that means the end of what little semblance of privacy the living rooms provide. At least temporarily, because suddenly everyone becomes incredibly neat.

Staff has called a special meeting. The ward buzzes with rumors as the doctors, Woodridge, even Gidro-Frank himself, file solemnly into South living room. Sly and R.J. accompany Nick, Bobby, and Jack, all stony-faced. The door closes behind them. An hour later, they emerge, flushed and silent. Bobby keeps his eyes on the floor; on his pale cheeks two pink dots blaze. It seems that Bobby had dressed up in girls' underwear in Nick's room, where he performed inappropriate oral acts on Nick, and possibly with Jack. Such manly men! All three have privileges revoked and are put on observation. Then Bobby is sent as a "guest" to the seventh-floor ward. When he returns several weeks later, he tells me what really happened.

For a while, Nick had been offering to help Bobby explore his feminine side. He was gently, persistently, persuasive. "Would you rather repress it, or act on it?" he'd ask Bobby.

One day Bobby borrowed a dress and makeup from Alyssa and appeared in Center in full drag. Later, Nick approached Bobby and said he felt attracted to him. Bobby had to admit he felt attracted to Nick, too. They planned an after-hours tryst in Nick's room. After some kissing and caressing, Bobby tried going down on Nick, but quickly realized this wasn't for him, and opted out. Shortly after, he lost his virginity with Lena, a new adolescent patient, behind the large chalkboard in Center. But this didn't stop Jack, the predator, from moving in for the kill, hounding Bobby day and night, trying to convince him to blow him. That was when Bobby decided to tell the whole story to his shrink. All of it. Including one detail: the panties he was wearing in Nick's room were mine. Nick had asked me to give him a pair so he could think of me when he was alone in his room. I never suspected how he'd use them.

Bobby laughs off the entire incident. "I was experimenting." He shrugs. "What can I say? I didn't like it! I'd rather smoke a cigar! And I looked pretty stupid in those panties."

Harold can't forgive Bobby for what happened in Nick's room. For a while, he can't even bring himself to speak to his former close buddy. Knowing that Nick used his charismatic power to get Bobby to "role play" and that Jack had egged him on makes no difference—he can't get past the homoerotic implications. He can't even say the word without a distorted emphasis: "homo-SEX-sual." "Homo" is usually more than enough for him. Heaven help the person with effeminate mannerisms; his days on the ward will be a torment of taunts and insults.

Here's what I find out much later: In his entire time in the hospital, Harold never breathes a word that during puberty he had fooled around with another boy, causing him to obsess over the unspeakable question: *Am I homosexual?*

In the aftermath of the Manly Men incident, Harold and Bobby are questioned about homosexual activity, which they both vehemently deny.

But Harold finds a way to get back at Bobby. In a gesture of friendship, Harold offers to trim Bobby's hair. Bobby wears his hair in a bowl-shaped Beatles/Prince Valiant style. One of his trademarks is shaking his head double-time to music, so his hair shimmies straight out from his head in a centrifugal hair halo. When Bobby emerges from hiding, all that's left is a short ragged fringe, almost bald in places. He looks like what my mother would call a "flicked chicken."

"What happened to your hair?" someone asks. Bobby looks up from lighting a cigarette, his eyes shining with tears. "Do you like it?" He manages a smile. "Oh well, it'll grow back. Maybe the rest of me will grow too."

Marjee's been scratching her crotch all the time. She can't figure out what's making her itch, until one day, inspecting her pubic hair, she sees something moving, and screams. A nurse comes running. It turns out she has crabs. She's not alone. Nick has them too, and Harold. This is one club I don't mind being left out of. They have to shampoo twice a day with Qwell, a special shampoo designed to kill head lice and crabs. The minuscule crabs look like teensy white spiders, but Marjee says they bite like hell, burrowing in under the cover of pubic hair to lay their eggs in their nice, warm adopted environment. Their eggs, or nits, get into clothes and sheets, so everything has to be washed repeatedly in the industrial-strength hospital laundry. It takes several rounds of Qwell to get rid of them.

Craziness is contagious too. We're all connected, a big rolling wave of emotion. When one of us is upset, it spreads faster than crabs. The same thing goes for rebellion.

Harold has been getting into so many fights on the ward that he's spending more time in the Quiet Room than out. Marjee is worried about him. When he won't talk to her about it, she starts crying a lot, especially when Harold starts eloping. He runs away again and again, running out the staircase door when someone unlocks it, or sneaking onto the elevator. He gets as far as the front door and almost makes it outside, wearing his pajamas. He's fast, and he's strong. Once he punches out the guard at the main entrance and has to be subdued by three men.

Harold finally tells Marjee what happened. His parents are getting divorced. His mother doesn't want custody, so Harold, if he's ever released, will have to live with his father in his new apartment. His younger brother will live with his mother. Harold is devastated. His childhood is over. He'll never go home now.

We continue to "act out." We are determined *not* to behave, *not* to comply, *not* to shut up. Plenty of patients on our ward were told by uncles, fathers, cousins, brothers, mothers to not breathe a word of what really happened. Certain things are never directly spoken of, but all around us are signs: this one's love of her brother, fear of her father, hate for her uncle.

The real stories, the deep dirt, are hidden from view.

Rachel is a few years older than me and has kind brown eyes. After we get to know each other she tells me she was sexually abused by an uncle, her mother's brother, since she was a child. The first few times it hurt horribly and she was so scared she couldn't breathe, but it soon became much more complicated than the physical act. As much as she was repelled by what her uncle was doing to her, she also liked the attention, the closeness, the forbidden excitement. For a long time Rachel told no one. She knew what she'd done was very bad, too bad to talk about. It was years before she finally told a psychiatrist, but she could never tell her mother. She feared it would destroy her.

At first I don't know whether to believe Rachel's story. I've never heard such a thing before. It's almost inconceivable. But I can tell she's telling the truth, because I feel her pain. I know how it feels to love and be betrayed. Next to Rachel's my own troubles seem insignificant.

"But that's not the main reason I'm here," Rachel tells me. "I'm here because my brother is getting married . . . to my best friend." Tears well in her eyes. "The thing is, I love my brother—I mean *really love* him, more than like a brother. He's my whole world." Tears roll down her cheeks. "I introduced them. My best friend, my brother—my two favorite people. I thought they'd like each other, but when they fell in love, I wanted to die."

I think about it. Whey shouldn't she love her brother? But I shiver with the same feeling of wrongness as when she told me about her uncle. Taboos like that run deep in the blood.

Relationships that shouldn't happen. Steps that shouldn't be taken. Lines that shouldn't be crossed. Questions that shouldn't be asked. Once you cross that line, how can you go back? You can never undo it, never really forget, even if you try. Compared to the stories I hear from some patients, the inappropriate behavior we're accused of is nothing but fun and games.

Rocky used to wash her hands twenty times a day. She reminded me of Lady Macbeth, scrubbing and scrubbing. Once, while taking a shower, the room thick with steam, I saw Rocky washing herself under very hot water, her skin bright red. Finally the nurse came in, turned the shower off and handed her a towel. What was Rocky scrubbing away? I never found out, because I didn't ask and she didn't talk about it.

DESPERATE MEASURES

5/12/68 Patient continues on C.O. in pajamas. She now tolerates the full 30 minutes in session reasonably well. The main issue that has evolved over the past weeks has been her angry denunciations of me for being "impersonal." Dr. Gidro-Frank feels the main issue is her fear of involvement with me. I will try to focus more on the transference.

A S MUCH AS WE SAY WE DESPISE THEM, we're in love with our doctors. Before therapy sessions we dab ourselves with perfume. Marjee wears Je Reviens, very sultry and sexy. I like Khus Khus, "The Fragrance of Jamaica"—flowers and spice. I dab it behind my ears and at the base of my neck, put on lip gloss and long, dangly earrings.

Our shrinks are the older men in our lives. We are their passive, powerless subjects; our fates are in their large male hands. It's exciting, scary, sexual; an ongoing, extended flirtation that can lead nowhere. We talk about them in private, fantasizing about what their wives or girlfriends are like and what kind of fathers they'd be. Marjee makes endearing comments about Stanley's bald spot, while I dub my all-powerful shrink "King Arthur." Each time I look at the wedding band on his finger, I wonder what his wife is like and whether they really love each other; I imagine them making love, then imagine myself in his arms.

Each time I see Dr. A., I'm confused and embarrassed, torn between wanting to please him and wanting to seduce him, be good or rebel. So I act out, doing all sorts of things, showing how bad I am, how indifferent to his opinion. I want to crash through his remoteness, shake him up, make him angry, make him love me. More than anything, I want him to see me as a person, instead of a patient.

Dr. A. says there's a chance that he can keep me as his patient, even though he'll be moving to a different ward. When he asks how I feel about this, I blush to my roots and shrug. Mostly, I'm surprised. It takes the wind out of my sails; I'd kept myself going partly by hating him. But I guess it's a good thing not to have to go through the embarrassment of getting to know someone new. I try not to look too pleased.

> 5/18/68   Patient has been put on C.O. in clothing. She is very happy about this. On the ward a heretofore repressed playfulness has emerged. If her behavior continues to improve, she will be given staff walks.

Just when things are finally going better, Dr. A. informs me that next month I will be getting a new psychiatrist. Then he asks how I feel about that. The look I give him is enough to let him know how I feel. I hate him for letting me believe there was a chance he might keep me. They're all a bunch of liars, and he's no different. Now I'll have to start all over again, telling my story to someone new. The same tired descriptions of my mental states. The same boring questions shooting at me, bouncing off the target, or missing altogether.

I walk around the ward fuming.

One afternoon Jack stops me in the hallway. "This place is a fucking drag. Why don't we just split?" I look at him, speechless.

"Why not?" he asks, smirking. "You scared?" Jack's hawk-eyes glimmer at me. His acne-scarred face looks craggy, with its beak nose and jutting brow. There's something almost Mafia about him, tough and scary. Sometimes he changes, chameleon-like, before my eyes, from a streetwise seventeen-year-old kid to a dangerous, evil criminal.

I come up with all sorts of reasons why I can't do it, but Jack wipes out every one, ticking them off on his fingers. He guarantees he can get us out. He has enough money for both of us and a place to stay.

Jack's lips twist into a smirk. "You really want to stick around, now that Nick's with Alyssa and your shrink's dumping you?"

When I think about it, he's right. I don't want to be here anymore. My shrink is leaving. Why shouldn't I leave too?

Jack takes care of everything. He bribes an attendant to let us into the staircase, tells me to be cool, and squeezes my shoulder hard as we stroll out the front entrance. We take the subway downtown to his friend's

apartment, where he lives with his mother and sister in a high-rise building. The mother knows Jack, but my presence would be inexplicable, so
they lock me into a storage room in the basement overnight, in the dark,
where I shiver my way through endless hours in pitch blackness, not
knowing whether they'll ever come and let me out or if I will perish in
that locked room. When they finally unlock the door I am completely
traumatized and have a cold. My one sheet of Kleenex is soaked through,
spread out on my knee.

As I have no money, I am totally dependent on Jack, who seems to be
enjoying his custodial role. He takes me out for breakfast and looks in the
yellow pages for a low-cost hotel. I wait outside while he rents a room,
then he smuggles me upstairs. After we settle in, Jack says he has some
things to take care of and instructs me to lock the door behind him.
While he's gone, I take a hot bath and try to calm down. I don't know why
I'm so afraid of Jack. When I hear the door unlock, I jump out of the tub,
towel off, and get dressed fast.

Jack's been busy. He takes a card out of his wallet and hands me a fake
ID—a Social Security card for Nancy Somebody-or-other. He also has
drugs: pot and hash, some pills, and a bottle of vodka. After we smoke a
joint, I wash down a couple of Seconals with vodka. I want to get as
stoned as possible. Because here I am in a hotel room with Jack, with one
double bed. I know I owe him, big time. Even though I'm nodding out,
Jack puts the moves on me anyway. When I don't respond, he gets more
forceful. He feels huge and painful and I, to say the least, am just barely
going through the motions.

"What's the matter—don't you trust me?" he asks, his eyes glinting in
the dark, and I lie and say yes.

The next day I'm so depressed I can't talk. I feel raw and bruised, so I
take another soak in the tub. In the afternoon, to cheer me up, Jack takes
me out for a walk. I want to run from him, but I'm afraid he'll come after
me. I scan the street for a cop, then realize I'm wanted as a runaway. In the
middle of the crosswalk I gather my courage and tell Jack I want to go off
on my own. He sneers and tells me to go ahead, I'm a drag to be around,
anyway. He hands me the ID and five dollars, says "See ya," and walks
away.

I call a high school friend, the one who's always telling me he wants to
make me his superstar. We hang out in his apartment until his mother
comes home from work. When I tell my friend I'm not going back to the

hospital, he makes some calls. It turns out that his older brother has friends I can stay with, a married couple with a railroad flat in the East Village.

My hosts, a hip couple in their twenties, are very nice to me. Soon after I get there, they light up some joints and pass them around. By this time I am completely out of it with paranoia and weariness. My fake ID says my name is Nancy, and whenever the couple calls me by my new name—"Nancy? . . . Nancy!"—I don't respond. My anxiety has reached a new level of disembodiment. Luckily they don't ask me too many questions. I go to bed early, but I'm having stoned thoughts even in my sleep, along with paranoid dreams that the police are in the apartment looking for me.

In the morning, over coffee and cereal, they tell me I can stay with them as long as I need to, at least until they find someone to rent their spare room—unless I'd like to rent it. Will I get some kind of job and pay rent and live in their spare room? I don't think so. It's only been a day, and already I know I can't keep it up.

> 5/25/68 Doctor's Note: Since her return to the ward, patient has been furious at me. Her standard comment is that if I really understood her, I would realize that she couldn't possibly be upset that I will be leaving in July. I find her more paranoid in her transference attitudes than ever before. She has been started on Haldol 1 mg bid which will be gradually increased.

Jack shows up on the ward a few days after me, brought back by the cops. I can't help gloating that he's in pajamas. When nobody's watching, he grins nastily and pulls his finger slowly across his throat. I tell my shrink I'm afraid of him, and he writes an order restricting us from having contact. For once, I'm grateful to be restricted.

In solidarity with Jack, Nick won't have anything to do with me. He looks daggers into my eyes when he sees me but won't say a word. I start to feel scared of him too.

The new medication makes me jumpy. It's harder than ever to sit still. And that's all there is: sitting, sitting, and more sitting. I feel more like a thing than a person.

Suddenly I'm frightened, like something terrible is about to happen.

In the dorm the blue bedspreads ripple like seas, and the baby doll on

Maryann's bed turns into a skull surrounded by flickering flames. I want to blink and shake my head, but the thought gets stuck before it reaches my muscles, just echoes inside the empty garbage can of my mind. I get up, slowly, and everything goes sparkly like embers, hundreds of little glow-worms squirming in the wall, incandescent white maggots eating up the dead world, peeling away the surface to show the glowing energy under-neath. When I walk down the hall the floor is full of shadows; the floor tilts and warps under my feet. I lean my shoulder against the wall to steady me.

What if they're right, and I *am* crazy?

> 5/31/68 Much of patient's paranoid rage has given way to feelings of hopelessness and depression. It appears she is beginning to realize how much sicker she is than some of the other patients. We are not dealing in session with my leaving in July. I have attempted to make it clear to her that this deci-sion does not mean that I don't like her. Increasingly she expresses the desire to see her mother. I do not feel that such contact should be allowed until after the change of doctors has been made. Doctor's orders: Haldol 2 mg. bid.

I stare into darkness. If only I could sleep. My mind won't stop think-ing, won't let me rest. I remember things I don't want to remember, revisit an innocence I'd rather forget.

The happiest time of my life was when my mother and I shared her bedroom. At night I went to bed knowing she'd soon come in, slip into her nightgown and kiss me good-night. On weekends I woke to the sound of her breathing and played quietly with my stuffed animals or read until she woke. Sometimes I'd bring her breakfast in bed—scrambled eggs and toast on a tray—as a surprise. She'd kiss me and call me her helper, her good girl. When my stepfather moved in, all that was ruined.

My mother. I ache when I think of her. In spite of everything—all the anger, hurt, and misunderstanding—our connection is still strong. The misery between us is deep and pervasive; layers of guilt so woven together that it's impossible to know where one of us begins and the other ends. Even without any contact, we feel each other's feelings. Now that I'm back on observation, she must be worried sick about me. If anything were ever to happen to her, I'd want to die.

Once I was afraid my mother would die. When I was eleven, the same year she remarried, my mother went into the hospital to have a lump removed from her breast. While she was there I stayed at a friend's house. The week was a pretense of meals, school, playing . . . but all I wanted was to see my mother. I was sick with fear, afraid I'd never see her again. I knew if that happened I couldn't survive.

I've made myself believe my mother doesn't care about me anymore, but I know she must be wondering every minute if I'm okay and when she'll be able to see me again. It's like everything else in this place—now, when I finally want to see her, they won't let me.

I'm awakened by sharp pains in my stomach. I try to go back to sleep but the pain is insistent. I stagger out into the hallway. It's 2 A.M. and the ward is desolate.

"Stomach cramps," I gasp to the attendant, who goes to phone for the night nurse while I curl up into a tight ball on the hallway bench. It's an eternity before I hear the jingling of the nurse's keys. The pain grows impossibly stronger.

The nurse asks me about the pain. "Dull or sharp? Constant or intermittent?" How can I describe this pain? It's everywhere, inescapable as air, beyond the bounds of any physical sensation I've ever felt.

"Probably gas," the nurse says. She doses me with Gelusil and Donnatal. I down it and wait, but the pain doesn't want to be tamed. It feels like punishment for all the awful things I've done; a karate chop from the hand of God that brings me to my knees. I pray for it to stop. It doesn't matter that I'm a self-proclaimed agnostic. I pray to the God of my childhood to please take away the pain. *I'll be good, I'll change my ways, I promise, I swear, I beg you, please just make it stop.* I'm crying aloud, moaning, trying not to scream. The nurse unlocks the Quiet Room and goes to call the doctor, leaving me to burrow and squirm on the mattress.

Soon I'm being wheeled through corridors to the emergency room at Columbia-Presbyterian. They x-ray and examine me, but aside from a fever and abdominal tenderness, they can find nothing wrong. Back on the ward, I'm dosed with chloral hydrate and manage to drift off to sleep. In the morning, the pain has been replaced by a less-intense version. I'm drained, weak, and feverish. The nurse takes my temperature and tells me I've been scheduled for a gynecological exam. I've never been examined *down there* before.

I sit on the exam table naked from the waist down, a sheet wrapped around me, while the doctor asks me questions. "When was your last period?" About three weeks ago. I remember I had it when I ran away with Jack; I'd had to ask him to buy some Tampax on one of his supply runs while I waited in our hotel hideaway. "When was the last time you had sex?" Also three weeks. "Did you use protection?" I shake my head.

He looks at me disapprovingly. "Aren't you concerned about getting pregnant? You could have contracted a venereal disease." *Venereal*—an awful word. The doctor tells me to lie down, loosens the sheet that covers me, places my feet in the metal stirrups, and pulls my knees apart. He turns his face to the side as he feels my belly for tenderness—yes, ouch— then slides his lubricated, gloved fingers inside me. I cover my face with my hands and bite my lip.

"You appear to have an infection." The doctor talks to me over the oracle of my exposed lower half. Once again he pushes his fingers deep inside me and in a moment withdraws a Tampax, tinged a foul greenish gray. It's been in there all this time. It must have gotten jammed deep into me when Jack and I had sex. No wonder sex was so painful. I'm mortified. What an idiot I am, so out of touch with my own body that I'm a danger to myself.

The doctor tosses the dirty evidence of my stupidity into the trash. "Your stomach cramps were a warning. You could have become very ill. In the future, if you're going to use tampons, please remember to remove them."

"I will," I whisper, dry-mouthed, flat on my back, my naked idiocy exposed for him and me and all the world to see. It's clear I'm mentally as well as morally deficient. My face burns, but I'm grateful that the horrible pain, and the thing that caused it, are gone. I wish it was that easy to get rid of whatever else is wrong with me.

6/1/68 Patient continues much the same. She is very fragmented, and thus far I have found it difficult to think of her as a complete person rather than a series of different personalities. She ranges from angry adolescent, to sociopath, to frightened child, to poorly functioning autistic girl. She can tolerate the full time in sessions but has difficulty being verbal. She does not respond to comments about her nonverbal manner. She is doing extremely well in her English class. C.O. in pajamas.

Marjee came bouncing out of session today with great news: she's off observation and back in clothes. She'll get to go outside with everyone else, while I have to stay on the ward. Now it's just me on observation. I beg my shrink to at least let me wear my own clothes, but he says not yet.

Through the open window, I catch a whiff of spring air, a curlicue of delicious green. My solar plexus contracts; my head throbs. To go outside! To smell the air, see the tiny buds on the trees, feel the *sploosh* of raindrops on my face. It's a physical longing I feel in every cell.

I try to sit still but can't. My nerves rule my body, and they're jumpy. As if on its own, my leg starts to jiggle. It's automatic. When I sit and even when I stand, I jiggle my leg up and down really fast; a kind of vertical shimmy. Other patients do it too, but I jiggle faster than anyone else, even Alyssa. I pride myself on how fast I can jiggle, almost as fast as the speed of my thoughts. Even if I'm not the most beautiful, even though I'm so self-conscious I can't speak, even though I have no opinions of my own, there are some things I can do better and faster than other people, that set me apart. My jiggling, my visions, my fears and crazy thoughts, my swearing, my sensitivity. These are my trademarks, the things that make me *me*.

Jane and Marjee are hanging out a lot, going on walks, telling secrets. I don't like this at all—my two best friends becoming friends. I do better with one friend at a time. With more than one, I have to work too hard to fit in and always wind up feeling left out. Before Marjee, my best friend was Jane; before Jane, Wendy; before Wendy, Janice; before Janice, Susie. "Don't put all your eggs in one basket," my mother used to say, but one at a time is the only way I can trust people.

I go back to the dorm and find Marjee and Jane sitting on Jane's bed. My body goes electric with jealousy. Marjee pats the bed and invites me to sit down, but I turn and walk away. Let them be friends. I'll just ignore them. But as hard as I try not to care, I can't help it, especially when I see them all together: Jane, Marjee, Alyssa, Nick, Harold. I hate them all! And there's nothing I can do. So I just clam up and start spending more time alone.

———————

The heat is like a slow alarm spreading through me, another drug nailing me down. The air is syrupy; it distorts, like looking through a lens. Time drips like Dalí's clocks. Everyone is slower than usual, trying to avoid the friction of air on our skin. We are moody. Weepy. Explosive. We argue and snap. In Center, two fans standing on tall stands whirl like large metal pinwheels, moving the hot air.

Just when it's time to go outside, when the sultry air coming through the window torments me with its invitation, I'm stuck on the ward. As if that's not enough, my doctor wrote an order that I'm not allowed to take off my bathrobe if I'm not wearing a bra. As if he has any idea what wearing a bra feels like in this heat—like wet rubberbands wrapped around me. Sweat rolls between my breasts and wells in my navel. I roll up my pajama sleeves and legs as far as they'll go. I swear at the nurses, swear at my shrink, vow not to speak another word, then can't help swearing some more.

With school over for the summer, the days are uninterrupted torture. The other kids get to go on neighborhood walks and trips to the park, but the closest I get is the caged-in roof. Weekends are the hardest, with no activities to break the routine—just meals, and watching other people's visitors arrive. I can't concentrate, can't read. I drift off, but instead of falling asleep, my thoughts just get louder. I dig my nails into my arms and thighs to stay awake, only to find myself sitting here, the same as a minute ago, and hundreds of thousands of minutes before that.

There must be something I can do to end the dreariness.

In the shower, I ask for a razor to shave my legs; then, when the attendant isn't looking I remove the blade and hide it under my soap. Suddenly I'm awake, focused, excited, with a new sense of purpose, something to look forward to.

Alone at last in the bathroom stall, I roll up my pajama sleeve, carefully unwrap the blade, and hold it between thumb and forefinger, enjoying the feel of its almost dimensionless thinness, the flexibility of the metal. The razor's edge—a zen koan of a concept—a weapon not against myself, but against them, those who have denied me my freedom.

I test a corner point on my finger. Sharp! Sharp and precise enough to part molecules of matter. I hold the edge against the smooth surface of my upper arm, but can't make my hand move. What if I can't do it? It's urgent that I do.

I slice, then open my eyes to look at the two-inch slash. I see the spongy white fat cells on either side of the cut—just for an instant, before the blood wells up from inside and drips out, a crimson tear. All I feel is a slight stinging, but no pain. Mostly I feel relief. My headache is gone, along with the bad thoughts. I am able to see inside myself and find flesh and blood—not just emptiness and confusion.

After making a second, parallel cut, I place and replace wads of tissue until the bleeding subsides, place a pad of paper towel over the cuts, pull my pajama top carefully over my arm, flush the toilet, and walk past the nurses' station, savoring my secret triumph.

I repeat this process several times on both arms and thighs until one day a nurse notices a red line seeping through my pajama sleeve.

"I wasn't trying to kill myself," I protest when they put me back on observation. "If I wanted to do that, I would have cut a vein." They don't understand. I do it because the blade lends me its power.

The hospital does not know what to do with me. The nurse's notes are filled with entries like, "Patient is not making progress. I do not see that she will ever improve."

One by one my friends are getting outside privileges, while I'm sitting in the living room in pajamas. I'm tired of being here, sluggish and confined, mired in the daily routines, the bland food, stale air, the buzz and whine of consciousness.

One morning while brushing my teeth, I become aware of a voice droning in my head. I've been hearing this voice subliminally for some time; this morning, for some reason, it's loud and insistent. I can't quite make out words, but what really speaks to me is its nagging, critical tone. At first I can't tell if it's male or female; then suddenly, I recognize the voice. It's my mother, inside my head. She speaks in the same tone of voice she used when I was a child. "Miserable kids . . . so selfish . . . only thinking of yourself." The voice continues: "You're stupid. You're horrible. I hate you, I hate you." That's my voice. That's what her voice has done to me.

In occupational therapy I notice a jar labeled "POISON: Contains Petroleum Distillates. DO NOT DRINK." I look closer. The bottle contains grout sealer, a silicon-based cement used to set mosaic tiles in place. Each time I go to O.T., I stalk and court that jar, waiting for the right moment. What do I have to lose?

Finally my opportunity arrives. Left alone for a few moments, I lift the jar from the shelf and unscrew the lid. Pungent fumes sear my eyes. The stuff smells horrible, but I take a deep breath, bring the jar to my lips, tilt back my head, and pour the vile, viscous contents down my throat, gulping it down like a high-octane malted. Gagging, I do my best to drain the jar. Almost immediately I am in trouble, lights flashing before my eyes, pain that's light-years beyond mere headache. I can't contain my retching. They make me drink an antidote, after which I vomit long and thoroughly, saving them the effort of pumping my stomach. I wish I'd never seen the jar or chosen to go that route. But I had to. It's just another passageway marked DO NOT ENTER that I'm compelled to take.

> 6/15/68 At approximately 4 pm this afternoon, patient drank 2 ounces of silicone grout sealer, apparently on impulse. What I find most disturbing was that we had had a session about 45 minutes prior to the episode. She was depressed about her lack of progress but otherwise gave no indication to me of being unduly suicidal. I have spoken to her since. She is extremely apologetic and worried that she has let me down. She cannot give any reason why she did what she did. She is now on tight S.O.

Being on S.O. is a status symbol. I feel elevated above the other patients, a step further along in the dangerous game of seeing how far I can go. But going all the way is another matter.

On occasion we are herded into the elevator and transported to a rooftop on the eleventh floor where the building narrows, forming a stepped-back tier, caged in on top and three sides with a chain-link fence. When the nurse unlocks the door, I am hit in the face with a blast of light and fragrant air. The concrete floor is painted green like pretend grass; along the edges, begonias and geraniums wilt in their planters. Below us, the Hudson stretches north-south along Riverside Park. On the highway cars zoom past. The silver span of the George Washington Bridge arches over the Hudson to New Jersey. The sight is dizzying.

I feel a subtle pull downward. If it wasn't for this fence, I could jump. I imagine doing it, leaning over the edge, letting my body be taken by gravity; but once I'm flying through the air, aware of the inevitability of the ground coming to meet me and the rock-hard irreversibility of that fact . . . It's too terrifying. I refocus my eyes on the chain-link fence that holds us in, holds us back, and drop my gaze past my hands laced in the fence to my feet on the concrete floor.

One day in the rooftop cage, I meet a girl a few years older than me. An unfortunate girl, I can see—bad skin, thin hair, face a mask of pain. She picks at her lips and face, scratches her arms. The others avoid her. Yet when I smile, she smiles back, transformed.

"Hi," she says softly, her pale blue eyes looking up at me.

Her name is Helen. She used to be on our ward, but now she's on the eighth floor, the one with the very skinny girls and people who scream a lot. As we talk, Helen shifts her weight from one foot to the other, rocking from side to side. She clutches her arms, her voice rising in tremulous questions, crying in little bleats. "Do you think there's hope for us? Will we ever get out of here? Will you be my friend?" Though my heart moves toward her in sympathy, I take a step back in fear.

"I like your ring." Helen peers wistfully at my hand. The ring, a black stone in a silver setting, was a birthday present from Jane. I take it off my finger and give it to Helen, telling her to keep it. She obviously needs it more than I do. As I hand it to her, a pang of regret vies with the compassion and revulsion, empathy and fear battling in my chest.

Back on the ward, when I feel the empty place on my finger where my ring was, I remember our conversation. *Is there hope for us? Will we ever get out of here? Will you be my friend?* I ask myself.

The next time I see Helen, she is recovering from a broken back, in a body brace from hips to shoulders, after jumping from the sixth-floor roof of a neighborhood building. They move her to our ward and give her a private room. She keeps to herself a lot, but I often hear her little bleats, see her picking at the scabs on her arms, legs, and face. Sometimes she erupts into screaming, which issues for hours from the Quiet Room. The ward becomes too quiet at these times. We tap and jiggle, smoke and pace, until her screams become a mere annoyance.

"Where is Helen? Has anyone seen her?" They search the ward to no avail. Then we hear the news: Helen has jumped again from a building. She's alive, but broken, in the ICU upstairs. No visitors allowed. When she's better, she'll be sent back downstairs.

I'm not sure which is worse—the fact that Helen jumped, or that she survived. That in itself seems punishment enough. But she isn't finished. Word filters down: Somehow Helen has gotten hold of matches and lighter fluid, and set herself on fire in the ICU. I shudder to think of the flames dancing over the surface of her skin, that sensitive boundary that defines the self, leaving it even more raw and scarred, covered with burns. If it was hard for her before, what chance at life will Helen have now?

"Did you hear about Rocky?"

We are in Mrs. Gould's classroom. The phrasing of the question contains within itself an answer; it ricochets impossibly around the room and settles inside each of us. Rocky has hung herself on some ward in Rockland.

It is horrible to imagine Rocky's life-filled body a dead weight. Our own bodies sag heavily. Nobody can offer any insight, except the obvious: how alone and abandoned she must have felt in that awful place. Tears flow; we hug each other, weeping. Mrs. Gould takes a handkerchief from her pocket and blows her nose loudly. She hands out tissues, little white flags of loss that become transparent with tears. One by one we remember Rocky aloud, reciting all we loved. We band together like the remaining survivors of a forgotten regiment. All but Nick.

Nick is devastated by Rocky's death. He is not simply depressed—he is angry at everyone and everything. Nick's usual cynicism hardens into bitter meanness. Abandoned by humor and wit, his silence sucks up the air around him. When he does speak, he is vengeful and nasty. Brown shadows appear beneath his eyes, making his sockets appear deeper, almost skeletal. His jaw clenches and his nostrils flare. Marjee steers clear of Nick's smoldering hatred; he still blames her for Rocky's being shipped. There's nothing anyone can do or say to help him—not even Alyssa, and certainly not me. He looks right through us, hating us for being alive when Rocky's gone.

It's hard to know who the enemy is. It's easy to point to *them*—the hospital staff and all they stand for. It's much scarier when it becomes apparent that the enemy lurks inside each of us.

Each suicide confirms my darkest feelings. Where others go, I can go too. I can get out of here, escape this place and the mess I've made of my life, the unendurable weight of the present, the blankness of the future. At the same time, it's tragic, senseless, scary. Another Vietnam, quietly happening all around us.

Suicide is our Olympic specialty. People here go to great lengths to succeed. Liz survives an overdose of sleeping pills, wrist-slicing, and an

attempt at suffocating herself in the utilities room with the gas-fueled
clothes dryer. She holds the all-time record for continuous months in
pajamas (more than two years straight) and total time spent on S.O. But
the hospital can't watch over her forever. When Liz's doctor feels she's
making progress, she's taken off E.O., gradually given privileges, and
finally discharged. A few weeks later, the news hits home. Without telling
anyone where she was going, Liz drove to her family's cabin in the woods,
held her father's shotgun to her head and in an instant blew away the thing
that troubled her most, her mind.

When someone succeeds, we are grief-stricken, tearful, frightened.
Frightened to death. Frightened of death. Frightened of life. Stuck here
with our cowardice, our inability to act. Suicide is an alternative, an
attainable choice. I'm in awe of those who make serious attempts and survive. They are miraculous beings, our saints and angels, an air of holiness
about them.

Gary, a quiet, personable redhead (his bright orange hair and flamboyant freckles their own miracle) threw himself in front of a moving subway. The entire train passed over him, yet he survived without a scratch.
He cheerfully describes the details. "I tried touching the third rail but
somehow missed it, and I guess I rolled into the middle where there was
just enough room. I felt very calm, even though I was conscious of the
train going over me. It seemed to take a very long time." He tells it like
he's describing a particularly challenging circus stunt. He never talks
about why he did it.

Nancy flew like a bird off the George Washington Bridge. They found
her floating downstream, broken but alive. I can imagine the awful contradiction she was driven to: the weightless arc of flight, followed by
crashing into water hard as stone; the strange horror of waking from her
death. But I can't imagine what drove her to it, what could have been powerful enough to propel her from that height. It's something she never
speaks of, a secret between herself and her doctor. The raised pink scars
on Nancy's back where she was stitched up look like they removed her
wings. Perhaps they did. One morning we wake in the dorm to find that
Nancy has disappeared. The police are notified, but Nancy has already
been found, shattered on the sidewalk following a plunge from a neighborhood brownstone.

Tina goes at it with gusto, in intermittent attacks. Stripes of scar tissue
cross both wrists; at the base of her throat a pink tracheotomy scar marks

where she was intubated following an overdose of barbiturates. Tina does not fool around; she took enough Demerol and Seconal to kill a horse. Due to some fluke they found her in time, and had to dig deep to bring her back. When she isn't committing suicide, Tina is passionately alive. She has a fairy princess's pale skin and long, silky strawberry-blond hair. She's also hotheaded, prone to red-faced explosions ("That's bullshit! Fuck you!") that clear the torpor of the ward like small but powerful thunderstorms. When she is upset, she is inconsolable, moaning, "I want to die," mascara streaking down her face in black rivers.

Tina has an irrepressibly irreverent sense of humor. When she launches into her rambling, complex stories, I have to listen hard to understand. Vocal-cord damage from the tracheotomy has made her voice hoarse and breathy. As she speaks her pale skin flames hot pink and laughter bubbles through her in wheezy brays. Tina has the kind of mouth that when she laughs, reveals too much of her gums; her stories become a spectacle of saliva, gums, and teeth, accompanied by the most unlikely symphony of wheezes, gasps, snorts, and shrieks. Sometimes she weeps with laughter— a sibyl of life force and emotion. But she is also utterly determined to take her life and pursues her goal with unswerving intention. Dead serious, she finally succeeds.

These are my family members; it hurts to lose them. Sometimes it's so painful I'm tempted to follow, but I've come to realize I'm not willing to ferry myself across that river. As if the decision's been made for me, I resign myself to stay among the living.

BACKLASH

THERE'S AN ODD ALLIANCE BETWEEN STAFF AND PATIENTS. They hold the keys, dispense the meds, tell us what to do and when to do it, enforce the rules, subdue us when they decide it's necessary. We sit around and do what we're told; or we rebel, curse them out, go off the wall. Ultimately we follow their orders. They follow us like shadows. They get to go home when their shifts are over, while we're here round the clock. Yet the boundaries separating us are thin.

Eric and C.T. are playing Ping-Pong. Eric wears hospital pajamas. C.T. wears a white uniform. They're a good match, both tall and thin with long limbs and quick reflexes. They stand a couple of feet back from the table, volleying, until Eric puts some spin on the ball, which whizzes just over the top of the net and bounces off the edge of the table. In the next volley C.T. slams it so hard it ricochets off the walls.

"You jive turkey!" C.T. laughs, rapping his paddle on the edge of the table. "Now tell me: Who's the master? Who's the master?" Eric concedes, laughing.

Bobby and R.J. join them for doubles. The game is tense, close, breathless. Long volleys end in whooping laughter and high fives. These guys can really play.

The male attendants are big brothers to the guys, full of wisdom about life—and love. They're men of the world, young and handsome, with a certain strut in their stride, a certain male pride. Tall, skinny C.T., with his "processed" hair and dark eyes, exudes warmth and humor. Sly is a babe magnet. He's irresistibly sexy. Under the curliest eyelashes I've seen on a man, Sly literally has a wandering eye. A glass eye fills the hole left by a bullet during his stint in the army—the armed forces, as he calls it. You can hardly tell, though. If anything, his faraway gaze just makes him more attractive to "the ladies."

"Let me tell y'all something . . . if a woman rejects you, don't let it get you, there's plenty more out there who'd be happy to have you. Yeah, I kid you not!" When Sly laughs, rasping rushes of air release against his palate like bursts of steam from a radiator.

They're workingmen, family men, but that doesn't stop them from telling tales of their exploits. They release their stories slowly, a scandalous bit at a time. Tall tales, probably, but it doesn't matter. The boys follow them around like ducklings, begging for the next detail. It's an ongoing education.

When they're not busy hustling patients off to the Quiet Room, the attendants like to joke around. R.J. does verbal riffs on his namesake, Raymond J. Johnson. "You can call me Ray or you can call me Jay, but you don't have to call me Johnson. You could call me James or you could call me Johnny, but there's no need to call me Sonny . . ." Playing cards or telling stories, R.J. maintains a poker face for as long as possible before breaking into laughter. He's even and openhanded with patients, dignified and respectful. But there are certain lines you should never cross.

One day Bobby, in a fit of temper, makes the mistake of calling R.J. a "black bastard motherfucker." That's it for him. R.J. grabs Bobby, picks him up, carries him to the Quiet Room, throws him in, and locks the door. A couple of hours later, when R.J. unlocks the door, Bobby says, "What'd you do that for? I was only joking, man."

R.J. looks straight ahead, unsmiling. "There are some names you never call a man. Don't you ever dare say that to me again, or I'll whip your ass."

The same racial tensions that exist outside permeate our lives inside. News seeps in each day in newspapers and on the news. Within months of each other, Martin Luther King, Jr., and Robert Kennedy are assassinated. The shots that killed Malcolm X in '65 still resonate. Dissidents raise closed fists; Afros bristle with Black Pride. The Black Panthers, Bobby Seale, Angela Davis make their voices heard. However calm racial issues inside the hospital are on the surface, they are tangibly present beneath.

When Jane asks R.J. how he came to work as an attendant, he tells her he was trained as a mechanic but couldn't find a good-paying job—

because he's black. There's a distinct difference between R.J. and the other black attendants. R.J. holds himself more apart—with some exceptions.

R.J. and Jane, whose snub-nosed, blue-eyed whiteness is coupled with a radical political awareness, are close friends. They spend hours sitting together, talking, laughing, playing cards. R.J. is fiercely protective of Jane. One day Izzy, in a confused state, comes over to Jane, puts his hands around her neck, and squeezes so hard she starts choking. In a flash R.J. is on top of Izzy, pinning him down in a stranglehold, with Jane yelling: "Stop it, please stop it!"

The attendants generally exercise restraint, but they've been trained to use force if a patient gets violent or out of control or simply to make a recalcitrant patient obey. It's a weird feeling watching an attendant subdue somebody. There's an unconscious identification with them because they, like us, are an oppressed class. You just don't see any black doctors, psychologists, or social workers. Even the nurses are mostly white. The attendants are third-class citizens in the hospital hierarchy; the only ones lower are the kitchen workers and maintenance crew. So when they turn into strong-arm men exerting the will of our oppressors, it feels like a real betrayal. They hold the keys, and they're aware of their power—a different kind of black power.

It's terrible when an attendant is angry at you, making you wait to go to the bathroom or refusing to let you watch TV, answering your demands with stony silence. We depend upon their good graces. They bring us news and energy from outside. You can smell it on them, a faint whiff of life, adventure, the street. They carry it on their clothes, in their bodies and attitudes.

"Tighten up now!" Sly warns when one of us is acting out or falling apart at the seams. Sly's muscles are taut bulges under his uniform even when he's at ease. When we have ward parties, Sly dances the Tighten Up, exaggerating the jerking robotlike movements to make us laugh.

But trust can only go so far. Attendants are expected to report back to nursing staff about what's going on with us. If a student nurse or attendant sits down next to you all friendly and asks how you are, beware. You may think you're just having a conversation until a couple of days later, when your doctor says to you in session: I hear you were feeling depressed, or angry, or missing home, or whatever it was that you confided to that staff member. Likewise, when attendants take our money to cop us drugs or booze, they could get their asses seriously fired.

It's an intimate connection. We're together constantly, except when they go home to their families and real or fictitious extramarital adventures. We talk, joke, horse around, play cards and Ping-Pong, laugh, yell at each other. They get frustrated with us and we get frustrated with them. They may hold the keys, but we're locked together in extremes of emotions.

My favorite nurse, Julie, is young and pretty. She sits and talks with us, brushes our hair, tells us about her boyfriend. She asks about our lives, listens to our stories. Sometimes she cries with us, passes Kleenex around, blows her nose. I sometimes wonder if she identifies with us too much for her own good. Julie spends a lot of time talking with Joe, a chain-smoking nineteen-year-old with curly blond hair and blue eyes. There's a tightness in his face, a twitchiness in his jaw, that relaxes as they talk. The word spreads that Julie and Joe have fallen in love. The implications are thrilling. If staff and patients fall in love, anything can happen. Insurrection. Anarchy. Shortly after the rumor of their affair surfaces, Joe is shipped to Bronx State. Julie wanders the ward red-eyed and pale, and is soon transferred to another floor.

We hear rumors that Luis, the physical therapist, is getting it on with Laurie, though we never know for sure. When asked, Laurie takes a deep drag on her cigarette, throws her head back and exhales slowly, working her jaw to pop out a few smoke rings. "Oh really? Where'd you hear that? I'm not saying it's true or not, but I do like those Latin lovers," she says, laughing. When Luis gets fired, Laurie goes into a rage that lands her in the Quiet Room.

Staff-patient relationships are the ultimate in subversion. Like interracial marriage, it challenges the heart of the system, undermining the basic divisions of hospital society. Crazy versus sane, us versus them, staff versus patient . . . and never the two shall meet *as equals.* To do so would make us too much alike, and the whole system would collapse.

Laura, day-shift head nurse for a while, has a facial tic and chain-smokes just about as much as we do. In the morning, her makeup is perfect, but within an hour perspiration has turned it into a shiny, oily mask. The more tense she becomes, the bitchier she is toward us. There are rumors of problems in her personal life, a relationship that came to an end, an affair with one of the attendants. She quits abruptly to move in with and nurse her sick mother. After her mother dies, Laura has a nervous breakdown and winds up on a psych ward. "How awful," we say . . .

but can't conceal a glint of satisfaction at the weird karma that's put Laura at the mercy of nurses like herself.

———————

The attendants call this place "the country club on the Hudson." From their point of view, we have it pretty good; we don't have to work, and our every need is attended to. From our point of view, we are prisoners shackled by their helping hands. They're here to make a living, whereas we don't have to work—or can't. Who is more privileged?

The patients, with one or two exceptions, are white, from middle-class homes. We have one Hispanic patient, but he is soon shipped to one of the other state hospitals. Two black patients are on the ward for a while, and one or two Asians. The attendants are mainly black and Hispanic, with a few Irish and Italians, and some odds and ends, like Oliver—a conscientious objector doing his mandatory public service stint. Who else besides a crazy person would want to spend their days and nights in a nuthouse?

In a way, we are a suburb of the ghetto. The Columbia-Presbyterian complex is a white-collar enclave bordering Harlem. The hospital provides employment opportunities for the locals, and they provide labor. We, the patients, provide both with occupations.

The night attendant making the rounds with her flashlight can't tell that Jane is not in her bed, but we know those lumps under the covers are towels. Jane has been smuggled out by R.J. and Sly to a party in Harlem. The next day when we corner her, Jane shields her dark-circled eyes from the light, mumbling something about coke and cool music. She won't say more, because she doesn't want to jeopardize anybody's job. I envy her special place in the staff's inner circle, the underground elite.

At night, dramas unfold. Overdoses and suicide attempts, elopements and psychotic breaks. I wake up to hear someone screaming, keys turning in the Quiet Room door, someone being carried off on a stretcher. In the morning, rumors fly. I feel like I've missed something when I've slept through something really big.

In the wee hours the insomniacs come out. When patients can't sleep, they pull up a chair and commune with the night attendant until the nurse or doctor on call arrives to write an order for more meds. You can see them from the dorm door or if you get up to go to the bathroom, sitting together quietly talking or trading newspaper sections. Sometimes it's me sitting on the bench, listening to the buzz of the fluorescents, the night pressing endlessly down. Maybe that's why so many bad things happen at night. I don't know how the night attendants stand it.

Other things happen at night: romantic trysts, drug parties, card games, kitchen raids, social gatherings in Center. Night attendants are easy to bribe and even easier to delude.

When Noel hears from his doctor that they're thinking of transferring him to one of the state hospitals because he isn't making progress, he goes about systematically enlisting the support of attendants and nurses he knows he can trust. All the time he's been at P.I., Noel's been such a model of good behavior that he hasn't even been given meds. His only crime is that he's underage and on Court Remand. They all agree it's in Noel's best interest to elope and are even willing to turn a blind eye to his efforts— though nobody is willing to go so far as to help him outright.

Noel plans a brilliant elopement with the night staff's unwitting help. For two weeks he stays up late and sits in the hallway reading the employment ads, shaking his head and muttering. When the night attendant asks what's wrong, Noel says that his doctor has ordered him to find a job. "Not much around these days," he sighs, shaking his head. Finally, when he feels he has the attendant fully conditioned, Noel gets up at dawn, showers, shaves, dresses, and walks out in his overcoat with the newspaper under his arm. "Today's the day," he tells the attendant. "Wish me luck." He glances at his watch. "Would you mind unlocking the staircase door?" The night attendant unlocks the door, and fifteen-year-old Noel is gone for good. Nobody reports him missing until late in the afternoon. An underground railroad of former patients—and Julie, our former nurse—spirits him safely out of New York City to Philadelphia, where the police won't look for him.

My favorite evening attendant is a diminutive black woman who calls herself Nana. Nana stands about five feet tall. Everything about her is round: round cheeks, breasts, hips, eyes—everything round, warm, comforting.

"Come sit by Nana," she says to me, patting the chair next to her. She sits demurely, hands crossed in her lap, legs crossed at the ankles. Her legs are slim and shapely, emerging from her white skirt and tapering into white shoes. I sit beside her, and she smooths my hair out of my face, tucks it behind my ears. She smells sweet, like peaches.

"What's the matter, honey? I see you're not feeling good. Tell Nana what's the matter."

I tell her how tired I am of it here, and that I'm afraid I'll never get better, never get out of here. She puts her arm around me, draws me close.

"You'll get out of here, honey. You'll be just fine. Trust Nana."

Nana is so nurturing I can't rebel. She reminds me partly of my little Jewish grandma who fed and fussed over me, and partly of Marie, the black woman who cooked and cleaned for my mother and taught me to tie my shoes and write my name. Aside from Marie, my mother's world was as homogenous and white as milk.

One night when Nana is going off her shift, she stops at the staircase door, keys in hand, and turns to wave. "Bye, now. Have a happy!" she calls out in her high-pitched Munchkin voice.

I crack up laughing, completely lose it. Have a happy? A happy *what?*

Christmas holidays approach, a turbulent parting of the waters. Some patients get passes to go home to their families. Among those left on the ward, spirits are low. It's too quiet; the minutes drag. Rooms seem huge and empty. Handel's *Messiah* fills the living room with its power but can't touch the emptiness inside. Little acts of kindness help get us through the day, coming from certain staff members—a few nurses and attendants who are especially warm and caring.

We are surprised on Christmas day by gifts under the tree—beautifully wrapped, with our names on them. A group of staff members—several nurses, Sly, R.J., C.T., Mrs. G.—have chipped in to buy gifts, personally chosen for each of us. Marjee gets a book of poems. I get a pair of glass bead earrings, blue and green, bringing out the green in my hazel eyes. I'm touched. The mood on the ward lightens; for a few hours it feels almost festive. We eat an early dinner—turkey, stuffing, and yams—that tastes surprisingly delicious. We toast each other with alcohol-free eggnog, sing carols, watch *Miracle on 34th Street* on TV, and go to bed peacefully.

A week or so after the holidays, the administration takes action against the staff members who gave us gifts. Carrie, the nurse who organized the gift-buying, is fired; the other nurses, R.J., C.T., and Mrs. G., are transferred to other wards, and Sly is forced to work the late-night shift. They have broken a cardinal rule—gift-giving between staff and patients is strictly forbidden.

But this was so personal, so human, so *needed;* not a trace of wrongdoing or coercion, just kindness. We protest, and are told, like children, that the hospital knows what's best; rules like this exist for our own protection. Protection from what—*human kindness?* What they really object to is the breakdown of our established roles. The hand reaching out for any other reason than prescribed duties gets slapped.

We decide to engage in some civil—or uncivil—disobedience. Someone suggests a hunger strike, but we know we wouldn't be able to last long at that. Then someone suggests a sit-down strike. Perfect! Putting our passivity to work is easy; we've had lots of practice. We sit on the floor and refuse to get up to go to activities, school, meds, meals, or bed. When they try to physically pull us up to stand, we are all dead weight. Let go, our arms flop back limply. But pacifism can go only so far. Gidro-Frank's henchman sends word that they will not consider our demands.

"Inappropriate behavior," the Catch-22 of life inside, has backlashed against those of our keepers who were caring enough to show it. I suddenly see these staff members in a new way. They're not just my jailers. At least some of them are human beings with feelings, not so different from us. For a brief moment, we're on the same side.

Old staff is replaced by new, and life on the ward is subtly changed. Over time, R.J., C.T., and some other staff members return, and life goes on.

CELEBRITIES

ONE DAY THERE'S A BUZZ OF COMMOTION AROUND THE ELEVATOR. We're being visited by the Finn Twins. George and Charlie Finn are world-famous idiot savants, mathematical geniuses with perfect numerical recall. Their gifts are a kind of barter: The twins are autistic and severely retarded. Regular retarded people are a dime a dozen, but the Finns are endowed with an extra function that compensates for their deficits.

I wait on the outskirts of the cluster of admirers to see what the fuss is about. I see two pale, round-faced, pudgy men somewhere between young and middle-aged, like Tweedledum and Tweedledee. Both wear slacks and shortsleeved shirts, with pen guards in their shirt-pockets, like accountants. They bask in the attention, unself-conscious and childlike.

Mrs. G. motions me to come closer. "Charlie, this is Mindy."

"Hi." What else does one say to an idiot savant?

Charlie's eyes are huge, magnified by Coke bottle eyeglass lenses. He gives me a big smile, with breath that smells like sour milk. He rocks from foot to foot. "Tell me your birthday."

"March 4th, 1952."

"Tuesday. Rain in the afternoon," comes the instantaneous answer. "Thirty-eight degrees low temperature," his brother chimes in.

"That's amazing," I say to the twins. "How do you do that?"

Charlie beams with pride. "I see it," he says. The twins, talking in tandem, explain that they read the *Farmers' Almanac* and mentally "photograph" the pages. In other words, they have perfect, instantaneous visual memory. What artist wouldn't give an arm for such a skill?

In a way, they're like machines, with some really amazing, weird wiring in their heads. It makes me feel like a very ordinary, low-functioning machine. As amazing as it is, though, I feel sad for them. Their exceptional ability doesn't make them any smarter. And though they're big celebrities in the hospital world, they'll never have a nor . . . I try to stop myself before the word hits the wall in my brain. I know there is no such thing as a "normal" life. I despise the very concept. Anyway, what difference does it make? The twins don't even know they're oddities. They think everybody—the doctors and nurses and people gawking at them—is their friend. They live an exciting life, playing the hospital circuit.

It makes me uneasy. The twins aren't the only specimens to be observed. We're also being studied, only we don't have any exceptional gifts. And *they* get to go off the ward, with all sorts of fanfare. I guess if you're unusual enough, you get rewarded.

Soon it's time to say good-bye to the Finn Twins. They shuffle onto the elevator, grin at the elevator operator and passengers as if they're old friends, and the traveling circus moves on.

There's excitement on the ward before Harry arrives. Staff calls a special meeting to inform us that a patient with a severe disability is being admitted. The adolescent boys are warned not to tease him. He suffers from a rare condition, a five-syllable word: "hydrocephalus," which Ted informs me means "water-on-the-brain."

Harry is a middle-aged man with a huge head that wobbles dangerously atop his rotund body. He's nearly blind, and eyeglasses magnify his eyes so that he looks like a large, bespectacled owl. Tufts of hair on his balding head stand up like wispy feathers. Harry's head is constantly filling with fluid, which is siphoned off by a plastic tube, called a shunt, that actually has a little plastic faucet. Harry does seem to be filled with water. His head is like a balloon filled to bursting. His eyes tear; his lips are livery and wet.

Harry has a surprisingly stodgy personality. He speaks in an exaggerated patrician drawl and likes to read the newspaper while smoking his pipe. He's usually polite, unless he has a headache, and then he's grumpy and snappish.

What, we all want to know, is he doing on a psychiatric ward? Other than being a guy with a huge head, Harry seems no crazier than most. At least his big-headedness is visible.

"Need to have your head shrunk?" Harry is the constant brunt of unkind remarks from the adolescent boys. In spite of the doctors' warnings, this is too hard for them to resist. They mimic everything about him: his enormous, slow-blinking owl eyes; the tremulous turn of his head; his deep phelgm-rattled hacking; his Frankenstein gait, arms held straight out to keep him from bumping into things. The boys start small, and slowly work Harry into a frenzy. They've discovered that their best laugh comes when Harry defends himself. "Cut that out!" Harry yells, swatting blindly at the air. "Go away! Leave me alone, for Chrissakes!" The boys scatter, laughing. The ultimate success is riling Harry so thoroughly that he curses them in his aristocratic New England drawl. "You little bahstahds! Go fuck yoaahselves!"

But during the three months he's on the ward, Harry and the boys develop a rapport. It turns out that Harry is a natural raconteur and loves telling jokes. The boys stop being cruel and start having conversations with him. They discover that he is a compendium of unusual historical facts and dub him "The Professor."

Every now and then Harry erupts into spasmodic coughing. It sounds like he's dying, and in fact, these fits could be fatal. He could asphyxiate himself or suffer a heart attack. "Easy, my man," Sly says, pounding Harry's back while someone steadies his head and someone else runs for a glass of water. Harry turns a deep purplish red, and the staff springs into action. Nurses come running. The clattering blood pressure contraption is wheeled in. The head nurse puts a stethoscope to Harry's chest and listens as his wheezing slowly dies down.

It's humbling to have somebody with such severe disability among us. Next to Harry, we barely register on the scale of dysfunction. It makes it seem like we're all just slackers, just kidding around. And it puts suicide in a completely different light. Harry could go at any moment. Even in his awful condition, he's lucky to be alive. From this perspective, every day is a gift—broken, imperfect, and poorly wrapped, but a gift, nonetheless. Self-destruction becomes a meaningless concept. For Harry what matters is survival.

One day Harry has a severe respiratory crisis and is taken to the hospital. Everyone is stunned and saddened, including the boys. The ward grows silent and introspective. One of the nurses brings in a get-well card that we all sign. In a week or so we hear that Harry appreciated our card and is doing better. But he never comes back to the ward, and after a few weeks people stop asking about him. People come, people go, and we forget them. Except for the boys, who on occasion still lumber down the corridors with their arms straight out in front of them, calling to each other, "You little bahstahd! Go fuck yoaahself!"

What I like about people here is that they have a sense of the absurd. They know the world is full of hypocrisy and horrors. Visionaries, in a sense. Their eyes are open.

Many patients on the ward are artists: musicians, painters, writers. Or they used to be. Most people don't do much anymore. It's part of the basic nihilistic requirement of admission. We are people who used to do things but have stopped. In some sense we are all artists. Depressionists, if you will. Our canvas, our clay—our selves. We are our own creations.

Victoria is a great big name for a very skinny girl. She's thirteen but looks like a seven-year-old, with arms and legs so thin her knees and elbows are the thickest parts. She's the skinniest girl I've ever seen, but she's always worried that she's getting fat. She's whittled herself down to almost nothing, a bizarre, semihuman, walking sculpture. We all treat her with deference, speaking softly and gently, afraid she might suddenly shatter, or disappear.

Jason carries in his wallet a dog-eared photo of his masterpiece, a beautiful classical marble sculpture of a female nude. He takes it out several times a day to show people. She's more than his muse; she's his protection, the passport to his other life. Fortunately, the occupational therapist takes an interest in Jason and allows him to go to O.T. whenever he wants, to work in plaster or clay.

Judith scribbles in her notebook most of the time. If I come near her while she's writing she slams her notebook shut. She's angry at everybody—the doctors, nurses, her shrink, her parents—especially her father: "That bastard! May he rot in hell!" She's like Botticelli's depiction of Wind, cheeks puffed out, issuing forth strong gusts that make everything shake, blowing the world away.

Not everybody here is a creative type. Some patients are just really out there. Psychotics. Zombies. Vegetables. Lost in dreams, trapped within themselves.

The loony bin is like the bins in my mother's refrigerator—one for fruits, another for vegetables. The vegetables are pathetic. I'd rather be a fruit than a vegetable. Fruits are juicier, more interesting. Right now I'm a fruit, but maybe after I've been in here awhile, rotting away in the bin, I'll become a vegetable.

Aram, firmly planted in the vegetable bin, suddenly surprises us. After shock therapy, Aram undergoes a startling metamorphosis into a vivacious, friendly, regular guy. He laughs about how funny it was to think he was falling from a great height when he flung himself out of his chair . . . until depression nails him again, and the sitting and sliding resume.

Then there are the nuts: cracked, but not yet vegetablized. Nuts talk in images and symbols, like poets. Fred is always prophesying the end of the world, California falling into the sea, ultimate cataclysm, and the Second Coming. He backs himself up with quotations from the Bible, the Kabbala, the Beatles, Dylan, and Dante's *Inferno*. Fred is way out there, a garden-variety nut. But couldn't they have said the same thing about William Blake, or even Jesus himself? Sometimes, after watching the display of atrocities on the evening news, I wonder if Fred is right.

Fruits and nuts. A delightful combination. And democratic too. We have bizarros from every walk of life: a lawyer, a college professor, several teachers, a policeman, a former nun, an antiques dealer, an accountant, an engineer, a nurse, a social worker, even a former doctor, Marvin, whose insider status gave him full access to the morphine he self-administered until he lost his license.

Substance abuse is big here. Several adult patients have drinking problems. They look a lot like depressives, but with a difference. Carl had been drinking for years before he tried to kill himself. His suicide was carefully planned to succeed. He took a massive amount of barbiturates, washed it down with vodka, and fell heavily—all 240 pounds of him—onto his left leg, and into a coma. By the time Carl was found, the circulation had been cut off for so long his leg had extensive nerve damage. He awoke to a prolonged, painful, medical hell. After several surgeries the leg was saved, but permanently damaged. Carl has no sensation in his leg—a swollen stone column impaled with metal pins and encased in braces—so when he walks he's like a clumping Eiffel Tower. Carl is from a wealthy family of media barons. He's disgraced himself in the eyes of his family. No wonder he wants to drink. He gulps down Thorazine as if it's cocktail hour.

Ron, another drinker, is easily the most lethargic patient on the ward. He stretches out his long legs and dozes in his silk bathrobe, his specially delivered *Wall Street Journal* spread across his chest. He's been here for years and doesn't seem to care. In a way it's a continuation of his past circumstances. Because he has a trust fund, Ron has never had to work. Here, where he's not expected to do anything except take his meds and go to therapy sessions, he can focus on his full-time job of being depressed.

It's a game of substitution, changing one form of incapacity for another. The drinkers are on meds instead of alcohol. For a brief time, they're also given the option of voluntarily signing up for an experimental new therapy: daily doses of an antibiotic that induces nausea when combined with alcohol. So when Carl or Ben slip off the wagon, they become violently ill. Too violently ill. After several weeks the experiment is discontinued.

There's nothing sadder than a dried-out drunk on Thorazine. Their skin is sallow. They're too resigned; they could do with a dose of rebelliousness. You can sense the suicide impulse storing itself up inside them, waiting to bust out.

Life on the ward can be as filled with nuance and crisis as literature or theater. We play our illness like musicians, actors, tragedians. No wonder they call our eruptions of emotion "episodes" or "acting out." We deliver soliloquies, have scenes, make dramatic gestures, threaten to exact our revenge on the world . . . and on ourselves. We are eternally pissed off. There is so much to be angry about, so much to be depressed about. The world has gone psychotic, and it would take millions of gallons of Thorazine and a Quiet Room the size of the solar system to calm it down.

Outside, the whole world is erupting. We've been blown inside like debris, seeking shelter from the storm. Napalm and carnage, entire villages slaughtered. Assassination and revolution. Tear gas and senseless acts of violence. Buddhist monks and nuns immolate themselves, sacrificing their lives for peace. And here we sit in a state of perpetual internal combustion. What are we doing? We're destroying ourselves for nothing, for nobody.

During a brief period when funding for state hospitals is temporarily cut, our ward fills with spillover patients: genuine psychotics. We are suddenly very aware of the difference between *us* and *them*. Though we're curious, we don't mingle—except for the adolesent boys, who now have a new crop of unfortunates to torture. Beds are set up in Center and line the hallways for a couple of months, until the visitors are carted back to where they came from.

One day a real celebrity arrives. Edie Sedgwick, Andy Warhol's superstar, famous for her poor-little-rich-girl presence in his films. Edie has an appealing, dreamy spaciness, a waif fallen from the society pages to the druggy avant-garde art world. She is stick-skinny, hipless and flat-chested, swimming in the big T-shirts she wears as mini-dresses over black tights. Her blond hair is in a tousled, two-toned pixie cut. Her eyes, accentuated by black eyeliner and false eyelashes thickened with black mascara, are like headlights. Even without makeup, she's luminous. Before Warhol, Edie used to model for *Mademoiselle* and *Vogue*—the same magazines my mother reads. I suddenly understand the word "model" differently. Everybody (secretly even me) wants to model themselves on the beautiful creatures in the fashion pages and in the movies. They seem to have what we don't. So why is Edie here?

Right from the start Edie brightens up the ward. Every morning she spreads her blanket out on the floor and practices yoga, gracefully bending her torso over her legs, then straightening, lifting her head like a sunflower on a skinny stalk. "I love doing my exercises," she says. "My best thoughts come to me when I do yoga. It gives me a glow."

Like a sunflower, in the middle of Edie's golden aura looms a large dark center. Beneath her sunny exterior, she seems fragile, lost. There's a rumor that she's the sad-eyed lady in Dylan's "Sad-Eyed Lady of the Lowlands." I don't understand what she has to be depressed about—she has everything: wealth, beauty, fame.

Just because Edie is a celebrity doesn't mean she gets special privileges. She lives in the dorm with the rest of us. I expect her to be snooty, but she's friendly. At first I feel extra-shy, but Edie's openness is hard to resist.

"What would you be doing," she asks, "if you weren't here? What were you doing *before?*" My face blazes when I tell her I'm an artist, or used to be—I mean, I like to draw and paint.

"I like to draw too." Edie tells me she majored in art in college. "People said I was pretty good. What I liked most was drawing animals. Do you know Beatrix Potter? Kind of like that." She rummages through her bureau and shows me a drawing of a mouse. It's perfect. Little eyes and nose, whiskers, tail. I'm impressed, and discouraged. I've never done anything that good. And she's so blasé about it. "I could have been an illustrator, if I wanted to. But I got bored." Artistic talent runs in Edie's family. I'm envious when she says her father is a sculptor, until she tells me he's the one who had her committed when she was eighteen. She understands how terrible it is to be sent away by your parents and locked up.

Jane and I sit on Edie's bed passing a hash pipe, concentrating so hard on being quiet that we're soon choking on smoke and laughter. Later we talk. Edie is interested in our life stories, and very open about sharing hers. She tells us about growing up on the ranch in California, running wild with the horses, raised by servants under the egomaniacal eye of a father who dominated her mother and everyone else, and about her passionate love for her brothers. She cries when she talks about them. Two of her brothers died, one by suicide, one in an accident.

"What a fucked-up family," she says. "I had to get away from them, but it's impossible to really get away."

Edie's life has been filled with mixed blessings. She's survived overdoses, fires, and other bad scenes. She gets teary describing how beautiful it was galloping bareback over the California hills, and tells us about the younger brother she loves—*really* loves. Edie is a wildflower; a free, unbridled spirit. She generously shares the hash she managed to smuggle in, as well as any drugs she can get on the ward, and we share ours with her. She tells us she used to mainline heroin. There's nothing else like it, she says, like a blissful, soothing snowfall, better than sex. The only thing is that she overdoses all the time. In her attempts to recapture the bliss of her first experience, she always does too much.

The shrinks keep Edie doped up on Thorazine. Her blood pressure drops so low that she periodically blacks out—then they accuse her of taking drugs. But Edie takes therapy seriously and soon gets privileges. When she's allowed out on "adult pass" she beelines straight to the local bar and drinks herself stupid. Then her privileges are taken away, and she's back in pajamas, hungover and contrite. Edie sits talking with her favorite nurse, who listens, holding her hand. Mascara streaks her face. She wants to get better. She vows to be good, to talk to her doctor, to obey hospital rules. She's been warned that the next time she's caught with drugs, the hospital will have to discharge her.

One day something goes drastically wrong with Edie. She blacks out, vomits, and has seizures. There are meetings and conferences. The doctors assume she's been using drugs, but Edie swears she wasn't. It doesn't matter what she says. They ship her off to Manhattan State, that hellhole in the East River. Life on the ward feels sadly ordinary without her.

There are rumors of other celebrities in our midst. Jane says she saw Robert Lowell on the fourth floor on his way to the outpatient program where a new experimental drug called Lithium is given to patients who are "manic-depressive." An illness of highs and lows, of deep feeling—a diagnosis befitting a poet.

Lowell isn't the only poet who was here. Allen Ginsberg and his friend Carl Solomon, whom he wrote about in *Howl*, were both here in the 1950s. Right here in these harrowing halls. And I'm here too, right at home among the nuts and bolts, fruits and vegetables, in the P.I. Freak Show and School of the Absurd.

PROCRUSTES IN
COCONUT GROVE/
THE BUDDHA/HIC PHAT!

*I*T'S REALLY TRUE THAT NOTHING MATTERS, *no mad mad world and no mad hat-ters, and no one pitchin' 'cause there ain't no batters . . . in Coconut Grove."* Ted strums his guitar, softly singing the Lovin' Spoonful's lyrics, lingering on the lazy syllables. As I listen to the melancholy tune, an overwhelming longing rises up within me. What am I longing for? Perhaps my freedom, a life in which I feel I belong. Some kind of reassurance that I am okay, not just an endless well of pain.

In our microcosmic community, we have something basic and undeniable in common: We all look directly into the well of suffering, while it seems the rest of the world is in denial. Everyone—parents, teachers, shrinks—is busily, stubbornly, callously determined to deny what those of us inside insist upon feeling. Why is it that we see what the others so easily ignore?

No matter how much they medicate us, we can't stop mulling over the same questions philosophers and theologians have pondered throughout the ages: Is there a soul? Life after death? Heaven and hell? What is the purpose of existence? Is life worth living? What is the nature of time?

The real question is, are we crazy, or visionary? Self-indulgent, or sensitive? Self-destructive, or philosophically inclined outcasts of a material-istic society?

Ted was a gifted student at one of the Ivy League colleges until he started gliding through his classes with arrogant insouciance. Required to write a term paper describing his idea of an urban utopia—the ideal city—Ted handed in a paper consisting of one sentence: "Surf City, where it's 2 to 1"—referring to the Beach Boys' lyric: *"Two girls for every boy . . . Surf City, here we come!"*

In the process of outsmarting himself, Ted slid out of school, down a mucky slope of family expectations and sanctions, finally landing on his butt in the living room of P.I.—at home among similar self-styled scholars, busily contemplating the insides of our brains.

One of the concepts in which Ted takes great delight is the "Procrustean bed." Procrustes, also known as The Stretcher, was a robber who roamed the woods, waylaying travelers whom he tied to an iron bedstead and tortured. If they were too short for the bed, he stretched them; if they were too long, he lopped off whatever parts hung over—limbs and other appendages—to fit the bed's dimensions.

When Ted first tells me about it—enthusiastically miming the chopping, slicing, and stretching from the point of view of both victim and tormenter—I immediately recognize how it applies to us. As we contort ourselves to our families' plans and needs, unsuccessfully suppressing those parts of ourselves that don't fit, whatever can't be eliminated becomes ingrown and infected. Unfortunately, whatever our parents most deny is unavoidably evident in us. Misshapen by the procrustean expectations and fears of our families, we now need to be cleansed and neutralized, through medication, boredom, renunciation, and removal from the world.

Despite the energy with which we fling blame at our families, it's hard to make it stick. Have they punished us too much or indulged us too much? Smothered us or withheld their love? Have their faults been grafted onto us? Or are we just bad seeds, damaged, dysfunctional, spoiled? Are our problems the fault of stubbornness, bad chemistry, or genetics? We have plenty of time to contemplate these questions. We aren't going anywhere.

"Be Here Now," Ram Dass instructs, but I don't think this is what he means.

———————

Richie is a practicing Zen Buddhist. The only problem is, he can't sit still. He's in a state of perpetual nervous reaction and has a dicey relationship with all things physical, beginning with his own body.

"Do I have B.O.?" he asks me five, ten, twenty times a day. "Do I smell bad? I'm very clean, I shower every day." He sniffs his armpit, cups his hand in front of his mouth and breathes. "I have bad breath! Please tell me, does my breath stink?" In spite of this annoying habit, Richie is endearing, and funny, with a vaudevillian physicality. He sits down, jumps up, paces, sits down, jumps up, talks in staccato bursts, laughs, and then . . . "Does my breath smell bad? Go on, you can tell me, I can take it!" He laughs, reddening. "But it's not my fault. The medication makes my mouth dry. Halitosis!"

Richie's last name is Kestenbaum. "That means 'nut-tree' in German!" he says, laughter shaking his thin frame. Self-denigrating, sweet, bright, and loving, he just cannot sit still. Yet his primary obsession is Buddhist sitting meditation, zazen. He sits three times a day for at least twenty minutes. He reads Buddhist texts and likes to recite zen koans.

"When I say I, who is the I who is asking?" Richie's thoughts assault him with a manic insistence. The only time Richie is quiet is when he's doing zazen. The rest of the time he's as neurotic and loony as can be. His stories are interrupted by fits of laughter, which are highly infectious. The two of us clutch our sides, jaws aching, tears streaming, until the nurse orders us to calm down.

Richie falls in love with one actress and model after another. "Do you think she might like me?" he asks, showing me his new love in a magazine ad or on TV. "I'm kinda cute, don't you think?" He pats his hand over his hair and sticks out his chin like Dudley Do-Right.

As a teenager, Richie almost died of a brain tumor. He has a soft spot on the side of his head from the surgery. "Here, feel," he says, guiding my fingers over the plastic tubing just beneath his skin. It's an eerie sensation: something missing, something extra. Someone who has come so close to death and survived is already partly enlightened, in my estimation. He's had a glimpse of the other side. And as uncomfortable as he seems to be on the physical plane, however anxious and itchy, Richie is glad to be alive. He is just aware enough of mortality to want to prepare himself.

Ted is reading the *Tibetan Book of the Dead*, the Evans-Wentz translation with the red and black cover. The book is tucked under his arm as he shuffles into the living room and settles into a chair next to one of the four dented, cylindrical, standing metal ashtrays—prime real estate.

Slipping into the chair next to his, I can see that he is unusually absorbed. His hair hangs low on his forehead, just over his glasses. His ever-swinging leg is crossed at the knees; a scuffed loafer hangs poised from the toe of his bare foot. He sits with his mouth slightly open, his cigarette, which has burned away unsmoked into a straight column of ash, held languorously in one hand. I pull my feet up under me so my chin rests on my knees and wait for the ash to fall, wondering whether surface tension is a concept that applies to solid matter as well as to liquid, and to people for that matter.

Ted flicks the ash into the large bowl of the ashtray, which at 10 A.M. already holds a dozen or more butts. He glances at me, smiles for a millisecond.

I crane my head toward his book. "What's that about?"

"Pretty wild stuff. It's an ancient Buddhist text that tells you what happens at the moment of death, when your soul leaves your body. Apparently there are these realms where demons come to taunt you and lure you into illusion, *samsara*. The *Book* tells you what to expect and gives you step-by-step instructions."

I consider this. Here I am in a place where everyone is obsessed with death—longing for it, courting it, yet at the same time fearing it. A rendezvous with *lethe*, eternal sleep, adds excitement to existence. It's the ultimate game of chicken. Having sought the kingdom of escape through drugs, alcohol, or sheer self-destruction, we've been locked up to protect us from ourselves. But what do we really know about our elusive love—is it just nothingness, the void, the cool darkness of oblivion? Is it a fiery pit? Or maybe a holding pen for confused souls . . . sort of like the hospital.

Death's emblems are everywhere, tattoos marking our tribe like the sign of Cain—scars on wrists and necks, burns and broken bones—wherever the attempt has been made to break the ties between spirit and body. My own attempts have been paltry; more the proverbial cry for help than anything serious. Yet I'm curious to know what awaits us. I certainly don't believe in heaven. Maybe it's more like the grotesque hell of Hieronymus Bosch, or the concentric rings of Dante's Inferno—perfect metaphors for life on earth. Or is it just oblivion, worms munching on our remains?

The hospital staff approaches everything on the physical level. Aside from talking about our turmoil with our shrinks a couple of times a week, our spiritual malaise is treated with pills, shots, and shocks. "Grandiose ideation," they say when they overhear us philosophizing.

Ted approaches me on the lunch line. Even slouching he towers over me. The *Book* is tucked under his arm.

"I learned something interesting. Evidently there are times when the soul doesn't want to leave the body, sort of refuses to let go. When that happens, the guide, an advanced monk, strikes the person sharply on the crown of the head and says the words 'Hic Phat!' Then the soul, taken by surprise, leaves the body through a space that opens above the third eye." Ted peers down at me. "You want to try it?"

I giggle. I know he's playing with me, but a little thrill of fear runs through me. What if it actually works? Then I hear a familiar rumbling— the sound of the lunch cart being wheeled off the elevator. On cue, everyone turns around. I turn to Ted. Oh, what the hell, why not?

Ted gathers three fingers of his right hand into a tight bunch and strikes the crown of my head sharply, loudly intoning the words "Hic Phat!" We wait a few seconds, but nothing happens. No chanting of elders or dematerialization. I'm still standing in the corridor waiting for the line to the lunch cart to start moving. I exhale, relieved. I guess it isn't my time; I'm just not ready to leave. But playing with death gives me a little thrill at being alive.

It becomes a joke between us, our code for "Let me out of here!"—a sort of morbid "When You Wish Upon a Star." As if wishing could make it so. When we pass in the hallway, we greet each other with a three-fingered salute and two breathy syllables.

"Hic Phat!" Our existential hiccup.

PROGRESS

3/5/69 Patient is trying very hard now. Last night the patients gave her a birthday party. Mindy appeared to be enjoying it very much. With all of her friends getting their own clothing back, maybe she will try harder. She's 17 now.

I
T'S FUNNY ABOUT DR. A. LEAVING, like having a tooth pulled; the fear of it is almost worse than the thing itself. When it's finally yanked out it hurts, but then it stops and you wonder what you were so afraid of.

When I meet my new, pleasantly ordinary-looking shrink, I'm relieved. He seems shy and has a funny way of slurring his S's. Starting new with Dr. R., even though he has a folder full of notes telling him how fucked up I am, I feel I have a new chance. When I talk to him, he listens and responds warmly, and even seems interested in what I say. He sits with me through my silences and smiles at my pun-ridden humor. When I say or do something outrageous he is just as embarrassed as I am, reddening and stuttering, lifting his shoulders in a stymied shrug. If I do something bad enough to make him disappointed or angry, I feel awful. When I act out and he threatens to take away my privileges, I can tell he feels bad about it.

Maybe because he's shy too, I feel that Dr. R. understands some of what's bothering me. When I tell him about the painful emotions I have listening to other people talk, feeling I have nothing of my own to contribute, Dr. R. tells me, "Being a good listener is a talent in itself." That little bit of support is a talisman I carry with me, a touchstone of self-worth. So much more than their drugs and restrictions, I need someone I can trust, who's nonjudgmental, on my side.

Finally I'm off E.O. It's a little weird hearing everyone congratulate me. It's not as if *I've* changed—my shrink just decided he could trust me enough to say it was okay. It's like I've been telling them all along—if they'd just leave me alone, everything would be fine.

I pull my clothes from the laundry bag they're stored in. My old sweatshirt with the holes chewed in the cuffs. T-shirts, flannel shirts, work shirt, army shirt, poor-boy sweater. My jeans! I bury my face in the denim and inhale its musty smell. But when I try them on, they're so tight I can't zip them. Between the inactivity, the starchy food, the birth-control pills, and the meds, I've gained forty pounds. The nurses notice too and tell my doctor, who writes an order to put me on a low-calorie diet.

Dr. R. says if I keep up the good behavior, I can have unaccompa-nied building privileges. "Whoop-de-do!" Ted says sarcastically when I tell him, then pulls his index finger from his mouth to make the sound of a popped cork and twirls his finger over his head. Now I can go to the vending machines all by my lonesome. No big deal, but when I go off the floor I realize how enclosed my world has become. The build-ing, with its pipes, accoustic tiles, and painted walls, depresses me. It makes mournful sounds, rumblings and grumblings, as if it's hungry, or lonely.

The ward has become a real world for me because of the people who live there. Seeing the rest of the building is like seeing the facade, or maybe the scaffolding, of our reality. It's an artificial construct: We're here because we're "sick." The doctors, nurses, attendants are here to cure us, and until they do we can't leave. *Sssssssstay* . . . That's the message that hisses through the air vents and hums through the pipes. *Sssssssstay* . . . *Insssside.* It's spooky enough to make my heart pound as I wait for the elevator to take me back to five, back to the illusion of our fake community.

Sometimes I get out on the main floor and stand there as if I'm wait-ing for someone, looking out the front door. I stand stone-still and let the forces play it out inside me. In or out? Stay or leave? Submit or rebel? Do what they say or make my own rules? It gives me a terrible feeling in the pit of my stomach. When I go back downstairs, I feel defeated and tired and have to lie down.

There are occasional brushes with normalcy, even in here. In the heat of the summer we take a trip to a local swimming pool; I get in quick and stay submerged as long as possible so nobody has a chance to see me in my suit. They let me stay up for late-night pizza parties on Friday nights—the ones I always used to miss because I was restricted. We order whole pies from the pizza place on Broadway (delivered to our representative waiting at the main entrance), gobble them up until nothing's left but the drips of cheese we scrape with our fingernails from the empty cardboard box, and wash it down with cold cans of Coke.

There are trips to a local movie theater that happens to show surprisingly good films: *Alfie, The Graduate,* and *Morgan*—the latter about a guy who can only feel good when he's dressed in a gorilla costume. Most of the films we see are about weirdos trying to find their way, or who don't quite fit in the world . . . like us.

I'm finally allowed to go to the picnics in Riverside Park. Marjee and I prepare buckets of egg salad and tuna salad, chopping bits of pickles and olives into the mix to spice it up. We're taken in groups down to the deserted Riverside Drive entrance, the bowels of the building inhabited by the hospital's laundry, food preparation, and maintenance crews. A warm wind from the highway rushes into the corridor when the door is unlocked, like air sucked into a vacuum.

In the park, the air is sweet with grass and pollen. Sunlight sparkles on the river. We unpack bags of food, unfurl sheets, and settle into groups. Jane, Laurie, Sly, and R.J. play bridge; a group forms around Luke and his guitar; Luis organizes a softball game. Later, when Marjee and Harold disappear into some tall grass, I wander off to explore the park. The fresh, fragrant air saddens me—though I'm out in it today, I'm just a visitor; it is air meant for others, not me. The hot sun glares in my eyes; I feel a headache coming on. I walk to the base of the George Washington Bridge. It's cool in the bridge's shadow. I place my hand on the massive piling into which the bridge is planted, look across its span, feel the bridge's power. It seems impossible that the structure can support its own weight across such a distance. I shiver and return to join the others, fill myself with tuna and mayo and egg.

In session, Dr. R. looks stern. "There are reports that on the picnic you went off on your own. There is some suspicion that you used drugs. Do you have anything to say?"

The openness I'd been feeling toward Dr. R. evaporates. No. I have nothing at all to say. It hurts that he, too doesn't trust me. He's just one of *them,* after all.

I don't give in easily. It's still up and down, round and round. But in general, the spiral seems to be pointing up.

In the fall, Dr. R. gives me the go-ahead for neighborhood walks. I'm reunited with the navy peacoat I bought at the army-navy surplus store. I run my hands over the soft, dense wool, admiring its utilitarian beauty. It's like a part of me I'd forgotten.

"Who wants to go for a walk?" Mrs. G. calls out. She stands, hands on hips, as if she's asking nobody in particular, then turns to look directly at me, a huge smile on her face. "I thought you might," she says when I raise my hand. "Go get your coat!"

Mrs. G. escorts Marjee, me, Eric, and Fred. My first steps outside are in slow motion, the ordinary street sounds and smells a weird déjà vu. The unfamiliar sensation of cool air on my face and hands wakes me up—unless I'm still dreaming. A few people walk down the street, mostly hospital employees, judging by their uniforms. Do they realize how lucky they are to be able to walk down the street powered by their own free will? I wonder if they can tell that we're patients. I feel like I might as well be wearing a ball and chain, my difference seems so obvious. If anyone looks at me, I look away.

We walk two blocks to the Shangri-La Diner, where we crowd into a booth. On the table is a metal bowl filled with pickles, which we almost polish off before the waiter comes. The sting of salt and garlic brings a rush of saliva, waking up my taste buds. Everything on the table looks like an old friend—the Heinz ketchup bottle, the paper placemats with the map of Greece. The air has that great greasy, steamy smell of coffee and hamburgers. The clanking clatter of dishes and talk brings unexpected tears to my eyes. Ice-cold glasses of water. Hot cups of coffee. Heaven.

"Seven times seven," Fred says, going off on his own wavelength, starting with his prophesies again.

"Calm down, Fred. Or do you want everyone to go back?" Mrs. G. says.

"I'm just getting ready for the end of the world. All right, all right, I'll be quiet." Fred says, and mostly keeps his word.

When the waiter comes over, I watch him carefully. Does he know where we're from? Mrs. G., her white uniform sticking out from her coat, is a dead giveaway. But the waiter is friendly, and I can't detect anything unusual in his eyes.

I never thought a hamburger and chocolate egg cream could taste so good.

We order coffee and sandwiches with extra pickles to bring back for those unfortunates who aren't privileged enough to go outside. I never imagined walking a few blocks would feel like a privilege, but it does. Then the bland blond building at the end of 168th Street draws us to it like a magnet, and our temporary powers of locomotion evaporate as we descend in the elevator.

The very fact that I'm being "granted" privileges says that these are things I've been denied all along. I'm not sure whether I want to lick or bite the hand that's offered me the treat.

My next walk is with a group that includes Marjee, Harold, Bobby, Eric, Jane, Alyssa, and Nick. Just as we're heading down the front steps, I suddenly see . . . *my mother.* I can't imagine what she's doing here at four in the afternoon, when she's usually at work.

"Min?" My mother's mouth forms the shape of my name as she walks toward me. She looks just as surprised as I am. I freeze. It's been so long since I've seen her. I don't know how I feel about her, and I don't want to interact with her now, especially in front of my friends. So I do the easiest thing. I turn away and pretend I didn't see her.

I rationalize it by telling myself that I was too surprised to react, but I don't feel good about walking away like that, and become so depressed that I ask for a special session with Dr. R. He asks me if I'd like to start visiting with my mother again. I say yes, provided it's without my stepfather. When my mother comes to see me, she reaches across the dining room table to tell me she's proud of how well I'm doing.

After several visits, Dr. R. asks me if I'd like to go on an outside pass with my mother. We could spend an afternoon together. Since I've grown out of my clothes, my mother suggests lunch and a shopping trip. We do it, and I even survive the multiple reflections of myself in the dressing room mirrors. But we have a tense moment when my mother asks me about what I want to do with my future.

Dr. R. has been talking with me about the future. I should be graduating from high school as soon as I have enough credits—probably sometime in the fall or winter. I was worried about graduating from Loony Bin High, but it turns out I'll be getting my diploma from George

Washington High School. It's not the same as getting a diploma from Music and Art, but as stigmas go, it could be worse. I tell Dr. R. I'd like to get a summer job outside the hospital. He says he'll bring in up in Rounds. If I continue to do well, he says, perhaps we can start looking for an outside residence in the fall.

For the first time in a long, long while, I feel a ray of hope.

For a long time we've been complaining that there's no library on our ward. In response, the O.T. department organizes a bookshelf-building project. A group of us design, measure, saw, sand, hammer, and nail a floor-to-ceiling bookcase for the North living room—a day-long project. We order in sandwiches and soda, draw diagrams, wipe our sweaty brows, suck bruised thumbs, bicker, laugh, and lose ourselves in work . . . and the satisfaction of seeing the finished product, built by our own hands. It's better therapy than years of sessions and meds.

Mrs. Gould organizes trips to plays and concerts. We see *Man of La Mancha* on Broadway and hear Nina Simone perform at Lincoln Center. From our seats way up in the balcony, Nina Simone looks tiny and remote, but her big voice fills the hall as she moans, trills, and shouts her way through songs like "Mississippi Goddam!" and "I Wish I Knew How It Would Feel to Be Free." I feel every word.

One day Mrs. Gould announces that she has an opportunity to get tickets to a cabaret show called *Jacques Brel Is Alive and Well and Living in Paris* at the Village Gate. She asks for a show of hands. I hesitate. I'm afraid this will be some uncool event, some superficial, foolish pop music. But everybody's going and I don't want to be left behind, so I raise my hand.

On the ride downtown, we have most of the subway car to ourselves. Across from me is Bobby, looking very neat and brushed. Harold's next to him, then Noel, Fred, and Eric. It's a long ride from Washington Heights to the Village. We've been sitting a long while when a matronly looking woman gets up and walks over to Bobby. Uh, oh. What now?

The woman says to Bobby, "Excuse me, I've been watching you, and I must tell you what a well-behaved young man you are. I just wanted to compliment you on your behavior." Without a word, Bobby reaches into his jacket pocket, pulls out a pack of cigarettes, takes one out and puts it in his ear, so the cigarette sticks straight out from the side of his head. He folds his hands in his lap, looks straight ahead . . . and stays like that for the rest of the trip. The attendant accompanying us is aghast, but Mrs. Gould shakes with laughter. It embarrasses me, though. Why advertise the fact that we're crazy? Whenever we have a group excursion, I always half expect some version of the scene in *David and Lisa* when a jeering crowd taunts the group of mental patients in the neighborhood railway station, shouting over and over, "Bunch of screwballs, spoiling the town!"

I try to look unimpressed and ultracool as our group is ushered into the smoky, semidark room past rows of couples sitting knee to knee, talking intimately over drinks. Oh, to not be part of a group! We're seated at a long row of tables and order drinks; no alcohol, of course, so I order a ginger ale. As the overture begins, spotlights illuminate a small, formally dressed ensemble. Oh, brother, I think. This is going to be terrible.

At first I don't know what to make of it. The sound of the performers' voices ringing out in the intimate cabaret startles and embarrasses me. But the lyrics are amazing. Goose bumps rise on my skin as I listen to a ballad, "The Desperate Ones":

> *Just like the tiptoe moth they dance before the flame*
> *They've burned their hearts so much that death is just a name. . . .*
> *They watch their dreams go down behind the setting sun*
> *They walk without a sound. The Desperate Ones.*

When the song is finished, the room is quiet for a minute before applause breaks out and the band launches into a rollicking number. I hardly hear it; my heart still aches from the last song. Jacques Brel knows us, speaks for us, maybe even is one of us. We exist in his songs, and people are moved, and applaud. My eyes fill with tears, and even though I clench my jaw hard, they spill down my cheeks.

The program ends with an anthem of peace: *"If we only had love, we'd destroy all the bombs, and we'd build a new world for our daughters and sons . . ."* It's the same message everywhere these days: peace and love, truth and beauty. These are the important things. Everything else is just greed, materialism, and people trying to control you.

One by one, my friends are leaving. Discharged or permanently eloped, one way or another they leave, and I am still here. At seventeen years old I've become a career mental patient.

Nick elopes and doesn't return, and life on the ward feels empty without him. For a while I become a resistant lump, retreating into myself. Then I notice something else: The tension I feel in his presence has gone with him. In its place, an opening. A new space in which I can focus more on different people, instead of living in fear of, and desire for, the attention of one.

Alyssa is discharged soon after; strangely enough, I miss her.

Ted left months ago. For a while he spent time out of the hospital on weekend passes. Then he got a job and was here only at night. Finally, he was discharged. He came back to visit the ward a few times, then that stopped too.

When Bobby returned to the ward after his time on the seventh floor, he seemed subdued, more grown-up. He says he's decided to get well and get out of here. If the summer goes well, they're planning to discharge him in September.

Now everything is changing very quickly.

Jane's doctor feels she's ready to be released from the hospital, but it's up to Loathsome Lothar to judge whether or not that's true. They schedule Jane's discharge conference. She'll appear before Gidro-Frank and a panel of residents, and if she answers their questions to their satisfaction, they'll let her go.

Before the conference Jane is worried. Her fate is entirely in the hands of a roomful of male psychiatrists. If she looks too nervous or says something they don't like, they can decide not to let her go. Jane is more than ready to leave. She's been working at a job outside the hospital and plans to share an apartment with Anne, who was recently released. After forty-five minutes the living room door opens to let Jane out. When the door opens fifteen minutes later, the doctors are smiling.

Jane promises she'll write. "Just do what they tell you and maybe you'll get out of here soon," she says when she hugs me good-bye. "I will," I tell her, but I'm not sure I can. I'm too accustomed to misbehaving.

Harold really wants to get out of here too, and he has a plan. He picks a fight with Jack outside the room where the doctors are having Grand Rounds—a down and dirty fistfight so conspicuously loud that the door bursts open and the doctors themselves break it up. A few days later Harold is shipped to Harlem Valley.

"Don't worry, babe," Harold consoles Marjee. "The state hospitals don't keep you for long unless you're really whacked out." It may be a few hellish months living with hard-boiled loonies, but after that they'll release him. Otherwise, P.I. might keep him forever. He's been here over a year and has eloped thirteen times in as many months. As he predicted, Harold is released from Harlem Valley after three months—during which he learns how to defend himself against the hard-core criminals there on temporary vacation from Matawan prison.

Marjee cries buckets when Harold goes. They promise to write letters every day, and even when their correspondence dwindles to twice a week, it keeps her going. She stays off observation and gets neighborhood privileges. But lately we've been drifting apart. Marjee's gotten very friendly with Hillary, a former fashion model who's into the avant-garde art scene. Hillary, with her porcelain skin and expertly made-up pale blue eyes, wears silk kimonos splashed with vivid reds and purples, a matching sash tied around her head. Marjee starts wearing one too. Marjee's like a chameleon. When she hangs out with Hillary, she's cool and glamorous. With Jane, she's intellectual. When she hangs out with me, she's her old creative self.

Marjee has a series of involvements. Among the new patients are several guys she deems cute enough to date. Blond, blue-eyed, blue-collar Dave flipped out after some bad acid, but after a while on the ward he calms down enough to go back to work at the Post Office. He's good-hearted, but when Marjee realizes he's not exactly up to her standards of intelligence, she's bored enough to break up with him. This doesn't break his heart, because another patient already has her eye on him.

Next Marjee gets involved with Rodney, who is bearded, mustached, sardonic . . . and ten years older than she is. I dislike him intensely, but to Marjee, he's sexy. I can think of an O-word for him: obnoxious. I can't bear the thought of his slimy hands on Marjee's beautiful body.

Marjee attracts guys like flies. Who can blame them? She's beautiful. Her only problem is she thinks she's too fat. She constantly asks me about it. But what would be ugly bulk on me is curvaceous beauty on Marjee. I get exasperated. Can't she see what she's got?

Marjee puts up a cool exterior, but her feelings are easily hurt. She can be cuddly and affectionate one minute and coolly self-possessed the next. But so often at the end of the day she comes back to the dorm with tears dripping from panic-stricken eyes. "I humiliated myself," she sobs, confessing that she'd bragged or said something stupid. "How can I show my face again?" But in the morning, after putting on lipstick and eyeliner and scrutinizing herself in the mirror, she presents herself, wide-eyed and smiling, and asks, "How do I look?" And I assure her, as always, that she looks fine, not fat at all, just perfectly beautiful.

June approaches. Time for the change of doctors again. The new residents tour the ward and we check them out. Whispers and gossip fly: Who's cute or ugly, sexy or square, intelligent or dense, kind or mean, who has the nicest eyes.

Dr. R. tells me that since we work well together, and as he'll be staying on at P.I. for the last year of his residency, he has been granted permission to keep me on as his patient. I'm so embarrassed it's days before I can talk to him. Finally, three sessions later, when he asks me why I'm so embarrassed, I stammer, hot-cheeked, looking at the floor, that I'm embarrassed because the fact that he's keeping me as his patient must mean he likes me a lot.

What I can't tell him is that in a funny way I'm also disappointed. It could be exciting to have a new doctor. Some of the new residents are really nice-looking. I've already picked one out. He's tall, dark-haired, and intelligent-looking, with soulful brown eyes. Once, passing through Center, he smiled at me and my heart jumped.

The change of doctors is especially hard on Marjee. It's only three months since Harold left, and now Dr. G. is leaving. Marjee's gotten very attached to him. When he tells her she'll be getting a new psychiatrist, it's the last straw. "I can't do this anymore," she says. She's been crying; her eyes and nose are red. "I think it's time for me to split."

Even though her new shrink looks nice, she can't go through it again. She just doesn't want to deal with the whole getting-to-know-you thing. Repeating the same stories, winning him over, getting to trust him and vice versa. I ask where she'll go. She says she could move in with Rodney, who was recently released and has a great apartment in Greenwich Village where she can stay rent-free until she finds a job. This time, she says, she's not coming back.

"Come with me," she says. But I can't say yes. By now I've run away half a dozen times and have never managed to stay out even a week. I would just be a drag, another problem for her to deal with. I tell her she'd be better off on her own.

"You can always come later. I'll write to you." Marjee reaches for my hand. "Will you help me?"

I'm in a muddle. I don't really want to help Marjee escape, because I don't want her to leave me here alone. But I feel honor-bound to help her. If I don't help, what kind of friend am I?

We devise a plan—I'll create a diversion so the staff won't see her get on the elevator. And I help her another way, so she doesn't have to move in with Rodney. I call my friend Larry, who now shares a friend's apartment on the Upper West Side. Larry met Marjee when he visited me. As soon as he met her, he was bowled over. Larry says he'd be happy for Marjee to come live with him. "She's the most beautiful girl I've ever seen," he says on the phone. I try not to be jealous.

Eleven days after the change of psychiatrists, Marjee is gone.

Marjee's departure feels like the turn of a page. One less person who knows me. One less reason to be here. A little chink in the walls of my prison. An unspoken challenge. Change.

Summer of '69. We feel the pulse of what's happening outside—the heat, the excitement, the music. A kind of external telepathy broadcasts what's happening in the world, bringing it to us.

We crowd into the living room to watch the moon-launch broadcast on television. It's perfect: a roomful of lunatics, lost in space at the edge of the universe, watching Neil Armstrong bounce weightless off the surface of the moon. At midnight, just after we hear the famous line: "One small step for man, one giant leap for mankind," the attendant snaps the TV off. I, too, want so much to make that leap out into the unknown. But the gravitational pull of this place is strong.

We watch Woodstock on the news. I get glimpses of ecstatic, tripped-out faces, kids in body paint dancing with abandon, sleeping happily in the mud. My entire generation is showing up for this event, and here I sit.

I thought my negativism was a kind of beatnik-cool, that optimism was for squares, that being in the hospital was a statement, like dropping out. But there's a new energy in the world, a creativity and freedom that I'm just too frightened to join, and I'm miserable to be missing it.

I get postcards and letters from Marjee and Jane. They're both doing well. Jane is sharing an apartment, working, and having a good time. Marjee and Larry move from his uptown apartment into Hillary's empty Soho loft. Marjee calls to tell me she's doing great. Larry's really good to her, and she has a waitressing job in a fancy ice-cream parlor called The Flick.

Each time I hear from Jane or Marjee, they tell me they miss me and worry about me. There's always a lump in my throat when I tell them I'm fine. I feel deserted, like a lone shipwreck survivor stranded on an island. I try to be happy for them, but I'm filled with envy. Phone privileges, weekend passes, and neighborhood walks are a far cry from having a real life. As usual, Simon and Garfunkel put my feelings to music: *"I know I'm fakin' it . . . not really makin' it."*

But it also gives me hope. If Jane and Marjee can stay out and live on their own, maybe I can too.

PARTING SHOTS

I'M SORRY TO HAVE TO TELL YOU THIS, but I will be leaving P.I. next week."
I stare at Dr. R., but in place of his eyes I just see the fluorescents reflected in his eyeglasses. His forehead is shiny with sweat. On this hot July day everything is a little distorted anyway, a little too still. His words fall flat in front of me, and lay there.

I sigh. What else can I do? Even so I feel my fists clench. It's exactly what happened a year ago. After all this time, all this talk, it's the same thing all over again. Why don't they just tell me what they mean at the beginning, instead of telling me one thing and then another.

"We still have a week to work together, during which I'll also be meeting with your new doctor—Dr. S. Perhaps you've seen him on the ward." Dr. S. is the handsome, sad-eyed resident who'd smiled at me in Center. I guess I have to be careful what I wish for.

I ask if I'll still be able to find a job outside the hospital.

"Yes, certainly, if you continue as you have been. But that will be up to your new doctor." Always, it's up to someone else. I resent being passed from hand to hand, like a *thing*.

I ask where he'll be going.

"I've taken a job at another hospital. I'll be working with young children."

I envy those children. They get to have the benefit of Dr. R.'s care and concern, his shy abashed gentleness. Lucky them. I guess I was lucky to have him for a while.

7/17/69 Patient seen for the first time. She was distant and tended to look at the desktop except for occasional glances at me as if to see what I was feeling. She expressed some guilt about having wished I was her therapist before Dr. R. told her he was leaving but was unable to express any other feelings about his leaving. Because her past history involves elopements and self-destructive behavior after her previous therapist told her he was leaving, patient has been restricted to the ward and placed on E.O. When she begged to be taken off observation and out of pajamas, I explained to her that she would remain on E.O. until I feel she is better able to deal with her losses.

—Dr. S.

I hate having to begin seeing my new shrink wearing pajamas. It's bad enough to have to start with someone new, but it's even worse to have him see me in these ugly damn things. I hate them. I hate him. I should have run away for good a long time ago.

The worst part of this whole thing is having my privileges taken away—not because of something I've done now, but because of what happened last year when Dr. A. left. Just because I ran away and drank grout sealer a year ago doesn't mean I'm going to do it again. If they're going to judge me by my past actions, they might as well just throw away the key.

This time, I'm being restricted for someone else's mistake. I didn't ask Dr. R. to say he was keeping me and then decide to leave—but I'm the one who winds up back in pajamas.

Before he left, Dr. R. told me to be patient, but he doesn't know what it's like to be stuck here, and summer is the hardest time. I was hoping I could get a summer job and start planning for outside school. But now it's all on hold. It's as if I've made no progress at all.

When my mother comes to visit, I'm afraid she'll be disappointed because I'm back in pajamas. Instead she tells me she won't be seeing me for the next few weeks because she's going on vacation. She's had this planned for weeks. I resent that nobody told me until now. Did they think I couldn't handle it?

8/11/69 Patient made a 1-inch superficial cut on her leg with a razor blade this evening. She was seen immediately afterward. She was tearful but reticent to talk about why she did it. The immediate precipitant was a male patient asking her to go away. After elaborating on other rejections of the past few weeks and months, she expressed her anger at me for keeping her on E.O. We then turned to her mother's going on vacation. Attempts to elicit her anger and feelings about the mother's departure were unsuccessful. Patient denied suicidal intention and does not seem so at present. However, I will place her on S.O. as a precaution.

—Dr. S.

Now I really feel like the Incredible Shrinking Patient. Back on S.O. Restricted. In pajamas. As if that's not enough, I have to play getting-to-know-you with this new shrink. Cutting myself didn't even make me feel better; it just felt like going through the motions.

Dr. S. keeps bugging me to talk to him. He says I have to talk in order to "get better" and to get my privileges back. That's bribery! I'll talk when I feel like talking. Does he think relationships are so arbitrary that you can will them into being instead of just letting them happen? I tell him I'll talk to him when I get my clothes back.

Besides, why should I have to state the obvious? I'm sure he already knows what's going on with me. He should know, if he's at all sensitive. If not, what kind of psychiatrist is he?

One thing I liked about Dr. R. was that if I didn't want to talk about something, he didn't push me. But this new one is pushy. Sometimes in sessions the pressure gets so intense that I make up things to tell him, just to get him off my back. When he asks why I wear my pajama sleeves hanging down over my hands, I pull them up to show him my clenched fists. I wear short sleeves to our next session, and that seems to make him happy.

He keeps bugging me about how I feel about Dr. R. leaving, when all I want to do is get over it, get my clothes back, get a job, and get out of here. It's infuriating. I'm trying to be strong, but he wants me to open a vein so he can see the crazy stuff inside me—the things I'm struggling to leave behind.

Each time I get a phone call or letter from Marjee, she's living somewhere else. First she leaves Larry—she says she fell out of love with him because he was too possessive. Then she moves in with Rodney in the Village, gets a fake ID and goes from waitressing at The Flick to working as a barmaid, which she likes much better. ("The uniform's sexier, and the tips are great.") After Hillary is discharged from P.I., Marjee ditches Rodney ("He turned out to be a real pain") and moves in with Hillary in her Soho loft. Hillary, a real jet-setter, is thinking of spending the winter in the Caribbean and asks Marjee to come with her. I prickle with envy.

One day I'm handed an envelope addressed in red felt-tip pen. The envelope is a work of art, with an enormous 5 in the lower-left corner, and the stamp on upside down (a sixties protest thing). The postmark is from the Virgin Islands. The letter is filled with news, illustrated by Marjee's drawings of ocean waves, palm trees and cactus, chickens and sea urchins. She's sharing an apartment with Hillary in St. John, Marjee writes, and she's waitressing and going to school. Not bad for a sixteen-year-old. I flick away a tear that splatters on the page, blurring the red ink. I hate myself for staying on at P.I., for being so weak and unsure of myself, so fearful of life.

———————

At some point I make up my mind that I will survive this place and move on. Maybe because my eighteenth birthday is in sight, my freedom seems less remote. Maybe because I've seen too many people come and go, I feel the time approaching for me to take my own place outside. I keep a low profile, go to school and activities, take my meds. The higher powers lower my dosage and give me neighborhood privileges.

By now I'm an old-timer. The nurses call on me to show the new patients the ropes. I don't mind helping out, especially if I can help someone feel less scared, but I also feel like a hypocrite. Who am I to reassure them?

In response to my complaint of boredom, the social worker offers me a volunteer job within the hospital complex. I could work in the library, but the job is mostly filing, and I don't like clerical work. I agree to a job accompanying schoolchildren on tours of a medical research facility. I'm excited and nervous. What if I'm too shy to relate to the children I'll be escorting? What if they're more confident than I am and sense something's wrong with me?

The interview goes well. Afterward, a technician shows me the lab. There, stacked against the walls, are cages filled with mice and rats of different sizes and colors. Then—my heart freezes—I see cages of cats, piled one on another, floor to ceiling. And these are not normal cats; they are missing the tops of their heads, onto which some kind of machines have been affixed. The cats are meowing, and their eyes don't look right. Some crouch open-mouthed and drooling; others lay motionless.

I have a cat at home; my germ-o-phobic mother finally allowed me a pet when I was fourteen in a desperate effort to normalize me. But a cat with a machine on its head? This is not what a cat is supposed to look like, or be. An alien thing confined in a cage. Isn't this what they're trying to do to us? Replace our ability to think for ourselves with an external attachment that regulates our actions? A staring cat seems to catch me in its blank gaze, drool dripping from its open mouth. I know that look. I've seen it often on the ward.

The technician places his hand on my arm and asks if I'm feeling okay. Yes, I tell him. I'm determined to stick with it.

The following Tuesday I arrive early so they can prepare me for my first batch of kids. When they arrive, I'm relieved. I like them and they seem to like me, clustering around with their braids, braces, lunch boxes, and questions.

In the morning we tour the lab and watch a film about medical research. After lunch we are to witness a dissection. The technician wheels in a cart with a large something lying on top, covered by a sheet. A strong chemical smell fills the room. He pulls back the sheet to reveal a big black dog, lying on his side. It's a black Lab. He is beautiful, but so still. I want to see him wriggle onto his belly, get up, run around. The technician pulls back a paw to show the degree of rigor mortis, then points out the location of the organs, and, after tracing a line on the dog's belly with his finger, picks up a scalpel and begins to cut. The children watch, their eyes large. They're doing better than I am. It's too much for me: the big black dog, the smell, the stillness. A wave of nausea takes me. "Excuse me," I mumble, and run from the room. I never go back.

"Are you sure?" the staff asks, then tells me it's okay. To me it was a cruel exercise. How could they have sent me there, where I was sure to fail?

———

The social worker finds me a job as a cashier in a midtown art-supply store. As I hurry through the autumn morning wearing stockings and a skirt, the air is chilly against my legs. The sounds, sights, and smells of outside are extraordinarily vivid, almost surreal. They assault my senses, too long accustomed to blandness. Walking east on 46th Street in the early morning, I rush past large plastic bags of restaurant trash, holding my breath but gagging anyway on the stench of rotted food. The locked facades of restaurants seem to be sleeping off last night's debauch. But even reeking of garbage, the air is filled with new possibility.

The store manager explains the routine patiently and doesn't get upset if I make a mistake. I learn to work the cash register, but I am slow, and I feel shy and muddled when I talk to customers. The job is repetitive and boring. It's hard to stay awake.

When I'm not at the register, I straighten the merchandise and dust the shelves. I run a feather duster lovingly over the tubes of oil paints, watercolors, boxes of pastels and colored pencils, brushes of all shapes and sizes. I love being near artists' materials, and long to be using them. If only I felt confident enough to be an artist. Art is the antidote to meaninglessness, the medicine that will save me. I only have to wait until I have the courage to become an artist, until I have something to say.

At lunchtime, I eat my sandwich sitting on a stool by the cash register. I look out at the surging traffic, wondering if I will ever feel like part of the busy crowd—or if I really want to. At twilight I take the subway back to the hospital, where the walls suddenly feel less solid and opaque. It's a strange sensation. Neither world, inside or out, is quite real.

Moods come over me from out of nowhere. I'm suddenly swept up in waves of despair, then feel old and weary, as if I've survived a war. And I have. I can't help thinking of my friends: Liz, Rocky, Tina. I haven't forgotten them. I can't, I won't forget.

I continue my daily traverse between the hospital and the outside world. On the subway when panic threatens to engulf me, I sing a prayer of my own, to the tune of the Beatles' "Let It Be": *"Give us God, give us love, give us peace and give us hope. Take away all fear. Give us love."*

One morning, the store manager takes me aside to tell me that business is too slow to afford to keep me on, and wishes me luck. I'm paranoid that he's lying to let me off easy, but his eyes are clear and kind. After that my mother comes up with a new job: a clerk in a variety store in the Empire State Building. Every morning I navigate the surging masses on 34th Street. I hate this job, the junky merchandise, and the low-level mentality of the personnel, who seem just as institutionalized in their work as the patients at P.I. Must I always be trapped among the downtrodden? At lunchtime it's a toss-up between wanting to escape the claustrophobic dreariness of the store and dealing with the anxiety of going out into the crowded streets. I am carrying so much grief that the slightest thing can tip the bucket. I panic in the crowds on 34th Street and don't return to work.

For a while they've been letting me go home on weekend passes. It's like being in the hospital, only at my mother's apartment. I can't go out without permission and have to be on best behavior. There's my stepfather to put up with, with his lectures and fake affection, and my mother telling me what to wear, what to eat, when to wash my face. After a few hours I start to feel like my inner self is being eradicated, absorbed into the Muzak drenched upholstery.

In January I graduate from high school. Mrs. Gould hands me my diploma from George Washington High and hugs me tight. My eyes brim as I leave her classroom, now filled with students I don't recognize. Mrs. Gould sometimes talks about the terror an artist or writer feels when facing a blank canvas or page. I know that terror. It's how I feel about my life.

The days on the ward are long. Dr. S. agrees to let me get a full-time job outside the hospital. The idea of going out into the regular world is exciting, and a little scary. What if somebody asks me where I live? I'll have to pretend I have a normal life.

Soon I'll be eighteen—of legal age. Old enough to drink, to drive, to be called an adult. I wait to find out what the doctors plan to do with me.

Dr. S. won't let me apply for a residence until I have a steady job. Since the art-supply store and the variety store, it's been one big zero. I'm not sure I want to go through it again.

My mother takes matters into her own hands and finds me a job at a midtown boutique. The owner of the store is gruff and gives me busy-work like dusting the shelves and folding blouses. I'm no good with the customers—too shy and nervous—but the other girls help me out. I get up in the mornings and take the subway to the stop near Bloomingdale's, and surface in the heart of my mother's world—the world of shopping. It all seems so meaningless.

The hospital and I are in a stalemate. They want me to sign myself in voluntarily when I turn eighteen. I can't believe they're serious. After waiting so long to get out of here, I'm not about to stay. It will just be a transitional period, they say, just a matter of weeks until they find me a residence. I'll continue working outside and going out on passes. As if I have a choice. Once I'm eighteen, I'll be a "voluntary" patient. What would happen if I insisted on leaving? I know the answer—I've seen it happen too many times. If they don't want you to go, forget it. It just takes the signatures of two psychiatrists to keep you here against your will.

> 3/28/70 Patient has begun a relationship with a patient who is a former addict and a marked psychopath. In sessions she has been angry and secretive—so that it is difficult to know what is going on. Part of the problem is her indefinite plans for the future and the counterphobic way she handles it by saying she hates the hospital and me. In family session her mother has tried to be unintrusive and for the most part is managing well, but Mindy's recent boyfriend and her vague way of talking about him have gotten to the mother, and she has become angry and guilty.

Dan is half Puerto Rican and half Spanish, twenty-two, and very handsome. His skin is the color of light coffee, and he has the most beautiful eyes. It's funny how a stranger you hardly notice can suddenly become an important person in your life. When I come back to the ward after work it's Dan I look forward to seeing. We sit in the living room and talk. Just the sound of his voice relaxes me.

Dan was at the top of his class at Dartmouth for the three years he was there, until he decided to drop out. "You can't imagine what it was like to be the only Spic in a white-bread college." As a fucked-up mental patient who doesn't fit in anywhere, I can imagine very well.

People misunderstand Dan. Because he's Puerto Rican, they assume he's some kind of criminal. This just makes me love him more. I love his cinnamon skin and his dark, liquidy eyes. I love his strong hands and velvet touch, the way he lifts my chin and looks me in the eyes when we kiss. He melts me.

Dan is discharged, but we continue to see each other when I'm out on weekend passes. When Dan comes over to visit, my mother, in spite of herself, is impressed by his charm, good looks, and perfect manners. Who could resist him? She's even a bit flirtatious. One night when he says good-bye to my mother, she kisses him full on the lips. Dan looks amused, but I am not.

Can't I have anything of my own? Must she be in the center of everything?

Things are getting serious between me and Dan. But of course my shrink doesn't want me to be spending time with him, on account of his drug use. Dr. S. pokes and prods me about using drugs. Now they suspect that I'm some kind of junkie, just because I'm hanging out with Dan. Let them believe what they want!

"Marry me," Dan says. "I'll take care of you." I shiver at the touch of his hands on my bare arms. His kisses fill me with fear and desire. I have to admit we look good together, brown on blond. I bet we'd have beautiful babies.

I tell my mother that Dan asked me to marry him and I'm immediately sorry I did. Of course she tells Dr. S., who brings it up in our next session.

"You realize that Dan is a heroin addict. . . ."

"*Former* heroin addict, in case you've forgotten. All he does is some grass and a little coke occasionally. I've done it with him. It hasn't hurt me, or turned me into a heroin addict."

"So you admit you've done drugs with him. How am I to believe you aren't doing more?"

"Because I'm telling you!" He expects me to do what he says but doesn't trust that I'm telling the truth. Why should I listen to him? I'm over eighteen—an adult. I can do what I want. Legally, he has no control over me. I pull my eyes away from his and stare at the wall.

"As a matter of fact, I noticed as soon as you sat down that your eyes are red and glassy. Have you been taking drugs?"

I laugh in his face. If I was on drugs, does he imagine I'd say yes? Yet when I tell him no, he doesn't believe me. He ought to know there are other things aside from drugs that turn eyes red.

Dr. S. says he'll bring it up in Grand Rounds and see what Dr. Gidro-Frank has to say. I don't give a shit what that towering cadaver has to say. I've had enough of these men controlling my life. I shut my mouth and don't say another word for the rest of the session.

Later that afternoon Dr. S. takes me aside. "It's been decided that the situation with Dan puts you too much at risk. Dr. Gidro-Frank agrees that for your own good you are to be restricted from seeing him. Unfortunately this means that for the time being your outside privileges are suspended."

"Fine." I turn on my heel and walk away. Back in the dorm, after I stop crying, I put on a sweater, blow my nose, and try to figure out what to do. When the dinner bell rings, I walk slowly down the hall toward Center. Patients are lined up, as usual, placing silverware on their trays, waiting to be dished out the daily dose of sustenance. I only know a few of them. It suddenly hits me—I've been here far too long. I never want to line up for another meal, another dose, another activity. I casually push the elevator button—nobody seems to notice—and when it opens, I get in and say, "Ten, please," in a firm voice. I watch the elevator door close and try to breathe normally. The elevator operator knows me by now, anyway.

I cross the lobby and am at the front door when the guard stops me. They must have phoned from downstairs. "Where do you think you're going?" The guard puts his beefy body between me and the door. I try to sidestep him, but he grabs my arm.

"Let go of me!" I yell. I try to twist away but can't. He's stronger than me. They're always stronger than me, damn them!

I sit on the table in front of the staircase door, back in pajamas once again. The nurse orders me to get off the table.

"Why? I'm just sitting here." As far as I know there's no law against sitting on a table.

"Because it's *inappropriate. . . ."*—my favorite word—"Go sit in a chair." I ignore her.

She walks away and returns with R.J. I don't move, except to swing my legs a little faster. R.J. hitches up his pants and walks toward me. I jump off the table. Too late. R.J. tackles me with his full weight and drags me to the Quiet Room, where in spite of my tearful pleading they restrain me, shoot me full of sodium amytal (a cousin of Sodium Pentothal), and lock the door. Every few hours they come in to take me to the bathroom or give me another shot. Time shuts down. It's at least twenty-four hours before they release me from seclusion and break the news: *They're shipping me to Manhattan State.* Without letting me speak to anyone, they dump my belongings into a laundry bag and send me to the seventh floor, still out of it from the drugs they pumped into me.

When they tell me where they're sending me I try not to cry. But it's impossible. I sob like a child. How could they do this? They talked me into staying here past my eighteenth birthday, and now they're shipping me! So much for their wanting to help me. So much for my efforts, their promises, their concern for my welfare.

This is the final insult, the ultimate betrayal. It's as if the hospital has to have the last word; if they've been unsuccessful at "treating" me, they can at least show me who's boss.

4/9/70 Patient discharged to Manhattan State Hospital. Diagnosis: Chronic Undifferentiated Schizophrenia 295.20. Condition: Improved.

———————

Manhattan State Hospital is a warehouse for lost souls located on an island in the middle of the East River. From the Queens side of the Triborough Bridge approach ramp, you can see the sun shining clear through the windows, not a moving body in sight. The other structures on Ward's Island house prison wards for the criminally insane. Criminals on one side; long-term, hopeless cases on the other. The whole island is a prison, just like the TV show. As the hospital car crosses the bridge, I'm filled with dread. What will happen to me now?

The intake interview would be humorous if it wasn't so terrifying. The East Indian doctor who examines me has a comically incomprehensible accent. "What is your name? Do you know what day it is? What year?" His questions echo those I was asked as I emerged from fever more than two years ago. "Do you hear voices?" Yes, I want to say . . . yours! But I know my freedom is seriously at stake. The doctor will not listen to my request to be released.

"The doctors at the other hospital have sent you here. There must be some reason, yes?" If I do not sign myself in voluntarily, he will get two psychiatrists to commit me.

The ward stinks of urine and unwashed flesh. At night I lie awake on a cot listening to the snores, snorts, sighs, whistling breath, and night terrors of the thirty women I share the dorm with. The staff is uncompromising—I witness an attendant cruelly shove an elderly woman against a wall for not wanting to wait in line for her medication. At breakfast, rubbery powdered eggs are eaten in complete silence. Toilets have no seats or stalls dividing them; shit is smeared on the walls. Compared to this place, P.I. *was* a country club.

There is an unfathomable dreariness and hopelessness in the air; it is all I can do to hold on, not panic. Marjee was right—this is Hell.

I'm different enough from the other patients that people notice. The occupational therapist makes a point of getting me off the ward for several hours each day. I design and construct a jacket of orange leather, with green crocheted seams. I hammer holes in the leather with an awl, throwing my energy into each blow, depending on the loud thumps to clear my head. Thinking of the fatal slip of the awl that blinded the man who later invented Braille, I suddenly fear my own hand will slip. It seems to have a life of its own, as do my thoughts. I feel a force pulling me down. Then I drag myself back up. Fuck them! I refuse to sink. I'm medicated, and I'm in this place. That's enough to make anyone screwy.

Working on that jacket keeps me going, one stitch at a time. I have to believe I'm getting out of here—deeply, religiously believe it—or I'll be lost forever.

One day I see a ghost in the dining room. At first I can't believe it's possible, but to my horror, I see . . . Helen. She shuffles along with terrified eyes. I recognize the tough pink scars from the fire on her neck and arms. When I try to talk to her, an attendant stops me. ("No talking! Sit down!") After breakfast I intercept Helen in the hallway and say her name. She takes both my hands and cries noiselessly, her face bending into a mask of tragedy. But I can tell she's happy to see me, someone who remembers her before her body was scarred by flames. She's been through so much, and lost so much; fallen from rooftops through flames, landing in the hopeless hell of this place. Every time she sees me, her face contorts in grief. When you've fallen this far, it must be painful to be reminded that there are friends to be found in the world.

"I'm sick," she weeps. "Will I ever get better?" This makes me angry. "It's not your fault," I tell her. "You're not sick. It's them! They're crazy for sending you here." Helen cries all the harder. I kiss her cheek and wipe the tears from her face before the attendant comes to pull her away.

The staff is brutal to Helen. Every day they lock her in seclusion and won't let her out, no matter how much she begs. I find ways to talk to her: tapping on the door, whispering through the keyhole, pressing my face, my hand, against the door. Though I fear she'll never get out of this place, I tell her over and over that she *will* get better, she *will* get out.

I pray day and night—for Helen, as well as all these women who have lived here for months or years, and for myself, young and healthy enough to walk out of here and never be locked up again. Within a month I am free.

II

LIFE AFTER

RELEASED

IT IS SCARCELY A MONTH SINCE MY RELEASE FROM MANHATTAN STATE. I am back in my old bedroom in my mother's apartment, shell-shocked, wounded, out of place. The spotlessly clean room, smelling of furniture polish, could be a stranger's. The bedroom set, mustard-gold with eggshell-white bamboo trim, which my mother carefully picked out for her eleven-year-old daughter when we moved here seven years ago, seems absurdly, uninterestingly frivolous.

One of the first things I do is flush my medication down the toilet. Watching the little yellow tabs swirl and disappear, I think of all the pills I've swallowed over the last twenty-eight months. I have swallowed enough. I refuse P.I.'s offer of outpatient therapy. I just want to be left alone.

Finally free, I am at a loss. "Normal" life seems weightless, diffused, insubstantial. My hours at home drag like a too-long afternoon; the silence echoes my vacant state. Even the apartment, semidark, seems to be asleep. My mother tiptoes around me—her almost adult, truculent daughter, so different from the child who used to live here, plopped down in the middle of her immaculately ordered life, a gargoyle among the knickknacks.

A few of my old friends are still in the city, but most seem to be moving away. Josh, finishing up at City College, has been accepted for graduate school at UCLA. Jane, dividing her time between a new apartment share and upstate New York, is contemplating moving to Ohio.

Everybody seems to be moving freely through the world except me . . . and my old boyfriend, Dan. My handsome Latin lover hasn't forgotten me. He phones me at my mother's and asks if he can see me.

In my bedroom, Dan and I recline on my bed, his head cradled in my lap. I trace the angular line of his jaw and look into his soulful brown eyes. His sleeves are rolled up, his white shirt unbuttoned to a tanned, deep V. I notice some dots of dried blood on his sleeve.

"What's that?" I ask.

"Cut myself shaving," he murmurs. "Come here." He pulls me down for a deep, deep kiss. His hands slip under my shirt, then down into my tight jeans. But we can't do much; my mother is right outside.

"Min, will you let me know if you need anything?" she calls.

"Yes, Ma." Dan and I slowly, reluctantly untangle.

Dating Dan is a way out of my mother's apartment. He has a car—at least, his father's car, a baby-blue Volkswagen. Dan picks me up and we drive to Coney Island. We walk the boardwalk, stopping for long kisses that flow through me like melted sunshine.

"I dig Dan," I say to myself when we're apart. And I do. We do unusual things together. Sleep under the stars on the rooftop of a friend's tenement apartment in Harlem. Drink cold Lancer's with Cuban sandwiches, followed by café con leché and flan. Snort coke in his father's apartment, while his dad is out. It amuses me that we inhale it through a rolled-up dollar bill, thinking it very imaginative of him to invent such a metaphorical method.

When Dan renews his offer of marriage, I hesitate. The idea of marriage, instead of feeling like a door opening, feels like a door closing on a frighteningly narrow space. But then I think, why not? I have nothing else on my horizon. Here is a chance to love, to be loved and accepted. Dan understands my past. He knows how it feels to be an outcast. He's been called Spic; I've been called Crazy.

"We need each other," Dan says. He gives me a gold-rimmed jade band as an engagement ring, because he knows green is my favorite color.

My mother is skeptical. "You're too young. What do you know about love? I thought I loved your father but that doesn't always mean it will work out." At some point she resigns herself. "If you're sure that's what you want, I won't stand in your way." She knows how stubborn I am: maybe she just wants to avoid an argument.

"My fiancé, Dan." I like the sound of it. Like a real person, with a real life. I should be happy. But something in my gut is uneasy.

I catch Dan nodding off in the middle of the afternoon, more than just normally sleepy. When I ask him again about the marks on his arms, he accuses me of not trusting him.

I feel stricken. I'm supposed to be his oasis; if I don't believe in him, who will? And without him, I have no moorings, no connection to anything real. But the bad feelings won't go away, and I become more and more depressed.

———————

Harold phones. We chat for several minutes. Then . . .

"Have you heard about Marjee?"

The question knocks the breath out of me. "What do you mean?" I gasp, trying to fend off his meaning, but it has already reached me. An alien sound rips from my throat. My mother appearing at the door, immediately sees the grief I'm in and takes the phone until I get myself together.

"She overdosed," says Harold.

They found her on a rooftop. Dead at seventeen.

Marjee, gone from the world. Impossible. She was just a girl; a beautiful, talented girl, filled with energy, mischief, fun—but also pain and need, her driving forces. Did she know where she was heading when she swallowed the pills, snorted the powder, stuck the needle into her arm? She didn't leave a note. Maybe it was an accident. . . .

It doesn't matter. She is gone, forever.

Dead. Dead. The word itself a heartbeat. Did she listen to her heart's struggle to keep beating? Did she want to undo it? Did she cry out for help? Questions, pounding in my skull. Maybe she just went to sleep.

Sleep. I cannot sleep.

I remember Marjee's postcards from the Virgin Islands: "Having a wonderful time, wish you were here," showing seabirds swooping over a turquoise ocean. I dig out her last letter, addressed to me at P.I., postmarked February 1, 1970. Three pages torn from a steno pad, written in red felt-tip pen in Marjee's lovely loopy script, illustrated with drawings of waves, hearts, flowers, a big red sun, a rooster, a sailboat, an island with a single palm tree. I remember reading this letter in the hospital, stung by pangs of envy and self-loathing. She'd been courageous enough to run away and stay out, while I was too fearful. She was living an exciting life, while I chose the living death of the hospital.

Now, looking at her letter, I see, literally, the flip side. On the back of the last page, Marjee had scrawled in dark black pencil some notes about Heidegger's *Being and Time*. "*Da Sein . . . being . . . Human Being . . . Being there . . . people . . . healthy . . . NON-BEING . . . beyond . . .*"

Why did I never consider that Marjee was seriously flirting with death? Maybe because dark thinking was the medium in which we all swam, it was in a sense invisible to me. I'd helped Marjee escape from the hospital, thinking I was helping her find freedom. Never did I imagine I was helping her end her life.

I plunge into a sea of remorse, loss, and grief. I cannot stop weeping . . . at home . . . on the bus . . . at work. In the midtown boutique where I work as a salesgirl, each interaction is a challenge. Women try on sweaters and blouses, asking my approval before buying—as if I were an authority on fashion. Me, a loony tune in disguise. Can't they see? I am numb, I am dumb, I am dying.

One of the other salesgirls enjoys telling me stories of the poverty and deprivation she endured as a child in the West Indies, living in a house overlooking the graveyard where her mother worked—including the precise details of how her mother prepared corpses for burial. Can it be that Marjee's beautiful body is now rotting in the earth? I dig my fingernails into my palm, trying not to cry, until I have to rush out on the sidewalk to breathe. The screeching traffic mocks my loss. What does it matter to the world that my friend is dead?

Days and weeks of grief. I go with Dan to see the movie *M*A*S*H*, and at the sight of the carnage I am so overcome I cannot watch the film. I identify with the soldiers' yawning sense of loss—of time, of innocence, of life. The theme song taunts me: "Suicide is painless . . ." Is it? What do they know? How dare they speak its name lightly?

I don't know which world I want to stay in, the one with dragging days and sleepless nights, or the unknown one where my friend has gone.

At first Dan is sympathetic, but then things start to go sour. He's tired of my bad mood, and tells me it's time to get over it. Later he apologizes and promises he'll make it up to me by taking me camping in Montauk over the July 4th weekend. But the weather is against us. We set up our tent on the beach in the midst of gray drizzle that quickly turns to torrential rain. It storms all night. The next day, on our way back to the city, the cops stop us. They arrest Dan for auto theft and impound the car. I catch a bus back to the city, while Dan stays overnight in the local jail.

When I phone Dan's father, he tells me he had not given Dan permission to take the car, that he has been shooting heroin again, that he's always broke and borrowing money from him and is probably dealing drugs. He'll pay Dan's bail, though he says some jail time might do him good. "He's a very troubled boy," he adds, and tells me I'd do better to find someone else.

With Marjee gone and Dan out of my life, there's no reason to stay in New York. My mother hears of a small liberal arts college in Denver that will accept me on short notice. When the brochure arrives in the mail I look at photos of a manicured campus with mountains in the background. It looks nothing like any reality I know of. But any reality has got to be better than this one, so I agree to go.

My application includes a letter from my mother explaining that I had problems in high school but am now doing fine. Together we go to the bank and take out a loan for my first year's tuition. In August I leave for Denver.

As soon as the plane takes off, something lightens in me. Lifted above my life, suspended in air, I wonder, *what now?* Will I be an oddity in this new place? Will there be anybody there I can talk to? When the plane descends from the mist, I'm looking down at the Rocky Mountains.

To a coastal person, middles are foreign. I'm comfortable with extremes, with edges. I've always lived near water; even at P.I. I could look out over the Hudson into the unfathomable blue-gray horizon. But it's not the landlocked, mild middleness of Denver that gets to me, it's the mile-high altitude. It takes two weeks for my headaches to go away, longer for the sense of strangeness to dissipate.

Loretto Heights College is going through its own transition. This year it has gone coed, importing students from the East and adopting an alternative slant. Until very recently a Catholic women's college, it is still run by the Sisters of Loretto, a progressive order of nuns active in the antiwar movement. Some sisters still wear the habit; others wear blue jeans.

Following in my brother's footsteps, I decide to major in philosophy and theology. I long for a spiritual understanding, to make of the world a *Thou*, rather than an *it*. My adviser, Sister Marie Antoinette, is a spare, ascetic woman with nearly transparent skin. Delicate hands and the fine bone structure that forms the triangle of her face are all I can see of the woman beneath the cloth. Black and white suits her. I find her austerity calming. She is a disciple of rational thought, whereas I am tempestuously emotional. One week into classes, I become upset when Heraclitus, my favorite pre-Socratic philosopher, is misunderstood by my classmates, who interpret his cryptic aphorisms solely with logic. His is a mystical teaching: *"The upward way and the downward way are one and the same."* I know this, I feel this. Why don't the others understand?

"There is no place in philosophy for emotionality," the good sister says, enfolding herself in the heavy cloth of her habit like a chrysalis. She is right. But there is a place for it in literature. I sign up for a literature survey course: "Search for Self." The first book assigned is *Till We Have Faces*, C. S. Lewis's interpretation of the Cupid and Psyche myth. As in Lagerkvist's *The Sibyl*, the book's main character contemplates the inscrutability of the gods.

"What is all this but cat-and-mouse play, blindman's buff, and mere jugglery? Why must holy places be dark places?" Orual, the heroine, rails against the gods, who have taken the life of her beloved sister, Psyche. I feel her anger in every fiber of my being. Orual eventually comes to realize that she has not yet earned the answers she seeks because she is not yet fully human. *"How can they meet us face-to-face, till we have faces?"*

With new passion, I immerse myself in my studies. It's easier than socializing.

From my first meal in the cafeteria, it seems that all the students already know each other. They seem so innocent, with their easy smiles and sparkling eyes, their man-tailored shirts and ironed jeans. They drink milk and go skiing and have nothing to be ashamed of, no dark pasts. I might as well be from Mars.

People seek me out anyway. The midwestern girls surprise me; they seem more open-minded, more mature than the eastern students. They accept me with all my peculiarities: my pained silences, my ratty fur coat. They adopt me, affectionately, like a pet. But I'm still wary. I feel that I am sitting on a large egg, which, if exposed to too much warmth, will crack open, and the loathsome secret of my difference will come bursting messily out, frightening people.

Not at all sure where I stand, I cloak myself in a persona of mysterious sadness, with a whiff of tragedy. I'm different, I tell myself, nuzzling into a familiar, comforting loneliness.

After classes, I sit in on rehearsals of the rock opera *Tommy*, played by two guitarists and a drummer, who practice the songs over and over until they know each note. In New York I would have cynically dismissed this corny stuff, but in the fresh midwestern air I'm touched by their faithful rendition. Although it's not original material (originality being high on my list of requirements, especially because I fear it's a quality I lack), I have to admire their persistence. Witnessing three longhaired nineteen-year-old blue-jeaned, flannel-shirted guys fervently singing, *"See me, feel me, touch me, heal me"* in tremulous, reaching sopranos, it's impossible not to be moved.

Denver is beautiful. The mountains' humped backs encircle the horizon like sleeping beasts, changing color with the hours: green, blue, purple. Below Loretto Heights lies the valley, a wide bowl filled with minute houses and curving roads dotted with shiny cars—a well-ordered, self-maintained system. On campus the sprinklers go on and off at regular intervals, startling me with their hiss and splash. Summer's green burns away to gold and rust among the dark, unchanging evergreens. I've never experienced such beauty, such space. As I look up at the night sky my mouth drops open, as if the stars—more stars than I've ever seen—might fall into my mouth like snowflakes.

At sunset, pastel and gem-colored light floods the silhouetted mountains. As the sinking blaze throws its spectral rays into space, I talk to Marjee. *I wish you could see this,* I tell her. The sky is like a painted depiction of heaven, rays shooting in all directions. I find myself wishing that there really is a heaven, and for an instant I see Marjee in it. Not that she would want to be there. I'm sure she would much prefer oblivion. I remember our conversations about reincarnation: How was it, we wondered, that everyone with past-life recall was once Cleopatra or Napoleon but never a lowly peasant? We wound up rejecting the idea as too egotistical. Now I hope we were mistaken. I would love the world so much more if there were a chance that Marjee might again be in it.

Where are you? I ask. The sky, impassive, gives no response. Instead of Marjee's presence, I feel only her absence. The last of the sun dips behind the mountains, throwing a carmine afterglow into the purple sky. What is a person but a light that dazzles and illumines . . . and in a moment is gone?

There is something spiritual in my hours of solitary study, the hushed library a place of deep renewal. One day, walking across the quad in the late afternoon, the trees casting long shadows across the snow, a sense of well-being floods through me. My thoughts are quiet, my mind alert. I'm not sure what this is, or if I can trust it.

I talk with my mother on the phone every week or so. She worries if she doesn't hear from me. "Are you eating? Do you have friends?" She tries to filter the anxiety from her voice.

"I'm fine," I assure her, but don't go into detail. I have my own life now. I don't need to share it with her.

When I fly home for Christmas, I carry back for my mother a bunch of dried wildflowers I gathered in the hills above Boulder. As the plane gains altitude, little worms emerge from them, writhing in their death throes. I shudder with apprehension at what awaits me; I fear New York will seem small, dismal, suffocating. But as the plane descends the city glimmers like an old friend. As much as I might criticize the crowded, noisy, fume-drenched city, we know each other well. Too well. Before long, the old feelings return. I feel trapped in my mother's apartment and can't wait to return to Denver.

The second semester I make a new friend. Emily, from Indiana, is almost as sad as I am. Our pain reaches toward each other like phantom arms. Like me, Emily's been seeing a shrink since she was fifteen, but she considers her therapist a friend and surrogate mother. When I take the plunge and tell her about my recent history, the confidence cements our friendship.

We are a study in contrasts. Emily conceals her soft curves behind pinstripe denim overalls. Next to her, I feel all edges. But we share a common language: emotion. For both of us, the world feels daunting and unreal. We roam Denver high on speed-cut acid, convinced we're in Oz, wondering why all the lakes have fences around them.

I'm one of eight people piled into someone's beat-up car. We're on our way to the mountains. The radio blares Crosby Stills Nash & Young. The roach that's being passed around is too hot to hold; I drop it on the floor and double over to look for it, groping among the candy wrappers and empty cans. The car hits a bump, and its old shocks send me flying off the lap I'm perched on. When I land, my bony butt and his bony thighs collide, hard.

"You're a woman. Why don't you act like one?" Tom is humorless. It's our first real date, and already things are sour. I flip my hair over my shoulder and snake my arm around his neck, like I'm supposed to. What's wrong with me that these things don't come easily?

It's especially difficult in a group. I worry so much about what to say, I can hardly get the words out. When I do, it takes me so long to recover, I've lost the sense of the conversation. Then I say something stupid. If I say something other people respond to, I'm so relieved I could cry. Laughter sticks in my throat. It's worse when I smoke dope. I turn in on myself. The others talk, but I can't follow. If I try to say something, the distance between one word and the next is too far.

We arrive in Aspen late and crash in a heap of down jackets and sweaters on the floor of someone's friend's ski house. Tom is nowhere near me; he's off with the other guys. I take advantage of the bottle of red that's being passed around to drink myself into a stupor. The next morning everyone but me is up and out early to go skiing.

I've always thought skiing was a sport for rich kids. I don't consider doing it for a second. I can't imagine moving that fast, out of control. For me, just being in the mountains is dizzying. All that beautiful snow; smoke curling from wood stoves. I take long walks until I'm frozen, then find a place to thaw out with a book over a cup of coffee or hot chocolate spiked with Irish whiskey. Something for the cold, something for the soul.

On the way back from Aspen, we stop to visit someone's friend: Jeff, rugged in his flannel shirt and soft brown beard. He has his own little cabin in the mountains, complete with wood stove. A self-sufficient mountain man, with one unique feature: Jeff has only one leg. He lost the other below the knee in an accident. When he's clothed, wearing his prosthesis, you can barely detect Jeff's disability. He can do everything other guys do; he even cross-country skis. But there is a difference. Jeff understands loss. Here is a guy who does not intimidate me. A truly gentle guy. Unbelievably, he sees something in me too. Soon he is my boyfriend.

Let the others go off to the slopes. We stay in, snuggling. Jeff's a good kisser, and sex promises to be nice, but I cannot ignore that stump of a leg, and I can't fully embrace it either—though I try. The first time I sleep with him, before bed, I hear him unbuckling his plastic limb. I peek through half-closed lids to see him unwrapping several feet of ace bandage, finally exposing the blunt evidence of his loss—more obvious than mine, and more forgivable. His accident was something that just happened, whereas I feel a deep complicity with my flawed character. Still, my heart goes out to him. I admire the way he's accepted his fate. I hope I can learn to be as strong and adaptable as he is.

But something gnaws at me. Am I with him because I love him or because I feel pity for him? Or is it because I identify with him? The conflict continues to nag me. When I come to the conclusion that Jeff's disability reflects my feeling of not being whole, I no longer find refuge in the relationship and gently break up with him. Jeff cries. I feel like a girl Judas. I wonder, will he always expect people to reject him because he is not whole? That's exactly how I feel. I'm a coward, a hypocrite. How can I accept him when I can't accept myself? *Till we have faces* . . . I can't let anyone get too close until I understand myself better.

I've been summoned away from my studies to Neil's room down the hall. Neil is one of the popular guys, a jock who's also a good student, nice, and dauntingly good-looking. I knock on the door, then open it. It's dark in the room; all I can see is the glow of some candles.

"Happy birthday!" The lights come on; the room is filled with people. Speechless, I clap my hand to my mouth, pressing it over the smile that's spreading across my face. The next minute tears well up. I hang my head, but friends circle round me, laughing. Someone puts a paper cup of wine in my hand and points to the lopsided, home-baked chocolate cake, the candles melting into the icing. Time to make a wish. I take a deep breath and close my eyes. I wish for health . . . happiness . . . peace . . . and love. Then, *whoosh*, I blow them out. Nineteen candles, plus one for good luck.

I'm feeling pretty lucky. This is the first birthday I've celebrated since the hospital. Only a year ago the doctors were convincing me to sign myself in, only to ship me off to Manhattan State. I still don't really believe I'm out. I never imagined my life going on, let alone a birthday party in a dorm room in Denver.

People help themselves to hunks of cake. There's a gallon jug of Mountain Chablis, lots of beer, nachos, and bean dip. Neil puts a Youngbloods record on his stereo and turns up the volume. The room is thick with marijuana smoke, talk, and laughter. People cluster in little groups. I feel myself shrinking, a small island in a sea of bodies. I gulp wine. Someone hands me a joint. I look at it, wanting to pass it on, but change my mind and lift it to my lips.

In an hour or so people drift back to their rooms, but I linger, too drunk and stoned to feel like moving. Soon it's just me and Neil. I look up from pretending to study his record collection, surprised to feel his arms around me. Soon we're naked in his twin bed.

"Was it good?" he asks. I try to answer, but I'm spinning. I drank too much; how could I have done this on my birthday? "I'm sick," I moan and the worry inside comes bubbling up and out of me and, suddenly ill, I try to aim it over the side of the bed.

A blur of voices and movement and I'm back in my room. I'm sick all night and I swear if the room ever stops twirling I'll be good, I'll be careful, I'll try not to do stupid things. How naive to think I could leave the old me behind, just like that. They throw me a party and look what I do. My roommate tends me through the night, cleaning up after I'm sick, wiping the damp hair from my forehead. "I'm terrible," I cry between retches.

"No you're not," she says, "you're just drunk."

———————

Schoolwork is my refuge. I love to study. I love the immersion, the discovery, the connection between what I read, what I feel, and the new thoughts spawned. Inspiration, revelation. I stay up all night writing papers. The words just seem to come. A little amphetamine doesn't hurt. The sun rises to *Rhapsody in Blue*. In the morning my teeth ache.

"Let me know what kind of typewriter you'd like." My father's handwriting, as always, is neat, clear, uniform. I write back and tell him not to bother to get me a new one, a used one would be fine. He phones. "I'll get you whatever kind you'd like. How about electric? Are you sure you don't want a new one?"

"No, Dad, don't bother. I don't want you to spend a lot of money. A used manual typewriter would be fine."

It sounds humble, but I'm really a reverse-snob. I would hate to appear to be materialistic, so I force my father to hunt around until he finds the antique Smith-Corona—perfect, except for the stuck Y key. It's black and gold and beautiful, but it takes some solid pounding to get those papers typed.

I haven't seen my father since he visited me in the hospital. There is a conspiracy between us: I don't mention the hospital and he doesn't ask. My father wants to hear I'm doing well, enjoying myself, having a good time. So that's what I tell him. His letters are filled with pleasantries and news. When I get one, I tear it open and read it over and over, especially the ending: "I think of you and miss you. Your everloving Dad."

Since I've been in Denver, I am geographically closer to my father than I've been in years. Our contact becomes more frequent. Phone calls and letters pass back and forth between us, a kind of courtship, as we slowly get to know one another again.

At spring break I get a ride to California with an older student, a voice major with a well-worn Volkswagen. I don't drive—Driver's Ed wasn't offered in the loony bin—but she's happy to have the company. We eat diner food and fast food with lots of Coke and coffee. Halfway across Utah, as the sun sets over the desert, she rolls up the windows and sings at the top of her voice an aria so piercing that the hair rises off my body in its own hallelujah. Orange and gold beams fan out in all directions through a green and violet sky. I'm as happy as I've ever been.

My driver loops through San Francisco to drop me off before heading south. I've made plans to visit Larry. Now an aspiring photographer and sometime carpenter, he shares an apartment in the Haight with an inde-terminate, fluctuating number of roommates. A huge cauldron of soup boils on the stove; nearby a pot of brown rice is cooling. Larry's hair, an orb of frizz, has doubled in size since I last saw him. Larry takes a look at me and offers me a bath. Before I get in he lights a candle, hands me a bottle of Dr. Bronner's peppermint soap and offers me a joint. Welcome to San Francisco. A hilly, trippy haven for hippie artist dropout poets. I love it immediately.

In the supermarket, Larry casually slips every other item into his shirt. I question him with my eyes. "Too expensive. Food stamps only go so far. We have to eat!" We wind up with enough for a feast, which we cook in a campfire with some friends in the hills. Walking in Golden Gate Park, we watch the sun set over the bay. I taste my first soul food in a tiny restau-rant with bare wood floors, walls, and tables; we wash down collards with Anchor Stream. Where have I been all my life?

Back in his room, I'm momentarily uneasy.

"You can sleep here," Larry says, pointing to his mattress, "or here," pointing to the floor. "No pressure."

Of course I want to sleep with him. Don't I? He's my old, dear friend, whom I've loved for years. How could I not want to be close to him? We start to get into it, but something's wrong. However much I try I'm not really turned on. So I just kind of . . . submit. Then I realize what's wrong. It's Marjee. Her ghost is in bed with us. It occurs to me that I've never told Larry about Marjee's death. Whenever he'd asked about her, I just changed the subject. I just didn't have the heart to go through it all again. And since their breakup, Larry always sounded pained or wistful when her name was mentioned.

"What's the matter?" Larry asks.

"It's Marjee," I answer, and burst into tears.

Then we are both weeping, tears and snot all over our faces, hugging and sobbing, holding on to each other for dear life. Both of us, in our own ways, are Marjee's former lovers. Although I never would have defined it as such back then, I was bowled over in love with her—not in a sexual way, but it was love, nonetheless. That was what she'd inspired in me. And that was why, though I'd tried to be magnanimous, I felt distanced and hurt when Marjee and Larry became lovers. Larry had been in love—or in lust—with Marjee. How could he not? Men were always all over Marjee, throwing themselves on her beautiful body. Sorting out love and lust is hard enough at nineteen, but at sixteen . . .

Marjee had an unfillable, voracious hunger for love. She could never get enough. Always hungry, always empty. I remember her playfully singing the Oscar Mayer wiener theme song: *"Oh, I wish I was an Oscar Mayer wiener, that is what I really want to be, 'cause if I was an Oscar Mayer wiener, everyone would be in love with me,"* followed immediately by, *"I'm glad I'm not an Oscar Mayer wiener, that is what I'd truly hate to be, 'cause if I was an Oscar Mayer wiener, there would soon be nothing . . . left . . . of . . . me."* Then she'd start the song over again.

As bereft as I am, I'm mad at her too. How like you, I think, to abandon us, so we can't abandon you. How easy for you to disappear, leaving those who loved you here to deal with the mess of our emotions.

The next day Larry gives me a photo he'd taken of Marjee. She is naked, stretched out along the floor, hugging her breasts, looking up at the camera. Her voluptuous body, her face filled with pain, her huge eyes, her self-critically sucked-in cheeks. Even in grainy black and white, she is too much for this world.

I sit on the dock of the bay where Otis Redding once sat. Sun sparkles on the water, a breeze ruffles my hair. Tourists and natives bustle around me, but Otis and I have nowhere to rush off to.

I have a date . . . with my father. He's flying up from L.A. to spend the day with me. Waiting for him to arrive, I'm just as self-conscious as if it were a real date. Afraid it will be awkward. Afraid we will be strangers. Wishing we hadn't planned this, wishing it was over.

Any figure in the crowd could be his. But each time I single out a man's conservative form, it is that of a stranger. Then the shock of recognition: This handsome face, tanned, with crinkly brown eyes and wavy hair, is my father's. We hug and kiss. "Look at you!" he exclaims, and I am glad he's here. We don't have much to say, but the chemistry's there.

My dad is an organized tourist, with an itinerary. First, Fisherman's Wharf. A ride on a trolley car. Then lunch. He's a man of simple tastes: an egg-salad sandwich and a malted. Like most Brooklyn boys who survived the Depression, my father is a conservative spender, but he enjoys treating me.

"Order whatever you want." He leans across the table and pushes my hair behind my ears. "It's important in life to look presentable."

My dad is full of social parables.

"I never liked the taste of olives, but when I socialized with successful people and saw them eating olives, I taught myself to like them, and now I do."

To my dad, any setback can be overcome by diligent, persistent effort. His earnestness is so pathetic, it's endearing. If he weren't my father, I'd dismiss him as boring, square, one hundred percent establishment.

"Your father is not very sophisticated," my mother has always said. She's right. He's cultivated an International House of Pancakes persona. But still there's a connection, a spark between us. I listen to his instructive stories, laugh at his jokes.

"You should try harder to get along with your mother," my father says.

"We don't get along. She drives me crazy." I immediately regret using the C-word.

"Your mother is just very high-strung."

I picture my fashionable mother strung up high where everyone can see and admire her, the ultimate fashion statement. As if reading my thoughts, my dad asks if I'd like to go shopping.

Although I generally avoid department stores, I decide to let my dad take me shopping. I'm very particular about what I wear. Nothing flowered, flashy, or bright; I prefer dark, simple, understated. I refuse to wear anything that might compromise my identity. I'll wear Earth Shoes or clogs but never heels. I want in no way to resemble my mother. Intent on spurning fashion, I won't admit that my deliberate, studied rejection of stylishness is the epitome of fashion-consciousness.

My father patiently stands by while I reject everything I see until I find something that speaks to me—a soft, woven midnight-blue shawl. I wrap it around me, and we stroll in the late afternoon. Arm-in-arm, one-step-at-a-time communion. When it's time for him to leave for the airport, we have one last, long hug. Inhaling his wonderful smell of shaving cream and cigarettes, his arms around me, I feel: This is simple, this is good.

Back at school, the semester barrels toward a close. In April the snow melts, revealing green grass. Tulips pop up out of the earth. Then it snows again, and the red and orange flowers sit atop a field of white.

I join in a flurry of antiwar efforts, painting banners and distributing leaflets. The closer the end of term draws near, the faster it goes. Lots of coffee, a variety of white powders. Term papers. Finals. For the second semester my grades are 4.0; I make dean's list.

This sudden success feels uncomfortable. Now what? Summer's approach is unsettling. What will I do next year? I've done well in Denver, but why repeat the experience? I'm approaching the edge of a cliff, with no idea which way to turn.

Emily and I discuss the possibilities. It's a big world, and we both want to explore it. Why not drop out for a year and travel in Europe? We could go to museums in Rome, Florence, and Paris; relax in Provence or Tuscany; maybe even go to Greece, where I could visit the site of the oracle at Delphi. Emily is enthusiastic. We agree to work out the details over the summer.

May, 1971. New York City. Bedrock. Reality. The city, unbeautiful, harsh, has a cerebral energy that, after my mountain mellowness wears off, I hook into like an addict. This is a city of thirst, of thought. In June, the city air turns sultry and fills me with longing.

Already there's a split in me. Did I make a mistake deciding not to go back to Denver? No, I decide, that's not reality. That was just a dream. A cheerful little bubble in the mountains.

I hang out, see whatever friends are left in the city. Once again I'm in limbo, on extended vacation. My mother looks at me questioningly, not wanting to push. I tell her about my plans to travel with Emily, see her check her response. "If that's what you want to do . . ." She seems to think I'm capable of making my own decisions now.

Then Emily's letter arrives. "Dear Mindy, It's hard for me to write this . . ." She doesn't think she can go ahead with our plan. It isn't that she doesn't like me or that it wouldn't be fun. Her psychologist thinks that she always bonds too much with women, particularly women with problems.

It isn't healthy. She needs to be more independent. She's decided to stay in Indiana, get her own place, work, and go to school.

Of course. Emily must have told her therapist about me. And of course her shrink would convince her not to associate with me.

Noel is back in New York, living in his mother's Upper West Side apartment. After two years in Philadelphia, he's finally eighteen and no longer a runaway. A scruffy little beard has appeared on his chin, and he's full of stories about his misadventures in art school.

One day Noel calls to ask whether I'd like to visit Mrs. Gould at P.I. I'm a little spooked by the idea, but I'd love to see her, so I say yes. It's a weird, weightless feeling, entering the building as free citizens. We sign in at the desk (Noel signs in as Norman Mailer) and take the elevator down to the fourth floor. Mrs. Gould has just dismissed her class; kids are filing out as we walk in. Mrs. Gould welcomes us with a big smile and open-armed hugs. She's beautiful and filled with energy, just as I remember her.

"Look who's here!" she says to the students still gathering their things, showing us off as living proof that people do get out of this place. "Let me look at you!" Mrs. Gould holds us at arm's length, wipes her lipstick off Noel's cheek, then embraces us again, demanding to hear everything we've been doing. Noel tells the story of his elopement and exodus to Philadelphia. I tell her a little about Manhattan State, but mostly about school, philosophy, art, my college literature classes. She beams at us, picks up the phone and dials two digits. "There are two former students in my classroom I know you'll want to see, so come right down," she says, and hangs up. Noel and I exchange glances. I hope she's not calling the head nurse. In a few minutes there's a knock on the door and in strolls Dr. S.

Dr. S. is understated, as usual. "I'm surprised, and pleased, to see you. You look well." He chats with Noel, who was also one of his patients, until he learned he was going to be shipped to a state hospital and ran away. When Dr. S. turns to me and asks how I am, I'm not sure what to say. I'm still angry at him for having had me shipped. I've got to show him once and for all that I'm okay—in spite of the hospital. I stand up tall and face him. "I'm fine, thank you. Manhattan State was no picnic . . ."— I stare meaningfully at him—". . . but that's all behind me. I just spent a year at college, majoring in philosophy. I made dean's list."

"I'm very happy to hear that," Dr. S. says.

It's strange to be standing here shooting the breeze with him, pretending to ignore the big ugly blob of our former experience of each other. Unlike me, Noel seems relaxed, talking with Dr. S. in an almost conspiratorial tone. "I want to thank you for threatening to ship me. It gave me the motivation to claim my freedom."

"My two successful failures," Dr. S. says with an odd smile. In his face I read his bafflement: Here are two kids he'd been powerless to help but who nevertheless, in spite of our poor prognosis, seem to have turned out okay.

So what was all the fuss about, anyway?

There is something about the summer in New York. Just surviving the heat emanating from the sidewalk feels like an accomplishment.

I sign up for summer session at Hunter College, work part-time and take a couple of philosophy classes. I think I might enroll as a matriculated student in the fall, but can't decide whether to continue in philosophy, return to fine art, or do something more useful. Hunter has an Institute of Health Sciences that offers degrees in nursing, social work, occupational and physical therapy. Maybe helping others would help me get out of myself. More than that, I want to do something to help people in the situation I was in.

Who am I kidding? As if I could help someone else. I'd probably just be as big a hypocrite as the people who thought they were helping me. But I apply anyway, to keep the option open.

Meanwhile I set about healing myself. Psychology seems a more humanistic alternative to psychiatry. I investigate current trends. I find Fritz Perls's humorous approach to the idiosyncrasies of the psyche refreshing. Jung's *Man and His Symbols,* a layman's introduction to Jung's theory of archetypes and the collective unconscious, also speaks to me. I relish his synthesis of art, literature, popular culture, and psychology. But I long to find a real live mentor, a teacher, a spiritual guide.

My mother comes with me to the midtown brownstone that houses Albert Ellis's Institute for Rational-Emotive Therapy. I fill out application forms, then return solo to attend one of the guru's group-therapy sessions. The atmosphere is highly charged. Ellis, a compact, dapper, gray-haired man, initiates in a nasal New York accent a kind of psychological neo-Socratic dialogue. I tremble violently when called upon to speak. I'm intimidated by the other group members, as well as by Ellis himself. His method of reasoning people out of their neurosis seems too superficial. My anxiety goes deeper, where reason can't reach.

There are days when I am so filled with an anxiety that approaches terror that I can scarcely function. I am tyrannized by thoughts, tricking me at every turn, judging and condemning. Depression is always sucking around my ankles, threatening to pull me under. In order to not fall apart or into a panic, I hold myself rigidly and speak in measured sentences.

I don't talk about the hospital. To do so would be to trivialize my own experience, as well as the deaths of my friends. I hold my grief and outrage within me, cultivating it into my personal brand of moral superiority. To speak of it would be to expose the purity of my pain to dissolution in the corrupt superficiality of the world. Instead I assume the stance, the posture, of the wounded. I jump at loud noises, sniff at trivial pleasures, shake my head at idle chatter, sneer at insensitivity. I hold in disdain anything that comes between me and my sacred suffering. Anybody who hasn't suffered, in my opinion, has the moral depth of a fashion model. So it is with everything. To talk about anything other than art and ideas would be trivial. Yet to try to give voice to the ineffable would be a defamation. Better to keep my thoughts to myself.

I find some release in drawing and painting, when I'm not paralyzed by my own perfectionism. Besides, most art classes are freewheeling and offer little instruction. Teachers like my work, and I glide by, unchallenged.

Wanting more structure than fine art offers, I sign up for a six-week course in stained glass. The two brothers who own the studio are master craftsmen and artists in their own right. I marvel at the delicacy with which my teachers handle the glass, gently tapping in just the right place to deftly snap it along a scored line. By comparison, I am clumsy, shattering piece after piece of gem-colored glass, apologetically sweeping up the shards.

"Don't worry, just try again," my teacher reassures me. I practice, progressing from straight to curved cuts, learning to solder the lead without burning or melting it. I love the challenge of working with the sharp, brittle glass—a little like my thoughts: fragile and potentially dangerous, but if handled with patience and care, they can become things of beauty.

My final project is a lampshade of my own design. But I'm critical of the design, and the execution is less than flawless. I lose heart and don't complete the project in time for the student exhibition. I make up an excuse: My cat knocked it over and it broke. My face flames as I tell this lie. I know my teacher sees right through me. He doesn't seem angry, just disappointed. I leave the class feeling ashamed. The bad me, the liar, is too strong for me. As much as I'd like to, I can't seem to change.

"Why work?" asks Sheila, my wild and irrepressibly rebellious friend from P.I. It's the first time I've seen Sheila since she was sent to Chestnut Lodge. She eventually ran away from there too, and has been on her own ever since: doing some acting, making films, living life on her own terms. Sheila thinks I'm selling out. I explain that I have to contribute to my parents' rent until I make enough to afford my own apartment.

"You don't have to live by their rules. I'm going out to New Mexico to live in an artists' community. Why don't you come?"

I can't, though. I don't want to live with a bunch of people I don't know. I just did that for a year, and before that, at P.I. I wish I could be different, more adventurous, but there's nothing I can do.

I answer an ad in the *Village Voice* and land a job as secretary in a law and real-estate office, a family operation. The Blumenthals—the dutiful, silver-haired son ("Mr. B.") and his ancient, shrewish mother ("Mrs. B.")—have their office in the storefront of their brownstone on Irving Place. The work—mostly filing and some light typing and bookkeeping—is boring, but the office is quiet, which allows me to indulge in my favorite activity: daydreaming. I watch the sunlight drifting through the dusty windows. It's a long stretch until lunchtime, when I can explore the neighborhood, find a stoop to sit on, browse in the shops.

I circumnavigate the crowd of tough, noisy girls from Washington Irving High School and find refuge and sustenance in the cavernous Schrafft's automat on 14th Street—the height of Art Deco modernity during the forties, now a relic of a dying breed. At the end of the serving line contained by gleaming brass handrails, hot food is ladled from steam tables by aproned, hair-netted workers, but the major feature is the wall of coin-operated, chrome-trimmed glass windows displaying sandwiches, side dishes of creamed spinach and macaroni and cheese, and slices of pie. Amid the clatter and bustle of the busy cafeteria, I settle down with a "bottomless" cup of coffee, read my book, and sometimes sketch the people around me.

One exceptionally busy lunchtime, I carry my tray around trying to find a place to sit, when I notice an empty chair next to a peculiar-looking

character—a mountainous man, tall and robust, with long, white hair
flowing out from under a knitted cap, and an equally long, white beard. A
real-life Mr. Natural. He glances up from his newspaper and nods as I sit
down. After finishing my pie and coffee, I reach for my pencils and
sketchbook.

"Are you an artist?" my tablemate asks, raising his bushy eyebrows
slightly.

I'm not sure how to answer. As much as I aspire to become an artist, it's
presumptuous to call myself that. "Um, well, yes, I hope to be."

He looks at me a little severely, then proceeds to query me about who
my favorite artists are, and why. I mention Dürer and Leonardo, Blake and
Daumier, Manet and Cezanne, Goya and Siqueiros, Klee and Kollwitz,
hoping he doesn't notice the glaring gaps in my knowledge.

"Are you an artist?" I ask, and he answers that he is. His name is
Benjamin Benno, and he has been an artist since before I was born.

I ask if I can see some of his work. He pulls from his rucksack a gallery
announcement and newspaper reviews of exhibitions, with reproductions
of boldly painted still lifes. He tells me a little about his years as a struggling artist in Paris and the progress of his career after returning to the
States. This is a man whose art is taken seriously, by himself and by the
world—the first artist I've met who's had some success and recognition.

Then he asks about my life. I tell him my few tellable facts: the schools
I've attended, where I was born and where I grew up. When I mention
Stuyvesant Town, those "little boxes made of ticky-tacky" I couldn't wait
to get away from, he leans forward. "It used to be a swamp," he says. As a
conscientious objector during the Korean War, Benno worked on the con-
struction team that laid the foundations for the sedate middle-class housing development I grew up in.

He asks to see my sketchbook. Somewhat reluctantly, I show it to him.
He leafs through my sketches of buildings, rocks and trees in Central
Park, people's faces, my own face and hands.

"You have talent," he says, and I am thrilled to my core. An artist—
that is who I want to be—not a person working in some dusty office,
moldering in a safe, sterile little box of an apartment, but an artist—who
sees and creates beauty, powerful with truth and meaning, someone who
builds foundations for the future.

I'm accepted into the Institute of Health Sciences but decide to enroll in the regular college as a liberal arts student. I just can't see myself as a nurse, giving people injections and holding bedpans, and I'd be kidding myself to think I could become one of the therapists that I couldn't wait to get away from.

I work part-time and matriculate at Hunter, majoring in fine art. I maintain my 4.0 average, taking only those classes that interest me: philosophy, art history, studio art, French. Terrified by the prospect of written self-expression, I refuse to take expository writing, the prerequisite for all other English classes, and have to take the literature classes I love through the foreign language departments, in translation. I avoid the math and science requirements, but try some history and social science. I burn and hyperventilate through one semester of psychology before dropping it. *What do they know?* I think, *what do their textbooks know?*

My sense of being an outsider—outside the norm, outside the rules—continues.

ROOTS

THOUGH I TRY, I CANNOT BURY THE PAST or forget where I've been. I'm
not sure I want to. I cling to my pain like a raft. Without it, life is
hollow, and I'm lost.

A friend of Jane's tells us about a grassroots political action organization dedicated to informing patients of their rights, lobbying to change
legislation so that mental patients can no longer be held in institutions
against their will. After attending one meeting, I become a member.

Mental Patients Liberation Project (MPLP) rents a storefront in the
East Village for a dollar a year from the city-funded Cooper Square
Redevelopment Corp. We hold weekly meetings in which we discuss
philosophical, legal, and political aspects of the treatment and mistreat-
ment of the so-called "mentally ill."

The storefront is raw space. Bare bulbs dangle from wires. Our furniture: sawhorse tables, orphan chairs. There's always coffee and hot water
for tea, and packets, cubes, and lump-ridden bowls of sugar to feed our
excessive craving. Ashtrays overflow onto the larger ashtray, the floor.
Someone donates a small refrigerator; it fills with beers, sodas, and the
occasional moldy sandwich.

I've never joined an organization before, except Girl Scouts: a brief for-
gettable blur. This is the first organized group to which I truly belong.
Self-government, at last. We have a president, a vice-president, a treasurer,
and a secretary, and follow *Robert's Rules of Order*, sometimes absurdly to the
letter. Meetings begin with the reading of the minutes, then motions are

raised and the floor is opened to discussion. We may be united by a shared moral indignation, but as our president often reminds us, we are first and foremost a political action group, not group therapy.

I am amazed to hear the assortment of tales. A rambunctious southern woman, not content to be a housewife, committed by her mother and husband. A young woman whose controlling father taught her a lesson by having her locked up. A blind man who claims some of his "symptoms" were misinterpreted behaviors stemming from his blindness. An Eastern European immigrant thought to be insane because nobody from the rural town he wandered into could understand what he was saying. Artists, musicians, and writers who were too headstrong, sensitive, rebellious, cantankerous, or unhappy for the taste of those around them. People whose depressions or breakdowns evolved from disturbing, sometimes horrific personal circumstances who followed their doctors' orders and went trustingly inside, only to find the gates locked behind them. Their stories make my own seem tame.

Everybody here has been misunderstood or victimized. Nobody seems "crazy"—but then, we're the ones who got away, and we don't forget it. We don't say "hospitalized," we say "incarcerated." Psychiatrist is synonymous with Pig.

I become militant. Books by Thomas Szasz, Erving Goffman, and R. D. Laing strengthen my conviction that so-called mental illness is a construct, an imaginary wall built by society to barricade people against their own fears that inside, though they dare not admit it, they may also be weak, different, freakish, unacceptable. To Laing, insanity is a logical reaction to prolonged, unreasonable demands or an unendurable difference in temperament from one's family. To me, it is the hallmark of a special sensitivity, an unwillingness to conform. Just read Van Gogh's letters, I tell anyone who labels him insane.

We are part of a subculture that has its own resonance in the arts. Peter Brook's experimental *Marat Sade* is playing down the street at La Mama. Frederick Wiseman's chilling *Titticut Follies*, as well as the offbeat film *King of Hearts* ask the same question: Who is crazier—the so-called lunatic, or those who hold the keys?

We subdivide into factions: the uncompromisingly radical proponents of the anti-psychiatry movement, the milder "we can all learn to get along if only we can educate people" advocates of patients' rights, a contingency of Maoists who see incarceration as an offshoot of capitalist oppression, and the hecklers who get a charge from disagreeing with everyone. There are gay men and lesbians who were locked up because their homosexuality was diagnosed as mental illness—and listed as such in the DSM2. We even have a psychiatrist who joined us because his conscience led him to disagree with the injustice he'd witnessed and the training that perpetuates it.

This is my new family. The only problem is, it's a dysfunctional family. MPLP is beset by power plays, infighting, politics. Heated arguments erupt, and the spirit of contentious rebellion overflows as conflict escalates into high drama. This is a group rich in verbal skills and highly imaginative use of expletives. Shouting. Fistfights. Beer cans flying across the room. Who could possibly be more dramatic than former mental patients? We are licensed for ruckus.

"That's a pile of crap!" "Shut up! You're as bad as they are!" "Go fuck yourself, capitalist arsehole!" "Come on, come on, have at me!" Chairs overturn as we scramble to get out of the way.

We appoint a sergeant-at-arms, a muscular young man whose job is to toss unruly members out onto the sidewalk. It can take the collective strength of four men leaning on the door to keep the ejected one out, but sooner or later the pounding and shouting dies down. A couple of times we call the police, an action that always raises intense dissent. Once during the hubub the storefront window is smashed. Occasionally some fainthearted spectator is pushed over the edge and bursts into tears.

"You'd think they're crazy or something," a musician friend stage-whispers in my ear during a particularly raucous meeting. One man won't relinquish the floor. The secretary stops taking minutes, throws down her pencil and pad, stalks out of the room. The president and vice president are both drunk. I sit on the periphery trying to decide whether it's scary, funny, or tragic. At least ours is not a dangerous kind of lunacy. If we can help one person locked up against their will, it's worth it.

In spite of all the drama, we get things done. We draw up a patients' bill of rights and travel in small groups to state hospitals to inform inmates of their rights, and try to give them some hope.

On a trip to the State Hospital in Harrisburg, Pennsylvania, four of us, two men and two women, stay overnight on a locked ward for acute patients. The sour smell of the drab ward is unsettlingly familiar, bringing it all back—the endless days, the total absence of freedom and joy.

We arrive with just enough time after dinner to give a talk. Feeling tongue-tied, I let the others speak for me. At bedtime I'm locked into a small room for my own safety. I twist restlessly on the institutional cot with its squeaky springs and lumpy mattress that smells of urine, listening to the screams and mutterings of my neighbors. In the morning, tired and anxious, I wait for the sound of the keys that will unlock my door.

After breakfast we talk with patients. My heart breaks for the lifers, most of whom are uninterested in what we have to say. One very medicated teenage girl softly touches my hand and asks: "Do you think I'll ever get out of here?" She reminds me of Helen—and of my former self. I encourage her to be strong, to have hope, and she hangs on my words. How strange to be an emissary of freedom. When the weekend is over and I walk out into the day, I greedily breathe the fresh air.

We start to attract media attention. Mental health is becoming a hot issue. *Parade* magazine, syndicated in Sunday newspapers across the country, does a story on the rights of mental patients that features MPLP. I agree to be interviewed and photographed. When the article appears there is great excitement among the group. We are finally making an impact. Several MPLP members are quoted. There are three paragraphs about me, which I'm not sure are entirely accurate, but they have a poetic quality—I describe the effects of medication as "the kiss of oblivion." There is also a photo of me staring challengingly at the camera, for all the world to see—including my father's relatives in Long Island, where the Sunday papers include *Parade*. I know they will be shocked by my coming out publicly as a mental patient, but I try not to think about it. It's part of my brave new persona.

I get fan mail, love letters. This is my first experience of going public with this private part of my life. Although I generally feel my hospitalization as a stigma and a source of shame, it is also the source of my anger, a force that keeps me going: to work and to school, to meetings and demonstrations. Something new is beginning—a sense of mission, a taste of pride in myself.

———

I have to get away from my mother or I'll disintegrate. Everything about her life negates mine, and vice versa. The contention between us, barely concealed, grows more dangerous every day. I start looking for other places to live. On my way home from work I check out the Salvation Army residence for young women near Gramercy Park. The lobby seems a little grand and formal. Then I read the rules. There's a curfew. A dress code. Visitors' rules.

The only apartments I might afford are in the East Village, but the places I see are rat- and roach-infested tenements with airshaft windows, on dangerous blocks, side by side with shooting galleries. No, I realize, standing in a debris-littered room, fighting an urge to flee, I can't sleep here.

December 1971. I move into my apartment, in a prewar high-rise on the Upper West Side. My stepfather grew up in this apartment, and until recently his parents still lived here, until the death of his mother. When his father moves to a senior's hotel, my name is put on the lease. It's the best thing my stepfather has ever done for me.

I feel like a pioneer, living uptown in an area completely unknown to me. At first the Upper West Side looks dingy and depressed. The once-grand buildings could use a good washing. The avenues look too wide. Then I discover some of the local delights. The New Yorker bookstore is a comfortable place where I am welcome to sit and read. I spend hours browsing, the faint strains of jazz filtering in from the music school next door. Local theaters like the New Yorker and the Thalia feature foreign, art, and vintage films.

The neighborhood has a history of change. Once a haven for prosperous middle-class Jewish families, it's now a mix of black and Hispanic families, and elderly Jews. The kosher butcher shop is next to a *botanica* whose windows display statues of the weeping Virgin and Christ dripping blood. I eat dinner three times a week at a local Cuban-Chinese restaurant where the food is delicious, abundant, and inexpensive.

Central Park is just two blocks away. I explore the unfamiliar uptown paths and discover they connect to my familiar turf: Bethesda Fountain, the Sheep Meadow. I walk off some of my melancholy in the healing presence of trees. In Riverside Park, where George Bellows painted the poetry of winter trees overlooking the frozen Hudson, I find vistas I didn't know the city had, here at the city's edge, close to water, my sustaining element.

I strip away my step-grandparents' dusty carpets and sell or give away most of their furniture, keeping only a few favorite pieces. Soon the place is so empty I can ride my newly acquired secondhand bicycle around the living room. I rip up layers of old linoleum: black-and-white squares, ugly speckles, multicolored Wonder bread balloons. I scrub the floors, paint the walls, wash the windows. I sew rudimentary curtains with my step-grandmother's old Singer, an experience that reminds me that sewing is not my talent. Determined to do things the hard way, I sand the floor with squares of sandpaper, a few inches at a time, revealing the oak parquet hidden beneath the darkened wax.

As exciting as it is to have my own place, it's also daunting. At night I lie frozen in terror, certain that I've left the door unlocked and someone is already in the apartment, on his way to my bedroom to rape or murder me. And though the recently decontrolled rent is low, it's still a stretch. I find the first in a series of roommates. Some don't last long—like the roommate who gets up in the middle of the night and eats entire sticks of butter standing in the kitchen in the dark and moves out one day without a word while I'm at school.

I'm not good at being a roommate. I'm not flexible enough. I can't bear another person's mess in my space. I can't go to sleep if there's a dish left in the sink; everything has to be in order. Watching myself, I'm reminded of someone—my mother.

"How are you? Why haven't you called me? Are you feeling okay?"

"I'm fine. I've been busy."

"Are you eating?"

"No, Ma, I'm starving to death."

"Don't get smart with me. I just want to know you're all right. When are you coming over for dinner? Or we can go out to eat."

I don't want dinner. I don't want to eat out at fancy restaurants where the cost of dinner could feed me for a month. I don't want to make small talk, or hear about how well her friends' kids are doing—the ones whose parents have sent them to expensive colleges and bought them cars, who have good jobs and boyfriends and are getting married and having babies and whose parents are so proud of them. I don't want to hear any of it.

But I do go, because she expects me, because she's my mother, because she gets angry and hurt and worried if I don't, because I'm her daughter, because she loves me and worries, because it's our habit, because we're tied together, because she's my mother, because I feel guilty, because she feels guilty, because she's my mother.

In her peach-colored apartment, windows closed and air-conditioning on, lights dimmed and mood music on the stereo, I feel muffled, blotted out. I can't bear the small talk, the excess, the inert heaviness. The smell of my mother's perfume sticks in my throat.

I retreat to the bathroom, check myself in the mirror. My skin is bad, bumps popping up everywhere. I think of my bad skin as a spiritual condition, a telltale eruption of my inner state. I squeeze a couple, leaving them red and nasty, then wash my face and try some of the dozens of cosmetics lined up next to the sink. Lipstick, eyeshadow, a whole new face. But my mother's makeup is wrong for me: Her bright red lipstick and black mascara don't work with my complexion. I try a dab of perfume. Whew! Too strong, makes me choke. I wash it all off. Check myself again. I look like hell. My pores are huge, my skin red. Maybe I should try some of my mother's foundation makeup. It's no use. I sit on the padded toilet seat, my head in my hands.

"Min! What are you doing in there?"

We are going through a charade. I'm trying to pretend I'm fine. She's trying to pretend we're a normal family. But even though she's a great cook, the food's delicious and I eat until I'm stuffed, I can't digest the suffocation I feel being back in her world.

My mother presses cab fare into my hand as I leave. I hate myself for accepting it, and the leftover food, hand-me-down clothing, and cosmetics waiting for me in shopping bags. Things that look great and sexy on her look ridiculous and ill-fitting on me. Even if I look fine when I try them on in my mother's apartment, when I get home I see in my mirror an awkward schoolgirl playing dress-up.

My mother is endlessly generous about buying me clothes. I let her take me shopping, an ordeal I emerge from shakily, not just because of the crowds and mass consumerism, but also the mad lust of it, clothing piling up on the fitting-room floor, my mother running to get this in that size and that in this color. Then there's the irksome contradiction of defining my own image with clothing paid for by my mother, along with guilt at taking money from the very person from whom I am attempting to declare my independence. Each time I see the multiple images of myself in the fitting-room mirror, I face my uncertainty about how I want to present myself to the world. I return home with several shopping bags of sweaters, skirts, slacks, and shirts (some her style, some mine). Before I hang up my new clothes, I admire them in the mirror, forgive myself the compromise, and vow to be nicer to my mother.

During the week I work and go to school, long days that start early and end late. I'm driven to do as much as possible, as if to make up for the years I've lost. Saturdays I'm busy doing errands, cleaning my apartment, seeing friends. But Sundays, beautiful quiet Sundays, are my time to rest, reflect, and feed my spirit. I read in bed, walk in the park, listen to music, do some painting.

I adopt a cat; she's white and fat—Moby Dick, my great white whale. We respect each other's space; I'm glad for the company. I keep my windows always open for fresh air. Moby catwalks ten floors up, crying at the pigeons. I trust her to keep her balance.

In a moment of weakness I go to bed with a friend I've known since junior high. We're at it for only a couple of minutes before he collapses on top of me, just as I'm mulling over in my head when to tell him I'm not using anything. Within a month I know I'm pregnant.

There is no doubt in my mind what I have to do. My friend agrees to give me half the money. I go by myself to the Margaret Sanger clinic, not far from my mother's apartment. In the waiting room I'm surrounded by charts of female anatomy, pictures of diaphragms, posters of smiling mothers with their babies, and young women with bellies in various stages of roundness. Not everyone has come here to destroy the life within them. I feel like a criminal.

"Do you want to have the baby?" the woman interviewing me asks. The question startles me. Of course not. How could I? I can hardly take care of myself.

"Does your mother know?" Absolutely not. I would never tell her. She'd be furious.

I arrive on the appointed day. The waiting room is filled with young women; some girls my age or even younger. Many are with their parents, or boyfriends. A few, like me, are alone. A group of us are called into the next room, where we're given hospital gowns in exchange for our clothes. Then I'm in a room by myself; the doctor introduces herself, the instruments are cold, I feel a twinge. I'm shaking with cold and fear. The anesthetist, smiling down at me, tells me to start counting backward: 100 . . . 99 . . . 98 . . .

I hear crying. At first it's soft, a kind of whimpering, then it turns into sobs. I open my eyes. I'm lying on a cot, surrounded by other cots. Most of my neighbors are sleeping, but a few are stirring. The crying continues, such a sad sound. I want to get up and comfort whoever's weeping, but I can't move. Why doesn't someone go help her?

A white blur appears in front of me. I feel a hand on my arm. "Are you in pain?" a voice asks. No, I try to say, not me . . . but then the two images come together and I realize the sobs are coming from me.

It would have been a boy, they tell me.

I'm sent home with sanitary pads and painkillers and told not to strain myself. After a day in bed, I'm bored. Time to begin again. I decide to paint my kitchen new colors. I buy the paint, empty the room, borrow a ladder, get to work. It's hot outside and I don't have a fan, but with each trickle of sweat I earn a drop of self-respect.

My mother calls. "How are you?"

"I'm okay. I had the flu, but now I'm better."

There are many ways in which I deny myself. I deny myself sleep, food, and comfort. Four hours sleep ought to be enough. Dark circles grow beneath my eyes. How far can I push myself? I stay up all night painting, then after several cups of coffee and cigarettes, head off to school. I allow myself the meagerest of lunches, usually too tense to finish them. After school I walk home instead of taking the bus. I love the power and rhythm of walking fast, outstripping the plodding crowd. As I walk, thoughts flood my mind with a speed and clarity that astound me.

I find creative ways to overcome my fears. Taking the subway home from downtown at 3 A.M., alone, afraid of being mugged, I pull my raincoat hood over my face, singing aloud and talking to myself, to scare off anyone who may think I'm an easy mark.

How strong can I become? I often walk up the ten flights of stairs instead of taking the elevator, and do barre exercises when I'm alone in the elevator so as not to waste my time just standing still. I rearrange my few pieces of furniture each week so as not to get too comfortable. Before long my bed has been in every position, parallel and perpendicular, along every wall in the bedroom and the living room. Likewise, I alternate my pillow between the head and foot of the bed each night so I'm never sure which direction I'm facing when I wake. I will do anything to keep from feeling dull, heavy, and habitual. I will be different: alert, light, awake.

For days at a time I function like a well-oiled machine. But always, inevitably, comes The Crash. Anything can set it off. It could be a nasty look or knowing remark that makes me realize I've said or done something arrogant or foolish. Or it could be the cumulative effect of sleep deprivation, a diet of doughnuts, coffee, bananas, and eggs, or just the wild monthly hormonal swings I've never learned to be prepared for. Sooner or later, I fall off my streamlined, brilliant high, and crash into the pits of depression. Hell, I call it. A punishment for my sinful, arrogant sham of a self. I stay in hell for as long as it takes, sleeping, weeping, reluctant to go outside where the world can behold my puffy, heavy, ugly, stupid, lazy, crazy self. Sooner or later I venture out, breathe the air, walk a little faster, and before long, I'm off and flying again.

To keep myself going, I chain-smoke and drink: coffee all day and alcohol at night. I keep on hand a bottle of Slivovitz, the fiery Yugoslavian brandy my grandfather drank. The scorch of smoke in my lungs and the alcohol burning its way down to my gut remind me that I exist. Each night I drunkenly vow to be strong, not weak; impulsive, not passive; solitary, not dependent.

I carry a full course load and work part-time. The N.Y.S. Department of Vocational Rehabilitation pays my tuition—thirty-two dollars per semester, plus money for books. As much as it bothers me to think of myself as someone in need of "rehabilitation," I think of it as a reparation, like tuition paid after military service.

In art history survey class I sit in a state of bliss, watching slides of great art projected on the screen in the darkened auditorium. In one semester we cover the art of ancient Egypt, Greece, and Rome through the Renaissance. At the end of each class I leave the auditorium with tears in my eyes, awed. As I walk home through Central Park, the sky softening into twilight, little shoots poke through the winter crust and tiny buds dot the branches. The earth is alive, the trees breathe with me, and life and art seem entwined together into one sacred living entity.

I start drawing in the park, like I did during my truant times in high school: rocks and trees—but now I also draw people sitting on benches or in grassy stretches. I always have my sketchbook with me. If I'm not drawing, I'm writing lists of imperatives: "Draw. Paint. Love. 2 feet on the ground. Be. Respond. Move." If anyone approaches me—it's always some man, checking me out—I ask if I can draw him. That way, even if I'm scared or I sense he wants to come on to me, as long as I hold the pencil, I'm in charge.

I sign up for printmaking, life drawing, and painting, and soon am fully immersed. I draw everything: the plants in my window and the buildings outside it; the white metal stool sitting on the radiator looking like a skeleton; myself in the mirror, my face unflinching, my face sad; my room from all angles; my hands held this way and that; my foot on my bed, the sketchbook on my knee, my foot on my bed and sketchbook on my knee in the sketchbook in the drawing, like the endless reflections of the anxious girl in the department-store dressing room, but this time it's the real me and I'm not anxious, I'm in control.

"You have something here. I'd like to see you do more writing about art. Please make an appointment to see me," my art history professor writes on my term paper. But I can't bring myself to see her. The idea of a conference, and possibly being called upon to back up my intuitive insights with solid performance, is too scary. I can't imagine myself on a career path, writing research papers, doing serious scholarly work.

The beginning of each semester is a crisis of indecision. The courses all look so inviting. Who will I be—a philosopher with a social anthropological/historical twist, or a fine artist grounded in art history with some literature and French on the side? The permutations are endlessly delicious. I roll them around in my mind. It can take a couple of weeks to sort it out, and by that time half the classes I'm interested in are closed out anyway.

———————

For a while I work as a mother's helper taking care of two little girls, three and five. The older girl goes to preschool in the mornings and I am left with the baby. I hold her on my lap, inhaling the fresh scent of her hair, while we watch *Sesame Street*. After lunch, when her sister is home from school, I read them a story or watch them dance to their favorite record. It amazes me how unself-conscious and secure they are. It's hard to imagine that I used to be just as innocent as these little girls. I envy their peaceful, happy childhoods.

One day in the playground I meet Carole. Doe-eyed, dark-haired, quick to laugh, she easily handles a play group of five children, while I have my hands full with my two girls. I admire her outgoing, joyful presence. We discover we're the same age and are both enrolled at Hunter.

Carole has a small studio apartment but isn't happy living alone. When my roommate moves out unexpectedly, Carole moves in. We are the proverbial odd couple: Carole, relaxed and messy, loving bright colors and creative chaos. Myself, spare and controlled, unable to go to sleep if things are in disarray. "Olive Oyl" Carole jokingly dubs me when I stand, arms crossed, tapping my foot, surveying whatever mess needs cleaning.

We watch George and Gracie on TV, eat gallons of chocolate pudding, rely heavily on fried liver for nutrition, switch to the same brand of cigarettes, laugh, cry, and confide. It soon comes out: Carole had a breakdown in high school shortly after her older sister attempted suicide. Deeply depressed, she admitted herself to a hospital, grateful for the brief period of isolation in which she could fall apart, then reassemble herself.

Like me, Carole is fragile, the split in herself not fully healed. Strangers to ourselves, we navigate the ways of the world. We go to parties and drink too much, seduce and sleep with men we don't feel anything for, wonder why we feel so bad at times, so ecstatic at others. In spite of our different styles, we form a sisterhood that withstands fights, silences, misunderstandings, and ultimately, years, geographical distance, Carole's marriage, the birth of her sons, her divorce, the rise of her career as a poet. She is as close as any family I've ever known.

I meet a young man at a poetry reading. His eyes are deep, dark pools, his face pale and handsome. He asks for my phone number, and after writing it down, says slowly and with intentional emphasis, "I will *call* you." Anticipation colors my days until the phone rings.

David is a student of the occult, a poet who plays the guitar. We soon fall in love; the sleepless, up-all-night-talking-and-making-love, telepathic kind of connection that dreamers pine for. It's a love affair of two intelligences that merge perfectly.

From the start, it's different with David. When we hug, I feel like I hold the world in my arms. My gaze grazes the top of his head; half a head taller than him, I feel exotic, powerful. I inhale his smell: clean T-shirts, cigarettes, a familiar maleness, like my father. His chest is covered with soft dark hair, his face a pale moon with long-lashed, wide-set eyes. He is gentle and nurturing, a true poet.

David introduces me to the teachings of G. I. Gurdjieff, the Russian mystic whose esoteric "work" is compiled from various occult and major religions. I attend weekly group meetings in which we are given exercises and report on our efforts to "observe ourselves"—becoming conscious of habitual behavior, especially wasteful negativity. Impulsiveness and emotion are frowned upon. Having cultivated negativity to a fine art, I struggle with this new orientation. At group meetings I assume a straight, gravity-defying posture—the opposite of my adolescent slouch—and try to appear aware, while underneath my heart is pounding fearfully and below the table my legs jiggle like mad. Instead of manifesting higher consciousness, my agitated thoughts judge every move I make. Always my shameful secret threatens to betray me.

When I tell David about having been in the hospital, he opens his arms and holds me close. With David I find an oasis, encircled in his arms, his intelligence, his poet's heart. He values my sensitivity and sees it as a strength, not a symptom or failing.

David moves in. For a while there are four humans, a dog, and two cats in my one-bedroom apartment: my current roommate, her boyfriend, David and I, and and our various pets. When my roommate moves out, David and I set up house.

The apartment becomes our project. I like things open and airy, the furniture flat against the walls for more floor space. David has a cozier aesthetic: carpets, bookshelves extend into the room as subdividers, tables kitty-corner. We work it out, making the place a home. In the bathtub, a red-sailed wooden sailboat, my gift to David; on the wall, a Persian tile his parents gave us—a young girl ("She reminds me of you," says David) with a bird on her shoulder. The bird symbolizes thought, David informs me. Me and my ever-present thoughts.

Living with David brings out my domesticity. I make pancakes and eggs for breakfast, chicken and mashed potatoes or pasta for dinner. We both put on weight: the accrual of contentment. Even the laundry is proof of our bond. I watch our socks and underwear tumble together in the dryer. His, mine. Ours.

Our lives blend effortlessly. Our days and nights are filled with work, meetings, culture, films, friends, and one another. We are best friends who never argue or tire of each other's company. Sometimes, sitting in the living room reading, we look up at precisely the same moment and smile. I draw David reading, David talking, studies of his hands and feet. An avocado I grow from a seed shoots up two feet; before planting it I do an etching of it, roots dangling as long as its stem, interestingly, intricately entangled.

At the edge of our oasis is the cool criticism of his mother, who seems to sense something is wrong with me. I wonder if she's the only one. David's friends are older, hip, well-adjusted. At parties I stand staring at my hands, mortified at my self-consciousness. The gulf between us is great. Students of the occult, they are striving to be less a part of the world, while I'm just learning to be comfortable in it. But there's a catch: to be happy, to be part of the world, would be forgetting—and that is inconceivable.

I don't understand how other people just seem to live their lives, while I have to constantly navigate the gulf. On one shore is a life in which I am happy, loved, creative—my life with David. The other side is inhabited by grotesque sadness, failure, loss—the life I've come from. Between them rush all my anxiety and despair, in great gusts. When the conflict becomes too great, I weep wordlessly, unable to express to David the reason for my pain. Sooner or later he will leave me. Like my father, like Marjee, like everyone I've loved. I don't talk about it. I just know.

Sunday afternoon. David is sprawled on the carpet, watching the World Series, drinking a beer. I clean around him; stepping over him, I straighten the couch cushions. I'm restless. I take a walk around the block, but it doesn't dispel my anxiety. I go around again, running this time, then stand breathing deeply, looking at the sky. Clouds are gathering, but I don't feel like going back upstairs. I could go to the supermarket or browse in the bookstore, but I know when I come home, it'll be the same problem. I don't know where "we" leave off and "I" begin. The more melded I feel with David, the more my own outline seems to fade.

We have our separate heroes. David emulates those people in the Gurdjieff community he sees as evolving toward higher consciousness. They are his buddies and his role models. I gravitate toward artists. David's friend Joel is someone we both admire, an artist who explores concepts like identity (making his own shoes and clothing with hand-made tools) and time (using papermaking as a metaphor), documenting everything with eclectic, brilliant texts. Joel defies classification. His life, like his art, is an exploration, an exercise in awareness.

"You should be with someone like Joel," David tells me repeatedly. "You're so alike." I can hardly imagine how. It's clearly not because of my mind, a muddle of subjectivity and metaphor, whereas Joel's is like a swift, clear stream.

In the seventies, anything goes, even between me and David. It's understood: We're together, yet we're individual entities. It's clear that we love each other, but where we go from here is unclear. Outwardly, I scorn marriage. That's what my parents did, and it didn't keep them together. Inwardly, I'm an unadulterated romantic. We fumble around the blurred edges of our relationship. At dinner with a couple of David's friends, I fuzzily decline the invitation to be a foursome, hating myself for being so square.

When Joel invites me to come with him to Nova Scotia, where he's been invited to teach a week-long seminar at an art college, David urges me to go. Why not travel to a beautiful new place? Why not spend a few days with this free-spirited artist I admire? We share a bedroom in his hosts' house in Halifax, twin mattresses beside each other on the floor. When I emerge from the bathroom in my nightgown, Joel is already under the covers. I lie on my mattress for a moment, body pulsing, before we turn to each other and Joel pulls me into the warmth of his body.

I drift mutely through the rest of the visit, welcoming the cleansing shock of immersion in the bone-crunchingly cold Atlantic, the only thing aside from sex that has the power to penetrate my confusion. I love Joel, but I've betrayed David. Or have I? It was David's suggestion in the first place. Then why do I feel so awful? Joel doesn't seem to feel any qualms. When I return home and David asks about the trip, I tell him everything but what's really important. Betrayal, an irritating grit eroding my self-esteem, swirls into a cloud of depression.

For a while I've been losing interest in school. I've taken all my electives and now only requirements remain. I sign up for biology, then drop it when I realize it includes dissections. Astronomy starts out well, but the other students irritate me, endlessly asking the teacher to repeat himself. I fidget and hyperventilate through classes and bolt when the bell rings, racing through the halls in a state of righteous indignation.

When David leaves his bookstore job for a corporate gig as an assistant editor for a group of industrial trade magazines, I feel betrayed. How could he join that world, abandoning the values I thought we shared? I meet him for lunch at a midtown restaurant. Looking across the table, I see a stranger. This person in his suit and tie is not the poet I fell in love with.

I feel left behind, aimless. What's the point of going to school if I have no goal? I could become a teacher, but the education classes lack humanity, poetry. I want to be an artist . . . but how do artists make a living? I refuse to study commercial art—a subject beneath contempt, its very name an oxymoron.

David tries to help. "Maybe you'd feel better if you got a full-time job, Min."

"*Get a job . . .*" I wake in the mornings with the old rock 'n' roll song playing in my head.

I drop out of college and start looking for a job. Plenty are listed in the *Times:* gal Friday, secretary. I dress up for job interviews, make a good enough impression, and have no trouble getting hired. The problem is keeping the jobs. How can people sit all day? After a few hours, days, or weeks, I quit—if I'm not fired first.

Why not do what common folk do? I'm hired as a waitress at a midtown burger restaurant. I'm a terrible waitress, running back and forth, apron askew. Reaching for a dish, I accidentally bop a customer on the nose. Serving a family of five, I forget to give the chef their order. After forty-five minutes they march out, justifiably indignant, and I'm told to hand in my apron.

Temp work is even worse: every week a new place, not knowing anyone, moving on just as I'm becoming familiar with the office machines or where the bathroom is. I file documents in a windowless, closet-sized room in a law office; at night I dream I am filing the events of my life in a manila folder that will be on permanent record for posterity; I wake in tears and don't go back.

Next I get a job as a file clerk at the public library. Even in the midst of all the books, my work—replacing index cards in the card catalog—is numbingly mindless. By midday I am claustrophobic, by the end of the day, desperate. Late to work every morning, I decide to quit before they fire me.

Back to job interviews. But something is malfunctioning. I can't get my clothes on. I try on everything in the closet, but nothing looks right. Clothing all over the floor. My arm aches from brushing my hair. Why am I even trying? What happened to the girl who loved to read, think, create? Why is she dressing in skirts and blouses, going off to secretarial jobs? I swore I'd never be like my mother, and here I am, living her life.

David sits and talks with me, trying to understand my distress. To him it's simple—either I do this, or I do that. We make lists of options, with pros on one side and cons on the other, but they always seem to cancel each other out. David draws a cartoon of me: a stick figure with long hair trying to tuck hospital corners around a mattress on which sits a large brain. The caption reads: "Just making up my mind."

I don't want a job, I want a sense of purpose. I don't even want a career, I want a reason for being. Every option I think of falls short; either I feel inadequate for the task or it feels inadequate for me. I'm not a free spirit, I'm not an academic, and I'm not a nine-to-fiver. I'm a poor excuse for an artist. Why do I have to be the way I am? I wish I could be anybody else.

"You can't make a flower grow by pulling it up by its stem," a friend wisely advises.

Instead of going to job interviews, I see therapists. One offers medication, another suggests meditation. One advises a trial separation from David so I can experience myself apart from him. When I mention this to David, he is stunned and saddened. He never imagined our splitting up. But he agrees to a six-month separation and finds a loft on the Bowery. A new life begins for David. A new neighborhood, and new friends. He makes an effort to include me, but everything has changed. When news reaches me that David has slept with someone we both know, he assures me it meant nothing.

"We'll get back together once you calm down," David promises. But I don't calm down.

I can no longer sleep at night. If I turn out the lights, I fall into an abyss. I catnap, lights on. I can't eat, can't work. I have no money. I can't bear to see my friends. My skin has been sandpapered raw, every contact excruciating. I wander supermarket aisles looking for bargains, quaking in the fluorescent glare. I take buses and subways to nowhere in particular. I call David from phone booths, crying. I have ruined my life, destroyed my one happiness, pulled the rug right out from under my feet—the same way I dropped out of high school, into the loony bin, out of college, out of the one place I'm loved. What will I do now? I'm a fragile shell.

A social worker/psychotherapist prescribes jogging. "It worked wonders when I was going through my divorce," she confides, her makeup crinkling into a smile, sitting in the makeshift office in her newly decorated Upper East Side apartment. "Call me anytime." Her charm bracelet jingles good-bye.

David stops by after a business trip to California and vacation in

Mexico. Kneeling on my living-room floor, he confesses that he took the trip with a new girlfriend. I feel somehow vindicated. What else could I expect but betrayal?

Then David asks me to marry him. "I thought of you the whole time, Min. It was always you I loved."

Too late. I'm frozen. Can't go forward, can't go back.

CRAZY

I'M NOT LIKE OTHER PEOPLE, and I know other people can see it.

Early one Saturday morning, my building's resident superintendent, a hardworking Eastern European immigrant with three small children, rings my doorbell. Surprised, I wonder whether the building's old valves are leaking again, silently drenching the walls. Or maybe my downstairs neighbor complained that I let the bathtub overflow, something I do regularly. My form of wetting the bed, my unconscious overflowing its banks.

"Yes?"

The super looks down at his feet, then at me, then away; clears his throat, takes a breath.

"I come to apologize."

I look at him, puzzled. As far as I know he has nothing to apologize to me for. But he looks upset. He takes a breath, continues.

"If someone, like the handyman, tell you I say you're crazy, it's not true. I never say that." Now that it's out, the words tumble faster. "So in case that's what you heard, or if anybody say that to you, I'm sorry. But I never say any such thing."

I feel my face reddening, my hands suddenly sweaty, my chest tight. Now he's off the hot seat and I'm on. That's okay, I tell him, nobody said anything like that to me. But the cat's out of the bag. Here, in my new life, in my own apartment, people *still* think I'm crazy. They talk about it— why else would the super have dragged himself to my door early on a Saturday morning? His denial indicts him. I feel sorry for him, for the worry that propelled him up here to confront me, both of us wriggling on the hook of his indiscretion.

How can they tell? What do they see? My eyes reveal my inner turmoil in spite of myself. I'm too transparent, every emotion visible, as much as I try to cover up. The composure I practice in the mirror fractures under pressure. Maybe I smile too much, a tense, twisted grimace pasted on my face. Or maybe it's the frequency with which I go rushing in and out, in and out, anxiety rising off me like steam. It shouldn't take a genius or a psychiatrist to see that something is wrong with me.

When I pass through the lobby, I try to put on an impervious surface, smile politely, look normal—whatever that is.

Normal. Is that what I want to be? Normal is the prison I've tried to escape from; normal is everything I don't want. Normal is an office job, and I aspire to be an artist. Normal was the fifties, and I'm a child of the sixties. Now, in the seventies, my brand of emotional angst is rapidly becoming outdated. Being the victim of one's emotions or circumstances is too Victorian for these times. Women's lib has filtered into daily life. Helplessness is passé.

I list my flaws: I am too emotional, impulsive, fearful, indecisive, sad, depressed, negative, compulsive, judgmental, angry, uptight, confused, stuck in my head. I have low self-esteem but at the same time I'm too intense. And too sensitive, like I'm missing a layer of skin or some protective coating.

Sensitivity isn't a deficit, I tell myself. It's a hallmark of the creative spirit, a highly desirable quality. Sensitivity is my protection, the ultimate alibi. Too sensitive to make a decision. Too sensitive to go into midtown, to work at a boring job, to be in a crowd of people, to take criticism, to handle rejection. Too finely tuned, too highly strung, wound up tight, ready to snap.

When *The Exorcist* opened, David and I were among the first audiences. Sitting in the dark watching the film, I was terrified yet transfixed by the image of the innocent child whose mind, possessed by evil, had become an alien thing. So it is sometimes with my thoughts. It's as if they are not my own. A malevolent voice undresses people, picks out their flaws, and makes crude, cruel comments. Or it does the same about myself. The voice emerges when I am in a dire state of depression, heavy as lead, sunk into the depths. When this happens, I wonder whether I too am possessed by dark forces.

There are times when, propelled by an irresistible impulse, I find myself walking straight out into the crush of oncoming traffic pouring down Broadway. *Hit me,* I dare them. Horns blare, brakes shriek, as cars swerve around me. Someone yells, "What the hell is wrong with you? You want to get killed?" And some driver always shouts as he pulls away: "Are you CRAZY?"

I look it up in the dictionary.

Crazy *adj.*1. full of cracks or flaws. Unsound; also crooked, askew. 2.a. mad, insane b.1) impractical 2) erratic 3) distracted with desire or excitement.

So far it's all accurate. I *am* crazed, cracked, flawed, impractical, erratic, distracted, desirous, too easily excited, though I'm still not sure about mad, insane. Poetically, at least, the word seems to fit. But I can't help searching for signs of a more serious condition.

One day while brushing my teeth, I notice my eyes look funny. My pupils are dilated; that is, the left is hugely dilated, while the right is contracted into a pindot. I look closer. The left pupil seems to be pulsing slightly. Maybe I have some neurological impairment. Or it could be my thyroid, or hormonal imbalance, or diet, or . . .

Mental illness is what I fear. How I hate that expression. As if I have a disease. Mental hygiene, like dental hygiene. Mental floss. That's probably what I need to clean my excessively worrying, negativistic brain; to scrape out the thoughts from where they shouldn't stick.

Once David took me to Nirvana, a luxurious Indian restaurant high above Central Park South. As we sat talking over drinks, a palm reader, complete with jeweled turban, approached us. With a flash of his teeth he asked if we would like our fortunes told. "Sure," David said, always willing to explore.

"I see you will have love in your life . . . you will excel in your career . . . you will travel far and wide . . ." Looking closer at David's hand, he found traces of David's interest in the occult and artistic endeavors. "You are, perhaps, a musician?" he inquired, to David's delight.

Then it was my turn. I wiped the moisture from my palm, and placed it face up in his. The palmist raised my hand and turned my palm this way and that. Wiping a new layer of dew off its surface, he looked up and grinned.

"This is one damn crazy woman!" he announced in a thick Hindustani accent.

I blushed. Did he really see this in my palm? Or was it just plain obvious?

The palmist pointed out two stars of crisscrossed lines under my ring finger, symbolic of creativity. "You are very artistic, talented in many areas, but cannot decide which direction to take, always torn in two directions . . ."

That's me, all right.

"You are extremely idealistic, a real dreamer, but with much mental agility—your thoughts are faster than other people's and this can get you into trouble. Your head line is very chained . . ." (that's for sure, I thought) ". . . and your heart line as well." He checked my left hand. "Were you ill as a very young child?"

Maybe there is something to this after all. How else could he have known that my first year was a succession of illnesses? Born seven weeks premature, I had no fingernails or toenails; my skin, covered with peach fuzz, was a jaundiced yellow. Visitors approached my crib wearing surgical masks, instructed not to touch me. Perhaps that accounts for my uneasiness in the world. Or perhaps, being jolted out of the womb too soon, I emerged radically unprepared for life.

The fortune-teller returned to my right palm. "You will have much trouble in your life, perhaps illness. You are prone to nervous disturbances. But with the proper care and understanding, you will do well and have much success." He turned to David and said, "You must take care of her! She is a precious flower. You don't want to lose her."

And David promised that he would always take care of me.

———————

David is getting married. I knew it was coming, but the shock, the sense of betrayal, defies words. It's the worst kind of pain, like everything rolled up into one: Once again my father moves to California; again I quake in the elevator's descent to the fifth-floor ward; again the abyss of Marjee's death. I am definitely being left behind, alone—proof that I am not meant to experience the pleasures and successes that others do but will always stand on the sidelines, watching.

Holidays are particularly difficult. David and I used to spend Thanksgiving with friends, afternoons as warm and delicious as the turkey and sweet-potato pie we savored. Even my sociophobic self relaxed into the spirit of the day, mellowed by brandy and hearthfire. Now Thanksgiving is an agony. I decline going to my mother's and go instead to my local coffee shop, where I order the holiday special and poke listlessly at the turkey and canned cranberry sauce. I'm one of the few customers sitting alone. Even the elderly are sitting in pairs, except for two old ladies, each in their separate booth, focused on their holiday plates, not a trace of animation on their faces. I wonder if I'm looking at my future.

Shortly after David and I split up, my mother and stepfather get divorced. Even though their marriage had been deteriorating for a long while, and my stepfather and I certainly have our issues, it comes as a minor earthquake. Nothing in life feels stable or dependable. Nothing stays in place, nothing lasts.

My mother moves into a studio apartment and starts a new life. She sees a psychologist and begins dating a man in her industry who was recently widowed. It isn't long before he moves in with her. Paul is a good man who's had a hard life. He nursed his late wife through debilitating illnesses, raised his daughter, and worked hard to support his family. This time my mother marries for the right reasons. They truly love and care about each other.

"Depressed." I say flatly into the phone, in response to my mother's anxious "How are you?"

"Why should you feel that way?" my mother pleads. "You're young. You have your whole life ahead of you."

"I don't feel young. I'm all fucked up."

"You're not all fucked up. You just think you are."

Easy for her to say. She didn't spend two and a half years in a nuthouse. Why can't she just hear that I'm upset and let me be? I know she feels threatened by my unhappiness. My failure means her failure as a mother. Her voice is edged with guilt.

"Put the past behind you. Move on. Why must you punish yourself? What have you done that's so terrible?"

I've ruined my life, that's what! Why is she always trying to talk me out of feeling what I feel? She wants to put on some kind of false face, but I won't.

She changes the subject. "Are you working?" Of course, that's the most important thing. Mental health is synonymous with holding a job—a boring, meaningless, demeaning job. Gal Friday, secretary, or that holiest of Jewish working-class holies, retail. My mother's dream come true would be for me to get a job as a buyer at Macy's.

I tried working at Macy's. After viewing the orientation film ("Macy's! It's like no other store in the world!"), I worked for two weeks as a file clerk in a large room filled with women silently flipping papers with rubber-tipped fingers. We were allowed two fifteen-minute coffee and pee breaks (we were expected to hold our bladders until break time) and a half-hour for lunch: bagged sandwiches and vending-machine coffee in a dingy, smoke-filled room that reminded me of Manhattan State. Some of the filing ladies were lifers; one gray-haired file nun was ceremoniously awarded a gold watch for her twenty-five years of faithful service. Too depressing for words. I requested a transfer and was sent to Fur Storage, where plucked and powdered ladies came to refrigerate their pelts. I didn't last a week.

I feel bad that I'm a disappointment to my mother. Can't she see that I'm equally a disappointment to myself? The combination of the two is too much for me.

"What the hell do you want me to do? I don't want to be a fucking file clerk!"

"How dare you talk to me like that!"

"I'm sorry, I'm sorry!" I shout into the phone, hating myself more than I hate her.

Half our conversations end with us screaming at each other. When all else fails, I hang up or throw the phone at the wall. I've hurled the phone across the room so many times it's dented and cracked. It gets to the point where we can't talk to each other at all.

My new stepfather, a kind and understanding man, intervenes. He calls me every few days to see how I'm doing, and we have a standing dinner date on Monday nights. At least I have one good meal a week, and some structure in the barren desert of my days.

I struggle to keep myself going. I'm alive, but barely "functioning"— another psychiatric expression I abhor. Functioning: the bare minimum of existence. I might as well be a snail or clam or some other invertebrate; a pathetic collection of biological functions. I have to find something to justify my existence.

I try painting, but I can't get the paint to do what I want—if I even know what I want. Frustration rises. If I can't paint, if I'm not creative, then I'm completely worthless. Outside the window, winter; inside, darkness, chaos, rage. I have to stop it. I turn to the window, crash my fist through the glass, shattering the pane. Blood wells on my hand, but it's only a little cut where the jagged glass caught my pinky. Cold air streams in from outside. The window! I'll have to call the super to have it repaired, and then he'll know. What can I tell him? I think up a story about a BB gun shot from across the street (there was a little hole in the glass from a BB pellet, so it's not a total lie). I practice telling him aloud, alone in my room. When he comes to fix it, I tell my story and can see he doesn't believe it, doesn't even want to hear it.

On buses and subways, streets and restaurants, eyes closed, tears seeping, I try not to sob out loud. If some kind soul offers me a Kleenex and asks me what's wrong, I tell them what I can. "My boyfriend . . . we broke up . . . he's getting married . . ." I'm amazed by how sympathetic people are. Complete strangers, taking the time to listen. Concerned, they ask me where my family is. We don't get along, I sniffle. It's pathetic. Panhandling for sympathy—a new way to humiliate myself.

"You're young," they tell me, "and pretty. You have your whole life ahead of you." The same words that make me bristle when my mother says them. As if youth isn't fleeting, as if I haven't wasted years, as if a pleasing appearance is everything, as if what's inside doesn't matter.

I don't understand why everybody is intent on telling me that what I'm feeling is not real. It's like a conspiracy of rationalization, or mass hypnosis. "You're young," people keep repeating, until suddenly you're not young anymore. I'm almost thirty—the age over which my generation is not supposed to trust anyone.

"Get some help," my mother says each time we talk. As if help exists. I don't trust that therapists can do anything for me. That's another sham of a conspiracy: paying a stranger to listen to me, so they can go out and buy some nice new clothes. But I have to do something.

I eventually call to make an appointment with one of the psychotherapy clinics my mother keeps recommending. But the idea of further self-humiliation is too daunting. After hours of agitated indecision, I call and cancel at the last minute, making up an excuse. In a week or so I try again. This time I make it to the appointment, but grow fainthearted at the sight of the forms they ask me to fill out and leave before I've completed the first page.

My friends have already referred me to therapists, psychologists, psy-
chotherapists, social workers, counselors. It's always a variation on the
same theme, ending with my sitting across from them in a stew of embarrassment. A familiar scene: the modest office with one window, two
chairs, a table, an oriental rug, and if the therapist is a psychoanalyst, a
couch. I never lie on the couch; too passive a position. I need to maintain
some control over my life.

Always, I unwrap and unload the burden I carry with me, exposing the
artifacts of my life: my mother, my father, the divorce, the hospital,
Marjee, David. Totems of loss and failure, my heavy load. After laying
them out on the oriental rug for the entertainment and edification of the
concerned or distant, intelligent or plodding, experienced or novice so-
called therapy provider, after summarizing their history and describing
some of their fine points, after several soggy tissues and some hard swallowing, our time is up. One by one I put my trinkets back in the bag,
relieved to have them disappear from view. We discuss whether or not to
work together; the therapists invariably say they feel they can help me (I
am so irresistibly in need of help), and I tell them I need to think about
it, that I will phone them. Then we settle up, whatever sliding-scale, low-
cost arrangement we've made. It irks me to no end to have to pay for the
ultimate booby prize of human relations, a hired friend or surrogate parent. After putting away my checkbook, I pick up my sack of woes, hoist it
over my shoulder, and stagger out onto the street, feeling somewhat
purged but mostly relieved that the ritual is over.

On my way to and from therapy sessions, I always spot a street loony.
On 57th Street it's the Opera Man, who stands outside Carnegie Hall
shouting arias in a frenzy of torturously discordant vocalizing, his face
twisted as if in pain. As I pass he approaches me, arms tensed, shaking his
fists at the sky, as if entreating the heavens to help him or strike him dead.
There's the Traffic Drummer, who runs into the middle of the street,
drumsticks to the ground, tapping out rhythms between the moving cars.
There's the Shitty Ass Man, pants dropped, exposing his dirty buns for all
to see, and lovely Mary who, though she smells like rotten fruit, sings
sweet ballads to the pedestrians on Broadway and 88th Street. I see them
as shamanistic figures—mediums or channels, expressing the craziness
buried in all of us.

The street crazies really begin to blossom in the hot weather. They
erupt into fits of raving, get into fights, run screaming into the paths of

cars. One particularly hot day on my way home, just as I emerge from the subway stairs, a street lady, arm outstretched, whirls around, swinging her clenched fist smack into the side of my head so hard I almost black out. I fall to the ground wondering why, out of the crowd of commuters, it was me she chose to clobber.

The street crazies seem especially attracted to me. They converge on me for change, bless me, or curse me. I give them what I can, which isn't much, and try not to gag at the stench or harden myself to their plight. They remind me that I do have some things to be grateful for. At least I have a bed and a refrigerator to go home to. Except when I forget to pay my Con Ed bill and they shut off my gas and electricity, much to the dismay of my current roommate, who is none too thrilled anyway to be living with someone as barely functional as I am.

A MEMBER OF MY TRIBE

FLASHBACK TO 1975. I am in the lunchroom of Hunter College. Never comfortable in crowds, I find an empty seat, open *Crime and Punishment* and disappear into its pages, pulled into Raskolnikov's intransigent choice of murdering not just the old woman, but his own future. It takes me a while to notice the guy standing over me.

"Excuse me," he says in a croaky voice. "I think you're in my philosophy class. My name is Zev." He stammers slightly, his prominent Adam's apple bobbing up and down.

The low roar of the cafeteria swallows his syllables. I look up at him. Gangly, nervous, thinning hair, black jeans, flannel shirt, bad complexion, darting brown eyes magnified by metal-rimmed glasses. Not very attractive. I fight against myself; why should I react to him solely on the basis of his looks? But he does look sightly familiar; maybe I'd noticed him in class.

The guy next to me picks up his tray and leaves, bequeathing his chair to Zev. Now I'll have to stop reading and talk. I fold down the corner of the page and reluctantly close the book.

"Great book," he says. I voice my agreement, but something about him makes me feel uncomfortable. I look at my watch. "Sorry, but I've got to get to my next class."

"Me too." He hastily gathers himself up and squeezes in beside me onto the cattle car of an elevator.

"Bye," I murmur as I fight to get out on the fourth floor, then hurry down the hall.

"I hope to see you again," he calls out as the doors close.

Over the next few weeks I see Zev everywhere. In the hallways, the stairs, the café and art gallery where I go to restore myself, the luncheonette across the street, the bookstore. Gradually we become friends. There is something endearing about him, a nervous desire to please, a sensitivity—not to mention his knowledge of literature and his bursts of philosophical irony. He tells me he's majoring in psychology.

I'm a little envious. "I thought of that myself, but I could never do it."

"Why not?" Zev asks. "You're such a sensitive person."

I hesitate. "I can't stand their generalizations, their formulas. They can do such harm . . ." My face grows hot. Not wanting to say too much, I stop.

Zev scrutinizes me carefully. "Go on."

He's looking at me as if he knows the secret I'm so bitterly fearful of revealing. I don't often talk about the hospital . . . though it sometimes bursts out unexpectedly, usually when I've been drinking. When I do talk about it, I focus on its initial shock value instead of going into detail.

When I finally tell Zev my story, he takes it in, resonating with my grief. "I know, I know," he croaks. "I was there too."

He had been hospitalized too, "cracked up," as he put it. Locked up, shocked, medicated. Zev's parents were German Jewish immigrants—Holocaust survivors. Fearful, overprotective, carrying a sense of powerlessness, they managed to infuse their son with a burden of guilt and pain.

Of course. Zev is one of my people. They flock to me—the hurt, the wounded, self-inflicted sufferers, oppressed of spirit. The disenfranchised. The ones others call crazy. They gravitate toward me, coming out of the woodwork, drawn to the subliminal buzz of despair and conflict that emanates from me like a termite call.

Maybe it is simply that there is no dividing line; that suffering and breakdown and despair are sprinkled about at random. Some doughnuts have powdered sugar, some cinnamon, some plain; all doughnuts, nonetheless. Still, I often find myself in the same box as the crumbly, broken ones, the ones especially in need of love.

Zev has become obsessed with me, waiting for me outside classes, showing up unexpectedly at my building, calling me too often, writing me letters declaring his love. "You know we belong together. We have so much in common."

I am in a bind. I don't want to hurt him, but beyond friendship, I am just not interested. I find the idea of his touching me repellent. However persuasively Zev tries to push me over the line, I stick close to my boundaries, trying to preserve what we have.

Gradually it becomes impossible. As Zev's frustration grows, so does his hostility, and so does mine. I fear answering the phone and think about changing my number. Whenever I find a letter in my mailbox addressed in Zev's tight hand, I cringe.

Over time he retreats. Each time I leave my apartment without seeing Zev lurking nearby, I breathe relief. I feel guilty about it, but what can I do? I'm not Mother Teresa.

One hot July afternoon I sit on the living room floor wondering if I should buy a fan. The downstairs buzzer rings. "A friend is down here," the doorman announces through the intercom. My heart leaps. Maybe it's David . . . lately I've been missing him so.

"Okay, send him up."

But it isn't David. Looking through the peephole, I see Zev. Flustered, I let him in. Time has passed, and he *had* been a close friend. It's only fair to give him a chance. So when my inner voice warns me, *Be careful,* I ignore it.

Zev looks different; he's thinner, his body more muscular. He seems taller. I look down at his feet; his cowboy boots have heels. He's grown a mustache and isn't wearing eyeglasses. And there's something else: He has more hair. It looks like he's wearing a rug.

"How are you?" I ask. "You look different."

"Yes. I look different." He does not return my smile. "I was tired of feeling unattractive. I decided to do something about it. I've spent too many years with my mother trying to take over my life. It's all been starting to make sense." Zev is distraught. His hands are shaking, and beads of sweat dot his forehead, nose, and chin.

"Would you like a glass of cold water?" I ask. "Or we could go get something to eat."

Zev stands in the middle of the living room. "We can go out, but not yet. I came to see you because there's something I need to ask you to do for me. I've thought a lot about this."

Something in me flinches, but I stand my ground. Maybe I can be there for him, as others have been there for me.

"Go on."

"I've gone through hell, years of hell. My mother has destroyed my life, and you . . . you've always pushed me away. But that's about to change. You're the only other person who understands what I've been through. So here's what I need to ask you . . ."

Zev stands facing me, his face pale and sweaty. His skin looks funny, like it is melting, and his mustache is bleeding black at its edges. Could it be? He is wearing makeup and it is starting to run. And his eyes, glaring at me, are blue! He's wearing tinted contacts. I take a step back, but he grabs my arm in a tight grip.

"I want to give you my pain, the pain my mother has planted in me, poisoning me. I want you to take it from me." He pulls me against him. I can feel his hard-on. "Kiss me."

I try to pull my face away, but he pulls it in front of his and presses his lips over mine, his tongue pushing against my teeth. Zev pulls his head back. "Why won't you let me kiss you?"

"Ouch, you're hurting me!" I try to free my arm, but Zev tightens his grip.

As frightened as I am, I suddenly smile. The situation is just too weird.

"It's not funny! I'm not fooling around. I'm tired of being the nice guy, the guy who begs and waits. I'm going to have sex with you, to give you my pain." Zev's voice is full of anguish, and he is trembling. "Will you help me?"

Feeling pity for him, I shake my head. "You need help, but I can't help you." It really is a lot to ask, even of a friend.

Zev pulls himself together and continues. "You have a choice. You can do it willingly or you can resist, but one way or another I am going to do this."

Oh God. Alone in my apartment with a lunatic who has just announced his intention to rape me. He could kill me if he wanted to, but I don't think that's part of his plan.

His whole body is shaking with emotion. "Will you do this for me?"

Terror has wired my mouth shut. An odd sensation tingles through my body, making me light-headed. Then I have an idea. My voice becomes smooth, soothing.

"Okay, I'll do it. But I'm really hungry. Let's go out and get something to eat, just a quick sandwich, and then we'll come back here. It'll be better."

Zev stares at me. "Okay. As long as you promise we'll come back here and make love."

I nod. "I promise."

He asks me to hold him and I do, then let him kiss me, opening my mouth to his tongue. Satisfied, he loosens his grip on my arm; his body relaxes. I turn away and wipe my mouth.

"I'll leave my jacket here, okay?"

"Sure." I hook my arm through his and lead him to the elevator. A neighbor gets on the elevator and smiles at us, probably thinking we're a happy couple. As soon as we are out the front door I break loose and run. Then I turn and yell, "Go away and never come back or I'll call the police. I never want to see you again." I turn to the doorman. "He tried to rape me!" My words surprise me, stamping into comprehension a larger meaning: He'd attempted to force himself on me, to *give me his pain.*

Zev looks puzzled, disappointed, wounded. "But you promised!"

How could he have thought I'd agree? He must have assumed that with such ample capacity for my own pain, I must have plenty of room for his.

"I was lying! Did you really believe I would have sex with you? I never want to see you again, ever!"

Zev suddenly realizes he left his jacket in my apartment. After warning him to stay away from the building, I go upstairs to get it, the doorman standing guard. In the elevator I tremble with rage. When I return I fling his jacket at him.

"Don't you dare ever come back here! Don't call me! Don't write!" I watch him back away. "I never want to see you again!" I shout after him.

I realize I am repeating myself. I search for new words and find two.

"You're crazy!" The words echo in my ears—the ultimate betrayal, against my personal code of honor. But it is a point of departure. No matter how many nuts and bolts roll in my direction, even if they're members of my tribe, I have to take care of myself first and stop taking on other people's pain.

THE CLITORIS OF THE HEART

THE FIRST TIME IT HAPPENED I WAS FIFTEEN. A beating in my chest, much too fast, as if a time bomb had been activated. I was in the high school locker room preparing for gym when it started. I pulled off my shirt and watched my chest vibrate . . . *fibrillating* was the word that came to mind. It felt like a million beats a minute, too fast to count. I put my hand over my heart. *Click, click, click,* a desperate Morse code. I tried tapping along with it, but my hand couldn't move that fast. The back of my neck felt hot, and dizziness enveloped me, making things look white and misty. I sank to the floor, then drifted in to tell the gym teacher I needed to see the nurse.

Upstairs, the nurse told me to lie down and wait. I lay on the cot with my hand on my heart, trying to calm its frantic beating. My chest was visibly shaking. I felt clammy and tingly; it was hard to breathe. Was I having a heart attack? I tried holding my breath; the beating slowed slightly, becoming harder and deeper, a painful pressure. I let go and it sped up again. I held my breath and pushed down. With a sudden *pop!* the beating stopped. Silence. Had my heart burst? Was I dead? I lay there for a moment in perfect stillness. By the time the nurse returned my heart was beating normally.

I'd been having trouble with my heart for a while, but nothing like this. Mostly it just hammered away inside my chest, so that from the outside it looked like my T-shirt was beating. Because I was so skinny, if I wore a camera or pendant around my neck, I could look down at my chest and see whatever was over it jump around. If this happened when I was with a friend, I'd point it out and we'd laugh. I just seemed to have a wild heart.

But starting with that first time in the gym, a few months before I was admitted to P.I., the wildness inside me had become frighteningly, inexplicably, dangerous. And ever since, the frantic beating has come on unexpectedly, sinking me to my knees at home, in subway stations, on the street. Nobody has ever been able to shed any light on it.

"Gas pains," the nurse at P.I. said, and gave me Gelusil. "Indigestion," said my internist. True, no doctor had ever observed it while it was happening. Like a ghost or a hallucination, it eluded physical science, as if I were imagining or inventing it. Symbolic of my weakness, an almost Victorian kind of faintheartedness, it was one more crazy thing to be ashamed of.

Since David and I broke up, I've been falling apart, unable to sleep at night and unwilling to wake in the morning. And there's something new: I can't seem to leave my apartment. I think: *I should go outside,* but the thought of the noise, the people, *the choices I'll need to make* is too much. Besides, I have no reason to go out, no purpose, nowhere I'm needed.

But there's nothing to do inside either. I've already scoured the bathtub and swept the floor. I've checked out my problems in Karen Horney's *The Neurotic Personality of Our Time* and reread *How to Be Your Own Best Friend* so many times the binding has started to crack. I pick up *Love and Will* but it depresses me—I possess neither. Even Rilke's *Letters to a Young Poet* feels like salt in my wounds. I list my flaws and what to do about them. I go from room to room. I check myself in the mirror to see if I'm still there, then look away, hating what I see.

When the loneliness and panic become unbearable, I'm propelled into the street, walking, not sure where. I could go to the New Yorker bookstore, where there's a chair waiting and books to browse—but it's too early in the day for that and I'm too restless. So I hurry down Broadway, trying to look purposeful. At some point, when the traffic gets too thick or I hit a red light, I turn around and head back uptown. I do this so many times I imagine my feet leaving tracks of erosion—at least that would be something, for I fear I'm a nonperson who'll leave no trace in this life.

Sometimes I stop at a phone booth (*pain booths,* I call them) to call a friend. I rotate calls among my friends, so as not to overly annoy anyone. It's usually a male friend, because sometimes just the sound of a calm male voice helps me get my bearings. And they're less likely to lose patience with me than my women friends. They're more . . . indulgent.

"I'm on Broadway, and I can't breathe and I don't know where I'm going." Pathetic, I think, seeing my distorted reflection in the scratched, metal phone plate. They advise me as best they can, before my dime drops or I run out of nickels or they're called back to work, to their wives, to their lives.

In my first torrent of grief after David and I split up, my friends were sympathetic. They invited me out into the world, for dinner or movies or parties; if I went at all, depression and panic soon caused me to flee, back to the safety of my apartment. After a while, my friends' patience grew short. How many middle-of-the-night weeping phone calls can a person tolerate? Now when they hear my voice, I feel something tense up on the other end.

Hell is other people. . . . Funny, all these years I've mouthed Sartre's words as an expression of my own self. I've pushed away my family, and David, and am starting to alienate my friends. Now, really alone, I find I'm in a new kind of hell.

A poet friend tells me about a psychologist she's seeing who is both a Jungian and a Tibetan Buddhist. Bernard Weitzman is on the graduate faculty of the New School for Social Research. Bernie, as my friend calls him, is a therapist who has taken a Bodhisattva vow, committing himself to the welfare of all sentient beings. She gives me Bernie's number and urges me to give him a call. What do I have to lose?

I wait in the anteroom outside his office. On the wall is a framed photo of a Tibetan monk dressed in a saffron robe, and on the table next to me a little brass bell. My heart thumps. What am I getting myself into? I've had enough of gurus and shrinks. This guy is both.

But when Bernie appears he looks ordinary enough in his plaid shirt and jeans and puts me more or less at ease. Though it's hard for me to articulate my trouble, I can tell he clearly sees the muddle of pain I am in. I tell him, through sheet after sheet of Kleenex, how lost I am, how I find every minute hell to get through. I struggle to control my feelings. Sitting rigidly, I tell him I think I am crazy. He tells me that I am not crazy, not beyond hope. His voice is quiet and unhesitating, his words like steady footfalls on a sure path. But I won't be reassured so easily. I unleash my final thunderbolt and tell him about my stint at P.I.

Generally when I tell psychologists I've been hospitalized, their ears perk up. Even if they try to act nonchalant, I can see them rolling up their sleeves, reaching for their clipboards and pens, aroused in anticipation of such an enticing challenge—or perhaps a bit fearful. And although I enjoy a perverse pleasure as the exotic center of their interest, of course I loathe them.

But Bernie's not impressed. I see him catch the thunderbolt and, without flinching, swallow it down into his belly. He says I can choose to stay in hell as long as I like, or I can choose a fresh start, something that is always available as long as we are alive. He says my situation is workable, like fresh clay, that it is a good thing my heart is tender and sore, as that is the best place to begin.

I've never heard anything quite like this. My mother has always tried to talk me out of my feelings. At P.I. they tried to medicate them away. The Gurdjieffians thought of emotions as irrelevant and wasteful. Bernie is the first person who's said to me, "Feel what you fear most."

"It's like riding a wild horse," he says. "Your hair may be standing on end and you may be peeing in your pants with fear, but as long as you hold on and sit upright in the saddle, you'll be fine."

As much as I like the image, I am dubious. I haven't proven to be courageous in the past; what makes him think a simple parable can make a difference? My weakness is deep within my neurons, in my blood. I'm still not sure it's not a clinical condition, a gross biochemical imbalance.

Bernie asks me if I'd like to work with him. I tell him I would like to, but that I have no money, that sometimes I can't leave my apartment and have a hard time planning ahead. He tells me that we will work it out and smiles warmly at me as I gather myself up to leave.

Bernie offers me techniques for working on my greatest stumbling blocks—confusion and indecision. Both involve a particular kind of circular thinking, an obsessive tendency to visualize endless permutations or possibilities. I derive maximum self-torture imagining all the alternate routes I might have taken instead of the one I'm on.

If only I'd done this instead of that, my life would be different. If I hadn't asked David to move out. If I hadn't helped Marjee escape. If I hadn't dropped out of high school. If I hadn't been sick as an infant. If I'd had different parents . . .

My instructions are to stop indulging the circular thoughts and "sit on a cushion"—just sit down, focus on my breathing, and turn my senses outward: hear with my ears, see with my eyes. Not an easy task for one so anchored to her thoughts. Just sit and observe the judgments and thoughts of doom and loss and failure and see if the panicky pounding in my chest subsides.

But no matter how straight I sit, I can't stop my thoughts. I close my eyes and they're off, running in circles, yapping and pawing the ground like a pack of wild dogs. They are insatiable, relentlessly sniffing down all the roads. I think everything to death, a pundit of confusion-inspired inaction.

Indecision is my absolute nemesis. I freeze at the simplest decisions, not knowing what I feel or what I want. It doesn't matter if it's something very small, like ordering lunch. Every item on the menu becomes symbolic. Burgers are macho and require a strong stomach. Salad means I'm lean and healthy. Egg salad means I'm sensible and simple, like my dad— wishful thinking, because of course I'm not. I imagine how each dish will feel sliding down my throat or sitting in my stomach. I sit at lunch counters perusing the menu, starved but unable to decide, and finally leave without ordering. And these are just the small things.

Bernie offers me a tool. He takes it out of his pocket—a penny. When you are really stuck, he says, just flip a coin. Because the answer doesn't really matter; what's important is to experience whatever road you wind up taking.

I have been ruminating about whether to go back to school or get a full-time job. I discuss this with Bernie endlessly in our sessions and on the telephone. My confusion has grown so all-encompassing that I can think of nothing else. I throw the I Ching, but worry over the interpretation, uncertain which are the moving lines and whether to follow the original hexagram or what it changes to.

Bernie takes a penny from his pocket and balances it on his thumb. "Heads or tails?"

I hesitate.

Bernie is dead serious. "Choose or I'll choose for you!"

"Okay, heads I go to school, tails I get a job."

Bernie tosses the penny. It flips upward in a graceful arc before its weight pulls it back to his palm. He overturns it onto the back of his hand and shows it to me.

"Tails. I get a job," I groan.

Bernie smiles, extending his hand. "Two out of three?"

He should have known better. I am about to abuse the little tool he's given me. I become a compulsive coin-flipper. From large to small decisions, I flip endlessly. As if I haven't "flipped" enough already, I've found new use for the word. I even collect special Lincoln pennies with wheat sheaths on the back—the only ones I endow with enough power to "listen" to.

In time the habit becomes so absurd that it neutralizes itself. The coin-flipping becomes more like taking my preferential temperature. I gauge my reaction to what the coin has "decided" and begin to listen to my feelings.

I complain to Bernie of my loneliness, but he is not sympathetic in the way I want him to be. "Alone-ness is our original state," he says. "It's all we ever have. We are born alone. . . ."

". . . And we die alone." I know this. It's the underpinning of my sadness and chagrin—and of every self-styled existentialist.

"Alone, we have nothing to distract us from our brokenheartedness." Bernie's voice is soft; it seems filled with breath from somewhere deep inside him. "Only when we are willing to accept our aloneness, and not try to escape, can we begin to heal. Then we can connect with the broken-heartedness of others."

"But people *do* things, have families and careers. If they didn't, they'd be just as depressed as I am."

"That's only secondary. Underneath, we all have to deal with our loneliness. Otherwise, we are just escaping . . . or nesting."

I've done my stint of trying to escape—through drugs, alcohol, sex, TV. I know it's not an answer. But *nesting*? I remember the years I lived with David. The sweetness of it. The memory fills me and I feel my throat constrict. It's undeniably in front of me: Underneath the sweetness, I was suffocating. Burrowed in too deeply for the wrong reasons, I was compelled to destroy what I most loved.

"What's wrong with me?"

"You're arrogant, and you have an undisciplined mind."

I know he's right, but it doesn't help, doesn't begin to touch the depth of my pain. But I'm in no position to reject what Bernie has to offer.

"What can I do?"

"You can start by sitting up straight, and stop picking at the scabs of your pain. The best way to do this is to sit on a cushion."

"I refuse to get on a subway to go to a place where a herd of people say prayers in Tibetan and pretend to sit quietly while my thoughts are running amok, and then even if I do get quiet, I have to get on a screeching subway to get back uptown. I don't like spiritual groups. I'm not a follower."

Bernie looks at me, just looks into my eyes, until I feel the slacker in me start to squirm. "You are very stubborn."

Exactly what my mother used to say. So they're right. So I am. So what? At least my stubbornness shows some sense of self.

"Suppose you were mortally ill and a doctor came and said, 'Here, take this medicine, it is your only hope.' Would you refuse because you didn't like the medicine's bitter taste?"

I think of the bitter taste of Thorazine, and how those drugs cut me off from my feelings, numbing me, making me even more a stranger to myself.

Psychology tells me that I am ill, and that the roots of my illness lie in infancy and childhood, that my relations in the world mirror my relationship with my parents. In order to change, I must analyze the causes. Bernie tells me things go deeper, and not so deep, that my "illness" is a universal condition, and that I can free myself—not by analyzing the causes or blaming my parents, but by stopping bad habits and cultivating compassion for myself and others.

There is a Tibetan Buddhist meditation practice called Tonglen in which, after quieting the mind, you work with the breath, inhaling whatever negative state you are stuck in—grief, loneliness, depression; you breathe it in and experience it, then exhale its opposite: joy, well-being. Breathe it in, feel it, transform it, breathe it out. This is the exact opposite of what our culture tells us to do: Run from your pain, and that of the world! Go to the movies! Go shopping! Eat a sandwich! Drink Coca-Cola! Have a glass of wine, a joint, some Valium or Thorazine. And then dump your negativity on your family, your cat, anyplace but processing it inside yourself.

Tonglen isn't easy, but I begin to develop a taste for it. It feels like good medicine; not just for me, but for the world. An important part of this practice is extending it to others: Breathe in the collective misery of humanity and exhale its opposite. Inhale ignorance, illness, hunger, hate. Exhale wisdom, health, fulfillment, peace. If only Tonglen were taught in schools and hospitals. If it had been taught to the resident shrinks at P.I. we might have learned a way of working with despair and depression, or at least a deeper understanding of the universality of our problem. This is Bernie's point; something the psychiatrists would never admit. There lies the connection between us and them, patient and doctor, crazy and sane, there in the common root of our aloneness.

———————

With my shirt pulled up I can see the small round depression at the base of my ribs beating. Bernie places his fingers lightly on the point in the middle of my chest where the false heart beats.

"This is not your real heart. It is another heartbeat that expresses your fear, your panic—a kind of self-protection. We need to penetrate, to tell it to let go, that it doesn't need to protect you any longer." He presses his fingers more firmly against it. The little place beats harder. Bernie keeps his fingers on it.

"Your real heart is up there. Can you find it?" I place my right hand under my left breast and find my beating heart.

"You think you are in danger. You are afraid that if you let go and stop protecting yourself you will die." His fingers push a little deeper. I feel the odd clicking sensations, the dizziness and heat that signal the onset of the crazy heartbeat.

"Relax," Bernie says. "You know one day you are going to die. There is great power in this knowledge, but the ego does not want to acknowledge it. It blocks it. It creates policemen, a militia, to ward off this knowledge because it is too threatening. This heartbeat is a sentinel. Let's see if we can get past it." His fingers push deeper. The pulse in my neck begins to throb and a familiar white cottony feeling spreads up into my head.

"On the other side of this guard it is soft and squooshy. It is where your feelings are, where you are vulnerable. It's a lot like sex. You can tighten up, or you can relax into it."

My muscles contract against his fingers. Taking deep breaths, I allow my muscles to open to his touch. With a little pop, the extra beating subsides.

"There, that's better," Bernie says and lightly withdraws his fingers. "You have the power to do that yourself. You have everything you need to take care of yourself. You just need to learn to discipline your mind and love yourself, as if you were your own loving parent."

"But I don't love myself. I've screwed my life up so badly. I'm such a bad person."

Bernie laughs. "Yes, you're just terrible! So what are you going to do? Lock yourself in your room without supper? Flog yourself?"

I slump in my seat, my head hanging from my neck.

"Sit up," Bernie commands. "You can't breathe properly when you're sitting like that."

I sit up, but I don't look at him. I pick lint from my pants legs.

"Look at me," Bernie says. I meet his gaze. "Here is what you need to do. You need to start loving yourself." I'm suddenly afraid. Is he talking about masturbation? I've tried that; it just leaves me feeling grotesquely sad and lonely.

Bernie continues. "You need to start saying to yourself, 'I love you.' "

"What, right out loud?"

"Yes, why not? Whenever you feel bad or need love or support or encouragement, you can say this to yourself. It's a good habit to get into. Will you try it?"

I shrug. "Okay."

Bernie laughs again. "You could be a little less grudging about it."

I muster a faint smile. "Okay, I'll try it."

"Good. I'll see you next week." Bernie hugs me good-bye, a big bear hug. I stiffen slightly as our bodies press together and look at him quizzically.

Bernie looks suddenly serious. "My feelings toward you are entirely wholesome. But you know, the heart is a very sexual organ. The first time I saw you, I felt a tickle, as if you had touched the clitoris of my heart."

For many months Bernie gives me pamphlets on classes and invitations to special events at his Buddhist community. Finally I give in and go to a group assembly honoring a high-end Tibetan Buddhist lama, visiting from Nepal.

The loft space, in a renovated industrial building, is immaculate and airy. I remove my shoes at the door and am directed to a large hall where hundreds of devotees sit quietly on round meditation cushions. The walls are hung with *tankas* and bright-orange banners with yellow Tibetan lettering. Up front, beneath a huge banner of a rising sun, a platform is draped with red silk. It's all so bright—red, orange, yellow—the colors I most dislike, too boldly ostentatious for my cowardly soul. And silk . . . that's my mother's fabric.

There are two cushions on either side of the podium; on one, a monk with a shaved head. On the other, a massive, bare-chested holy man, draped equally in folds of flesh and silk.

Prayers are said, a mumble of foreign syllables. Then a hush, and the great man begins to recite in a monotonous Tibetan drone. I understand none of it, and wonder whether the crowd of American disciples does. They're sitting motionless, eyes closed. I try to look suitably humble, but the longer I sit, the more uncomfortable I feel. I do not belong here. I want desperately to leave but to get up would be rude and highly noticeable. After a silent meditation that feels like an eternity, there is a break, and I find my shoes and leave.

It wasn't a wasted trip. I've found my truth: Whatever transformation I'm going to do, I'll just have to do it the hard way, alone.

New Year's Eve 1979. I've forced myself to go to a friend's party. I feel like a complete void, sitting there pretending to listen to the conversation, pointing my fake smile here, then there, hoping my eyes are in sync with the action. If they only knew how screwed up I am. Can they tell? Maybe they already know and are being kind. Or maybe they're just shallow and superficial. But no, they have relationships, marriages, children, interesting jobs. Several are artists—real artists, not failures like me.

In the middle of all this, a handsome guy with piercing blue eyes introduces himself. Bob is an emergency-room doctor as well as a jazz musician. Though his skin is pale from the New York winter, he exudes a whiff of laid-back California. He offers me a joint, but I refuse. I'm already having enough trouble getting my words out. When I finally deliver myself to the cold night air, I can't wait to get home and pull the covers over my head. I've had enough of New Year's. I can't bear the thought of another year alone, without love, without David.

A couple of months later Bob stops me on Broadway. When he mentions the New Year's party, I remember with some embarrassment how I'd slipped out while he was off getting some guacamole. I never expected to see him again.

We walk and talk for a while, then exchange numbers. I can't believe he's interested in me. He's a doctor, for God's sake. He even did a brief residency in psychiatry. He's studied and treated people like me.

The first time we get together we are in the middle of eating dinner when Bob reaches for my hand across the table.

"I'm all fucked up," I say. "I don't know if I can be in a relationship." But it doesn't seem to deter him.

Dating Bob is a real stretch for me, a good one. He is athletic and loves being outdoors, cycling and jogging. He lives on City Island—a little Italian fishing village in the Bronx. There's a beach at the end of his street, and his neighbors respectfully address him as "Doctor" and leave baskets of homegrown tomatoes on his doorstep. Sometimes Bob picks me up in his car and takes me home with him, airing me out in his backyard like a rumpled sheet.

One day, heading out of the city with Bob, I realize how good I feel. The sky is bright blue with puffy white clouds. Buildings roll by and are replaced by trees. We are talking about his work. I have never dated or even been friends with a doctor before. I don't usually have access to such privileged information.

"I have a question for you." Beginning tentatively, I describe the symptoms of the long-elusive heart palpitations.

Bob listens, then gives me a sidelong glance. "How do you stop it?"

I tell him about holding my breath and bearing down hard until the beating stops.

"I can't believe it! You've just described a textbook case of P.A.T., including how to stop it."

He explains that P.A.T. stands for paroxysmal atrial tachycardia, an electrical misfiring of the heart. Triggered by the autonomic nervous system, the heart beats at an enormous rate (150–250 beats per minute). There are three traditional ways to stop it: the diving reflex, where you immerse your face in a pan of cold water; massaging the carotid artery on the side of the neck; and holding the breath and bearing down on the diaphragm, which I seem to have discovered by pure instinct when I was fifteen.

Amazing. After all these years, I have a name for it. Now when it happens that my heart is hammering for my attention, I am doubly armed. Bob has given the problem a name and an explanation, and Bernie an understanding.

WORK

BERNIE ONCE TOLD ME TO THINK OF JOB INTERVIEWS as a way of seeing the world, and that I should think of myself as interviewing my prospective employer. This advice has helped me straddle my ambivalence and lumber through zillions of job interviews. I'm rarely interested in the jobs themselves. It's more of a pastime, a ritualistic purge, a repetitive acting out of what I think I'm supposed to do.

I come from a blue-collar background. My maternal grandfather, who grew up on a farm in Austria-Poland, arrived in this country, alone, at thirteen. After taking a series of factory jobs he opened a small factory of his own on the Lower East Side, where he manufactured leather wallets and key cases. My paternal grandfather was a housepainter back in the days of lead paint. My father, who never graduated high school, started his career as a stockroom clerk, worked his way up to salesman, and finally started his own business as a manufacturer's representative in electronics. My mother worked for many years as a secretary in the toy industry before becoming the first female vice president of a home-furnishings company. Though she earned respect in her industry, it was still a man's world. My mother was paid less than the male executives and was also still expected to run their errands.

Before my brother, the only people in my family who had attended college were my great uncle (a dentist), two of my father's nephews, and my mother's younger brother, an advertising executive whom my mother helped put through college.

My father scoffed at academic achievement. When my brother went to graduate school to study philosophy, my father was disgusted. He thought of intellectuals as ineffectual sissies, not real men who did real work in the real world. Both my parents were waiting for my brother and me to settle down and get jobs. Confirming their apprehensions, both of us, snail-like, have left a smeared trail of semiemployment. My brother has worked as a stock boy, waiter, gas-station attendant, postal worker, ambulance driver, and union organizer before moving on to public relations writer, translator, journalist, and management consultant. I've been a waitress, carpenter's assistant, housepainter, gal Friday, bookkeeper, secretary, mother's helper, and, sporadically, an illustrator. I've typed, filed, and answered phones for architects, writers, book publishers, museums, television producers, and dance companies, always the outsider coveting the creative lives of others.

I enroll in a two-semester certificate course in art therapy at the New School. The teacher is inspiring: creative, perceptive, dedicated. She teaches us to recognize the symbolism in children's drawings: a burning house with no doors or windows; a huge stick-figure mommy, much smaller daddy, and tiny child; a little girl with no mouth or hands. As the teacher describes the miracles of change that occurred in an autistic child she worked with, shivers ripple through me. Maybe through art therapy I can help others locked within themselves open the door to self-expression.

Seeing the intensity with which I throw myself into studying, the teacher allows me to begin an internship at a yeshiva for special education located in the Williamsburg section of Brooklyn. The all-boys' school is run by a rabbi. Many of the students don't speak English, while I know only a few words of Yiddish and not a word in Hebrew beyond *shalom*. But the boys aren't interested in talking. Without making eye contact, they choose among the art supplies I offer and quietly get to work. One boy scribbles over and over the same area, using only a black crayon. Another draws tiny people in pencil, then colors over them in red and yellow, and ends by tearing up the paper. I'm at a loss. Aside from being a dispenser of art supplies, I have nothing to give them. The problem is more than the language difference; it's the lack of a solid emotional foundation within myself. I'm too much like these boys, walled in by my own pain and inability to communicate. Beginning to suspect that I myself am in need of art therapy, I quit the program.

I decide to go to art school. I take classes in drawing and painting, but nothing really satisfies me. I want a more rigorous kind of training. Then I see a notice on a bulletin board for a nine-month course in art restoration.

Gregor Rosinov is a Bulgarian art restorer, trained in Italy, who promises a Renaissance course of study, including art history, what he calls the "fundaments" of drawing and painting, and restoration theory and techniques. Classes meet five days a week, six hours a day. The students are all women. Although he makes his living as an independent restorer, Gregor sees himself as an artist, and puts great energy into teaching us how to draw.

In his thick accent Gregor exhorts, "Valium, gehls!" ("Volume, girls!") He takes the pencil from my hand and darkens the shadows until they're black, demonstrating for the class. "This is what is! Dark, light, makes volume!" Gregor employs unorthodox techniques to loosen us up and focus our attention. We karate-chop blocks of wood. We draw with balsa wood sticks sharpened to a blunt point, dipped in sepia watercolor. In a few weeks my drawings have changed. They're more spontaneous, the gesture more fluid, the line stronger—and they have volume.

We also learn basic restoration techniques. Gregor demonstrates relining and how to painstakingly match colors to touch up abraded canvases. But this is not enough to become a professional restorer. I investigate graduate programs. The entrance requirements are stringent. You must be fluent in French, German, and Italian and have substantial art history credits. I don't even have my B.A. I'm discouraged, as usual—the kind of horse that balks at a hurdle. Maybe art restoration is not for me. I'd probably find the disciplined restoration techniques wearisome.

On my way to the subway from Gregor's studio I often walk through Washington Square, sometimes stopping to watch the portrait artists lined up on Sixth Avenue. I've always admired the ability of portrait artists to capture the human face, a tradition descended from the Renaissance. On the street it's almost performance art. Grace under pressure. When Gregor's classes end for the summer, I decide to try my hand.

I'm sitting in a folding chair on Sixth Avenue and West 4th Street, my easel and art supplies all set up. My sample portraits, matted and wrapped in plastic, are on display, and an empty chair awaits my first customer. It's early, only 7 P.M., so while the light is good, customers are sparse. The other artists try various means to get passersby to sit in for them: offering them half-price or even free portraits, hoping to attract spectators. I'm probably the only artist praying that nobody sits in my chair.

Each time I go, I tell myself this will be the last time. Schlepping my stuff on the subway is arduous, and the working conditions are challenging. We work late into the night, illuminated by streetlamp light, which has a greenish cast. That's okay when working in charcoal, but if someone wants a pastel it's almost impossible to distinguish certain colors. Then there's the street grit, the local kids' boom boxes, dogs peeing on trees (if you're lucky, not on your easel), and the wind knocking things over so you have to chase paper down the street, hoping nobody steals anything while your back is turned. And working under time pressure—twenty minutes—in public is not the easiest thing if you're a shy perfectionist.

Still, something keeps me coming out here. The challenge to do good work. The thrill of really capturing the person, oblivious to the crowd that's formed behind you until they burst into applause as you finish. A taste of show biz.

Then there's the flip side. The heckling from the dissatisfied crowd: "That doesn't look like him. The nose is too long. The face is too wide." They've hit upon a sore spot—I never measure, working instead from my gut, hoping to capture the spirit of the person. But the worst happens when I'm asked do a color portrait of a young girl as a birthday present from her father. Not a bad job, I think, until the girl looks at the finished portrait and cries, "My eyes are blue, not brown!" I fix it, but it shakes me up.

When the summer is over, I decide I need to strengthen my technique and enroll at the Art Students League, where I take classes in academic drawing. But the question remains: How am I to support myself?

While David and I were living together, I started doing illustrations for the magazines he edited. The early assignments were simple: pen-and-ink spot illustrations, a border of paper cups and plates for an article on disposables in the fast-food industry. His editor in chief was pleased with the results. My next assignment was a color illustration for a story on the fast-food labor force: a watercolor painting in which I used my own hands as models, shown in the act of assembling burgers. The illustration was so well received the editor decided to use it for the cover and titled the article, "The Hands That Do the Work." I did several more magazine covers, adding them to my growing portfolio.

I take my portfolio around to magazine and book editors. "Nice work," they say. "I'd like to see more. Come back and show me some new work." Or, "I'd love to use you but we have nothing right now. Call me in a couple of months." It takes months for me to realize that although they're sincerely trying to encourage me, I'm also a nice break in their routine. So be it, I say, burying my portfolio in my closet. Time to get a real job.

Just as I'm scouring the employment pages for ads, the phone rings. It's the art director for *The New York Times Book Review*, calling to ask me whether I'm interested in doing an illustration. I'd sent him samples of my work months ago and never heard from him. I'm so disillusioned with illustration, and so intent on sticking to my decision, that before I can stop myself I answer, "No, thanks." He asks if I'm sure . . . and I say, "Yes." After hanging up, I almost pass out with despair at what I've done. (It's years before I can get myself to tell this story to anyone. It still makes me cringe.)

After my short-lived careers as illustrator, art restorer, and portrait artist, I decide it's time to finally give in and learn a new skill—commercial art. One day I sneak into Parsons's library. There I find a book, *Agency and Studio Skills*, and spend a couple of hours copying its contents into my notebook. Armed with my new knowledge, I answer ads for paste-up artists—the lowly peons at the bottom of the graphic-arts barrel who prepare camera-ready art following the art director's layouts.

After a couple of hours at my first freelance job, I'm still struggling with the opening pages of a forty-page book. I can't seem to get the type aligned, rubber cement is everywhere except where it should be, and nothing stays where I put it. My employer calls in a dusty little man carrying a briefcase filled with special rulers, dividers, tweezers, knives, and blades and sends me home.

But I'm determined. No more waitressing or secretarial work for me.

My next gig is pasting prices set in four-point type (hard to read, equally hard to align) onto full-page newspaper supermarket ads. Then on to a catalog house, where the studio manager, a Native American with a ponytail that falls past his waist, calls everyone, male and female, "Babe" ("Hang loose, Babe" or, "You're up, Babe"). In each of these places I'm one in a "bullpen" of oddball artist types who have fallen into commercial art by default. Sometimes we go out en masse for liquid lunches at a local pub and dig into the deep dirt of office intrigues and affairs.

On the job, I'm weirdly accident-prone, slicing off bits of my fingers that hang over my T square or triangle—more homage to Procrustes. Plus I tend to lose things. "Has anyone seen Mindy's X-Acto knife?" the studio manager calls out. "It's the one with the blood on it!"

Over time I master the techniques, but it brings me no joy. It's just another industrial skill, like bookkeeping or manufacturing leather keycases. Just another straitjacket for my soul.

THE TRAIN TO BELLEVUE

SEPTEMBER 1983. I pace the subway platform, not knowing whether I am going uptown or downtown. I have accepted two jobs, both starting today: one as secretary to the head of the engineering department at uptown Columbia University, the other a steady freelance job in the bullpen of a downtown retail advertising art department. The job at Columbia is full-time nine-to-five and offers good benefits, including free tuition after six months. This would enable me to finish my B.A. without worrying about tuition. But it is boring secretarial work, something I've promised myself I would not do anymore. And it's full-time, so I'd be trapped there, disguised as a secretary, day after tedious day. The art job, though it offers no benefits, pays more per hour and would enable me to develop my graphic art skills . . . although at my level the work is so mindless and mechanical that a trained chimp could do it. I've learned that there is little or no upward movement in this art department. Also, the graphics job has no security; if work gets slow or I make too many mistakes, I'm out.

I've been mulling over these two offers until my brain is so tender and sore that I can no longer approach the problem directly. My friends—even Bernie, my therapist—refuse to discuss it with me anymore. We've been down every avenue, always winding up at the same cul-de-sac, going round and round. "It doesn't matter which you choose," Bernie insists. "Just pick one. Or flip a coin." By now I've flipped a million coins; they have no authority over my confusion. Every day I promise myself I will decide, but each night I fall into bed undecided.

Uptown or downtown? It's hot on the platform and I'm thirsty. I stand at the base of the stairwell, ready to run for whichever train arrives first.

A rumble slowly rises to a roar. It's the uptown train. I bolt across the platform, getting there just in time to squeeze into the crowded car before the doors close. At least it's air-conditioned. As we rumble north, I try to resign myself to my decision. I imagine the Columbia campus, the students carrying their books along the tree-lined paths—students years younger than myself, just beginning their studies, whereas I've already made such a mess of my life.

Have some compassion for yourself, I think, repeating what Bernie always tells me.

In my mind I go back to the campus, pass the library, and enter the engineering office. I see myself sitting there: the girl at the desk, filing, typing, answering the phone, taking dictation . . . I start to sweat. I suddenly realize I don't want to do it.

I get off at the next stop and cross to the downtown side, where I pace the platform until the train arrives. This time there's no air-conditioning. I try to yank the window open, but it's stuck. My skirt is damp and wrinkled; I smooth it under me and try to recover. The train, a local, is creeping along and stopping between stations. I'll have to get out at Times Square and call both jobs, telling Columbia I'm not coming and the bullpen manager I'll be late. Settled.

But I'm not feeling settled. I picture myself trying to explain to the head of engineering that I won't be taking the job. How can I do that? He hired me two weeks ago. I should have told him before this. He could have hired somebody else. I remember the warmth in his voice: "Congratulations. You've got the job, if you want it." Three times we confirmed the details of the position on the phone: salary, starting date. The last time was last week.

"You're an idiot!" I mutter venomously. "You're so fucked up."

The heat is getting to me. I'm breathing heavily, thirsty, for oxygen. I look around at the other passengers. They sit quietly with dull, glazed-over commuter expressions, preoccupied, half-asleep. Am I the only one going through hell on this train? I'll bet I'm the only one screwy enough to have accepted two jobs at once.

At last the train pulls into Times Square and I jump out and race to an unoccupied pay phone. But who to call first? And what will I say? Time to consult my oracle of small change. I scramble in my wallet for a penny. Heads Columbia, tails bullpen. Tails. Okay.

I feed two dimes into the phone and dial. The engineering department's voice mail answers. Shit! I hang up. I dial the other place; the studio manager answers. "Hi, it's Mindy. I'm on my way but I'll be a little late . . . subway delay. Sorry. See you soon."

Okay. I've made my choice. I imagine myself there, cutting and pasting, drinking cup after cup of coffee, pasting up ad after ad. Imbecile work! They don't call it "mechanicals" for nothing.

A sob rises in my throat. What am I going to do? I won't go back to waitressing or temp work. I flip again; this time it comes up heads. Columbia. Back to square one. Two out of three? Tails, art department. I have to stick to my decision.

I feed my remaining change into the phone and dial the engineering office. This time the department head answers. For a long moment I say nothing. Then I tell him it's me; I'm in the subway, there's been a delay. His answer is relaxed and kind: "No problem. I'll see you when you get here." How could I refuse? I say okay and hang up.

Oh God, what am I going to do? I am feeling very agitated, like I can't breathe. Then I hear the rumble of an approaching train. The downtown express pulls into the station, and I watch as passengers pile on. Why not me? Why can't I know where I'm going? If I don't do something I'll wind up nowhere, freaking out forever on this subway platform.

Just before the doors close, I squeeze on.

My skin feels clammy and my head tingles; little white dots flash in the edges of my vision. I close my eyes and sway. A man gets up and gives me his seat; I sink into it gratefully. I try to focus on what to do next—get out at the next stop and transfer back uptown? Or call Columbia and tell him I'm not coming?

Who am I? Where am I going? I look inside the space that is myself, but it is empty. My questions reverberate in that emptiness, clamoring and clanging like some mad Chinese gong.

I can't calm down. I am gasping for breath, and soon my gasps turn to sharp, rasping intakes of breath, then sobs. People look at me, then look away. My sobs grow louder. I know this situation is insane; yet it is the product of my whole life. I jackknife over in my seat and bury my head in my arms.

The man who gave me his seat asks if I am okay. "Yes," I gasp, then,

"No." Even this I can't decide. I hate myself and my confusion. I imagine getting out at the next stop and throwing myself in front of the train.

"Can you tell me what's the matter?" The concern in his voice helps calm me. I tell him I'm having an anxiety attack but that I plan to get out at the next station, and that I'll be fine.

When the man gets out at 34th Street, I watch him pass through the doors as if he were my last friend on earth. I'll get out of this infernal subway at the next stop, I promise myself, and straighten this out once and for all. I'll call Columbia, explain that I've made a mistake, apologize to the department chairman for the inconvenience I've caused. I don't deserve the kindness and forbearance he's shown me. I don't deserve the job, and he doesn't deserve to hire a fraud. I'm a horrible secretary, anyway, a real sham. Who did I think I was kidding?

The doors open at 14th Street; I take the stairs at the 12th Street exit. As I pass through the turnstile a policeman approaches me. "Excuse me," he says, "what seems to be the trouble?"

"There's no trouble," I tell him and try to walk away, but he blocks my path. I look at him in disbelief. Does he think I'm a pickpocket or something?

"We got a couple of calls. Apparently you were very upset. People thought you might try to hurt yourself."

"No . . . no . . . I was upset, but I wouldn't . . ." I stop, feeling for my footing on the edge of a precipice.

"How do I know that? What if I let you go and you do something foolish? I think you'd better come with me."

"No," I say, "it's really not necessary. I'm fine," but the cop slides a pair of handcuffs out of his pocket and slips one bracelet on my wrist and one on his. What can I say to him—that I was upset because I'd accepted two jobs and didn't know which to go to? Too crazy to be believed.

"Tell it to a professional," he says, clicking the handcuffs closed, "and let him decide."

People in the station are staring, watching the cop make his arrest. The situation has achieved cinematic proportions. Though I've observed scenes like this before, it's never been me. Suddenly I'm the star of the show—a tawdry real-life prime-time episode. Handcuffed to a man in blue.

My confusion is consumed by a flash of anger. How I hate cops!

Another cop joins us. They put me in the backseat of the police car, shielding my head from hitting the doorframe, just like on TV. Then we're moving through traffic. The streets are busy with people on their way to work. I wish I were one of them, able to go through the motions like a good automaton.

"Where are you taking me?"

"Bellevue."

Oh, shit! My worst nightmare come to life. Bellevue—the last stop on the loony train for the homeless, the poor, the psychotic. *Nowhere else to go? Send her to Bellevue.* How could I have let this happen? I wish I could go back to the train, the pay phone, last week . . . how far back would I have to go to undo this?

There is a surreal finality in this moment. A peculiar lucid calm comes over me. I no longer care about the jobs. Now all I have to do is save my skin.

The car pulls into the emergency entrance of Bellevue and I am delivered into a waiting area—a drab, dingy room with an institutional atmosphere. The courtroom where my fate will be decided. On the other side of this room is *Inside.*

My escort waits with me. He talks to a clerk; they get the paperwork going. The clerk asks me questions and jots down my answers, then tells me the doctor will see me soon. A few other miserable souls are draped limply in their chairs, disheveled, haunted-looking down-and-outers.

The cop is joined by his partner; together we wait. I feel like a child escorted to the principal's office, only these authorities can't be defied or reasoned with. They are Law.

A young man approaches us, slender, with dark hair and eyes, his shirt unbuttoned at the collar. Can this be the doctor? He doesn't look much older than me. I follow him into a smaller room where he gestures me to sit, pulls a chair around and sits facing me.

"Do you want to tell me what happened?"

"I had an anxiety attack. It was really nothing."

"That's not what the police officer reported. He said you were *very* upset, possibly suicidal."

He asks why I was upset and I start to explain about the jobs. He scrutinizes me, then starts asking me a million questions about my history. Have I been upset lately? Do I take medication? Do I use drugs? Do I see a shrink? Have I ever had a nervous breakdown? Have I ever been hospitalized?

We are playing a game in which my freedom is a house of cards. If this one, crucial card falls, the entire house will collapse in on itself. No matter how unbelievable a story I muster, if they know about P.I. they'll never let me go. Should I lie to them? What if he has a way of checking? If I'm not careful he can lock me up and throw away the key.

I tell him. He asks for more details and jots it all down, then looks at me as if he's trying to decide what to do with me.

I speak up, determined. "It's been over ten years since I was discharged. I've been to college, held jobs, rented an apartment. This was just one incident. I got upset, but really, I'm fine."

He chews the top of his pen. "Why should I believe you? What happens if I let you go and you do something crazy? Hmmm?"

There is something in his manner that jumps out at me. He seems flamboyantly . . . gay. *Traitor!* Oppressed minorities ought to respect one another.

"Look at me," I say. "Do I look crazy?"

"That's not enough. You have to tell me why I should believe you."

I lean forward and look directly into his eyes. "Look, I got myself into a bad situation and things got out of control. This is not something usual for me anymore. People make mistakes—don't you? All I can do is tell you that it won't happen again."

To my great relief he says okay and delivers me into the hands of the cops. They huddle for a moment, then escort me outside. I assure them I'll be fine, and they drive off.

Before I take the bus uptown, I find a pay phone and call Bernie. Fresh out of change, I call collect; fortunately he answers. As I tell him what happened, I start to cry. The thin tissue of my self-esteem seems irreparably torn.

"Go home and take care of yourself. Eat something. Take a bubble bath."

"But I can't forget this. How can I forgive myself? How will I face my friends? I have a date with Bob tomorrow."

Bernie's voice is firm. "Just take care of yourself, get a good night's sleep, and you can begin to clean up the mess. You'll know what you need to do. You may have a hell of a hangover, but it won't be as difficult as you think. It is an entirely workable situation."

Although I don't entirely believe this, I decide to take Bernie's word for it. I wipe my eyes, take a deep breath, and look up just in time to see the bus approaching.

Before stepping into the tub, I take a look at my face in the mirror. It is just my face, the same one that's looked back at me for years; the same one that's sat in a classroom, gotten hired at jobs, been kissed by boyfriends, labeled as crazy, and locked up.

A wave of shame breaks over me. I could tear myself to pieces over what happened today. What normal person would get themselves into such a situation? It suddenly hits me how close I came to jeopardizing my freedom. What did the psychiatrist see that convinced him to let me go? I take another look in the mirror. My face looks absolutely fine—still young and pretty, in my hippie-ish way. Maybe just a little too red around the eyes, a little too much sadness behind the hazel gaze.

Maybe with enough practice I'll convince myself I'm okay. I take my bath, eat some food, and go to sleep early. The next morning, remembering Bernie's words, I take a deep breath and pick up the phone. What's the worst that can happen?

PERSONAL MYTHOLOGY

In elementary school I was placed in an accelerated class that incorporated the third, fourth, and fifth grades into two years. The teacher wore a mink derby and had a booming theatrical presence and her own unique ideas about curriculum. In my two years in her class, we learned origami, basic Japanese, theater arts (torture for the shy), and how to play the ukulele. I managed to overcome my shyness enough to stand with my back to the audience conducting our ukulele orchestra's version of "Sing Along with Mitch" (I was Mitch).

In addition to all this, we had two periods a week of myths and legends.

I was immediately hooked. The pantheon of Greek and Roman gods, with their jealousies, cranky competitiveness, and manipulative interactions with their human playthings, was much more compelling than the stodgy Old Testament deity that put me to sleep in Sunday school. The gods were highly imaginative in their notions of justice, reward, and punishment.

Take the story of Pandora. In spite of being warned by the gods not to open the box that was entrusted to her for safekeeping, Pandora couldn't resist. The moment she opened the lid, a swarm of evil creatures flew out and afflicted human beings with all sorts of troubles: sorrow, envy, jealousy, anger, hunger, disease, old age. Even with little experience of the world, I understood sadness and hope with a child's heart. I already knew the disobedient curiosity that makes humans do things they later regret.

And although I wondered why the gods arbitrarily placed the world's ills in Pandora's care, I loved their wise beneficence in including the little winged figure of Hope, knocking to be let out of the box when Pandora felt the burden of all the world's troubles to be her fault.

Then I met Prometheus.

Prometheus, a member of the Titan race of giants, was punished by Jupiter for stealing fire from the gods. His punishment: to be chained to a rock while an eagle pecked away at his liver—which immediately regenerated itself, providing for eternal torment.

Why was I fascinated by this myth? At the time I couldn't have understood it. It was just an interesting story, a rather gory one at that. Later, as an adolescent, I related more to Sisyphus, his despair at a future of endless, meaningless repetition more accessible to my teenage self.

Still, there was something about Prometheus.

Entrusted by Jupiter with the task of making men from earth and water, Prometheus realized that these clay humans were lacking something essential: fire, the divine spark of consciousness. With the help of Minerva, the goddess of wisdom, he set out to get it. For giving to humans those godlike powers of creation and imagination, Prometheus was brutally tormented by the gods.

And each day, Prometheus's liver—his life force—grew back for more torment.

Going to work in midtown is my personal descent into Hades. It begins with waking in the morning. Half the time I don't. I just turn off the alarm, roll over and go back to sleep. Just about when I'm supposed to be arriving at work, I resurface, jump out of bed, fumble into my clothes without time to shower, my dreams bleeding into the day like wet paint. I make two or three circuits of my apartment before finding my keys and wallet, though I sometimes have to return for one or the other or to feed my cats, who wisely hide during my crazed leave-taking. But I'm fast. I can get out, if I have to, seventeen minutes after my feet hit the floor.

I run the five blocks to the subway, not stopping for red lights. At the subway entrance I hesitate for an imperceptible second before flinging myself down the stairs. If I have a token ready, I may make it onto the platform just in time to see the back end of a train receding down the tracks. I quickly position myself in what I think will be the optimal spot

for exiting the train and anxiously pace the platform, lengthwise and lat-
erally, so I can look down both the local and express tracks. The longer I
wait, the more frantic my pacing. Like everyone else, I avoid looking into
the eyes of my fellow commuters. Contact is definitely not what I want to
experience on the subway platform. When someone looks into my eyes,
my glance slithers away, like the rodents skittering along the rails, seeking
anonymity.

When the train finally pulls into the station and I maneuver my way
on, I heave a sigh of relief—until the train changes from a local to an
express, or stops dead, mid-tunnel. I don't know how everyone can sit so
calmly, so self-contained. I can't bear feeling this helpless, trapped belowground. When counting or mental bargaining (I'll only smoke ten cigarettes
today, I promise) no longer helps, my breathing turns to hyperventilating,
and I start to sweat. When at last the doors open, I take the stairs two at
a time and sprint, panting, through the streets, taking advantage of every
gap in the crush of people.

I make up some excuse to explain my lateness, and settle into the work:
a Sisyphean limbo of tedious repetition. Sometimes I manage to lose
myself in a hypnotic trance; if not, I count the minutes to lunch.
Bathroom breaks allow me a cigarette and time to commune with myself,
alone in a stall. In the fetid air, my privacy is sweet; I suck it in with the
cigarette smoke.

Whoever invented the notion that Hades is belowground has never
worked in a high-rise. The fluorescent lights cast a flickering, greenish pall
on my psyche. Maybe it's the electrical field (sparks snap from my finger-
tip when I push the elevator button) or the recycled air (I can hear the
coughing move from cubicle to cubicle along with the disease-of-the-
month), possibly even airsickness (worse on windy days when the building sways, creaking back and forth ever so slightly)—whatever it is, each
day I suffer from headaches and nausea.

Lunch is an obstacle course. From noon to two, all the workers in midtown pour from their offices to form one huge jostling mob scene, choking the streets. Cigarette smoke mingles with car exhaust and grill fumes
from shish kebab carts. And the noise! I press my hands over my ears to
dim the din of the gods of commerce.

Finding affordable food is a challenge. Midtown coffee shops are over
my budget. Company cafeterias, though affordable, offer lifeless food,
much like hospital fare: macaroni and cheese, mystery meat, deflated veg-

etables. The mass production weirds me out; the plastic packets of butter and salad dressing depress me. Alternatively, the lunch counter at Woolworth's has an institutional feel and a clientele that remind me of my hospital days. I imagine myself at one with the downtrodden waitresses, but they turn their backs on my smile to gossip and compare nail polish. I order the least offensive lunch special du jour, eat quickly, and go find refuge in a bookshop or art-supply store.

In the nearby vest-pocket park, I find a place to squeeze in among the bodies lining the benches and ledges like large, overcoated pigeons, eating their sandwiches and burgers, with their smaller versions vying for crumbs at their feet. I sit close to the architect-designed waterfall, hoping its hiss will drown out the dozens of conversations. I read, or write in my notebook, or do some sketches. On bad days, I face the fountain and cry, aware that nobody else seems to be spending their lunch break weeping.

Getting home is the worst part. I can't bring myself to get on the subway again, underground, bodies pressing against me, breathing other people's breath. A bus might be better. Perched high above the cars, with windows all around, at least I can look out and see patches of sky. But when the bus creeps along in traffic and I'm wedged between people, my nose in an armpit, someone's hand or bag or leg or who knows what pressing against my hip, their voices in my ear no matter which way I turn, I pull the cord and yell, "Getting off!"

I usually end up walking home. The traffic fumes bother me, but I count the blocks diminishing, and watch the blue-gray sky deepen to rose-tinted cobalt, then indigo. By the time I eat, bathe, and clean up, the night is gone.

As hard as I try to go to sleep by midnight, I'm always reluctant to get into bed. I straighten up, make lists of things to do and to think about, try to gather the bits of my psyche that go underground during the day like Persephone in winter. I need this small envelope of time, a netherworld between the days. I drink a glass of brandy and read, or sit in front of the mirror drawing the contours of my face, hands, body, trying to remember who I am. Before I know it it's 3 A.M. Just five hours before the wheel of work spins into motion again.

How do other people do this, day after day, for months, years? It's beyond me. I count each hour of each day, each day of the week, lined up like a long row of buildings along an endless avenue.

Sometimes on my way to work, just as the subway doors are closing, I hear, with dread, a familiar sound of wheels rolling from the platform onto the train. I freeze. *Please*, I pray, *let it not be him*, not the half-man.

I've seen him before: dark-skinned, handsome, a blue bandanna tied around his neck. He sits on a rolling platform, pulling himself along with powerful arms. His torso ends at the waist. He works his way, unperturbed, down the aisle, navigating gracefully, using the flat of his gloved fist alternately to steer and brake, pausing to receive coins in a cup he transfers to his other hand with his teeth. I cannot bear to look at him; just the sound of the wheels terrifies me. My eyes snap shut. *Please let him roll by.* The rolling sound stops, starts, grows louder, stops dead in front of me.

I fumble for coins, drop them in. He flashes a smile and thanks me; I try to smile back. His brown eyes look calmly, observantly, into mine for an instant before I look away, ashamed of my uncontrollably visible emotions. Always, after he rolls by, cool tears streak my hot cheeks.

What is it about him that fills me with such grief? It's not just that he has no legs—although that in itself speaks of terrible loss. But there's more, a yawning gap: What has happened to the organs below his waist? Where is his stomach; where are his intestines? Bifurcated, his lower half sacrificed to some terrible illness or accident. Truncated. Leveled. Cut down to floor level, at the mercy of people's feet. And yet his will is whole enough to get him to his work: panhandling on the subway. What extraordinary courage and dexterity it must require to navigate the subway steps, vulnerable to accident, carelessness, cruelty. To choose to be part of the crowd, even though he's at its mercy. My mind reverberates with imagined terrors. Someone could lift him, kick him, throw him onto the tracks. Just one hard shove . . .

I wince at this man's tremendous vulnerability. How can he survive? Whatever terrible accident bisected him, his daily life must be a constant exercise in persistent forbearance. I'm ashamed. I've had one bad thing happen in my life, and I can barely get myself out of bed in the morning.

He must have enjoyed his life before. He probably was attractive to women, judging from his handsome face and strong build. But now . . . I shudder. If only we humans could be equipped with prescience, to know ahead that one circumstance, one accident of fate will change our lives, and who we are, forever.

Each time I see him I'm reminded of life's random cruelty, as well as the losses we all endure to differing degrees—the loss of wholeness, and of hope. How can he roll along without feeling his loss, every second of the way, without asking himself the question I'm obsessed with: *What if?*

What if whatever weird twist of fate that stole his lower half had never occurred? The question gives rise to pantheons of distant cousins: What if Pandora had never opened that box? What if Prometheus had been content with his ordinary Titan duties without being compelled to possess fire? What if I'd never dropped out of school, taken drugs, had too many sleepless nights, gone into the hospital? Who would I have been if it had never happened? A whole person, with a whole will, without this conflict burning in me, wasting me. Trying to imagine who I might have been is my personal zen koan, as hard to fathom as the sound of one hand clapping. "What if" is only a hair away from its flip side, the mantra of self pity: "Why me?"

I've never been able to shake the feeling that I'm being punished for some unforgivable wrong—or for just being me. More likely, it was for going against the grain, trying to wrest myself free from my cultural/socioeconomic/genetic blueprint. For trying to be different (or for the prideful folly of imagining I'm different), for wanting some fire in my mud.

Maybe the gods are just playing with me, knocking me about for their own amusement. Since adolescence, I've become convinced (or convinced myself) that the gods were sadistic in giving that box to Pandora. They must have known she'd be unable to resist her curiosity, making their decision to include Hope seem that much more perverse.

Hope is a quality I've gone to great lengths to bury within myself. I've cultivated negativity like my own crop of evil flowers. Hope is uncool. Hope is for little girls.

The gods are jealous . . . and vengeful. They wreak havoc with mortals, stewing body parts, keeping the best bits for themselves. I've seen evidence. Cats missing the tops of their heads pile up in hospital labs. Strong men roam the subways without their lower halves. Teenagers lose whole chunks of their lives, and their peace of mind. Jupiter humbles those who would dare to reach beyond themselves; Procrustes gleefully lops and stretches his victims. As if I'd ingested the message I'd gleaned from Sisyphus, it's palpably real to me that even when we pit all our strength against it, the stone-heavy weight of despair will always win out.

I know I have to try harder. I have to prove them wrong—the psychiatrists who diagnosed me, as well as my own condemning voices. I have to tell myself, and the world, that I'm fine—even if I don't believe it. In order to "be," I have to act "as if." Not as if my incarceration in the hospital had never happened, but as if my experience is not so different than the stunning, leveling wounds we all endure at one time or another, no matter how privileged or protected.

I'm tired of regret. Bitterness and blame get me nowhere, just twist the wheel of my will, turning my stride into off-kilter circles. If the half-man considers himself whole enough to exist in the world, why shouldn't I? Like him, I need to push forward with whatever strength I have, and strive to become stronger, tougher, more resilient.

Wholeness—the ultimate myth—remains beside the point.

FOLLOW-UP

SATURDAY AFTERNOON, LATE FALL 1989. I lie in bed reading, savoring a day off from work. The phone rings.

"Is this Mindy Lewis?"

I ask who's calling.

"This is Dr. N. from the New York State Psychiatric Institute." Something quakes within my chest. I remember Dr. N. as a resident, somber and reserved in his jacket and tie. He later went on to become director of the adolescent program. He explains that he is conducting a series of twenty-year follow-up interviews as part of a long-term study. He wants to ask me some questions; would I consider setting up an interview?

Do I want to talk to him? Why should I—so I can give him data for his study? I've worked hard to bury this part of my past, and now I'm being asked to dredge it up again. I've built a life, haven't I? Suddenly it seems built on shaky foundations. My throat closes up—a panic reaction. Why should I be afraid? He can't lock me up just for talking to him. Then I notice another emotion: vivid, passionate anger.

I decide to do it. We set up a time the following day for a phone interview. Before his call I take a long walk in the park in the crisp fall air. Remembering. Thinking about what I most want to tell him. This may be my chance to settle an old score.

By the time the phone rings, I am ready.

We go over basic information, filling in blanks. Dr. N. invites me to

ask any questions I may have, which he answers within the limits of con-
fidentiality. His cordial tone intimates that we're coconspirators, as if this
were somehow an equal exchange. He pumps me for details about my
friends: Rocky, Liz, Edie, Tina. In a way I'm pleased he wants to know
about my friends, that he remembers them, that he might actually care.
I'm newly aware of my value as a source of data; an important link to
those who can no longer speak for themselves.

And Marjee. What depth of unhappiness drove her to destroy herself?
I recall Marjee's stories about her flighty mother, stern grandmother, and
alcoholic father, who used to beat her with his belt. Dr. N. asks if Marjee
had ever spoken of sexual abuse. I search my memory for clues, but if any
existed, they remain locked in the past.

Dr. N. is particularly interested in incest. "Nobody asked about it back
then," he says. But signs were everywhere: Rocky's scrubbing. Izzy's repetitive muttering, "I fucked my mother." Nobody ever imagined he might
have been telling the truth.

I inquire about Izzy; evidently he's alive and well, as is Helen, to my
great relief.

Dr. N. asks how my life has been since the hospital. I recap my signifi-
cant events: my work with MPLP, excelling in college but not graduating,
having long relationships but never marrying, living in my apartment all
these years. I tell him I am fine; I work, I paint, I don't take drugs or see a
shrink, I am completely fine! In spite of the hospital, I add.

"Is there anything else you'd like to tell me?"

I wind up and let him have it: how it felt to be confined, medicated,
misdiagnosed, traumatized; a shy, frightened, arrogant adolescent who
takes years to live down an early, unnecessary, too-long incarceration in a
loony bin. How hard it's been.

Dr. N. listens. "I'm sorry," he finally says. "We didn't know very much
about treating adolescents in those days."

And that's it. An hour and a half on the phone, and I have reached back
twenty years into the past and spoken for that girl who couldn't speak for
herself, and received an answer and an apology—skimpy and scant and
too late to make any real difference. But in doing this, I face that girl and
claim her, embrace her and love her, knowing that she is an important part
of me, that we are one.

———

When Dr. N.'s book comes out I order a copy. The book is a scholarly long-term follow-up study of more than 500 patients who passed through P.I. during a thirteen-year period, beginning in the early sixties. It's filled with charts and studies, surveys and trends, family histories and prognoses, tracing all sorts of behaviors (brutality, incest, verbal abuse) and symptoms (alcoholism, depression, antisociality, hostility, suicide). Divorce, violence, and abuse at home were common. The most horrific situations are described: a boy whose crazily abusive father used to dangle him by the heels from their high-rise apartment's window, threatening to let go; a mother who set fire to her child.

None of the people described are named. They are presented as statistics: the youngest female to commit suicide after having eloped (could this be Marjee?), an adolescent female who crisscrossed her limbs with superficial razor cuts (me, perhaps?). Did I know the young man who'd been dangled by his feet? Or the boy whose schizophrenic mother had tried to kill him? Or the young woman who survived incest with her father only to commit suicide years later following the termination of a sexual relationship with her psychiatrist? Were these the untold stories behind the people I knew? I stare at graphs and tables, pie charts and bar charts, and try to match the statistics to my friends. Two went to prison, one was convicted of murder—could it have been Jack, or Dan? Have all my friends been boiled down to statistics, mixed in among the others who came before and after? Are we equally interchangeable? Does it even matter who's who?

Not all our stories were tragedies. Most patients who didn't commit suicide went on to live normal lives. Many continued seeing therapists; others survived on their own "true grit." A minority never adjusted, living a marginal life on disability, locked away in their rooms. Some still have hope for the future. There is some doubt expressed about whether our extended hospitalizations were helpful or incidental to our recovery.

I can't stop looking at the book, searching for clues of identity, but the case studies remain anonymous—a final psychiatric excision of personality. Private lives are scoured away, leaving only the sediment of illness. At last, here are the stories we never talked about, but now they have no faces attached.

REUNION

Over time, my scars fade to the faintest of marks. I work, I pay my rent. I am just like everyone else . . . almost.

After years of bouncing about in the working world I've settled into a job as a graphic designer for a group of magazines. I have a good rapport with my colleagues, and my recent open-studio exhibition of paintings was a success. The stigma left from my hospitalization has eroded into such a thin crust that only the occasional bout of hypersensitivity or defensiveness threatens to give me away. One day I look around my office and take a metaphorical look at my life. Stacks of magazines I've designed are piled on shelves; photos of friends and my new boyfriend smile at me from the bulletin board; color xeroxes of my paintings are tacked up in neat rows. My Rolodex is filled with names of photographers, illustrators, typesetters. My mother, when friends ask, "What's your daughter doing?" can finally say "working," instead of uncomfortably mouthing "freelancing"—her euphemism for struggling.

I think about how far I've come and about those people who have helped and supported me. I remember Mrs. Gould, who taught our high school English class inside the Psychiatric Institute. A bright spot in our drab days, clothed in all the color and culture of the world, she drew us out of our silences, loving our energy and irreverence, hating whatever caused us pain.

I wonder where she is and what she's doing. A friend from the hospital mentioned her about a year ago, but I was too busy to follow up. He said she was no longer living with her husband and now had her own apartment in Greenwich Village. I call information; she's listed. I dial, and after a few rings a throaty voice says hello. That same familiar voice that used to recite Old English verse, making it sound fresh and juicy, infusing it with delight, managing to gather the attention of the handful of distracted, rebellious, depressed, or agitated adolescents in her charge. Only now that voice sounds as chipped as one of my grandmother's china teacups.

"Mrs. Gould?" I can hardly get the words out. "Is this Shirley Gould?"

"Yes. Who is this?" She exhales impatiently. I'd forgotten this aspect of her personality: wanting to get past the unnecessary formalities to the essentials, no time to waste.

"It's Mindy Lewis, from P.I. Do you remember me?"

"Do I remember you? How could I ever forget you? How are you, darling?" Her voice is animated. "Is everything all right?"

I assure her that I'm well and tell her I'm calling from work.

"What work?" she demands. "Tell me about your job."

I describe what I do, where I live—the essentials.

"And how are *you*? Tell me all about Mindy . . . who you are now."

I tell her a little of my recent news and promise to send her a letter going into greater detail, then ask about her. She tells me she stopped teaching at P.I. when they did away with the adolescent unit. Wow, I think. No more adolescents in P.I.—thank God.

"I taught at Bellevue for many years but finally retired. It wasn't like P.I., darling. It was heartbreaking. The kids didn't stay long enough to make any difference, and the bureaucracy. . . . Very frustrating."

I ask about her husband, why they no longer live together. "Did Mr. Gould pass away?"

"Good Lord, no! He's very much alive. We're divorced."

"Oh, I'm sorry," I say in my best condolence tone.

Her throaty laugh blows away my apprehensions. "Don't be silly! Leaving him was the best thing I ever did! I wish I hadn't waited so long."

Mrs. Gould had always spoken proudly and lovingly about her children, but I can't recall her saying much about her husband, a well-known composer, aside from brief references: Yes, yes, he was famous; he traveled frequently. Then, waving her hand in the air, bangles jangling, she'd signal us to get down to work, and the reading and discussion and essay writing would begin. If we were lazy or didn't want to work, Mrs. Gould would push and prod our intellects to their feet, and together we'd pull meaning from our shared experience. Our fearless leader did not shy away from difficult subject matter; denial was not her style.

"Thank you so much for calling me, for remembering me after so many years."

How could I forget her, smelling of musk and rose, welcoming us into her classroom, bristling with energy from her candid blue eyes to her curly brown hair. As we shuffled in, she always asked each of us how we were, her enthusiastic interest an antidote to our beleaguered bafflement. In her class, we were considered whole, healthy, and entirely welcome.

Mrs. Gould was our true ally, as close as the hospital brought us to an experience of unconditional love. Tough love, at times, demanding that we come out of our shells and join in experiencing literature. But always with humor, never to the point of invasion. If I was feeling too depressed or anxious to participate, I was allowed to put my head down and rest. Passing my desk, she'd stroke my hair from my face, or take my chin in her hand and look into my eyes. If I was fuming, she'd challenge me to express it in words, then laugh at my string of obscenities. "I know how you feel, darling; I've had days like that myself! Now what about Dostoevsky? Let's talk about rage as expressed in *Notes from Underground*. Not up to it? Okay, anybody else?"

Together we experienced Lady Macbeth's hand washing, Hamlet's indecision, Robert Frost's musings, Kafka's alienation, Emily Dickinson's longing, Chaucer's sensuous appreciation of winter melting into spring. The full spectrum of human experience, which we had just begun to explore in our young lives. But above all else, we felt her commitment to us, her "brilliant children"—and her belief that the intelligence and spirit of her group of adolescents on the fifth floor was worth more than all the psychiatrists in the world.

Although she never directly undermined the authority of the doctors and encouraged us to talk out our issues in therapy, when a psychiatrist took an unjustly punitive stance, increasing medication, denying privileges, or on occasion shipping someone to one of the state hospitals, Mrs. Gould did not stifle her disapproval. She didn't hesitate to voice her outrage directly, showing up at psychiatric rounds to confront the doctors if she thought one of us was being unfairly treated. She was unswervingly on our side.

In an atmosphere that classified rebellion as illness, Mrs. Gould taught by example that it was okay to challenge authority, to question, to think for ourselves and express our opinions, to grab hold of life with a passion.

After exchanging chirps of delight at having rediscovered each other and promising to stay in touch, we hang up. Immediately afterward I pen a letter, pack the envelope with magazines and photos of myself and my paintings, seal it, and drop it off in the mailroom.

A week later her letter arrives. I recognize the same legible scrawl that used to decorate the margins of my assignments and essays, commenting and encouraging.

28 January, 1991

Dear, dear Mindy—

I have been reviewing those years—those terrible, terrible, wonderful years. I can still see you clearly—your sweet face, the grace of your movements, your wit and intellect.

We were very bonded, weren't we? Never have I felt about any people the way I felt about that 5th floor class. . . . No matter how much time passes—I never have to try to remember—it is in my consciousness always.

Thank you for taking the time to send those things to me—"This is where Mindy is today."

Thank you, thank you for calling me—Be good to yourself—I do love you dearly.

Shirley Bank Gould

I'm moved, and surprised. It had never occurred to me that we'd had just as strong an impact on Mrs. Gould's life as she'd had on ours. Yet her letter confirms something I've always sensed: The love and commitment she emanated was not simply a routine part of her job. She delighted in us, and we felt it.

We speak a few times after that. I suggest getting together for tea; she says that would be wonderful, but why don't we wait until the cold weather passes. It's a particularly icy winter. The last time I phone her, her wracking coughing interrupts our conversation.

"Are you okay?" I ask when it subsides. "You don't sound good."

"What do you mean?" she queries, her voice rising. "How do you know?" Then she tells me. Cancer. This is why she postponed our visits. "You wouldn't recognize me; I don't want you to see me this way." That's why her voice has that thin, brittle edge.

I hold the phone and begin to cry.

"Cry if it makes you feel better, darling, but don't be sad for me. I've had a wonderful life. I have marvelous children, and grandchildren. I've enjoyed my work, and my life. I wish the same for you."

One more time she tells me she loves me, then we say good-bye.

FORGIVENESS

My mother's guilt about the hospital manifests in anxiety. She calls me almost every day to tell me the weather, to make sure I dress properly, and that I've eaten. And yet there is a large degree of denial. We've never sat down and talked about it. It's too hot a topic.

"Don't look back," my mother advises. "Go forward. What's done is done."

Over the years my mother has sent me dozens of Hallmark cards inscribed with sentimental messages, illustrated with romantic photos of girls with long hair like mine sitting in contemplative poses beside streams. It's her way of showing her love, maybe even asking for forgiveness.

I can't forgive her; but I'd like to, so I try to bury my anger. "Move on," I say to myself. But it's still there, throughout years of fraught interactions, arguments, apologies. For so many years I've lived with the stress and guilt of hating her whom I'm supposed to love, and loving her whom I have reason to hate.

My mother is moving to Florida. I look forward to impending liberation. My countless wishes for her to go away, leave me alone, are about to come true. A window is opening, and new, exciting, healthy, fresh air is about to blow in.

We plan a farewell lunch. She meets me at my office and I introduce her to the editor in chief and my coworkers. In the five years I've worked as a graphic designer for this midtown publisher, it's the first time I've invited my mother to visit. I try to keep my life out of her reach. But today I'm proud to have her. She's beautiful and charming, and everyone is happy to meet her.

I've reserved a table at a fine local restaurant, chosen with her in mind. My mother likes upscale venues; I'm more comfortable in low-key, low-priced places. Sometimes I wonder who I'd be if my personality hadn't been formed in reaction to my mother. In every area of my life, I've chosen to be what she is not. My mother's fingernails are long and polished; mine have paint beneath them. She is outgoing and confident, whereas I'm introverted and shy. It's an anima/animus situation: We are each other's shadow sides.

As the maître d' shows us to our table, my mother engages him in conversation, while I trail behind. It's never possible to be an adult for long beside my mother. But I've already promised myself that I'll do my best not to be defensive. Today I'll try to be the daughter she always wished she'd had.

My mother, after chatting with the waiter, asks for a wine list and orders a carafe. As usual, she's self-confident, assured, never a trace of indecisiveness. In spite of myself, I prickle when she reads aloud to me from the menu, suggesting I order this or that. But I know she does it out of love. When I can't decide between the tortellini and the salmon, we order one of each and share.

At some point, after the chitchat, the news, the ordering of food, our conversation grows serious. My mother is emotional at the thought of leaving New York, of being so far away from me. "I want you to be happy," she says. Her voice chokes with tears.

This sets me off, touching on my fear that I've missed out on having the happiness a "normal" life offers. Who, after all, doesn't want to be happy? But I can't help taking it as a personal failing. "I'm sorry if I've disappointed you," I say, unable to keep the bitter note out of my voice. "But I didn't exactly have an easy start."

My mother freezes, salad fork in midair.

Suddenly we are unveiling the unmentionable past, laying out all the gory details in front of us, right there on the table with our wine glasses and half-finished gourmet lunches.

I tell my mother I've never really gotten over being hospitalized, what an awful way it was to start out adulthood, and how much I feel it's set me back.

"You don't think I wish it could have been different for you? I keep asking myself, what did I do wrong? I did the best I could, and it wasn't easy."

I take a deep breath, then ask the big question. "How could you have sent me there?"

My mother puts down her fork and sighs.

"I honestly didn't know what to do. You'd become completely unmanageable . . ." Her voice trails off. "You were always so good, making me little presents and helping around the house. And then all of a sudden, you changed. You became a different child, almost overnight."

To my mother, the change in me must have seemed as sudden and inexplicable as demonic possession. Where had her little girl disappeared to, and who was this changeling in her stead? How could she know where I'd hidden her—deep, deep inside.

"Those were horrible years for me, too," my mother continues. "You can't imagine how it felt to have to send you to that place." Her eyes fill. "It hurt me so much."

It hurt *her* to have me put away? Does she want me to feel sorry for her? She's still unwilling to admit that she'd failed me in any way by locking me up. Now that we're into this, I'm not going to let her off the hook.

"I can't imagine sending a child of mine to an institution, no matter what." I watch the pain flicker in my mother's eyes, taking an almost sadistic pleasure in pushing her buttons. I want something from her, something she's never been able to give—an apology, reparation. Something.

"You signed me over to state custody."

"I didn't know what else to do. I was worried sick. Your psychiatrist advised me to send you to P.I., and that was the only way they'd accept you. Your stepfather and I thought we were doing the right thing."

My stepfather. We shake our heads, remembering.

"That marriage was a disaster," my mother admits. "I married him mostly because I thought you kids needed a father. He was a good man in many ways, but so manipulative, so financially irresponsible. He got me into terrible debt."

This was true. My mother had had bad luck with men. But again, it was all about her, about money, externals. I was just an appendage, existing only as a reflection of herself. So when her perfect, well-behaved child hit puberty and rebelled with a force equal to the strength of my mother's need to hold on, she couldn't handle it—but I was the one who was locked up.

"You don't know what it was like for me," my mother says, taking a sip of her wine, pinky outstretched. "The pressure of being a single mother. I worked hard to support us. Sometimes I barely had money to put food on the table."

I have friends who are single parents, and as hard as it is for them, they'd never have their kids locked away. They talk to their kids, even their truculent teenagers, so their kids feel loved even when they misbehave. My friends approach parenting as a bigger picture—perfect-looking children and tidy rooms are not their first priority. Besides, she enjoyed going off to work, where she could socialize and flex the muscles of her independence. It had to be a welcome distraction from staying home with two young children.

She blots her lips on her napkin. "Your father didn't always send the child support payments he was supposed to, and when I asked him for them, he'd threaten me."

I remember their tense phone calls, wondering why she spoke to my father so angrily while I waited in breathless anticipation to take my turn on the phone. Once, when I overheard my mother say into the phone, "Don't you threaten me with going underground! I'll take you to court!" I imagined my father digging a tunnel to Canada: my mental image of the Underground Railroad, which we hadn't yet learned about in school.

In my eyes, my father was always somehow beyond reproach. I envisioned him in a West Coast palm-tree and orange-grove heaven inhabited by fathers who'd abandoned their kids. My dad had his own "bachelor's pad." My dad dated lots of ladies, went waterskiing, and drove hairpin turns through the foothills. Where was my father when I was growing up? Conspicuously absent, except for his annual four-day visits to New York.

"Your father was no angel," my mother says, buttering a piece of bread. "He was the visiting parent. I was the one who was there. I was the one who took all the abuse."

Abuse? Doesn't she remembers how tense it was, how she yelled at us all the time?

"I did the best I could, under enormous pressure. Among all my friends I was the only one who'd been divorced. There was no daycare or outside support, no counseling for single parents. I had to do it all on my own. I kept a clean house; I put food on the table. You and your brother had nice clothes and clean sheets and never went hungry."

"You cared more about clothing and furniture than you did about our emotional security."

"Don't be silly. Yes, I cared that the apartment was clean and well furnished. But it wasn't just for me. I enjoyed trying to give you and your brother nice surroundings. I was playing many roles: homemaker, parent, dutiful daughter, wife, and breadwinner. A large package, sometimes tough to handle. But I never intended to hurt those I loved—and still love—the most."

I refuse to let her off easily. "There's more to it than that," I tell her. "We were all so unhappy." Doesn't she remember? The apartment was a minefield of misery. I mention my brother crying himself to sleep at night, and my mother and brother's horrible fights, as well as his and mine. I tell her how I used to excuse myself from the table and quietly throw up my breakfast before going off to fifth grade.

"I didn't realize it was that bad," my mother says. "I didn't have time to notice. I was too busy working, keeping the house together, just trying to survive. What did I know?"

Isn't it the job of mothers to *know?* True, all she had was Dr. Spock and Spic and Span—not much help for the true grit of familial relationships. In the fifties, there wasn't even *Sesame Street.* We were on our own—three people with very different needs locked together in an apartment. Just because we were related did not guarantee we were compatible. It was just a matter of time. Like my mother and father, sooner or later we needed to separate . . . or explode.

My father and mother had met in their late teens. My Bronx-born mother was a model for a knitwear company; my father, a Brooklyn boy, worked in the stockroom. It was the forties, the days of light romantic comedy and chic clothes: Lana Turner and Frank Sinatra, Judy Garland and Mickey Rooney, Humphrey Bogart and Lauren Bacall. My mom, with her auburn hair and hazel eyes, was a knockout. My dad's wavy hair, square jaw and cleft chin were an advertisement for romance. They were made for each other. Within their group of friends, they had fun times: movies at the Paradise, picnics at St. James Park, dancing at the Golden Gate ballroom in Harlem, swimming at Coney Island and Orchard Beach, double-dating. Then came the war, and my father was drafted. The young lovers were separated, just like in the movies. Before he left for Fort

Hancock, Virginia, my father proposed, and they quietly eloped to be married by a Bronx judge. Later, while my father was on leave, they had a second, "real" wedding, this time for their families.

I'd assumed my mother had always been obedient—the elder child, the responsible daughter. So I'm surprised to hear my mother confess that this example of her defiance was just one among many. As a teenager, if her mother said no, she'd do the opposite. But she was discreet. She didn't flaunt her misbehavior, so she didn't get caught.

"If I had acted the way you did, my parents would have beaten the daylights out of me," my mother says. My grandfather was of the old school of parenting, and my grandmother was also not above "lifting a hand." Occasionally my mother followed suit, usually with my brother, chasing him with the yardstick, the broom. My mother had rarely hit me— though sometimes, enraged, she'd dig her nails into my teenage arms.

Should she have been harder on me? Who knows. It might not have made a difference in the long run, but it might have discouraged me from some of my more flamboyant behavior.

I ask her what I was like back then, during the difficult years.

"You were so sullen. And foul-mouthed. And your temper—the bathroom door almost fell from its hinges, you slammed it so many times. You were so rebellious. I remember you wearing that horrible ratty army shirt on Yom Kippur, refusing to come to synagogue with us."

I was hospitalized for being rebellious and sullen? For refusing to go to synagogue? For being unfashionable? As usual, she only cared about the way I appeared from outside, never about what was going on inside.

"You just completely shut down. You stopped communicating. You stopped going to school."

She's right. But isn't that what teenagers do—shut down? In the sixties we wore army shirts and bell-bottoms, smoked grass, swore. I was an extreme example of a rebellious, sixties-vintage American teenager. I was definitely not an easy adolescent . . . but did I really need to be hospitalized? The fifties and sixties had collided in my mother and me with the same cataclysmic impact that was simultaneously wreaking havoc and change in politics, civil rights, values, attitudes, culture. The margins of acceptable behavior were narrow, and the birth pains of a new era intense. It was a power struggle of larger proportions than we'd then realized.

"I was afraid. I wanted to protect you."

"You *over*protected me." And she had, all my life. She'd instilled in me her own fears of the world, of bodily harm, of life. I was afraid to leave her side. I had to push her away. I was suffocating under her narrowness, her fear.

My mother had her own fears, impressed upon her by her own mother. When my mother was a little girl, my grandmother was in a car accident and sustained major injuries to her eyes. Her eyesight deteriorated until she was legally blind. Still, she navigated housekeeping and cooking, shopping and subways, and even traveled alone from the Bronx to look after me when I was little. But the world was a dangerous blur. "Be careful, *Mameleh*, stay in the courtyard. Don't go in the street," she'd warn me. My mother inherited my grandmother's fear of physical injury. But to me, my grandmother's concern was forgivable, whereas my mother's was overanxious, hysterical.

"You don't know what it's like to be a mother. To see your daughter using drugs . . ."

"And? I was locked up for over two years, Mom. Besides, you smoked grass yourself, later on." My voice is harsh with scorn. I did take LSD and pills, but I was mostly smoking marijuana—small potatoes in this day and age. By the seventies my mother was smoking pot at parties, or at least going through the motions; she never inhaled. But by then it was acceptable, even chic.

My mother's voice becomes insistent. "You don't understand. I was afraid you'd destroy yourself. There were so many articles in the newspaper about kids dying from using drugs."

I vaguely remember the press coverage when Art Linkletter's daughter jumped to her death from her apartment window, high on LSD. From this perspective, I understand how helpless my mother must have felt. She feared for my life. How could she have known what to do?

"I never stopped caring. When you were in the hospital, I wasn't allowed to see you, so I'd send you letters and care packages. I had regular meetings with the social worker to find out how you were doing. Once when I was on my way to a session, I saw you on one of your walks outside the hospital. I came over and said hello, and you just turned your back on me." Tears run down my mother's face. "You can't know how painful that was."

I remember the confusion I'd felt as I walked away from her that day, and the shocked expression on my mother's face. I imagine how she must have felt.

Now we both are crying, spilling our regrets and grief down our cheeks onto our napkins and dresses.

My mother takes a Kleenex from her purse and wipes her eyes. Then, taking out her compact, lipstick, and eye pencil, she expertly reapplies the face of composure. She was always so good at covering up. Always, to others, she was the good soldier, the fun gal. At home it was a different story, her frustration spilling over onto her kids.

It can't have been easy coming home from her secretarial job to two kids, with just enough time to kick off her shoes, make dinner, get the house in order, go to bed, get up, make breakfast, get us ready for school, and go back to work. Weekly visits to the hairdresser were her sole relaxation. Weekends were filled with grocery shopping, cooking, entertaining . . . all on her own. I don't know if I could do it.

All her life my mother had worked, struggling to support others. She'd gone to work straight out of high school, paid her parents for room and board, and contributed part of her earnings to help put her younger brother through college. After a brief period of full-time motherhood, divorce spun her back into the working world. As a child, I'd watched her tuck dollar bills into shoeboxes, coins into jars, a portion of her paycheck into savings bonds for my brother and me. She worked her way up through the ranks in her male-dominated industry, but never had time to fulfill her own dreams—of glamour, fashion, her own dress shop, a beautiful apartment—whatever her youthful dreams had been.

I look at the woman across the table from me, the mother I once loved and adored. Once, all I'd wanted was for her to be happy; her unhappiness was my worst punishment. Now the tables are turned. Can it be that all these years I've been punishing her by being unhappy, as if to say: Look what you've done to me?

What do I want? To drag my mother endlessly over the jagged edges of my anger, causing her the same pain I'd felt as a child when all I'd wanted was to please her? It suddenly hits me that what I'd wanted most as a child is exactly what she wants now—to be loved.

My mother reaches across the table and puts her hand on mine. "I'm sorry, Min. I wish it could have been different. If I could, I'd go back and change things. But what can we do?"

It's the first time she's apologized to me. I'm ready to take it in. What might have once sounded like denial now sounds sincere. I acknowledge her love for me, her bewilderment, and her pain. All these years she's put up with my rejection and blame, but she's never stopped loving me, never turned her back. It will take work, I know, but if she's willing to loosen her grip, I'm willing to let down my walls. Like swimmers surfacing from the depths, we acclimate ourselves to our new perspective, and slowly come up for air.

MY FATHER'S KEEPER

A PHOTO: MY FIVE-YEAR-OLD FATHER and his younger brother astride a pony, taken by a pushcart photographer. Such photographers were common during the Depression; for a penny he'd snap your portrait, and develop and print it right there. My four-year-old uncle sits in front looking tough and ready for trouble, my dad close behind, with his round face and sweet smile. Their short pants and stockings display ragged holes and ice-cream stains. The two boys are rough, ready, and inseparable— together they were called Twinny. Of the two, my father was considered the placid one, the handsome one, the charmer.

My father grew up on the streets of Brooklyn during the Depression, one of eight kids in a family so poor they often moved to a new apartment on the first of the month to avoid paying the rent. His father was a housepainter, his mother the family saint. No one was better than her children or good enough for her handsome son—not even my beautiful mother.

In some ways my father never left the early days of poverty and hard survival in Brooklyn. He was thrifty (or cheap, depending on how you looked at it), he idolized those who had "the finer things" (to him, the possessors of the "finer things" were such luminaries as Bob Hope, Bing Crosby, and Frank Sinatra). He worked hard, going from stock boy to salesman at Harvey Radio, and later, president of his own small wholesale electronics business. But in most ways he remained provincial.

My father had bad teeth. When I was little, he'd flash his gold crowns at me to make me laugh. By his forties, my father's teeth needed extensive work. To save money, he went down south on one of the weekend deals offered during the fifties to have all his teeth pulled at once and replaced by dentures. He didn't seem to mind being a forty-year-old man with false teeth. He called them his "choppers" and enjoyed scaring me, all in good fun, by dislodging them from his gums and rolling them around his mouth.

My father slept badly, grinding his teeth, flailing and shouting. He talked in his sleep. "Show me your ID card!" my mother once heard him shout. Sometimes he became physically violent during these nightmares. Once, fast asleep, he punched my mother in the stomach; another time he crashed his fist through their bed's wooden headboard.

My father was stubborn (as I am) and had a temper (so do I). On my brother's fourth or fifth birthday my father became enraged when my brother wanted to go out wearing the brand-new Hopalong Cassidy holster and guns he'd just been given as a present. My brother's joy turned to sobs, scorched to ashes by my father's withering anger. He often taunted my brother for not being athletic ("What are you, a fairy?") and later when my brother decided to major in philosophy: "What do you want to be—a professional student?"

My father was quick to make fun of people, pointing them out on the street or in the subway and restaurants.

"Look at that character," he'd say, pointing with his eyes to some poor soul he considered substandard. He'd go pigeon-toed or knock-kneed or cross-eyed and, flapping his hand forward, he'd lisp, "Ithn't he juth *adorable?* I'd like to go over there and give him a great big *kith!*" Then he'd spot another unfortunate specimen. "Look at her. Isn't she just *gorgeous?*" My father would screw his face into a grotesque parody of feminine wiles, then turn to me. "Wouldn't they make a great couple? They ought to get married! Should I go over and introduce them?"

It was the kind of fun my father grew up with on the streets of Brooklyn during the Depression. What else was there to do? They were so poor that for years he and his younger brother shared one pair of roller skates. They amused themselves in other ways: by looking at people, pointing out their shortcomings, laughing at their defects. By the time he was an adult, my father also knew how to frame people in the lens of his Brownie camera and engage them in conversation, smiling and animated, just before clicking the shutter, capturing them forever.

The same way he captured me. Whatever his shortcomings, I adored him.

He left when I was six years old and unable to understand why. Just a sudden fact, like cymbals struck close to my ear, a sound loud and startling, reverberating into an unfathomable silence. That soundless emptiness became a backdrop, invisibly influencing all my adult relationships.

The year I turned twenty-eight, one of my father's nephews phoned me after returning from a business trip to California. I rarely had contact with my dad's side of the family, so I was surprised to hear from him. After exchanging pleasantries, my cousin mentioned that my father's Parkinson's disease, which he'd had since his late forties, had progressed to a point where he was no longer able to properly take care of himself.

"You have to do something about your father," he said. "He's not well, and he's all alone."

My father had for many years lived on his own in a series of studio or one-bedroom apartments. Although he always had lots of girlfriends, several of whom wanted to marry him, my father eventually put them off. Years later he would confide that he always loved my mother, and when things didn't work out between them, he felt no reason to marry again— that is, until after he began to have serious symptoms of Parkinson's. But by then, the woman he'd been dating for several years, whose first husband had died after a long struggle with cancer, decided she could not take on another husband with a debilitating disease.

My father's life had boiled down to daily routines, and soon even those were disrupted. His hands shook so that simple tasks were a trial. His head and body lurched in tremors that made it impossible for him to drive. After his second accident, when he totaled his van, my work-loving father had to shut down his business. He stayed at home, eating sparsely, just surviving, his loneliness assuaged by keeping the TV and radio on constantly, often simultaneously.

Suddenly the onus of my dad's condition was on me. My brother had been living in Europe for many years. My mother was about to marry her third husband. Suddenly I was my father's next of kin.

Why me? I was filled with resentment. Where was he when I was in trouble? He visited me three times in the twenty-seven months I was in P.I. and I'd only seen him a handful of times since. Now I'm supposed to take care of him, when I'm just beginning to enjoy my life? As concerned as I was about my father, it still felt unfair. People my age weren't supposed to be burdened with such things.

"He's in terrible shape," my cousin continued. "I know you'll do the right thing."

The right thing? For whom—him, or me? Beneath the feeling of dread that lodged in my heart, I hit rock bottom truth. He's my father. I can't just abandon him.

What was I to do? I was not about to go to California. For one thing, I didn't know how to drive. My friends, my survival network, were all in New York, not to mention my rent-stabilized apartment. I decided to bring my father east. It would be an abrupt end to his autonomy, a return to his roots. Some of his brothers and sisters were still alive, though several had passed on, and his older sister and her husband had retired to Florida. But at least he'd have some family here.

I began researching possibilities, looking for residences that would provide my father with assistance, yet still allow him to maintain a sense of independence. I networked with friends and spent hours browsing the phone book for social-services organizations that could help me. Before long I had an arsenal of information on nursing homes, residences, and enriched-housing programs.

Finding a place for my father became my work. At first I felt shocked walking into these places, assaulted by the acrid stench of unwashed old people, sour food, disinfectant, and the ever-present stink of urine and feces. The more cheerful the name—Golden Years this, Sunny Acres that—the more depressing the place. Residents sat disheveled and despondent in rooms filled with shabby furniture, silent aside from the over-loud televisions. Too familiar a scene for me.

When I spoke with the directors of these institutions on the phone, they reassured me with phrases like "quality of life" and "dignity." But however hopeful I was when I arrived, I always left disappointed. After visiting two dozen places, I narrowed them down to half a dozen options. I was not about to put my father into a nuthouse for the elderly just because he had Parkinson's.

The symptoms of Parkinson's had come on gradually. When my father was in his late forties, he noticed a tremor in one hand and something not quite right in the way he walked. His letters from that time show a change in his handwriting, which had become jiggly and reduced, his loops

smaller and tighter than usual. In time, his gait became a kind of accelerated shuffling, as if he were tipped forward, running down an incline. His
facial expression, usually mobile and animated, grew mask-like and
frozen, his skin taking on an oily sheen. At first the changes were subtle,
but over time his illness would transform him into a grotesquely altered
version of himself.

─────────────

When my father finally arrives in New York for a four-week visit, I am
shocked. His body is wracked by tremors that twist his head and body
and shake his limbs. His walk, when it isn't the strange, shuffling run, is a
drunken lurching. His whole body is alternately frozen into immobility
and in a state of perpetual motion like some mad marionette.

It hurts me to look at him. Sometimes I stand behind him where he
can't see me, and cry.

The purpose of his visit is to look at several of the places I'd come up
with, and for them to interview him. The application process is time-
consuming and frustrating. Beds are hard to come by, and waiting lists can
be years long. I've already put his name on the list for state-subsidized
housing for the elderly.

"I should have planned ahead," he tells me, looking at me ruefully. "I
had a chance to invest in real estate, but I hesitated and lost the opportunity." He squeezes my hand. "Don't you make the same mistakes I did. Be
decisive. Take control of your life."

For the time being my priority is to take control of his life.

My father embarks on every visit with humor and grace. He doesn't
berate me when we inadvertently take the wrong subway to an interview
deep in the Bronx and end up in a godforsaken neighborhood miles away
from our destination. He jokes with doctors and nurses as he sits on the
examination table, wearing only his boxers, as they prod and poke him
with needles and withdraw tubes of blood. I marvel at his dignity.

"Look at that poor man," a blue-haired resident of one establishment
whispers loudly to her friend. "Must have had a stroke. And so young!" I
put my hand beneath his elbow and steer him clear of their gossip,
bristling with anger. Everywhere we go, people mistake my father's illness
for other conditions. On line in the grocery story, the woman behind us
disparagingly clicks her tongue and says, "Drunk in broad daylight!
Shame on him!" My entire body clenches in an effort to keep from

whirling around in his defense. "He has Parkinson's!" I want to scream, but my father would hate such a spectacle. He is self-effacing to the point of absurdity, never wanting to cause any trouble. He continues to smile and nod at people, who look at him like he's crazy.

"Do you know that person, Dad?"

"No."

"Then why did you say hello?"

"I can't help it. My head nods, so I might as well smile and say hi," he grins.

I admire the way he keeps himself buoyed on a raft of humor. I might have learned a lot from him if he'd stuck around.

What hurts more than anything is watching his functioning slowly decline. He can't tie his shoes. His head lurches so violently he can't read. This is the same father who sent me postcards from Japan, China, and Mexico, and snapshots of him waterskiing and downhill skiing in Lake Tahoe. My independent father has become dependent. If this ever happens to me, I swear silently, I'll kill myself.

Nobody knows what causes Parkinson's. They say it is not hereditary. (Is it just coincidence that my father's older sister and father both had it?) One theory links it with the encephalitis outbreak in the 1920s—the same virus that's said to have caused the sleeping sickness epidemic neurologist Oliver Sacks writes about in *Awakenings*. In fact, the L-dopa that Dr. Sacks used to revive his patients, frozen in a narcoleptic trance for a quarter of a century, is the same medication used to treat Parkinson's.

There is something about my father's symptoms that is eerily disturbing, something familiar that I can't quite pinpoint. The frozen inertness alternating with involuntary tremors—where else have I seen it? At P.I. and Manhattan State, patients suffering from tardive dyskenesia—an irreversible condition of involuntary movements caused by prolonged use of phenothiazine antipsychotic and antidepressant medications—exhibited similar symptoms.

There are other correlations between Parkinson's and depression. One of the side effects of the drugs used to treat Parkinson's is depression. The muscular rigidity and inertness associated with Parkinson's disease are also common side effects of Thorazine and similar antipsychotic drugs. People suffering from schizophrenia have also been found to have an excess of dopamines—the same substance that's deficient in Parkinson's.

Parkinson's patients tend to have difficulty initiating movement unless prodded into action by an outside stimulus. My father will freeze, his hand in midair, gazing fixedly at the salt shaker on the table. Yet if I just touch his hand, it glides forward to pick up the salt. Dr. Sacks noticed this same tendency in his sleeping-sickness patients, along with another impetus to movement: When patients emerged from their trancelike states, many spontaneously engaged in creative activities such as singing, dancing, or playing the piano. Creativity had the power to rouse them from immobility. My father, who has trouble walking and speaking, has little trouble dancing or singing, becoming at these moments fluidly animated.

One of the few things that has the power to pull me from depression is creative expression. It doesn't have to be painting; even the act of cooking a meal or singing along with a record can jolt me out of the depths. And like my father, I rely on contact with others. I'm an encouragement junkie, depending on friends or therapists to rescue me from crises of indecision and paralysis of will. I wonder—is my father's disease an elaborate expression of a weakness in character? It's so like my own dysfunction: a failure of will, but on the neurological level.

Just as I'd lost control of my thoughts and emotions as an adolescent, my father is losing control of his physical functioning. He's gone from being squarely situated in the mainstream of normalcy to an embarrassing aberration—one of the people he himself might have once made fun of. He's now on the outskirts of life. He has, essentially, dropped out. More and more he's living inside himself, in a semiconscious, trancelike state, locked in an internal neurological struggle. My once self-determined dad has become as avolitional and lacking in motivation as I was as a teenager.

After several visits to New York and various false starts, the time has come to admit my father to a nursing home. He rejected the enriched-housing program where he could have had his own studio apartment, assistance with shopping and daily tasks, and communal dinners served nightly. Now his functioning has declined to the point where they will no longer accept him.

When I finally find Morningside House in the Bronx, they promise that it won't be too long before a place opens up on their waiting list. Meanwhile, there's a nursing home just a few blocks from me that will accept him immediately.

The day I admit my father to Crown Residence is one of the bleakest of my life. My father has packed a small suitcase and accompanies me with dignity, fully trusting that I am taking him to a place where, though not ideal, he will be well taken care of. Rejecting the use of a walker, he walks into the nursing home falteringly, leaning on my arm. He makes pleasant conversation with the social worker while I fill out the required forms, filled with dread, feeling like a traitor. This time I'm the one who signs the admission papers, imprisoning my father.

The office is pleasant enough; only once you are on the ward do the true conditions make themselves known. The smell of urine hangs in the air, barely masked by disinfectant. The linoleum glares. Most of the patients are in their rooms, except a few, parked in wheelchairs in the hallway. An ancient black woman, so thin she seems made of ebony bone, sings constantly, in a loud, beseeching voice: "Have mercy, Lord Jesus, have mercy on my soul!"

"It's just temporary, Dad," I reassure him as I unpack his suitcase. He sits on the bed watching me hang up his clothes. His hands grip the sides of the bed; there is fear in his eyes.

The next day when I visit, my father isn't in his room. I find him tied into a wheelchair in the dining room, which is filled with patients. Those who are not asleep sit staring idly into space. A few mutter or curse loudly; the white-haired woman of the day before tries to drown them out with loud appeals to Jesus. I walk in just as one of the orderlies yanks down my father's jeans and boxers shoving a plastic urinal into my father's trembling hand. Evidently he had called out that he had to urinate, after having held it for as long as he could. He is visibly shaken and depressed. In the two days he's been there, his functioning has noticeably declined.

After a heated confrontation with the social worker, I decide that as long as my father has to be there, I will be there too. For the next three months—six days a week, three to five hours a day—I spend my days and evenings on the ward with my father. Mercifully, the occupational therapist makes a point of getting him off the ward several hours each day—just as the O.T. worker at Manhattan State had done for me.

At last I get a call from Morningside House telling me a space is available. When I arrive at 8 A.M. on the day of the move, my dad is sitting on his bed fully clothed, suitcase packed. We wait all day for Crown's ambulette, which finally picked us up at 4 P.M.; if they had waited an hour longer, we would have forfeited the bed that was being held for my father.

We arrive rumpled but relieved, and go through the now-familiar intake procedures.

Morningside House has a pleasantly modern feel; the patients' rooms even have little balconies. It's infinitely less depressing than Crown and offers many activities for those of its patients alert enough to participate. Its residential Bronx location reminds me of slower, quieter times. The old-fashioned bakeries, produce stands, and apparel and discount stores are reminiscent of the Brooklyn neighborhoods my dad grew up in.

At first I visit every few days. There is much to do: getting him settled in his room, meeting with the social worker, getting to know the nursing staff. We try to convince him to use a walker, but he resists, hanging on stubbornly to his independence. He's also reluctant to sign up for physical therapy and occupational therapy. I understand—I too had been resistant to such things when I was in P.I.—but I urge him to try, like a mom encouraging her child.

All too often, when I arrive on the ward, I spot my father parked in the hallway (where the staff situates patients so they can watch them), tied into his wheelchair with its brakes locked, jackknifed over, completely out of it. It takes me a while to rouse him. "Am I glad to see you," my father invariably breathes when he recognizes me. I bring him corned beef sandwiches, bagels and lox, and all manner of junk food. In good weather, I take him out on neighborhood pizza excursions or we sit in the rose garden and talk.

My father adapts. He wears slip-on shoes instead of lace-ups, and tries using special utensils with foam-padded grips. When fellow patients die, as they inevitably do, he is depressed for a while but sooner or later bounces back. Though he still finds people to poke fun at, he's friendly and well liked. He plays bingo and goes to most social activities. He flirts with the female staff members, who flirt back, and seems to enjoy the Sunday entertainment in the auditorium—especially the belly-dance performance (along with what seems to be the entire patient and staff population of the nursing home). Once he's caught escaping with his roommate, another Parkinson's patient, to the soft-core porn movie theater on Pelham Parkway. My father, the rebel, caught acting out.

But most of the time he's compliant. He grows timid and fearful, afraid to bother the staff even to ask for an aspirin when he has a headache. He doesn't complain when his wool sweaters are sent to the industrial laundry, returning shrunk to a child's size, whereas I hit the roof when I find these absurdly tiny articles stuffed into his dresser drawers. "Please don't say anything," he begs when I start down the hallway to complain to a nurse. I urge him to stand up for himself, but at the same time I understand his fear—his life is now in the hands of the attendants and nurse's aides who dress and bathe him, feed him, and put him to bed. His day can be made or ruined according to whether they are gruff and cruel, or gentle and kind.

My dad now becomes weepy at the slightest provocation. During one Sunday entertainment in the auditorium, he bursts into tears during the performer's rendition of "Sunrise, Sunset." A second later, so do I. The two of us look at each other and burst out laughing. To this day when I hear the schmaltzy chords and sentimental lyrics, my eyes fill.

It's not just sentimentality, but a softening into kindness he didn't have when he was fully functional. Some of this is directed toward me. "You're beautiful," he tells me each time I visit, then asks when I'm going to cut my long hair (he always preferred women with cropped hair). "How's your social life?" he asks as I sit next to him in the dining room, cutting up his food. My father wishes for me, more than anything else, to find a man to love and cherish me. He wants to leave this earth knowing I'm taken care of, enjoying a security he regrets not having given me when I was growing up.

Eight years of visits, Sunday afternoons with dad. As I watch him slowly deteriorate, my own life begins to take shape. I can afford to buy toilet paper *and* paper towels, keep my refrigerator filled and my soul at least partly sated. My fury at life's unfairness is balanced by the driving force to protect and nurture my dad.

Several times a year I take my father home for the weekend. Though I'm happy to liberate him from his prison, it's hard work. The days consist of constant meals and cleanup. I keep a watchful eye on my father to make sure he doesn't fall or become hungry or tired. I attend to him like a mother with a young child. At the end of the day I fall into my makeshift bed on the living room floor, exhausted.

But there are compensations. There's a calm rootedness I feel, just being together. My dad speaks openly of his regret at what he considers foolish choices—at missing out on being around to see his children grow up, for divorcing my mother and losing the women he loved after her, for remaining single, for hesitating to make investments that might have provided him with more than the meager savings that were quickly gobbled up in nursing-home payments. For caring more for his pleasure than for the important things—his family, his children. He must be just as surprised as I am to find himself suddenly dependent on me.

"What a fool I was," he says, shaking his head (is it Parkinson's or regret?), then lifts my hand to his lips.

My father disapproves of my relationship with Bob. "Don't waste your time," he tells me. When I say a few words in Bob's defense, my father interrupts. "I already know all about Bob. He's just like me." I'm stunned by his words. As much as I hate to admit it, Bob is a handsome, charming, independent, water-skiing, pleasure-seeking commit-o-phobe who will most likely return to California one day—without me.

Some of my duties are extremely intimate. My father can no longer urinate without assistance. Sometimes a pained look comes over his face, the signal for me to haul him out of his chair and trundle him off to the bathroom. While he steadies himself by holding onto the sink, I unzip his fly, take his penis from his shorts, and place it in his hand. When he's finished, I put it back in his shorts and zip him up. When he stays over, I wake a couple of times a night to my father's call: "Min, I have to go!"

I experience complex emotions when I help my father pee. My dad used to diaper me, wipe me, bathe me. Now here I am doing it for him, crossing a threshold I should not have to cross. He meets my eyes in the mirror with an apologetic glance. "I'm so sorry you have to do this," he says. I try to be matter-of-fact about it. It's impersonal and intimate all at once. This is the penis that helped create me, that joined both him and me to my mother. I'm not supposed to be touching it. The penis I hold, inactive though it may be, is the one and only, original, prototypical male model. It belongs to my first true love.

At night, exhausted from the effort of getting through the day, my father dozes off at the table or in a chair. I do my best to rouse him and half-carry him into the bedroom, seating him on the bed. I undress him, swing his body around, lift his legs onto the bed and push his body down as best I can into a somewhat prone position. His body is rigid; I have to push hard to get it to comply. If I push his shoulders down, his knees pop up, and vice versa. In order for him to be comfortable, I prop him up on a pile of pillows. After making sure he's covered, I kiss him goodnight, and turn off the light.

One night as I tuck him in, my father grabs my hand and pulls me down to him with surprising force. "How about a kiss?" he grins, his eyes unusually bright. As I plant a kiss on his cheek, he gropes for my breast, twists my face to his, and sticks his tongue out in a grotesque parody of an erotic kiss. I wrench away, shaking, and try to joke with him about it. "Come on, come closer," he insists, frightening me, but I can see that he's not really awake, unaware of who I am. I turn out the light and go into the living room, where I try to get a grip on what just happened.

For some time my dad has been experiencing bizarre hallucinations when he's tired, or as a result of medication. When I visited him in the hospital on a snowy December evening following his prostate surgery, I found my father, still slightly under the influence of anesthesia, intoxicated with love and altered consciousness. First he glowingly declared that he'd had a bowel movement, and that his turds had looked "so beautiful" as he flushed them down. Then, pointing at the window, he described a huge bison he saw outside in the falling snow. "I'm worried about him," he declared, his eyes filled with tears. "Do you think he's cold?"

In the nursing home he recounts elaborate stories of wild orgies involving staff and patients (most of whom were definitely not up to sexual misbehavior). Or he mentions that his old business partner from California visited him yesterday (unlikely, as they'd lost touch years ago) or that kids he'd grown up with in Brooklyn are living down the hall. After describing these things, he turns to me and asks, "Do you think I was hallucinating?"

But most of the time, aside from these twilight states, he is lucid. Too lucid—aware that his body and his senses are going out from under him, that life as he's known it is a thing of the past. This breaks my heart. I understand it; it's something I've experienced. But I was young when I'd suffered the powerlessness and despair of being locked away, while this will be my father's final experience of life.

After my father falls and breaks his hip, I no longer feel safe bringing him home. He's too heavy for me to lift; I can't risk another fall. He takes the news bitterly and is glum for a while. But to his credit, he rarely complains or tries to make me feel guilty.

Our bond is so strong that even when his speech becomes too garbled to understand, I usually know what he is trying to say. He speaks in a kind of code, substituting one word for another. His wheelchair is his "wheel." As his ability to articulate declines, he communicates with lone syllables.

"Shy, shy, shy . . ." he repeats, his head jerking and bobbing in all directions, and I know he wants me to shine his shoes—a habit he keeps up in a dogged attempt to preserve his dignity.

Caring for my father is like a weight on an old-fashioned clock. Without it, there would be no motion of the pendulum, no passage of time, no reason to be. He is the "man in my life" for the final decade of his life. It is often such a tremendous effort to visit him that afterward I fall dead asleep, totally drained, but there's also a feeling of being grounded, needed, in a way I have never been before.

Eventually my father falls ill with pneumonia. Each week the nursing staff phones to tell me he might not live through the weekend. I try to imagine what dying will be like for him, and how he'll experience it. One night before sleep I feel myself falling into darkness, then whooshing down a dark tunnel, at the end of which there is brilliant brightness. I lie as if paralyzed, unable to move or cry out, an odd calm between myself and my fear. Then I am above my body looking down at myself lying in bed.

The next day when I arrive at the nursing home, my father is asleep. I stand awhile watching the rise and fall of his breathing. When he opens his eyes and sees me, he murmurs, "I dreamed you died." Are we so bonded that we experience each other in our dreams? I feel afraid, and a little hurt. Both of us seem too complicity willing for me to take on my father's dying.

The pneumonia lands my father in the hospital. He lies in bed, unconscious. The doctors do not expect him to live. I grieve, not just for him, but for me. I've already lost him once as a child. Now I have to lose him a second time, when, after so much time and effort, I finally really have him close. Not fair, not fair. I pace the hallway with red eyes and clenched fists.

Miraculously, he rallies, recovering enough to return to the nursing home. Our weekend visits continue throughout the mild fall. We enjoy pleasant hours in the rose garden and eat sandwiches in the cafeteria. It's such a reprieve that I forget all about his brush with death.

When the phone rings at 2 A.M., rousing me from sleep, I know what it is before I answer it. The night attendant's voice is soft and gravelly, but there is no mistaking his words. I thank him, hang up, and lurch over to my desk, leaning heavily on my arms for support. I'm aware of a terrible pain in my left arm. Could it be a heart attack? I trace the source of the pain radiating up into my left shoulder through my arm and feel the severance of my father's life force as clearly as if a vein has been severed. Not knowing what else to do, I sit in meditation posture, breathing. Breathing, something my father can no longer do. I think of all that I know about my father, and how much I could not possibly know—all the memories, dreams, and secret thoughts of that young boy from Brooklyn.

I sit shiva alone. My father's relatives live out on Long Island; many are old and disabled. A rift has grown between me and my brother—an unfortunate loss; he's the only person who remembers my father as I do. My mother offers to fly up from Florida, but knowing that neither of us would feel comfortable staying together in my apartment, I tell her not to bother. Bob and I have recently parted. In a way, my grief is all the company I need.

I go through my father's things. Group photos taken at electronics conventions, snapshots of my dad with friends and various women. Love letters from one of his girlfriends culminate in a letter telling him she's decided to marry someone else . . . not because she didn't love him, but because my father couldn't commit. How alike we are.

For the last ten years, my link with my father has been my closest bond. At forty, it's a bit late to start thinking of forming a family of my own. I stare at a photo of my father taken when he was around the same age I am now. I know exactly how much time has passed since then. What will I do with the rest of my life, and who will be with me at its end?

———————

Several months after my father's death, I tune into a made-for-TV movie about a brother and sister who spend a summer with their divorced father in his beachside condo in Los Angeles, a trial arrangement to determine whether they'd like to permanently live there. It's a predictable tearjerker and I'm vexed with myself for watching, but I can't bring myself to change the channel. The scenario reminds me of me, my brother, and my father.

It hits me hard—the realization that my father had never expressed an interest in my coming to live with him. He never even offered to have me come for a summer. He kept me distant and estranged, aside from his celebrated annual four-day guest appearances. Though he was central in my life, he'd kept me on the periphery of his. He could have had me join him anytime he wanted . . . but he never did.

He hadn't wanted me! He'd valued his independence more than his relationship to his daughter, to *me*. He had not been able to find it within himself to do for me what I was more than willing to do for him. He'd abandoned me, in the largest possible sense. I feel like a fool for not having realized this before. But he knew it. I remember his gratitude toward me, his expressions of remorse and regret. The trickle of realization joins a larger flow—the underground stream running through me, endlessly whispering that I am unlovable, undeserving of love.

Then I'm hit by a wave that knocks me to the ground: *If I had gone to live with him, would I have wound up in the hospital?*

I know the answer. No, it never would have happened. I was too shy with my father to disrespect him. I didn't have the contempt for him I had for my mother. Plus he didn't believe in psychiatry and would never have had me institutionalized. My whole life would have been different.

My brother had gone to live with him. Why didn't he have me come? Was it because I was a girl? Did he think I'd cramp his unfettered bachelor's lifestyle? Maybe my mother didn't want me to go live with him—if he'd ever even asked. I wonder if the thought had ever crossed his mind. He probably felt relieved to be free to do his own thing. What did he have to offer me, really? We were strangers. I might have been miserable living with him. Whatever the reasons, my father kept his distance, until his illness brought us together. Ironically, my having to institutionalize him created a bond between us that would not have otherwise formed.

We had more in common than I'd realized. My father, with all his striving for acceptance, was, by his own choice, an outsider—to his own family. There is a certain marginality in living a solitary life; I know it well. And though we never spoke of it directly, we both knew how it felt to be locked on a hospital ward, irrevocably outside the mainstream.

FLOATING

AFTER MY FATHER DIES, I AM FLOATING. Without the pull of our connection I am like a hot-air balloon whose line has been cut. I moonwalk through my days, the air a strange ether. My new lightness is disorienting. I fear that if I don't find something to anchor me, I might float away. Now that my father is gone, feeding my cat and going to work are not enough. I need someone, something, other than myself to care about.

Following a friend's example, I become a volunteer for Common Cents, an organization that donates small change to good causes. I go door to door in my building collecting pennies, getting glimpses of neighbors I've never met. Through their open doors I catch sight of living rooms and dining-room tables in apartments that look more inhabited than my own.

Bob is no longer in my life. As we headed toward our final breakup, our relationship sprouted new symptoms. Bob had been losing me in crowds. Once, biking in Connecticut, he'd sped up and out of sight. He was probably just reveling in speed and strength, but I couldn't help feeling abandoned. Not trusting myself to navigate the unknown roads, I found my way back to the car and waited, simmering, until he returned. Another time he lost me deliberately in the massive gathering of costumed revelers at the Halloween Parade in Greenwich Village. I'd annoyed him by impulsively snapping photos, running out of film just when his friends, whom we'd come to see, appeared all decked-out in their costumes. I turned around and Bob was gone.

I could hardly blame him for leaving me. I'd disappointed him too often with my indecision and my inability to tear myself away from the security of known surroundings and routines to risk taking a trip with him. He loved to travel and frequently invited me, but even though I wanted to go with him, I could not bring myself to say yes. No matter how many positives I placed on the scale, they could not outweigh the enormous weight of my fears: of being social for hours on end, of being on unfamiliar turf, of not being able to retreat into myself.

This was the crux of it. I depend upon retreating into myself to recharge my easily depleted batteries. If forced to be social for too many hours, I become a soulless replica of my real self, like the pod creatures in *Invasion of the Body Snatchers*. A fake me, who says and does things I'd never say or do. I'd have to be constantly watchful to keep from annoying or alienating Bob. It could take days to recover from being on alert for so long. It was too much to risk.

Bob had broken up with me before, on a fairly regular basis. My method of dealing with these breakups was to lay low, making an effort to become stronger and a better person, and when I felt I'd made some headway, I'd write or phone him. We'd talk, and after a while begin seeing each other again. I knew that Bob still had feelings for me. But it wouldn't be long until I disappointed him once again.

The last time, however, I could tell it was different. Bob left me with a kiss and told me to take care of myself. A few days later he dropped off a box of my belongings in my lobby. This time it was final.

Each time a relationship is over, certain gifts remain, like the impression a fossil leaves in its sandy limestone host. David imprinted me with his quest for higher consciousness; Bernie with compassion, my father with simplicity and sincerity, Bob with a positive attitude and the desire to become physically strong and healthy.

Bob used to tease me that my constant smoking was like having an extra mouth to constantly shove food into. He was right; I smoked whenever I felt anxiety or the need for affirmation. I'd been smoking heavily since I was fifteen. Smoking was a symbol of my defiance and identity. We chain-smoked in the hospital to pass the time and to approximate some sign of life force. When David and I lived together, we smoked and talked until we went to bed, then lit up first thing in the morning. Smoking gave us mental energy.

True to my contrarian nature, I never declare to the world that I am quitting smoking. I think of it as merely cutting down, getting control over my habit. I'm tired of waking in the mornings with my mouth tasting like an ashtray; tired of coughing—the deep, juicy hacking that's alarming when you hear other people doing it. Recently I started swimming in a neighborhood pool, and though I love to swim, I can barely make it to the end of a lap without becoming winded.

I begin by jumping small hurdles: No cigarettes until 10:30 A.M. This is a radical measure that I sweeten with the doughnuts and extra-large coffee I bring to work. I extend the hurdles: No cigs until after lunch, 1:30, 3, 4:30 . . . until I'm down to three to five a day. I enjoy the sense of power and possibility I derive from my new control over my cigarette habit. I practice my "accordion method" of cutting down for more than two years. When Bob and I break up for good, I quit smoking altogether.

After our final breakup, I know that if I don't become strong, I'll fall apart. If I let myself be overwhelmed by self-destructive urges, I'll be the kind of weak, wretched victim that Bob would have wanted nothing to do with. I have to prove to myself that I'm worthy of his love. I'll become the kind of person he never would have rejected.

I've never learned to be at home or confident in my body. When attempting something physical, I seem to watch its movements from a great height, my thinking interfering with my coordination. When I try hiking, I'm not sure of my footing, and have to watch every step. I also feel shaky on my bike. I begin to cycle a lot, in order to get over my fears of falling off or getting lost. I go on bike trips and pump up hills, groaning from the effort. But I'm determined to grow stronger. I need to start taking pride in myself—aside from Bob, for myself.

I start swimming every day the pool is open, six days a week, about an hour a day. At first I struggle, straining to keep my nose above water level. I start watching other swimmers, the sleek and graceful ones, and ask them to correct my stroke. Once I learn to relax in the water and let it support me, I discover streamlined, efficient ways of swimming. I swim fast. If I'm upset, I thrash my anger and grief out on the water.

Water is a place of a natural meditation, a nonverbal, fluid world, a relief from the strictures of the working world and of the tyranny of my thoughts. With each stroke, they float away. When I swim, I follow my breath. The effort that too often felt forced and unnatural in meditation comes naturally in the pool. Underwater, I hear the *whoosh* of my breath, the beat of my pulse. Breathing in and out, syncopating arms, legs, and head. Moving forward while feeling precisely in the moment.

Other things help buoy me. My job as magazine designer, in its way, has contained and supported me, providing a community and a place to strengthen and develop my design abilities as well as my social skills. Though navigating the currents of corporate politics doesn't come naturally, I begin to learn not to take criticism personally, and discover among my co-workers several close friends.

The year after my father's death, my company undergoes a change in management. Under the new regime, the once-creative environment becomes stifling. With the change in staff, I feel as if the water in the pool has evaporated, leaving me flapping on the bottom. I want out but can't afford to just quit. One by one, many of the creative, free-spirited people I work with are fired and replaced. I pray to be similarly released, and after an agonizing year, my prayers are answered.

Once again, without the moorings of structure and routine, I find myself in that familiar floating state. But this time, my thirst for a higher purpose kicks in. Now that I have unemployment insurance, I decide to do everything I've put on hold or regret not having finished. I return to the Art Students League, where I study academic figure painting. Oil painting has long intimidated me (I was always more comfortable with the fluidity of watercolor), but I'm determined to master it—making a dent as well in my impatience, perfectionism, and limited tolerance for frustration.

After my first semester, I win a merit scholarship: a year's free tuition. I divide my time between painting and printmaking. In printmaking— etching and lithograph—the resistance of the materials acts like a focusing lens, channeling my imagination. I create a series of anthropomorphic images: trees as women, from puberty through adolescence and adulthood to maturity and old age. Young nubile trees, sexy adolescent trees, erotic trees, over-the-hill burlesque-queen trees. In Central Park I draw the gnarled, graceful limbs, trunks, and crotches that sheltered me as a truant adolescent seeking solace in nature.

Lithography is a particularly arduous—and mysterious—process. We work on heavy slabs of Bavarian limestone that first must be made absolutely level and uniformly smooth by rubbing two stones against one another in a constant circular motion, scouring their surfaces with a layer of fine carborundum and water. It's a rhythmic, repetitive process involving water. The meditative mermaid in me loves it. And though at first I can hardly manage the heavy stones, my arms and back soon become muscular and able.

Lithography makes me strong. It also teaches me patience. The delicate chemical balance (much like my own emotions) is oddly erratic and vulnerable to humidity and temperature changes. Lithography, with its interaction of oil, water, and stone, resonates with metaphor. The resistance and receptivity of the stone is the ground, the clean slate, that we are born with; the greasy image etched with acid, the circumstances that etch our characters; the water that extra something, the spirit that renews and protects us.

I keep my promise to tie up loose ends in my life. After a year and a half at art school, I reenroll in college for two semesters and do an internship in art therapy with acutely ill children before deciding to return to graphic design on my own terms. I work for a while at an educational publishing company before starting my own graphic design business. With the help of credit cards, I buy computer equipment and set up an office in my apartment, experiencing no qualms of conscience working for my nonprofit, arts-oriented clients.

I continue painting, exhibit my work in galleries and public spaces, and go away to artists' colonies where I experience the community of artists, and work for the first time in a studio instead of my apartment or a classroom. I join a painting group that meets weekly to paint from the model, eat junk food, and schmooze about art and life.

All the while I keep swimming, experiencing that steady forward rhythm of arms, legs, and heart through the fluid medium of my life. The chlorinated water in the local pool has absorbed my fatigue, confusion, anger, despair, and frustration of the last twenty years. It's a place of communion as well as a community. Years of conversations in the shower have formed friendships born of nakedness and frank talk.

Slowly, I do it. I become a swimmer, healthy and strong. I do it on my own terms, with a little motivation borrowed from friends and lovers, and lessons from the practice and craft of art, afloat in the element of my choice.

TOWARD OR AWAY?

TOWARD PEOPLE, OR AWAY? Psychologists like Melanie Klein, Karen Horney, and Erich Fromm agree that this is the core conflict of the neurotic personality. Neurosis, like the ferment of enzymes surrounding the annoying grain-of-sand-soon-to-be-a-pearl, revolves around the compulsion to recreate our childhood conflicts, over and over, because it is what we know, what we're "at home" in.

For years I struggled to sort it out: Is being a single a symptom of social/psychological disease, or is it a life choice? Though I consider myself a feminist, the question tugs at me, from deep inside my heart and brain—as well as my reproductive organs. I feel, literally, singled out. How could I hope to have a lasting relationship? My past is an invisible barrier between me and other people, always intruding, separating me. In spite of myself, I broadcast the message: "Don't come too close."

As much as I long for contact and closeness, as strong as my need is for love, I'm soon overwhelmed by the presence of another person. Even just a few hours tires me. Like a moon coming too near a larger planet, I'm pulled off course by their magnetic pull. If I don't get away, I'll be consumed. In love relationships, I do what it takes to get the other person to leave me if I can't bring myself to reject him first. After my initial relief at being solitary again, I return to my original state of aching, mournful aloneness.

I've had two long relationships; each lasted six and a half years. (Six and a half—the age I was when my father left for California.

Coincidence, or psychological fate?) David moved toward me and I pushed him away; whereas with Bob, I moved toward him and he pushed me away. I got to play both roles, but the end result was the same. Alone. Safe. Sad.

Such is life, I tell myself. Relationships are impermanent. You can't rely on other people for your sense of well-being. To thine own self be true. Et cetera. Ad nauseam.

What will it be? I ask myself. Toward, or away? Alone and isolated, or together and merged? The whole situation seems to carry an innate sense of failure.

There have been wonderful men in my life: kind, caring guys who loved me. A few asked me to marry them. I invariably rejected them. Their willingness to commit for the long haul scared me. What if I was unable to live up to their expectations? What if, once they found out who I really was, they fell out of love with me? What if I said yes, only to find married life too boring, confining, or abrasive? My freedom had been too hardwon. Better to remain at a distance.

Besides, nice guys didn't attract me. I preferred being treated like a temporary object of passion to the suffocation of being loved. When I'm with somebody for any length of time a kind of vertigo sets in. After the initial romance and the ensuing negotiations, misunderstandings, and reconciliations, the question inevitably arises: Why bother? A unique dimness of spirit settles on me when I contemplate this.

"What are we doing together?" I asked Bob one night after sex, nestled close to him, unable to understand my desolation. Bob thought for a moment. "We're comforting each other," he said finally. That made sense; I could live with that. But more commitment than that I couldn't handle. What did I need with someone criticizing and making demands on me?

Yet when a relationship ends, I'm shattered, overwhelmed by a sense of finality, severance, betrayal. I mourn the relationship as if it were a death. Then I reassemble my world. I clean and make order in my apartment. I listen to music, read, and paint, and slowly I'm reborn.

It's taken me years to understand that solitude is the amniotic fluid necessary to nurture creativity, and that my need to be alone is not simply an aberration. I've become used to living on my own terms. Even alone, I'm not alone. I'm in constant relationship with my plants, my cats, my friends, neighbors, even the city itself, in all its honking, screeching cacophony. When I read a book by an author I love or contemplate the work of a painter I especially admire, I feel a connection that traverses time and space. *This is your true family,* my inner voice whispers.

Yet the reality of being single can be wearying. Just me, my cats (on whom I lavish far too much affection), the television and telephone, the ever-increasing piles of books, the din of Amsterdam Avenue traffic. And on the street, in the park, everywhere: couples, families, children. I stare at women with swollen bellies, and couples apparently so in sync they could be one mechanism. Envy flows thick and heavy through my body.

I long for a family of my own. Family, like a handmade raft requiring constant attention and repair, ultimately keeps you afloat, whereas being single is like constantly treading water. As I age, I increasingly see that it makes sense to live for someone other than ourselves, to pass the baton, nurture another young life, give the best of ourselves, our wisdom, to those we love. But when I hear the screaming and whining of young children or the bickering of couples, I think maybe it's not so bad being single.

I think of the babies that I aborted in my twenties. At the time it was clearly the only choice; there was no way I was equipped to raise children. And yet I suffer a retrospective sense of loss. Sometimes I catch myself talking to the child I never had, clasping a small imaginary hand in mine, a dear little person I'll never know. At other moments I have a sense of how my children, if I'd had any, might have come to see me: what about me would they have loved, and what would they have come to hate—especially as adolescents. Just as how utterly unbearable my mother's expressions and mannerisms became to me: the tapping of her fingernails, the pursed upper lip when she felt insecure, the quiver of gathering anger, her fearfulness, her frustration. Her smell—the same scent I inhaled greedily as a child—became loathesomely familiar as a teenager. What in me would have driven my children to distraction?

I remember long afternoons visiting with family; the stiffness of my dress-up clothes, the discomfort of being on display. I'd fall into an almost drunken stupor, longing for the relief of being alone. In my twenties, friends teasingly accused me of having a Greta Garbo complex ("I vahnt to be aloone!" she moaned in *Grand Hotel*). Even wearing a turtleneck felt too confining.

Are there certain souls who are not meant to thrive within the confines of family—who need above all to be alone?

"You're too self-centered to have a family," one boyfriend accused me, angry that I'd been finding it hard to get home on time for dinner. I'd been painting in the park at sunset, unwilling to tear myself away from the spectacular, shifting light. Was he right?

Not a day goes by that I don't ask myself what my life would be like if I weren't so stubbornly *myself*. If I hadn't been hospitalized, would I be so fearful of commitment? Would I be happier if I'd let myself be carried more by my body's reproductive imperative and less by fears and defenses? Would my relationships have been different if my parents hadn't divorced? Could it have been any other way? If I had formed roots within a family, I might be wondering what my life would have been like if I hadn't. Would I have developed my creativity, or would I have channeled it into raising children? Would the human connection I crave have felt as much like a prison as my aloneness? If I'd been able to make other choices, *would I still be me?*

ROCKLAND REVISITED

I'm with you in Rockland . . .
—Allen Ginsberg

JULY 1999. The heat in the city is unbearable. I go for a drive with a
friend. As we head north on the West Side Highway, nearing the
George Washington Bridge, I crane my neck to catch sight of P.I., its
twelve modest stories now dwarfed by larger buildings. A year or so ago
Columbia Presbyterian added a modern, green-glass structure that now
obscures most of the old building, but if I'm quick I can see for a second the caged-in rooftops where they used to take us once in a while for
fresh air. I feel some dizziness—a residual vertigo—when I pass them
on the highway. But I always search them out. They are talismen of my
freedom.

We cross the bridge and head up the Palisades Parkway to 9W.
Country and western music twangs playfully on the radio. We're just a few
minutes from the city and already the air feels cleaner. I read the road
signs: Orangeburg, Pearl River, Rockland Psychiatric Center.

Rockland. The state hospital Marjee was shipped to shortly after I'd
arrived at P.I. Her crime: smoking a joint. She was there three months,
and when she returned she was not the same girl. She'd become bitter,
brittle, fearful.

It suddenly hits me that we are taking the same route Marjee must have
taken when she was shipped, driving along the exact same roads. What
must she have felt? I imagine her hand and face against the window, her
huge eyes watching.

My beautiful friend, armed only with your pout, your feminine curves, your humor and wit, your anger. How could they have sent you there, thirteen years old, alone and frightened?

I want to see Rockland in the flesh, experience the approach as Marjee had. I ask my friend if he would mind taking a detour. He agrees. "The place is enormous. Hard to miss it."

We take the exit—6W—and the road curves onto another highway. It could be Anywhere, USA: strip malls, restaurants. We miss the turnoff after passing a small sign that reads ROCKLAND PSYCHIATRIC CENTER.

"You know how it is—they don't want to make too much of it, ruin the neighborhood," my friend says. We turn around and double back. Soon after the turnoff, an easy-to-miss sign (HOSPITAL) marks a pastoral country road, dotted with residential houses, many of them boarded up. This must have once been staff housing, abandoned as staff was cut back in the gradual de-institutionalization taking place over the past few decades.

The guardhouse stands shut and unattended. As we pass through the stone gateposts, I see a large, hand-painted wooden sign, probably a project designed for patients: OUR MISSION: HOPE AND RECOVERY FOR PEOPLE WITH SEVERE MENTAL ILLNESS. The sign is embellished with flourishes and colorful flowers. I wonder how the patients who made it felt. Were they excited to work on such an interesting, fun project? Did they consider themselves hopeful survivors of severe mental illness? Or were they in a medicated stupor?

The tree-lined road curves and winds around for quite a while as we get further into the complex, which is nestled deep within the grounds. Finally we reach a clearing and a large sign with arrows pointing in different directions: Buildings 55, 59, 60 (right arrow); Building 57 (left arrow). The place is vast, a sprawling country estate. The buildings, roughly ten stories tall, are a modern Tudor design, with tan stucco exteriors. Pink rectangular lozenges beneath each window are inscribed with Xs, as if canceled out. The windows are framed by identical beige curtains, some open, some dawn; but nowhere do I see a human being. We drive slowly around the main cul de sac, past deserted picnic tables, bus shelters, benches; not a soul in sight.

INTAKE, NEW ARRIVALS—this is where Marjee must have arrived, her paperwork processed, before being placed on some ward alongside the "severely mentally ill." I can't bear to think of it. And Rocky, I can still see her, quick and graceful, her straight dark hair hanging past her waist, her gray eyes, her wry gaze. They sent Rocky here too, but she never returned. For only an instant I allow my mind the image of her slim body hanging lifeless from a noose made of . . . what? Maybe a belt, or institutional bedsheets. I scan the windows. On which of these wards did Rocky end her life?

The deserted buildings are a testament, a silent tomb of untold stories. My great aunt Gertie was one—a family secret, all hush and whispers. She lived out the last two decades of her life here.

My great-grandmother Minne (for whom I'm named) gave birth to six children. Two died young. Of those remaining, Gertie was the one Minne kept closest to her. Gertie was a handsome woman with pale skin, blue eyes, and black hair. She loved a good time and had no trouble attracting men. She married young, at fifteen or sixteen, but the marriage was short-lived. When Gertie discovered she was pregnant, her mother pressured her into having an abortion. She disapproved of Gertie's musician husband. The marriage was annulled, and Gertie never married again. For many years she had an affair with a married man who promised to leave his wife—until she sued for divorce. Gertie testified against him in court. After the trial, she became convinced that she was being followed and that someone was trying to poison her.

During the thirties and forties, Gertie lived with a widower, a retired engineer many years older than herself. Though he was good to Gertie, her family disapproved of him because he was Catholic. After he died, Gertie moved back in with her mother. She complained of headaches and depression and began to let herself go. "I won't always be here to take care of you," her mother warned. "After I die you're not going to have a home. Do something with yourself!"

When Minne died, Gertie signed herself in to Rockland. She was given medication and shock treatments, but nothing brought her out of her delusions for long. At first my mother and other relatives visited Gertie, but gradually the visits dwindled and finally stopped. Gertie died all alone on a ward in Rockland State.

You could say that Gertie's brain chemistry had gotten the better of her, that the illness was lurking in her, waiting for the proper conditions to release the chemical toxins that cause madness. Coming at it from another direction, you could point to the pressures and disappointments that might have pushed her over the edge. But the truth of Gertie's story is locked away in the past, as she was, behind these mute walls.

We drive on, passing smaller buildings. People sit here and there; alone, not in groups. A young woman carries a small suitcase up a path; a plump young man in shorts sits on a low stone wall, swinging his feet; a tall black man gazes up with a troubled expression beneath tense brows. Patients . . . I can tell.

We pass Our Lady Queen of Peace Chapel. But there is too much peace here, too much quiet. On a hillside, a large black woman sits eating lunch, a brown paper bag spread neatly on her lap. She is dressed all in blue and glances at her watch. Definitely a staff member on her lunch break, not a patient. I know these things.

The road curves back toward where we entered. I see a sign: GOLF COURSE. A golf course on the premises of a mental institution? I vaguely recall an attendant at P.I. saying, "It's not so bad there; they have their own golf course." Did they offer golf therapy? Of course not—it was for the staff. Probably a perk to entice them to commute or move to this isolated place, offering the doctors a way to refresh their spirits, the manicured greens washing away the craziness and negative energy that would accumulate, sticking to them like lint, during the course of their work day. Did they really play golf on their lunch hour? It seems obscene.

By now the silence has gotten to me. I remember it well: the sitting, the waiting, the negativity, the resignation, the despair. I hear beneath this silence the sighs and sobs, screams and shouts, confessions and vows—and silence—of the multitudes who lived and died behind these locked doors and windows; and not only here, but at Bronx State, Manhattan State, Harlem Valley, Creedmoor . . . and all the sad places like this whose names I don't need to know.

My friend swings the car around toward the gate. I close my eyes a moment and say to Rocky, to Gertie, to Marjee: You're not alone. I am your witness. I am here.

OLD FRIENDS

I HAVE BEEN REASSEMBLING MY LIBRARY from those years, making a daily pilgrimage to used book stores to search for my old friends: Dostoyevsky, Camus, Sartre, Hesse, Lagerkvist, Ginsberg, Plath. Over the years I'd given them away one by one. "I don't need this anymore; someone else might want to read it," I reasoned, as I divested myself of precious pieces of my past, making room for new books and new loves.

Lately I've spent hours searching my bookshelves for these old friends. "It must be here somewhere," I think, my heart filled with longing and panic, my search taking on a frantic, compulsive energy. I'm afraid I might never find the small hardcover volume of Buddhist aphorisms that I used to carry with me everywhere when I was fourteen. Can it be that I'll never see its brown-and-yellow cover again?

Sometimes I get lucky. When my bookshelf offers up the paperback edition of the *I Ching* Marjee gave me for my seventeenth birthday, I hug it to my chest. The inscription, all lower-case letters: "happy birthday '69 much love, marjee," goes straight to my heart. My tattered copies of Hesse's *Demian* and *Narcissus and Goldmund* are the same ones we'd shared in the hospital.

I discover Nietzsche's *The Birth of Tragedy and the Genealogy of Morals*, a birthday gift from Jane. The words she'd inscribed in green ink, "For Mindy, Be happy! Love, love, love, Janie," are spotted with my tears—a testament to the difficulty I had following her advice. Too bad I hadn't been able to see the humor in it: like giving someone *The Rise and Fall of the Third Reich* inscribed with a smiley face.

Sylvia Plath's *Ariel* is gone, as is a paperback of Zen koans, my Modern Library *Steppenwolf*, and dozens of others. I think of Esau, who foolishly gave away his birthright. How could I have thoughtlessly given away these links to my younger self?

In used book shops and at street vendors' tables I experience moments of success and disappointment. I want the original paperbacks, not new reissues. I want the pages yellowed and cracked, with underlinings and notes in the margins—books that have been loved, absorbed, taken to heart. I often have to settle for later editions, and even at half off the cover price I pay twice what they originally cost. When used book stores fail, I search online.

Like a detective on assignment, I am determined to unearth all clues, anything that will shed light on those years. I pull out things I've stuffed away in closets: letters, notebooks, diaries. I climb on stepladders to pull dusty boxes from dark cupboards. I empty bags and spread the contents out on the floor. Sometimes I can hardly look at what I find; it's too painful. On the blue-ruled pages of Marjee's high school notebook left behind when she'd escaped, following pages of history notes, I find a poem she'd written with Jane, and tucked inside, her last letter to me. I also find a photo of her taken by my friend Larry—her splendid body, her beautiful face, cheeks sucked in to look thinner, her huge eyes looking challengingly at me. I look at it a few minutes, then put it away.

I forage unsuccessfully in a closet for the faded red mailing tube that contained the carefully calligraphed and illustrated oversized letter my friend Josh mailed me for my first birthday inside, the paper so thick and curly I had to kneel on all fours to hold it open long enough to read it. For over two decades his letter stood in the corner of my closet until, declaring war on sentimentality, I must have put it out with the trash on one of my purges.

I find the hardcover copy of *Zen Mind, Beginner's Mind* given me by my twitchy Buddhist friend Richie. It was written by Shunryu Suzuki, his first meditation teacher; one of many he studied with after his stint at P.I. After the hospital, we continued our friendship, exchanging phone calls and letters, and getting together between Richie's zendo retreats. One balmy spring day in the early eighties he called from a Tibetan Buddhist community in Vermont to say good-bye: The cancer he'd evaded as a teenager had finally caught up with him, metastasized in his lungs. Richie comforted me in my grief, saying he was finally ready to leave this life, grateful to die attended by Buddhist monks. Surely he achieved an enlightened death.

Harold contacts me from California. We talk on the phone, exchange photos and stories. He visits me in New York. We reminisce about our outrageous behavior as adolescents. He confesses things: how he and his friends used to steal pocket money from the heavily medicated patients while they slept; how closely he'd guarded his fears and insecurities.

Harold describes what it was like being admitted to P.I.: "I was cutting school and taking drugs, and they brought me to Family Court and locked me on the ward. At first I was scared but then I discovered all these other kids just like me. We did whatever we wanted. What else could they do to us?" But he soon realized it wasn't fun to be drugged and locked up. Desperate to leave, Harold got himself shipped to Harlem Valley, which released him after three months. Afterward, he lived in a halfway house for troubled and delinquent teens in suburban New Jersey. (Coincidentally, Laurie was there too.) The psychiatrist who ran the place was like a surrogate father. When Harold complained of anxiety, he responded: "I'm going to put you on Valium. Do you know what Valium means? It stands for 'Valor'. We're going to give you courage." Harold left the program with a refillable prescription for Valium. Soon he was doing massive doses and selling the pills to friends. Before long he was mainlining heroin. The road back from addiction took years. Along the way he married, remarried, raised two families, and established a business and a part-time acting career.

I reconnect with Sheila, Bobby, and Noel; we spend hours exploring the past and catching up on our lives since then. Though they've all left P.I. far behind, traces remain. A decade and a half after P.I., Sheila cowrote, directed, and starred in her own version of Frances Farmer's story, a seventy-five-minute film entitled *Committed*. She now practices and teaches Chinese medicine.

Two years after he was released from P.I., following a bad experience with LSD, Bobby was readmitted to P.I. and given thirty shock treatments within three months, which he says helped him. Later he signed himself into a hospital where he was lucky to have a therapist he could work with in earnest. "Once I realized that other people had feelings too, I began to change," he says. "I started to learn to take responsibility for myself."

Bobby spent the next twelve years housebound, reading and meditating, determined to understand and heal himself. Now a family man focused on his wife and daughter, Bobby ventures out to do errands, but prefers not to stray too far from his "spiritual center." The spiritual healing techniques he developed have become his life's work.

To each of my old friends I put the question: Why were they hospitalized? The details of their stories vary, but their answers boil down to the same thing. As Bobby puts it: "My parents projected their own needs and fears onto me, but never saw who I was. More than anything, I needed to feel loved." Could it have been that simple?

I discover Loren, a former P.I. patient and the first lesbian I'd been aware of knowing, behind the counter of a feminist bookstore. One of the store's founding partners, Loren tells me she's doing well, is involved in her work and lives with her lover in their West Side apartment. I'm surprised to find her looking cheerful; on the ward she was always so depressed. Her situation comes into sharp focus: It must have been unbearable to have had her sexual preference diagnosed as illness, adding to and obscuring the sources of her depression.

Occasionally I run into former patients on the street. We exchange news and phone numbers, promise to keep in touch, and rarely follow up. Once I noticed the blind man from MPLP shuffling along the street talking to himself; feeling shamefully voyeuristic, I was unable to approach him. I was relieved to see him again a few weeks later, looking much better. I always feel shaken when one of my former fellow patients is in bad shape. After all these years, it still hits very close to home.

Judith, whose journal-keeping at P.I. kept her going ("It was the only privacy I had in that place"), later became one of the moving forces of MPLP, holding office variously as secretary, vice president, and president. Life hasn't been easy for Judith. Debilitated by chronic physical illness, she is now largely confined to her apartment, which she shares with her feline companions. An unpublished thousand-page novel about her time at P.I. is locked away in her desk drawer. Writing it didn't dispel her bitterness. "I feel like I died in there," she says.

Most of my old friends have put the past behind them. Their memories are of P.I. are hazy. Some don't want to remember, but for others, the intensity of those years is still alive. Harold says the relationships he formed at P.I. were deeper and more intense than any he's had since. Two of his three daughters are named Margaret and Jane, and his dog is named

after Alyssa—three of our fifth-floor resident Graces. And he's never forgotten his feelings for Marjee, his first true love.

Of all my old friends, Marjee is the one I miss most. Had she lived, it's
likely we would have drifted apart; still, I mourn the opportunity to know
the adult she would have become—and to simply know she is alive and
well. All these years, I've carried my grief at her death within me like an
unborn child, cumbersome and heavy. At times I think it's gone, but given
the right stimulus—too much alcohol or the ending of a relationship—it
kicks me sharply in the gut, fresh as ever.

In a telephone conversation with Mrs. Gould in 1991, I shared my
musings about whether Marjee's death was an accident. "What do you
mean?" she'd asked. "Of course it wasn't an accident. She jumped off a
roof!"—an explanation radically different from Harold's original account
of an overdose. The thought of Marjee hurling herself from a rooftop
was so shocking that I plunged into a horror almost identical to my state
when I'd first heard the news. Time may appear to heal all wounds, but
beneath the superficial skin graft, life's major losses are undiminished—of
that I am convinced.

I contact P.I. to verify the details of Marjee's death, but the hospital is
unwilling to offer any information. Until I'm able to find Marjee's
mother or brother, I will never know what really happened. Meanwhile,
I've chosen to believe Harold's kinder version.

Harold requests a copy of his records from P.I. and shares them with
me. Later Sheila does the same. Our records are filled with references to
one another, documenting our misadventures, bringing it all back in
amazingly vivid detail.

I search the internet for traces of Ted, James, Laurie, and other old
friends, without success. I hope they are alive and well, and that sooner or
later, our paths will cross again.

I listen to the music from those times: *The White Album, Sgt. Pepper,
Freewheelin' Bob Dylan, Blonde on Blonde.* (Dylan's "Sad-Eyed Lady" reminds
me of Edie Sedgwick, who briefly graced our fifth-floor ward.) I rediscover the Simon and Garfunkel album I listened to with Marjee the hot,
horrible summer I drank poison, playing over and over the sweetly melancholy *"Old friends, old friends, sat on the park bench like bookends . . ."*

I start seeing my old friends everywhere. The streets seem filled with
women with Liz's body type and bone structure, the sharp fox face cam-
ouflaged beneath fleshy curves. I could swear I see Marjee walking down

Broadway. My heart leaps, strangely hopeful. But when she turns toward me, an absurd disappointment breaks over me. It can be dangerous, recalling the dead.

Of all of us, Alyssa had seemed relatively well adjusted—maybe a little too fond of mind-altering substances, but basically okay. So I'm deeply shocked when I hear the news. Her body was found early one morning in the dining room of her father's house, not long after her divorce from a ten-year marriage. She'd written good-bye notes to each of her three young children.

Alyssa's death raises disturbing questions. I'd long been convinced that we were basically rebellious kids, unjustly incarcerated, acting out a clash of values like the rest of our generation—the ultimate rebels, in our druggy, self-destructive way. But perhaps it was more serious than I'd thought. We were at greater risk than we imagined . . . and only some of us survived.

In dreams, as in my waking life, I conjure up the faces I'll never see again. It seems urgently important for me to visualize every detail. Who else will remember my friends? I fear that if I don't, they'll disappear forever.

———————

One day I'm walking along Columbus Avenue when I notice a slim-hipped, broad-shouldered, brown-haired guy sashaying toward me. His longish hair is swept back from a high forehead. It's Nick. The same wide mouth, straight nose, hazel eyes—now behind horn-rimmed glasses. His lips curve into what might be a smile or a sneer. His eyes don't smile. He's carrying a large bag of laundry, scuffling his shoes along the sidewalk. His loafers are a more scuffed, his shirt collar a more frayed, version of the same style he always wore.

Nick doesn't seem surprised or especially pleased to see me. We walk along together for a while, then find a table at an empty café and sit and talk.

"The big event of the week," he says, unslinging the laundry bag from his shoulder. His sarcasm is familiar, but there's a bitterness, a flatness, in his voice I don't remember. I ask him what else he's doing.

"Nothing." Silence. Skin so pale his freckles and some red blemishes stand out sharply. He pulls his coat around him, returns my stare, a dull smolder in his gaze, then shifts his eyes away.

I try again. Is he working? Going to school? Did he graduate from college? Is there anything he's interested in?

"No." Nick hunches over his coffee, slurps a sip. "Nothing is worth doing. Nothing interests me. Not even sex." He arches an eyebrow, flares his nostrils.

I hope for a moment he's joking, then see he's dead serious. His eyes look hollow. And there's something new: every few minutes, his tongue darts out of his mouth and flicks around, exactly like a lizard trying to catch flies. (Later I learn that "fly-catcher's tongue" is a side effect of long-term use of certain antidepressant and antipsychotic medications.) The effect is disturbing, reptilian, almost evil.

This is the same guy I couldn't look at or speak to without trembling, whom I lay awake nights longing for. My first lover, technically speaking. He'd filled me, inside, making me gasp with astonished pleasure. Now, just a few inches away, he is separated by a wall of obdurate emptiness.

I try telling him that life has been hard for me too, but that I've found things I care about, things that make life worthwhile. My words, sounding foolish and naive, wither in the blankness emanating from him. After a few halting exchanges, we say good-bye. Nick shuffles off carrying his laundry bag on his shoulder, a solitary, diminished, fragile figure. There is such a chill inside me that when I get home I take a long, hot bath.

I don't remember how I heard or who told me. It wasn't long after our meeting.

"Have you heard about Nick?"

After the first shock, I felt a kind of relief. I knew when I saw Nick that he'd reached the end, that he had no hope, no fight, no struggle left in him. There was instead that deep, pernicious void. Nick's spirit had seemed flaccid, drained dry.

Where had his life force gone? Had it been medicated out of him? I remember his conservative, straight-arrow parents. Had they taken charge of his life, supporting him financially, undermining his motivation, telling him what was acceptable and what was unacceptable, so that the muscle of his will lost its tone and withered away? Or was this the legacy of having been hospitalized? That flicking tongue was evidence of years of swallowing, along with medication, the idea of himself as being sick and in need of medical help. Ending his life would have been the ultimate capitulation in Nick's dissolution of will.

What makes one person resilient, another brittle, another passive? Why do some people emerge from terrible circumstances filled with determination, while others come from the most advantaged backgrounds with sickened spirits?

Maybe Nick chose to poison himself with pessimism, willfully backing himself into a far corner of boredom, nihilism, and depression that medication couldn't touch. He must have been considering suicide right around the time I saw him. In retrospect, I can read in his face that he had already made up his mind.

I don't know how Nick chose to end his life. Perhaps he hung himself; that would fit with his youthful obsession with strangulation. Of one thing I am certain—his death was intentional. But I have no idea what had driven him to that point. When I knew Nick as a teenager, he never talked about what went on inside him. He appeared to be in perfect control, expert at manipulating the world, attracting and bending people to his will. I can only guess that his intelligence and physical beauty worked against him, becoming part of the wall that enclosed him, leaving him isolated and without hope.

With each suicide I pick up a grain of anger, of will, of stubborn determination to live. These are the gifts of the dead. This is what they leave behind.

SEDUCTION

JANE. MY FRIEND FROM OUTSIDE who joined me in the hospital, admitted to P.I. just three months after I was. Together, at thirteen, we started the trip down the rabbit hole of adolescence.

Jane knew Winnie the Pooh, Sartre and Camus, Dostoyevsky and Tolstoy, Yeats and Wordsworth. She was gifted with humor, irony, and a sense of the absurd—though she could also be scathingly critical. "What an illiterate fool!" she'd blast those who fell below her standards. I feared her judgment and did my best to avoid her criticism.

Compared to mine, Jane's parents were exotic: Trotskyites, labor organizers, intellectuals. Physically, Jane took after her snub-nosed Irish father, but her mind was more like her mother's, who always had an arch comment to make. When I visited Jane's apartment I did my best to hide my ignorance, covering up with the mysterious, silent persona I'd cultivated as my disguise. When her parents were out, we smoked filched packs of her mother's Kents and listened to albums on her parents' stereo. *There are places I remember . . ."* we sang, as if we'd both already lived a lifetime. I preferred sad songs, while Jane knew all the words to Brecht's "Pirate Jenny." We listened endlessly to Dylan's *Highway 61 Revisited*. Even though we lived in safe, middle-class Stuyvesant Town, inwardly we wandered the slums, ragged, hungry, lost.

"Queen Jane" the boys called her, intimidated by her aloof superiority. I thought the name suited her from a different angle, as in Dylan's "Queen Jane Approximately." Jane the World-Weary, the Brave, the Principled—fair-minded and generous, but discerning. Jane's high expectations of people were too often disappointed. To me she was the epitome of intelligence. To Jane, I was pure emotion, seeking freedom at all cost in a doomed world. She called me Ruby Tuesday, like the enigmatic free spirit in the Rolling Stones' song. I wanted to live up to this image, but couldn't. That's partly where my sense of tragedy came from, and I cashed in on it.

Being with boys was one way I could act freer than I felt, the heat in my blood a drug that could almost stop the clamor of my thoughts. I had an endless need to be held. If I could get someone to love me, maybe my fears would go away.

My behavior interested Jane. She'd always ask me the details of my flustered, flushed evening encounters that took place at dusk on the benches surrounding the Stuyvesant Town playgrounds.

"I'm so terrible," I'd tell Jane the next day, confiding that I'd let him do this, or that, even though I didn't want to.

"Why did you do it then?" Jane would ask coolly.

"I don't know. I was confused." I was used to not knowing what I was feeling. I didn't want to know. I wanted to be out there, desired, talked about. I was through being the good little girl. Seduction and sex—this was being a woman.

My head buried in some guy's chest, comforted by the pulse in his strong male neck, I was safe. Contained. I could feel my own heart beating, hear the whoosh of my blood. I clung to men for self-definition, for safety. Even when my inner voice told me I was doing something I shouldn't, I was driven by a blind urge into the arms of boys I hardly knew, like a mole seeking protection in the deepest corner of a dark burrow.

Not that it worked. I never found the comfort I craved.

I was taught from an early age to seduce. My mother dressed me for it, in pink and white frills and ribbons, all girl. A high premium was placed on adorableness.

My mother knew just how to pose for the camera. A photo: My mother, late teens, posed atop a rock in her swimsuit, head high, shoulders broad, chest proudly lifted, a slight arch in her strong back. Sunlight on her face and shoulders. Hazel eyes made sultry by makeup and youth. Her warm, open smile, all curls and curves. That smile, seducing the world. She was the sun, shining on us all, but I wanted her to shine just on me. I needed her light and warmth. Without it, I couldn't grow. Encouraged, my need extended to the secondary adult world—grandparents and uncles, my parents' friends and acquaintances, and finally to strangers on buses, in restaurants.

"What a little darling. How adorable." Innocent, but seduction nonetheless.

I seduced grown-ups in general but especially my father. I lived for the special thrill of being hoisted into his arms, or feeling the weight of his hand on my head, the warmth and security of it. Pretending to be asleep in the backseat of the car after a long drive home, I'd keep my eyes closed as my father lifted me from the car. Carried in his strong arms, savoring the feel of his shirt, his special smell of cigarettes and soap, the steady beat of his heart, I snuggled in, absorbing his warmth. Bliss.

I haven't seen Jane since the early nineties. She'd been living in the Middle East for many years, and I'd lost track of her. After getting her B.A. from Berkeley and her master's from Georgetown, Jane moved to Beirut in the late seventies, to continue her women's rights work in a place where it was really needed. When last I saw her she sat in my kitchen with trembling hands, shell-shocked. Her life in Beirut had been suddenly disrupted by political turmoil, and she'd returned to the States. Her husband, a journalist, had been thrown in jail. With little left in common, our conversation faltered. My old friend Jane was gone, replaced by this savvy, distant world traveler. Her name wasn't even the same; she'd changed it to the less gender-specific Lee.

Jane stayed in the States awhile, writing a book on the Palestinian political situation. We completely lost touch. When on occasion I thought of her, I quickly brushed aside the thought. I felt guilty but didn't know why. It felt like unfinished business.

It took some digging to find Jane, now living in Palestine, working for the United Nations and Oxfam International as policy adviser on the Middle East. Her reply soon arrived. In a few months, she wrote, she'd be visiting her mother in New York and would be sure to call me.

Over the phone we laugh and remember, reaching into the past somewhat cautiously. I feel as though we're unwrapping a package that might turn out to be a bomb.

Before she arrives, I dress carefully, choosing my clothes as if for a date. I straighten up a little, but not too much. After all these years, I still want to impress her.

We hug at the door. She hasn't changed much. Her face, creased from years of desert sun, is otherwise the same fair, freckled, snub-nosed, rosebud-mouthed face I remember. She still wears wire-rimmed glasses. "You look the same," we take turns saying—both of us just a bit worn, creased, faded. But in some ways it's as if no time has passed at all.

"I don't mind remembering," she says. "What worries me is that I really like to remember. Those times were so intense—in a way, more real to me than my life is now." For me too, present life seems pale by comparison.

There are things that remain hazy. "How did you wind up in the hospital so soon after I went in?" I ask. I'd always wondered, guiltily, whether she'd followed me, her best friend, inside.

"No," she says, "it was pure coincidence that we wound up on the same ward. I'd stopped talking to my parents, and I was cutting school, so they sent me to a shrink. I remember, I sat there in total silence; I just refused to talk to him. He asked if I was uncomfortable because he was black, and I told him no, it was because I didn't like him." Jane bursts out laughing. "He told my mother I was very ill and recommended sending me to P.I. They took me to court, told the judge I was subject to impulsive behavior, and put me on Court Remand." It's too bad they'd been unable to recognize in Jane's impulsive behavior the seeds of her resolve and independence.

I ask what else she remembers. She takes a deep drag on her cigarette, exhales. "Mostly I remember you having sex with Harold, with Nick—with all the boys."

I'm mortified. Had my behavior been so obvious? Crouching behind sofas, straddling chairs, standing behind doors, lying on tables, squeezed into the phone booth. I'd done it everywhere. I hate thinking about it.

"Oh, God," I say to Jane, "was I that bad?"

"Yes," she says, "you were. I thought it was funny, in an awful kind of way."

I cringe at how I must have appeared to my politically aware friend. Jane was a feminist much earlier than I was. She joined NOW and went to consciousness-raising groups when I was still heavily invested in unconsciousness. She was climbing mountains, wide awake, while I was still splashing around in the depths of my emotions, asleep.

We were so different, yet we'd been so close. We swore, along with the rest of our generation, to be true to our inner selves and never become like our parents. We were best friends, sisters . . . and competitors. Pert, pretty-faced Jane was small and round; I was tall and lean. She felt distant from men; I easily fell into their open arms. I was jealous of her friendship with Marjee; no doubt it was hard for Jane too. There was a rough edge to our friendship. We loved, hurt, and competed with each other.

Jane had been discharged from P.I. while I was still busy "acting out." She'd moved into an apartment with another former patient, then moved and kept on moving. She lived upstate, then in Massachusetts, and with a houseful of Antioch students on a farm in Ohio before moving back to New York, and then to San Francisco, where she finished her degree at Berkeley, then to Beirut. I, on the other end of the spectrum, am still living in the apartment I moved into in 1972. I've always envied Jane's ability to move around in the world—something that doesn't come easily to me.

When Jane wasn't in New York, we wrote and phoned and stayed in touch in other ways. Jane had always introduced me to her friends—intelligent, talented, creative people. She told them about me, as well, so by the time we met it was almost as if we knew one another.

In the eighties, our friendship evaporated. On the rare occasions we got together, Jane seemed annoyed with me. Intimidated, I gradually stopped calling. Her life had taken a different direction. We drifted apart.

"What happened to our friendship?" I ask her now. "I felt you were angry with me but never understood why."

"You're right, I was angry with you. Do you want to know why? It's because you slept with all my friends."

I look at her, incredulous. "Did I?"

"Yes, you did. You had sex with every single male friend I introduced you to." She rattled off a list.

It was true. I had been lovers with several of Jane's friends. Each of these relationships had seemed valid, at the time. Somehow I'd never connected the dots linking them to Jane, but she had. Yet she'd never said a word. I ask her why.

"I couldn't. It was too painful."

How could I have been so unaware, so insensitive? I apologize, explain that I've changed, I'm different now. She says she knows, and that she forgives me. But the betrayal is there between us, an obscene embarrassment.

"It was especially painful because sex was easier for you," Jane says. "I had such a hard time letting men get physically close to me."

I'd known this. I'd just been oblivious to my effect on her.

"Well, I guess we were all pretty unconscious back then," she offers. "I did it too. I finally slept with Nick—did you know that? He was after me for months. I slept with him once. It was no big deal."

No big deal? I'd stayed up night after night waiting for the attendant he'd bribed to come for me so I could join Nick in the living room after hours. I pined, longed, lost sleep over him. And to Jane it was no big deal.

We'd all done it. Marjee was lovers with my friend Larry, whom I'd loved since I was thirteen. I had sex with both of Marjee's boyfriends: Harold and Nick. Jane fooled around with them as well. It was as if we were trying to prove that nobody had the right to lay claim to anybody, and nobody could be trusted. The heart was a cutthroat country, but your first loyalty was to your man. Songs of love eternal poured from the radio into our adolescent ears. We pined and sighed over boys, but it was our girlfriends in whom we confided our secret feelings and the details of our adventures. Where were the songs that proclaimed loyalty to your friends?

Our deal had been that I slept with guys and told Jane about it, a kind of division of labor. Perhaps I'd imagined it as a trade-off. If I slept with her friends, she could experience it vicariously through me. I remember the glowing reports she'd given us about one another. By the time we'd met there was a preexisting intimacy. Had she unconsciously given me her male friends as gifts?

Of course not. I'd betrayed Jane's trust. I stole, or at least borrowed, the boys she loved. But beneath the betrayal was a larger seduction. I loved Jane but could never quite get her approval or feel assured of her love. So I did the next best thing. I slept with her friends. It was as easy as taking cookies off a plate.

All these years, I've been playing for approval. I've sought validation outside myself, in the eyes of others. Not getting it from my mother or father, I looked for it in the arms of men. Not getting it from Jane, I seduced her friends.

I recently dreamed that I was searching for Jane at a party. I milled around among strangers, asking "Have you seen Jane?" Among all these people, I couldn't find Jane. Or was it Lee? Since she changed her name, I haven't been sure what to call her.

"It felt so sad to lose you," I say now, surprised by a sudden burst of emotion. I tell her how I'd felt my old friend Jane had been replaced by a remote stranger, Lee.

"You can call me Jane," she says. "I don't mind. I'm glad we've found each other again."

I reach out and find myself in the arms of my old friend Jane.

FOR THE RECORDS

I N ALL THESE YEARS IT HAS NEVER OCCURRED TO ME to request a copy of my hospital records. I'd worked too hard to bury this part of my past. Occasionally a foggy notion arose in me that somewhere my records existed, there to incriminate me in case I ever have to go to court, or try to adopt a child, or want to become professionally licensed in some new career.

It takes several interactions with the Records Director (a suitably Kafkaesque title) to officially request and obtain my records. I fax formal letters explaining who I am and why I want them, mail a check, and wait.

The package, sent certified mail, awaits me in the post office. The outer envelope, stamped Medical Records, is torn—such a thin membrane, protecting my privacy. I carry it home, the truth and mystery of those years a tangible weight, finally mine. I paid for it. At fifty cents a page and 300 pages long, this epic record of my past cost $150. As if, by filling these pages, I had not already paid enough.

One and a half inches thick, between red cardboard covers, the volume weighs heavy in my hands. Inside, typed and handwritten, are endless descriptions of my interactions with staff and patients over those twenty-seven months. I leaf through it—it's all in there: medical reports, family history, psychological test results, medication charts, nurses' notes. The pages have been assembled out of sequence, different years mixed together—much the way I remember my time in the hospital.

DISCHARGE SUMMARY

The patient is an 18-year-old, single, Jewish white female who resided with her mother and stepfather until the time of her admission. Her problems at that time included depression with suicidal ideation, two suicide gestures with aspirin, several episodes of scratching herself or burning her arms with cigarettes, increasing social isolation, inability to concentrate in school with truancy, use of marijuana and LSD, and a complete breakdown in communications with her family except in a hostile, oppositional way. She also experienced frequent depersonalization and derealization.

Seeing myself objectified in writing is like the slap of a cold, bracing wave. My hospital years, a bad but distant dream, are suddenly very real, documented on the paper I hold in my hand, bringing home the fact that I was once labeled "mentally ill." Even the heading at the top of the page, "NYS Department of Mental Hygiene," implies that I am unclean or diseased. Yet so far the events described are tame. Much of the first paragraph could apply to many adolescents who'd grown up within the last thirty years. *Hostile, oppositional, use of marijuana and LSD*—the usual sixties stuff.

There are details I'd forgotten—my habit of always brushing a hand or shoulder against the wall as I walked, feeling I must always have contact with something stable and solid or I'd float off. And things I'd chosen to forget: my extremely profane speech (usually followed by an apology). My sexual escapades, seductiveness, and rivalries. My susceptibility to feelings of betrayal, so easily hurt in social interactions. Day after day are nurses' entries of my feeling "jumpy," "nervous," "depressed," "hopeless," "agitated," "angry."

In November, 1966, she was discovered using marijuana and was referred for private psychiatric treatment. Her behavior continued to deteriorate with the patient staying away from home, lying about her whereabouts, and being truant from school. She was admitted to the hospital on a court remand because it was felt that her family was too ambivalent to force her to stay.

It's clear: The hospital authorities, in their official capacity, had urged my mother to sign me over to state custody. I feel a flush of compassion; at least I know she was ambivalent about sending me away. There were other factors: the relationship between my mother and stepfather, and their individual pathology. I distinctly recall at age thirteen my stepfather telling my mother I was "disturbed"—my neurotic, ineffectual stepfather trying to gain some authority.

> The mother is an attractive, aggressive woman who, for the past few years has been the main support of her family. She is easily angered and has related to the patient either in a rejecting, competitive or guilty, overprotective manner. The stepfather is himself a divorcé and an unassertive, seductive man.

There it is in print: a concise description of the contradictions I'd experienced in my mother's behavior. This document is a double-edged sword; I had not been the only one under scrutiny. But I don't recall anyone at P.I. talking objectively to me about my mother's attitudes and behavior or how she affected me. It was all my problem. The psychiatrists abetted my tendency to take it all upon myself—my mothers' anger, frustration, rages. Reading this, I suffer in retrospect the same rage and helplessness I'd felt then. My behavior had been, in part, a pathetic attempt to claim some power. *"Depression, distrust of authority and nurturing figures . . ."* No wonder.

The records contain histories of my parents' childhoods and relationships with their parents (mostly from my mothers' perspective; my father refused to be interviewed). My relationship with my mother, in counterpoint to her relationship with my father and stepfather, is delved into and analyzed at great length—close to forty pages. It's all there, summed up in nuggety paragraphs—my mother, father, stepfather, described just the way I remember them. Certain words appear over and over: *aggressive, hostile, infantile, dependent, symbiotic, competitive, seductive, narcissistic.* Coincidentally, in Harold's hospital records, many of the same words were used to describe his parents. Are these common attributes of family dysfunction? Or was this the prescribed psycho-jargon du jour, used across the board by the social workers and psychologists who did the background studies?

In my hospital records, the psychojargon sometimes reaches heights of absurdity. For example, after I had confessed to my doctor my conflicted and ambivalent emotions toward my mother, my psychiatrist wrote:

> Patient talked about her ambivalent feelings toward her mother. She spoke of her dependency on her and her idealization of her. This gave way to feelings of rage and hatred for her mother and a feeling that she had been betrayed. Her own self-image was subject to the same fluctuations as her mother, went from an overvalued love object to a devalued one. In addition she described a feeling that she had lost something, that something bad has been expressed from inside of her. I believe this corresponds to the casting out of the incorporated bad-mother introject.

The entry begins accurately in the first three sentences, then shoots way over the top, embellishing and obscuring the simple truth. Procrustes at work once again, as our young doctors attempted to fit us to the iron bedstead of psychiatric definitions.

Parents as well as patients were subject to psychological misinterpretation. At Harold's follow-up conference after he had been hospitalized for three months, his father burst into tears at the sight of his medicated, despondent son and blurted, "I want my Harold back, just the way he was before I brought him here!" The psychologist, unable to acknowledge the father's rightful anguish, wrote: "Father's behavior delusional and paranoid." During another conference, his mother went berserk, hitting Harold and his father with her high-heeled shoe. Who was more in need of psychiatric attention—Harold or his mother?

Hospitalization placed enormous stress on families. The records document my stepfather's complaint that my mother blamed him for my hospitalization and that their marriage had suffered because of it. Their marriage continued to deteriorate and ended in divorce.

Under microscopic scrutiny, details are magnified. I read descriptions of my behavior: *"She was openly hostile . . . was self-conscious and unable to face the therapist, sitting with her head bowed while rocking in her chair . . . acting out and anger as a defense against her disorganized thought and intense dependency . . . secretive and withholding . . . anxious . . . autistic . . . severe feelings of depersonalization."* Page after page of notes describe my progress, or lack of progress, until my transfer to Manhattan State.

It sickens me to read it. Described from the outside, my behavior was extreme; if accurate, I'd been much "sicker" than I thought. Although the events are accurately described, my version and theirs are different. I'd experienced it all from inside, they from outside.

Diagnosis: III. Schizophrenia 295.90 Chronic Undifferentiated

I do not believe it. I was never schizophrenic. Not then, not now. How could they possibly have interpreted my rage and confusion as schizophrenia? Looking through the lens of psychiatric diagnoses, they subtly sidestepped the validity of the genuine crisis I was in. At the same time, the importance of my emotions became magnified. It became impossible for me to experience anything without classifying it as symptomatic of some larger illness.

On my application for admission to P.I., asked to specify the reason for hospitalization, my mother had written: "Rebellious behavior."

All my friends at P.I. were then diagnosed as schizophrenic (today none of us are). Were we so different from other adolescents? In the sixties, the margin of acceptable behavior was narrower. I retreated into my own private inner space by painting, reading, going to Central Park, taking drugs. I turned my undeveloped gifts against myself, defining myself as a lost soul; bad, weird, different, "disturbed." Making myself crazy was my own art form. Who's to say whether that was an indication of "mental illness," or a temporary response to an inner need?

Little was known about panic disorders when I was a teenager. The fact that I experienced such distress in crowds, confined places, and social situations—including school—led me to believe that I was defective, possibly crazy, adding to my sense of isolation and shame. Had more information been available, my frequent escapes to Central Park might have been seen as a homegrown solution to a problem that needed attention, rather than delinquent truancy.

These days, when I take a break from work, I bicycle to Central Park, where I draw, paint, read, and enjoy the trees and sky, just as I did as a teenager. What's changed? Aside from no longer using drugs, not much, except that I'm living my life on my own terms. Instead of phobias, I have preferences. Those things that were once so difficult for me—midtown, crowds, subways—are no longer a problem because I've structured my life in a way that works for me, something that unfortunately wasn't an option when I was fifteen.

I couldn't have known that some of my instincts were good ones. Without realizing it at the time, I gravitated toward the things that have helped me most: art, nature, literature, friendship. Ironically, the same traits that contributed to my incarceration in the first place—rebelliousness, distrust of authority, the need to create, and love for the life of the mind—were the very things that saved me.

> The patient is currently functioning at the bright normal level of intelligence. Although there was little discrepancy between her verbal and performance IQ scores there was a marked discrepancy within certain tests in which the patient answered more difficult questions correctly while missing more simple ones (she did not know how many weeks there are in a year but did know that Goethe wrote *Faust*).

Today, I know Goethe wrote *Faust and* I know there are fifty-two weeks in a year. Why did I not know it then? Was it due to lack of concentration, the negative voices in my head drowning out the world, or simply my vow to not cooperate? The records state that I was straining to over-achieve. *"She currently tries to achieve beyond her intellectual level, placing her under tremendous strain which is more than she is able to sustain."* A year later, tested again, the following comment was noted: *"She seems to be less driven and striving to show her intellectual ability, but she still likes to think of herself as an intellectual."* It is painful for me to read this. Why did nobody in the hospital environment except Mrs. Gould take seriously my desire to educate myself?

I decide to retake the test and compare the IQ scores in my hospital records with my present score. The results: in all areas except performance, my scores are considerably higher. In the Rorschach test I recognize certain familiar images in the inkblots. Others have changed. One inkblot, formerly viewed as an animal with its heart cut in two, I now see as *a person with a wishbone for a heart*—something I could never have seen at the time, because I didn't believe there was hope for me.

I become newly conscious of the power wielded by a profession that deals with the most sensitive stuff of the human psyche. Back then, the psychiatric residents were mostly young men in their twenties, focused on the rigors of surviving medical school, passing exams, impressing supervisors, learning the ropes of their profession. How could they have understood what we were going through or known how to help us? They must have felt helpless in the face of our depression, rage, and rebellion. Wasn't it easier to prescribe drugs—to distance themselves, as well as us, from our unruly emotions and self-destructive urges? They needed us medicated, not just so that we would behave, but to afford themselves a concrete way to deal with all the psychic pain. It probably helped them sleep better at night. I don't think they were evil. They probably believed in what they were doing. It was what they were taught in school.

I recently came to learn that Dr. A., my first psychiatrist at P.I., was then a second-year resident whose first year had been spent doing evaluations. The year he was seeing me was his very first experience of seeing patients. Yet he'd been put in charge of my life, under supervision, for the first six months of my hospitalization. I remember sitting across from him in session, engulfed by an uncomfortable silence. Could it have been that he, like me, had been at a loss for what to say?

For those of us inside hospital walls our so-called treatment could be baffling. Many of us were experiencing a crisis of identity and of spirit. Were we really "crazy"? Or were we the products and perhaps scapegoats of our parents, with their fears, anxieties, guilt, and feelings of failure at controlling their offspring? Were we simply being held in detention? Was it justifiable to have our rights suspended until the regimentation and daily infusion of chemicals somehow corrected our faulty wiring? To be diagnosed as schizophrenic was to be frozen in a moment of crisis.

On our fifth-floor ward at P.I. in the mid-sixties, medication was the greatest silencer: of fears and phantasms, anxiety and lucidity. True, it provided a semblance of peace to a handful of severely ill patients. But for the majority, it was an enforced lullaby that delayed our learning the ways of balance and health.

A few of my friends continue to see psychiatrists and take their prescribed medication. Some, recipients of disability compensation, have never learned to hold a job or manage their moods. For others, the drugs became less effective over time or spawned severe side effects (e.g., kidney dysfunction). I know several people who after many years developed unbearable side effects to Lithium, then suffered breakdowns when taken off it. Even the latest state-of-the-art medications for anxiety and depression list a host of side effects, including dry mouth, dizziness, fatigue, headache, nausea, insomnia, and loss of sexual response—symptoms oddly reminiscent of the conditions these drugs were designed to treat.

For many people, psychiatric drugs can be the difference between comfort and discomfort, normal functionality and severe dysfunction, or even life and death. But they can also be irresponsibly prescribed. One friend was so overmedicated as to render her speech incomprehensible. Two people I know were victims of iatrogenic (physician-induced) illness, in which drugs were prescribed in contraindicated combinations that resulted in full-blown breakdowns. Another former patient, routinely prescribed medication without being seen in person, became addicted to sedatives and dependent upon an array of drugs to regulate his moods, the same way he relied upon medication for diabetes while avoiding working on his addictions to sugar and alcohol. He died of complications from diabetes in his early fifties.

Once on medication, it can be difficult to stop. When a friend, stable on Lithium for many years, asked her prescribing psychiatrist to gradually lower her dose, she was advised against it, after being reminded with some condescension that she had a serious illness. She decided to skip half a pill every other day, and in spite of her fear that every thought and mood might be a signal of illness, felt fine—though ultimately, frustrated by the psychiatrist's unwillingness to reevaluate her condition, she decided it was too daunting to adjust her dose without professional support.

I've fought hard to resist the lure of psychopharmaceuticals. At times my anxiety and depression have grown so intense that I've considered turning to medication for help, but I always pause on the brink. By now I know that each dip of the roller coaster brings with it an opportunity to adapt and grow, that the fear of falling apart is transitory, and that life is vastly imperfect. I will never know whether I would have had an easier time if I had taken medication. I only know that I prefer the straight, raw experience of my own emotions and mental states to dependence on medical intervention.

I come away with a deep conviction that the dividing line between "sane" and "insane" is a construct that protects us from our fear of chaos and the dark side of the psyche. Instead I see the range of human emotion as a continuum of many shades of gray, to be experienced and embraced—not medicated to dullness. Being hospitalized reinforced erroneous beliefs that took years of hard work to unlearn: that my thoughts and emotions are my enemy, that I need to be rescued from myself, that I am different from other people, that I am powerless.

"You can provide yourself with everything you need," Bernie once told me when I needed encouragement. It turned out to be true. Since being released from the hospital, I've weathered depressions, grief, and intense anxiety without resorting to psychiatric drugs. Instead I've learned to listen to my own signals, to recognize when I need food, rest, and exercise, when I need to retreat from the world, and when I need human contact. Slowly I've learned that I am a person both unique and like all others—feeling, fallible, capable, vulnerable, strong. True, I lost some time. But a good deal of my strength is drawn from my past, from the compassion and understanding I've learned, by necessity, to feel toward myself, and from the love I feel for the others who were with me in the hospital—those who didn't make it, and those who did.

I've had help along the way. Friends and lovers, therapists and teachers. The alliance of others who understand or have lived through similar experiences. And other gifts: the creative work—painting and writing—instrumental both in maintaining psychic health and in cultivating a sense of mastery—and mystery.

Ultimately, recovering from incarceration and sorting through its myths has been the greatest education of my life.

FACING THE ENEMY

YESTERDAY, DECEMBER, 6, 2000, was thirty-three years since I was admitted to P.I. Thirty-three years ago today, I would have been stranded on the ward, terrified equally of the present and the future—taking my place among the screwed-up, disturbed, troubled, patients on the fifth-floor ward. I thought my life was over. Everyone was my enemy—parents, hospital staff, the other patients. No one could be trusted, especially the psychiatrists.

I dial and hang up several times before leaving a message on Dr. S.'s answering machine: "This is Mindy Lewis, your former patient from P.I."

Dr. S. was my final psychiatric resident at the Psychiatric Institute—the one who was responsible for sending me to Manhattan State Hospital. All these years I've harbored unexpressed, unresolved anger toward him. Here's my chance to set the record straight. I'll be fair, I tell myself. I'll simply ask him for his side of the story.

After a few days, he returns my call. I listen to his message on my answering machine, trying to interpret. Is his voice perfunctory or warm? I can't tell. After extended telephone tag, we set up a time to meet. It's all I can do to get to sleep the night before.

I arrive at his Upper West Side office on the dot of nine. He greets me at the door with his golden Lab, who sniffs me with interest. Dr. S. is a decade older than I am, and I can see the effects of time—his face is like a comfortable sofa, worn and lived-in. He's on crutches and has a cast on his left leg—a picture of vulnerability, far from the Oppressor I remember.

"Come in," he says. His office is spacious and airy, with paintings and pho-tos all around. What was I expecting? This is not the office of a Nazi jailer.

I explain that it's important for me to get his take on what the situation was back then, to try to understand it from his point of view.

"I remember you as an extremely feisty, independent girl, very rebel-lious," he says. "There was something very appealing about that."

Appealing? I'd thought I was many things, but never that.

"You were a waif. We all wanted to save you."

They wanted to save me? But they were the bad guys, my jailers; it wasn't possible that they were fond of me.

"You were something of a pet," Dr. S. continues. "Dr. Gidro-Frank was extremely fond of you. We all were." Again, disbelief. I'd hated him and assumed he'd hated me too.

"Dr. Gidro-Frank could be very tough, but he really got involved with the patients' cases." I just remember him as an immovable will pitted against mine. I never imagined that from his point of view I might be interesting or compelling. Once again, I express my surprise.

Dr. S. looks thoughtful. "Actually, I learned a very important lesson from you."

I'm mystified, and somewhat apprehensive. What could he have possi-bly learned from me?

"There was this incident when you called me a 'Pig.' "

I flinch. Did I really say that to him? If I did, it was just my natural way of protecting myself. I offer Dr. S. a retroactive apology.

"Not at all," Dr. S. replies. "As I said, I learned something important. When you called me a pig, I realized how great the gulf was between us doctors and the patients—especially the adolescents. Until that moment, I wasn't aware of how you saw us—not as people who wanted to help you, but as cops, the establishment, the enemy."

"I was an adolescent."

"We were adolescents too. As psychiatrists. We were very young, just learning. We made mistakes."

His openness surprises me. I'd only remembered the uncomfortable silences, his distance and inaccessibility. From where I sat, he was just trying to control me, by giving and taking away my privileges. What had he been thinking each time he confronted that girl silently fuming in front of him?

"I didn't know how to express myself."

"Maybe not in words, but you expressed yourself in other ways:

through body language and acting out. We were taught that the only acceptable way for adolescents to express themselves was by talking. In retrospect, I see that might have been a mistake."

Would it have made any difference if an admission like this had been allowed to filter through his professional armor? Perhaps it would have helped to know we were all, as humans, fallible . . . and forgivable. I might have felt less alone.

I remember what I'd come to talk with him about: what had happened during my final months at P.I. My records show I'd been given privileges and was working outside. When I turned eighteen, they convinced me to sign myself in for a short period. Suddenly I was back in pajamas and E.O.; then, overnight, I was shipped. What happened? Was it a final expression of the hospital's frustration at not being able to control me? Why then had they persuaded me to stay on?

"We probably kept you in an attempt to make a gradual transition."

"A gradual transition? And then you suddenly sent me off to Manhattan State?"

"Maybe we felt that was the best way to make a clean break. Separation was a big issue. It was very hard—not just for the patients, but for us too. We became very attached."

It had been such an intense environment. We were all thrown in together, the patients and our young psychiatric residents—the older men in our lives. I remember the anticipation and dread I felt before sessions. How sensitive I was to how he saw me, how he responded. My passivity, his power. An intimate connection that had come to an abrupt end.

We look through the records I'd brought with me and reconstruct those last few weeks: my working at a series of jobs, their disapproval of my involvement with Dan, their suspicions (unfounded) that I was using heroin myself, their shipping me to Manhattan State.

"I guess we felt it was in your best interest. We didn't think it was good for you to associate with him. We did what we felt was best."

"My mother was so overprotective that if I fell and skinned my knee she'd get hysterical. I needed to be allowed to make my own mistakes."

Dr. S. shrugs. "Perhaps we shouldn't have been so restrictive. But that was how we did things back then."

I ask about the hospital's widespread use of antipsychotic medication, even though it often didn't seem to help or even made things worse. Dr. S. confesses that he, like many of his colleagues, left P.I. leaning more in the direction of therapeutic talking than medication. Today, he says, a different problem exists. With the new tendency to medicate and release patients as quickly as possible, most psychiatric residents couldn't conceive of having the opportunity to talk with a patient over an extended period.

"Whereas we were kept much too long."

"Perhaps you're right," Dr. S. says. "I know several psychiatrists who share your view." He offers the telephone number of a colleague who is now a particularly vocal critic of P.I.'s policies—although as a resident, he was proud to be associated with such a vanguard institution. But there were those who disagreed with P.I.'s policies, even then. I'm surprised to learn that several residents left after stridently objecting to the extensive use of medication and long-term hospitalization of adolescents.

"Is there anything else you'd like to ask me about?"

I look around Dr. S.'s office at his artwork and books. I tell him how painful it was to read in my records that I'd been "trying to achieve beyond my intellectual capacity." Yet I was always reading. "It's even written in my records that on my first day I sat in the end room reading *The Dwarf*."

"Funny," he says. "I have a copy of *The Dwarf* from around that time." I'd read the book over a year before Dr. S. became my shrink. I must have told him about it. How odd that I'd possibly had some influence on the books he read. I wonder if he'd read it in an attempt to bridge the gap between us.

Now we are connected by our shared memories of those times. Dr. S. remembers some patients I'd forgotten (my memory of the early days is sharper than the later time). He also remembers Liz and Nick. When he mentioned their suicides, his face saddens—they too have left their mark on his life.

As I'm putting on my coat, Dr. S. says, "As I said, I learned an important lesson from you—that you can't cure someone simply by loving them."

I don't know if I've heard him right. Is it possible that our psychiatrists had feelings for us? They were trained not to show them, expressing their concern in physician-like ways—which makes sense, particularly if their feelings swung the other way. I'd been so angry at him—at all of them— that I'd never allowed myself to imagine that this man, who met with me several times a week for almost a year, might actually have cared. It's still hard to believe; yet it's as if I'd known it all along. Only the thinnest veil separates those two views. All I have to do is remove it.

APPOINTMENT WITH THE PAST

IT'S MORE THAN THIRTY YEARS since I've been there. I've caught glimpses of it from the West Side Highway on my way upstate—quick glimpses, blurred, Doppler-like. My reactions have varied: a sense of oppression, a sudden sting of tears, a shiver of anger. Once as I cycled by with my boyfriend on an outing to the Palisades, the hair on my body stood up as if raised by wind.

Today I go there on purpose.

I wake before the alarm, knowing, as I open my eyes to the morning, that this is a special day, like the first day of school—something more common to youth than middle age. Today I go back in time, to the scene of the crime, the heart of my life's drama, to the fifth-floor ward where I spent my adolescence.

It's dangerous. The past could devastate me, flood me so I can't contain it. When I revisit the ward, will ghosts join me? I hope not. Yet, I hope so.

It was a complex route that got me there in the first place. Today it's far simpler. Take the number 9 local north at 96th Street. Emerge into daylight at 110th; at 125th Street, peer over Harlem rooftops. Back underground, darkness. Soon, my stop.

The 168th Street station is a wide underground promenade with an arched ceiling. An overpass lit by green-globed lamps spans the tracks; people hurry across. I remember—a ghost of a remembrance—this same station, empty, ominous, on my way to my part-time job in midtown; I walked this same platform on my way back to P.I.

A sign on the station wall: COLUMBIA-PRESBYTERIAN MEDICAL CEN-TER. A crowd of commuters, many of them hospital workers, surge along to a bank of elevators that take us to street level. I'd forgotten the elevators. Seventeen years old, I'd listened anxiously for footsteps in the deserted corridor. But no longer—an elevator opens and schoolchildren run out, shouting, laughing.

Broadway and 168th is a wide wind tunnel of an intersection: people, activity, traffic. I look for familiar landmarks, but I'm completely turned around, unsure which way is west. Then, joining the flow of white-clad workers in lab coats with plastic badges, I can tell I'm going in the right direction. On my left: College of Physicians and Surgeons, William Black Medical Building (I shudder, remembering the laboratory cats). Beyond, next to a low wall blocking the river, literally a dead end, is the Psychiatric Institute.

The building dates from the 1920s, before New York's first World's Fair. Lofty ideals raised this structure, born of a grand idea. A new solution to an old problem: a modern Institute, where research will discover new ways to finally vanquish the chimera of mental illness. The state donated money. On the rocky Palisades they built His church: Freud's notebooks are housed in the library.

The lobby—run-down, almost antique, with its marble floor and dark wood—is unfamiliar. True, I rarely saw it. But the smell's familiar, a whiff of stale air from the past. The sullen guard, frowning, looks up from her newspaper, tells me to sign in.

Time: 9:44. Destination: third floor, North.

I've recently tracked down one of my former psychiatrists, Dr. R.—one of the few with whom I had a rapport. It is him I've come to see. After years of other employment, twelve years ago he was invited back to work at P.I. as director of a fellowship program. And although two years ago the wards were moved to the modern glass-and-steel building across the street, some offices, including his, remain in the old building.

Funny that I'm not afraid, though I remember what it felt like: the nightmare of being locked in. I still rebel at being confined, won't walk under the underpass, feel a fleeting panic when the subway's stuck in the tunnel. If I had come a year ago, I might have trembled, might have wept. But today I'm calm. I've come so far. I'm healthy, sturdy, mostly confident. And fortunate, alive, adult, free to do as I please—more so than the grumpy guard. A spirit catches me, clenches my jaw, just a hair. Some residual anger at authority. It must be her uniform.

The guard points to an elevator I don't remember. It's tiny, with barely enough room for four people. Today it's only me, no attendants dressed in white, no doctors with nametags. With a thrill of free will, I press 3.

The door opens onto what would be the common area between the North and South sides, the same layout as the fifth floor. It looks, and smells, like an old school, slightly decaying. I'd forgotten the dark wood doors with their little ventilation slits and brass knobs, the precise pattern of the linoleum. The same corridor I walked when I was taken for psychological testing. Recognition floods me: a pang, a sweetness. Youth. Fear. I find my way to his office, and knock.

I recognize him instantly, as he'd recognized my name on the phone. Now it takes him a moment. "I remember you as tall and slender, but with blond hair."

He remembers correctly. My hair has darkened with the years, though it hasn't yet gone to gray. And like my defenses, my personal architecture has thickened, grown more sturdy.

He looks the same, just older. I remember in an instant his eyes behind his glasses, his smile and manner of speech, the size and shape of his hands and feet, his gestures. He may be thinner, grayer, but his style of dressing is the same. He wears brown corduroy and brown suede chukka boots identical to the ones I remember staring at, sometimes for the entire length of our sessions. I remember awkward silences, flashes of anger, occasional laughs shared.

"I was just making tea, would you like some?"

I scan shelves of books, framed photos of his family, a hiking trip. I hear tinkling, coming from a miniature rock garden waterfall. He loves nature, I realize. A good quality in a psychiatrist.

As glad as I am to see him, I'm a little wary. Wasn't he once the enemy? Or was he my ally? It's confusing. After I phoned him, I wept, hard, for about an hour, surprised by the intensity of my emotions. I felt as if I'd contacted an old lover, or a father figure. Even our silences had been a kind of intimacy.

For a year he'd been responsible for me. He was a resident, still in training, only eleven years older than I was. I'd seen him for a full year, and when he moved on to do his second-year residency in child psychiatry, he decided to keep me as one of his patients. Then, abruptly, he'd had to leave P.I. I was crushed, though I never would have admitted it.

Now we sit across from each other and sip tea. I explain to him about my quest to rediscover my past. I dig in my bag for my pad and pen.

"Will it make you nervous if I take notes?" I ask. Now here's a role reversal.

"Not at all. I may want to take some myself."

I imagine I see in his eyes the slightest distrust. Maybe he sees me as someone who will twist and misuse his words. Another role reversal. I recall a remoteness, the imposition of his will over mine. A stranger, lording it over my life.

Then I remember. He invited me here to reestablish contact, to open the vault of the past. The apparition passes. Once again, he seems pleased to see me.

We reconstruct the times, each from our own perspective.

"You were very troubled back then, always getting into trouble. If I remember correctly, you were thought of as something of a ringleader."

How odd, when I remember being so scared, so timid. Again the adolescent trying to balance, overcompensating for qualities and abilities she lacked. Underneath the rebellion, I'd desperately wanted the approval and love of the parental figures closest to me. What better reason to push them away, to deny my need, to act out.

I explain what it was like to be locked indoors. How acting out was the one way I had to express myself, experience challenge, establish relationships—friendships stronger and more vivid than any I've known since. I describe my friends, hoping he'll remember them, and fish from my bag the few photos I have from those years—Marjee, Harold, Jane, and me on one of our Riverside Park outings—but Dr. R. says he's not sure he remembers them. I place the photos face up on the table, so my friends can be present, all of us here together one last time.

This is my opportunity to reassemble the hazy details of my past. I want to understand the way things worked. Why were adolescents kept in the hospital for so long?

He tells me there are trends in psychiatry, and that back then it was believed to be beneficial to take patients away from their families and put them in a controlled environment for an extended period. Contact with family was reduced dramatically in the belief, now considered mistaken, that parents were to blame for their children's illnesses.

I tell him how much I'd needed to get away from my mother, to separate myself from her. How my rebellion, essential for individuation, was

misjudged as illness. How symptoms were rewarded, almost encouraged—the way we got attention, a way to distinguish ourselves.

"How were you diagnosed?" he asks.

I take my hospital records, which I'd brought with me, from my bag
and point to where it's written. "Schizophrenic, chronic, undifferentiated."

"Obviously an incorrect diagnosis." His face shows concern, sadness.

That was how all my friends were diagnosed, all of us given drugs for
psychosis. Today, if we were to wind up here at all, we'd probably be given
Prozac or Paxil and sent home within a few days or weeks.

Dr. R. looks at his watch. "Would you like to go see the ward? I'm not
sure if we can get onto the fifth floor, but let's try."

The elevator rises . . . stops . . . the door opens. I am standing in front
of the kitchen where the food lady parked her cart and dished out our
meals. The swinging door with the little window that opens into the dining room will not open; it's barricaded by piles of discarded furniture.
The dining room is tiny; how could I ever have thought it large? I remember it filled with tables, chairs, patients silently eating, losing themselves
in food.

There, in the corner, like an abandoned vehicle, is the phone booth. Its
heavy glass panels are still intact, its chrome dented. The telephone apparatus has been yanked out, leaving a short umbilicus, its torn end frayed. I
try the folding door, hear its familiar squeak. I stand inside the booth,
remembering the sweat between my hand and the receiver, the feel of my
damp pajamas on the shelflike seat, my urgent need to make contact with
the world outside.

The deserted ward is a shambles. The fifth floor, like all the old wards,
is being renovated. Down the hall workmen are busy dismantling the
place, demolishing it before my eyes, bit by bit. As I remember, putting it
all back together, they are taking it apart. This will be my last memory of
the ward. If I come back in a month, it will be no more.

I have entered through an opening so narrow and fleeting, I might not
have found it. What are the chances that I would contact my old psychiatrist at a point in time when the ward, deserted yet still intact, was available to be revisited? Like Brigadoon, a door has opened briefly and let me
into a lost world. To my surprise, instead of the pain I'd feared, I am filled
with intense joy.

For years I've seen this place only in dreams—nightmares in which I found myself back inside. Now it's all here before me, details that until today existed only in the fog and haze of memory. I run my hand over the pebbly texture of the painted walls. Carpeting covers the linoleum, but there are places where it's still visible, a pattern of beige squares with gray flecks punctuated by gray squares with beige flecks. Details click into my memory like lost puzzle pieces.

I take out my camera; with Dr. R.'s permission, I take photos, so I'll remember.

Here's the utility room where Liz tried to kill herself with the gas dryer. The nurses' station, with its glass walls and metal cabinets, is unlocked, no longer off-limits. Around the corner, the Quiet Room where Helen screamed, and where I spent my last day on the ward. I kneel, push my finger into the firm foam floor. It gives a little.

Here are the private rooms: this was Laurie's, this was Judith's. Only briefly was I given the privilege of a private room, when I ran a high fever shortly after I arrived. There's the fan that blew on me, mounted high on the wall where patients couldn't reach. The mattresses, the beds are the same. I would lie on my stomach for comfort, fists tucked under my shoulders, my only wish to lose myself in unconsciousness.

A-dorm, its arched doorway now square, has been subdivided into smaller rooms. Here was my bed, I think, or there. This is where Liz slept, here was Nancy who jumped off the bridge, here's where I sat with Edie smoking opiated hash. Everything is deserted, long abandoned, furniture turned on its side, doors swung open.

I snap a photo. Just as I do a man strides down the corridor toward us. He is irate.

"No photos allowed! State law. Photos with advance written permission only."

His voice ruptures my dream. For the first time today I feel helplessness and fear, recalling the powerlessness I felt every day of my life on this ward, my inner balance tipping endlessly back and forth between defiance and passivity. From their point of view, the defiant me was "sick," the passive one "healthy." Today I see it as the complete reverse: My defiance was at least a misguided demonstration of life force, my passivity tantamount to depression.

What will he do, demand I give him the film? Deprive me of visual proof of my past? I apologize, and assure him that I won't use any photos without written permission. He seems satisfied, and walks away.

Here's the medical room where I sat shivering during my intake exam. The bathroom, the same sad sinks, the mirror. The stall doors now have locks.

I examine the creepy, institutional shower room, with its dingy white tiles, showers (where Rocky scrubbed and scrubbed), the tub with chrome fixtures and some strange therapeutic attachment. Peculiarly uninviting, not a place to enjoy the pleasures of a bath. For years this room has inhabited my dreams, yet here it is, a relic, stinking of mildew, tiles missing, ceiling crumbling.

The locker room, where inspections uncovered contraband items in our lockers, landing us back into pajamas. The end room where I sat and read, and sometimes had my therapy sessions. Thirty-two years ago I stewed in silent chagrin in this room, in session with the psychiatrist escorting me today, who no longer holds any power over me. I remember asking him to unlock the screen and open the window. Today I swing open the unlocked screen myself, push the window so it juts out into a V, and let in some fresh air.

We're finished with South side and head back to Center. The red-and-white EXIT sign marks the place where I sat on the card table, looking longingly at the door, just before R.J. tackled me. On the door a small sign: PLEASE BE SURE TO LOCK THIS DOOR BEHIND YOU. THANK YOU.

The living rooms are piled high with furniture, upholstered in neutral fabric instead of the orange, green, and gold vinyl I remember. With its modular, industrial furniture, the ward could be an abandoned office. It all looks so much smaller than I remember it. Yet it was my home, and my prison, for twenty-seven months. Tomorrow, again, it will be a dream.

For the first time I walk down the forbidden North side, the men's ward. I can still see boys coming toward me down the hall—sauntering, slinking, slouching, ready for trouble. Now, down at the far end of the corridor, where workmen kneel, instead of a wall, there is light. They've broken through to the new building, created a passageway connecting the new to the old.

For decades a part of me has been entombed within these walls. I've never fully lost the fear of winding up back inside, proving the hospital was right. I came here expecting to reexperience the pain of those dim days, but find instead an unexpected joy. This, I realize, is why I've come here: to break through walls of depression and fear and discover what I'd been determined to find even then, with all the energy and stubborn insistence of youth—that that girl, hell-bent on finding her own path, has ultimately succeeded.

Dr. R. escorts me out. We say good-bye in the sunshine, standing together for the first time on the sidewalk outside the hospital.

In the shadow of the new building, derelicts recline on benches. The bridge, glimmering in the distance, is partially obscured by the new Institute. The metal and green-glass structure shimmers futuristically, connected to the old building by external walkways. The parking lot is filled with cars. People come and go, walking the ramps. When the light hits just right I can make out human forms behind the tinted glass.

This is where the wards are now, where patients are treated with new medications, new ideas applied. I wish them luck, say a prayer for them. May they go home soon. May they not take drugs for long. May they have the courage to look inside and love themselves. May they learn to feel at home in the world.

Life will go on from here.

A NOTE TO THE READER

Although this is a work of nonfiction, the chronology of certain events has been slightly altered in order to produce a narrative that flows in a nonrepetitive manner. Because it is written in the present tense, the book poses problems: the point of view of the fifteen-year-old narrator is uninformed by the broader perspective of the adult. Thus, certain characters (e.g., my mother) may be represented especially harshly, through the lens of a youthful heart and eye. Also, as I was unable to locate certain former patients, or the families of those no longer living, I had to rely on my recollections and those of other former patients for certain details of their stories. Unless otherwise instructed, all names have been changed.

ACKNOWLEDGMENTS

From the moment I began writing this book, doors have opened. I am grateful to those people who helped open them.

I would like to thank my agent, Anna M. Ghosh, whose dedicated belief in this book helped make it a reality, and Russell Galen for his interest and behind-the-scenes work on my behalf. I am deeply grateful to my wonderful editor, Kim Kanner, who fell in love with my book on Valentine's Day, for immediately "getting" the spirit of this project and for her guidance and generous support.

Much love and gratitude to my mother for being willing to revisit a difficult time in our past and for her unfailing love and support, and also to my stepfather, Paul, for being a true father to me.

I am grateful to the following people:

Peter Bricklebank, mentor and friend, for his precise editorial eye and expert guidance, and for always being there when I needed support. Pamela Paul, my sister in new authorship, for her loyal friendship and editorial expertise. My writing group in its various incarnations, for the care with which they read and commented on my early drafts. My friends Irene Hecht, Carole Langille, Rachelle Rogers, Chrystie Sherman, Connie Sommer, Bob Sterling, Rain Bengis, and Karen Whitman, among others, for believing in me and seeing me through the perils of the pen. Amy Winter for editorial and moral support. The Freeman family for their love and support. Ed Sukman for twenty years of friendship. Elaine Wolff and Gary Bron for always making me feel welcome. Howard

Frazin for his feedback. Glen Goodman for research assistance. John Breitbart for adding music to my writing process.

My old friends Harold Green, Judith Greenberg, Geoffrey Heyworth, Spencer Lieb, Josh Lipton, Stephen MacDowell (thanks, Steve, for your detective work), Sheila McLaughlin, Lee O'Brien, Larry Plitt, Fern Seiden, Rick and Michele Widry, Janice Howard, Miriam Aliminos, and Wendy Thompson for time traveling with me. Joan Roselle for her candid recollections of her brother, Mike. Jackie Mooray for sharing her memories and photographs. Dr. Jules Ranz for his generous interest and editorial feedback. Dr. Michael Sacks, Dr. Allen Francis, and Dr. Arthur Shore for sharing their perspectives. Dr. Martin Lubin for his insight and encouragement, and for truly being one of the good guys.

Bernard Weitzman, Ph.D., for years of friendship and for showing me another way. Rebecca Barber, who graciously offered her psychological testing skills. Michael Weisbrot, who went into his archives and printed dozens of photos, for his friendship, support, and wonderful cover photograph. Ira Fox, for the author's photograph. Peter W. Goodman, author of *Morton Gould: An American Salute,* for putting me in touch with the family of Shirley Bank Gould; and her children, Abby Gould Burton, Eric Gould, and David Gould, for warmly sharing their memories of their amazing mother.

Elayne Clift, editor of the anthology *Women's Encounters with the Psychiatric Establishment: Escaping the Yellow Wallpaper,* whose call for submissions in *Poets and Writers* was the catalyst for the essay that was to become the seed for this book. Elayne's enthusiastic response directed me to the International Women's Writing Guild, an organization whose "Meet the Agents" session proved to be precisely that.

Thanks also to the bold, brave, inspiring writers who walked this path before me: Susanna Kaysen, Barbara Gordon, Kate Millett, and the many others compelled to write about their hospitalization . . . but especially Lauren Slater, whose writing gave me the courage to unlock the door to my past.

Finally, I would like to thank Banff Centre for the Arts, Byrdcliffe Colony/The Woodstock Guild (special thanks to Katherine Burger), and Jerry Paul and Carol Mayer for providing peaceful havens in which the writing could take shape.

SELECTED BIBLIOGRAPHY

Breggin, Peter R., M.D. *Toxic Psychiatry.* St. Martin's Press, 1991.

Casey, Nell. *Unholy Ghost: Writers on Depression.* William Morrow/Harper-Collins, 2001.

Ehrenreich, Barbara. *Fear of Falling: The Inner Life of the Middle Class.* Harper-Collins, 1989.

Farber, Seth. *Madness, Heresy and the Rumor of Angels.* Open Court, 1993.

Fox Gordon, Emily. *Mockingbird Years.* Basic Books, 2000.

Geller, Jeffrey L. and Maxine Harris. *Women of the Asylum.* Doubleday, 1994.

Glenmullen, Joseph, M.D. *Prozac Backlash.* Simon & Schuster, 2000.

Goffman, Erving. *Asylums.* Doubleday, 1961.

Gordon, Barbara. *I'm Dancing As Fast As I Can.* Harper & Row, 1979.

Gorman, Jack M., M.D. *The Essential Guide to Psychiatric Drugs.* Third Edition. St. Martin's Press, 1997.

Hebald, Carol. *The Heart Too Long Suppressed.* Northeastern University Press, 2001.

Herman, Judith, M.D. *Trauma and Recovery.* Basic Books, 1992.

Jamison, Kay Redfield, M.D. *An Unquiet Mind.* Vintage Books, 1996.

————. *Touched with Fire: Manic Depressive Illness and the Artistic Temperament.* Simon & Schuster, 1993.

Kierkegaard, Søren. *Fear and Trembling and the Sickness Unto Death.* Princeton University Press, 1941.

Laing, R. D. *The Divided Self.* Pelican Books, 1966.

————. *Sanity, Madness and the Family.* Tavistock Publications, 1969.

————. *Wisdom, Madness and Folly: The Making of a Psychiatrist.* Canongate Books, 1985.

Levenkrom, Steven. *Cutting: Understanding and Overcoming Self-Mutilation.* W. W. Norton & Company, 1968.

Luhrmann, T. M. *Of Two Minds: The Growing Disorder in American Psychiatry.* Alfred A. Knopf, 2000.

Maslow, Abraham H. *Toward a Psychology of Being.* D. Van Nostrand Company/Litton Educational Publishing Co., 1968.

May, Rollo. *Love and Will.* W. W. Norton & Company, 1969.

Miller, Alice. *The Drama of the Gifted Child.* Basic Books, 1981.

Millett, Kate. *The Loony-Bin Trip.* Simon & Schuster, 1990.

Moore, Thomas. *Care of the Soul.* HarperCollins, 1998.

O'Conner, Richard, Ph. D. *Undoing Depression: What Therapy Doesn't Teach You and Medication Can't Give You.* Little, Brown, 1987.

Pipher, Mary, Ph. D. *Reviving Ophelia: Saving the Selves of Adolescent Girls.* Ballantine Books, 1997.

Schneier, Franklin, M.D., and Lawrence Welkowitz, Ph.D. *The Hidden Face of Shyness: Understanding and Overcoming Social Anxiety Disorder.* Avon Books, 1996.

Schumacher, Michael. *There but for Fortune: The Life of Phil Ochs.* Hyperion, 1996.

Shannonhouse, Rebecca, editor. *Out of Her Mind: Women Writing on Madness.* Random House, 2000.